D1303296

FROM THE RISING
OF THE SUN

The American Society of Missiology Series, in collaboration with Orbis Books, seeks to publish scholarly works of high merit and wide interest on numerous aspects of missiology—the study of mission. Able presentations on new and creative approaches to the practice and understanding of mission will receive close attention.

To my wife, Ruth,
and our daughters,
Catherine and Marjorie.
"Love never ends."

American Society of Missiology Series, No. 3

FROM THE RISING
OF THE SUN

CHRISTIANS AND SOCIETY
IN CONTEMPORARY JAPAN

James M. Phillips

ORBIS  BOOKS

Maryknoll, New York 10545

The Catholic Foreign Mission Society of America (Maryknoll) recruits and trains people for overseas missionary service. Through Orbis Books Maryknoll aims to foster the international dialogue that is essential to mission. The books published, however, reflect the opinions of their authors and are not meant to represent the official position of the society.

Library of Congress Cataloging in Publication Data

Phillips, James M 1929-
  From the rising of the sun.

  Bibliography: p.
  Includes index.
  1. Christianity—Japan. I. Title.
BR1309.P44   275.2   80-24609
ISBN 0-88344-145-4 (pbk.)

Published by Orbis Books, Maryknoll, NY 10545, in collaboration with the American Society of Missiology

Contents

Preface to the Series

The purpose of the ASM Series is to publish, without regard for disciplinary, national, or denominational boundaries, scholarly works of high quality and wide interest on missiological themes from the entire spectrum of scholarly pursuits, e.g., theology, history, anthropology, sociology, linguistics, health, education, art, political science, economics, and development, to articulate but a partial list. Always the focus will be on Christian mission.

By "mission" in this context is meant a cross-cultural passage over the boundary between faith in Jesus Christ and its absence. In this understanding of mission, the basic functions of Christian proclamation, dialogue, witness, service, fellowship, worship, and nurture are of special concern. How does the transition from one cultural context to another influence the shape and interaction of these dynamic functions?

Missiologists know that they need the other disciplines. And other disciplines, we dare to suggest, need missiology, perhaps more than they sometimes realize. Neither the insider's nor the outsider's view is complete in itself. The world Christian mission has through two millennia amassed a rich and well-documented body of experience to share with other disciplines.

Interaction will be the hallmark of this Series. It desires to be a channel for talking to one another instead of about one another. Secular scholars and church-related missiologists have too long engaged in a sterile venting of feelings about one another, often lacking in full evidence. Ignorance of and indifference to one another's work has been no less harmful to good scholarship.

We express our warm thanks to various mission agencies whose financial contributions enabled leaders of vision in the ASM to launch this new venture. The future of the ASM series will, we feel sure, fully justify their condifence and support.

William J. Danker, Chairperson,
ASM Series Editorial Committee

21 2941

Preface

A book, like a baby, doesn't see the light of day until after much anguish. For this writer the anguish began with a prolonged and agonizing strike in 1969—70 at Tokyo Union Theological Seminary, where he was a professor of church history. The strike that closed down most of the seminary's classes and brought the barricading of the school's main building did not mean that the faculty and nonstriking students were free to take a holiday. Far from it! There were almost daily rounds of faculty meetings and innumerable consultations at which we tried to gain some perspectives on what had happened, and where we were to go from then on. This was a kind of intensive course in contemporary church history for all of us.

Nor was that all. During the time of our school conflict, the seminary was also besieged by requests from outsiders for information about what was happening. Schools and church leaders from around Japan and overseas wanted to know how this particular struggle had come about, for this was a season of school struggles around the world, and no one knew where the lightning might strike next and how one should respond when and if that fateful time came.

To meet such outside requests for information, and to help those of us involved in the turmoil get some perspectives on what we were doing, the writer began to distribute a series of mimeographed reports giving a running chronicle of events as they transpired, with the appropriately vague title of *A Seminary in Transition*. But, of course, such reports could tell only one small part of the story. It became clear that to do justice to an explanation of what was happening to Christians in Japan, a study of much broader scope was necessary. Such a study would deal not just with the Tokyo seminary, or with the United Church of Christ in Japan, with which the seminary was affiliated, but with the entire Christian community of Japan: Protestant, Roman Catholic, Orthodox, and others.

It also became clear that a much longer time frame would be necessary than the few years surrounding our era of conflict. The entire period of Japan's contemporary history, from the end of the Pacific War in 1945 to the present, would need to be surveyed. To be sure, the Christian community of contemporary Japan has its roots in past decades and centuries, but as several studies have already been written that deal with the story before 1945, it seemed best to focus on the contemporary era for the telling of this story.

The project of researching and writing this fascinating story has taken a full decade, and has sent the writer to all four major islands of Japan to meet and talk with the men and women who have been witnesses of and participants in the events of the period. The research meant reading Japanese and English books and articles of all sorts, interviewing hundreds of people who took part in that history, making tape recordings of many of those interviews, and discussing the results of all this both in informal groups and in classroom teaching. In time, what are now chapters 4, 7, and 8 appeared in the *Japan Missionary Bulletin,* chapter 1 in *The Northeast Asia Journal of Theology,* and the Bibliographical Notes in *The Japan Christian Quarterly.* There was much helpful "feedback" from many friends who carefully read and commented on these journal articles, and this led to a host of revisions of the material. Deep appreciation is due to the editors of these journals for their encouragement for this project, and for their willingness to allow revised versions of these articles to appear in the present volume. The book's additional chapters were written while the writer was a visiting professor of church history at San Francisco Theological Seminary, where his stay was punctuated with trips back to Japan to refine his data and observations.

This book has been written for those in Japan and in any land who wish to know more about both the triumphs and the heartbreaks that Christians in Japan have faced in recent years. It is the first attempt in any language to cover the subject in this fashion, to the best of my knowledge, although numerous works dealing with parts of the story will be referred to as we go along.

The writer sends this work of contemporary history into the world with no little trepidation, for he knows from his experience in teaching history that contemporary accounts of events are subject to all kinds of limited perspectives. He invites his readers to write him any comments and criticisms that occur to them. As a historian, he wants to make this account as accurate, encompassing, and fair as possible. And as a convinced Christian, he hopes that this study may commend itself to Christians of all communions, to people of other faiths and of no faith, so that their knowledge of and appreciation for the remarkable Christian community of Japan may be deepened.

Every effort has been made in the telling of this story to give as much background as is necessary to describe the period, but without overwhelming the reader with superfluous details. For the sake of consistency, both Japanese and Western surnames are given last, except in the Bibliographical Notes where for the same principle of consistency they come first. Long vowels in Japanese are marked with a macron thus: Kyōdan. The only exceptions are where people or organizations have preferred to spell their names without macrons, and with the cities of Tōkyō, Ōsaka, and Kyōto.

This book has been made possible by the help of so many friends that it is clearly impossible to give them all due credit. Even so, there are special people who simply must be mentioned. My colleagues and friends at Tokyo Union Theological Seminary have been most helpful, especially Professors Yoshishige Herman Sacon, Masaichi Takemori, Toshio Satō, Hideo Ōki, and Yoshinobu Kumazawa. Tatsuo Fujita as TUTS Librarian was of great help, and so were my students, in particular Teruo Kuribayashi, who served one year as research assistant. Special thanks also go to my Protestant missionary colleagues in Japan, especially to Newton Thurber, Sam H. Franklin, Richard Drummond, and John Hesselink. This study owes more than I can say to David Swain, who made very helpful suggestions for chapters 1, 4, 6, 7, 8, 9, and the Bibliographical Notes, and to Robert M. Fukada, who did the same for chapters 2, 3, and 5. Roman Catholic missionary friends have also had a direct hand in this study, for it was Joseph Spae who gave encouragement from the start, and Raymond Renson who published the three chapters in the *Japan Missionary Bulletin*. Numerous other Christian friends in Japan gave help, among whom I may mention John Masaaki Nakajima, Yuki Naitō, Yoshiro Ishida, Yoshiaki Iizaka, Toshihiro Takami, Masao Takenaka, and the late Takeshi Takasaki, Hidenobu Kuwada, and Ken Ishiwara. My colleagues at San Francisco Theological Seminary, President Arnold Come and all the rest, have been most supportive in everything. Thanks are due to Thelma Furste and Loel Millar for their skillful work in typing several chapters of the final manuscript. Philip Scharper at Orbis Books has been most patient and encouraging throughout. Above all, my personal gratitude goes to my long-suffering family, to daughters Cathy and Marjorie, and to my wife, Ruth.

A final word should be said about the title of this work, *From the Rising of the Sun*. It is, of course, taken from Psalm 113:3 (RSV):

> From the rising of the sun to its setting
> the name of the Lord is to be praised!

There are some who have maintained that these words were actually written by the psalmist with reference to Japan, "the land of the rising sun," but no such implication is carried here. Yet these words do remind us that the land of the rising sun in recent decades has witnessed developments within its Christian community that deserve to be better known. The purpose in telling this story is that mentioned by the psalmist: "The name of the Lord is to be praised!"

Abbreviations and Acronyms

ARI	Asian Rural Institute
AVACO	Audio-Visual Aids Commission, of NCCJ
BBC	British Broadcasting Corporation
CCA	Christian Conference of Asia
CLC	Christian Literature Crusade
CoC	Council of Cooperation
COTE	Commission on Theological Education (Taiwan)
CPJ	Communist Party of Japan (also, JCP)
CWS	Church World Service
EACC	East Asia Christian Conference
EMAJ	Evangelical Missions Association of Japan
Expo '70	Osaka World Exposition, 1970
FCM	Fellowship of Christian Missionaries
HOREMCO	Hokkaido Radio Evangelism and Mass Communications
IBC	Interboard Committee for Christian Work in Japan
ICSW	International Council for Social Work
ICU	International Christian University
IVCF	InterVarsity Christian Fellowship
JATE	Japan Association for Theological Education
JBS	Japan Bible Society
JCAN	*Japan Christian Activity News*
JCMA	Japan Christian Medical Association
JCP	Japan Communist Party (also, CPJ)
JCQ	*Japan Christian Quarterly*
JCYB	*Japan Christian Year Book*
JEA	Japan Evangelical Association
JEB	Japan Evangelistic Band
JEMA	Japan Evangelical Missionary Association
JMA	Japan Montessori Association
JMB	*Japan Missionary Bulletin*
JNAC	Japan–North American Commission on Cooperative Mission
JOC	Jeunes Ouvrières Chrétiennes (Young Christian Workers)
JOCS	Japan Overseas Christian Medical Cooperative Service
JPC	Japan Protestant Convention
JSP	Japan Socialist Party
KAATS	Korean Association of Accredited Theological Schools

KGK	Kirisutosha Gakusei Kai (conservative evangelical student group)
Kōmeitō	Clean Government Party
Kyōdan	United Church of Christ in Japan (also, UCCJ)
LARA	Licensed Agencies for Relief in Asia
LDP	Liberal Democratic Party
LIFE	Language Institute for Evangelism
LMC	Life and Mission of the Church
M.E.P.	Société des Missions Étrangères de Paris (Paris Foreign Mission Society)
Mukyōkai	Non-Church Christianity
NAB	New American Bible
NATO	North Atlantic Treaty Organization
NCCJ	National Christian Council of Japan
NEAATS	North East Asia Association of Theological Schools
NEAJT	*Northeast Asia Journal of Theology*
NHK	Nippon Hōsō Kōkai, (the national radio-television network of Japan)
NRK	Nihon Rūteru Kyōkan, Japan Lutheran Church (with historic connections to the Lutheran Church—Missouri Synod)
OECD	Organization for Economic Co-operation and Development
OPEC	Organization of Petroleum Exporting Countries
Rengō	The Federation of Evangelical Churches in the Kyōdan
RSV	Revised Standard Version of the Bible
SBC	Southern Baptist Convention
SCAP	Supreme Commander, Allied Powers (also refers to the entire American Occupation of Japan apparatus)
SCM	Student Christian Movement
SDF	Self-Defense Forces (Japan)
SDP	Social Democratic Party
SEAC	South East Asia Course
Seikōkai	Anglican Episcopal Church of Japan
TEAM	The Evangelical Alliance Mission
TEF	Theological Education Fund
TELL	Tokyo English Life Line
TUTS	Tokyo Union Theological Seminary
UCCJ	United Church of Christ in Japan (Kyōdan)
WCC	World Council of Churches
WCRP	World Conference of Religion and Peace
WSCF	World Student Christian Federation
YMCA/YWCA	Young Men's/Women's Christian Association
Zenkyōtō	All-Campus Joint Struggle Councils

1

The Historical Context
of Christianity's Development
in Japan since 1945

*Problems in Understanding Christianity's
Development in Japan since 1945*

For those concerned about understanding the present situation of Christianity in Japan, a problem very soon arises: that of deciding what historical context must be used. Most of the historical studies that deal with Christianity in Japan since 1945 treat that period as a continuation of developments which began with the introduction of Roman Catholic Christianity to Japan under Saint Francis Xavier from 1549, or with the reintroduction of Christianity under Protestant and Catholic missionaries in the nineteenth century from 1859. While an emphasis on historical continuity here is entirely valid, the fuller treatment unavoidably given the two earlier periods has sometimes tended to obscure the fact that Christianity in Japan has operated under quite a different historical context since 1945. An understanding of what that more recent context has been is helpful in order to understand the role of Christianity in Japan today.

Sometimes one gets the impression from an inadequate reading of psychology texts that the only lasting impressions a human being possesses in life are those from early childhood, as if the rest of one's life were determined by what happened when one was a child. This may be partially true, but there are also lives that have been significantly changed or altered, for the better or the worse, by events of adolescence or of young adulthood. Occasionally a life is decisively affected by something that happens in one's old age: consider the remarkable case of Cardinal Angelo Roncalli, who became Pope John XXIII just before his seventy-seventh birthday. Very significant and unexpected changes can also take place in the history of a mature Christian community in

1

a country like Japan. It is not enough to know when it originated and what were the early stages of its development. The fact is, the Christian groups of Japan were already fully mature when, in the period since 1945, they have had to face challenges from their society that have profoundly altered not only their ways of doing things but also their deepest beliefs. Perhaps sufficient time has elapsed since 1945 to be able to achieve some perspective on what a number of these societal challenges have been, and how Christians have responded to them.

Some Alternative Approaches to the Subject

To approach the subject in this way means that we must part company with other approaches to the subject that are entirely valid in their own ways. For instance, we cannot deal with this topic as a part of the "expansion of Christianity," for in 1945 Christianity was very much present in Japan. Nor can this subject be dealt with as merely an extension of "world Christianity," for many of the things that happened to Japanese Christians since 1945 had very little to do with what was happening to Christians elsewhere. Nor can one approach the subject in plain denominational or chronological categories, to state when a "mission was opened," when a certain "program was begun," or how a particular "territory was occupied." Let us hope that such quasi-military metaphors will be kept where they belong.

Another approach to the subject is to treat the history of Christianity as one subsection of "the history of religions" in Japan, as though Japanese religion were one broad stream, which coursed through separate channels called Shintō, Buddhism, and Christianity. Such an approach has its own validity, of course, from the standpoint of a government that seeks to draw up laws and procedures to deal with all religions equally, or for a study of the phenomenological aspects of religion alone. But such methods are not adequate for an understanding of the inner dynamics or the particular life-styles of various Christian groups.

Also, historical development can never be reduced entirely to sociological analysis. To be sure, historical research is helped at every step of the way by analyses of such things as the structural organizations, the value systems, and the functional relationships of Christian churches and groups seen primarily as social institutions. But a historical account must include more, by pointing out such things as the unique contributions made by individuals, the impact of unexpected events, and the strange interplay between ideas and the organizations that seek to give them expression.

Three Periods of Historical Development since 1945

If a historical approach is to be used, then the major periods of the entire time span under consideration need to be more carefully examined. Obviously, all attempts to divide history neatly into periods are artificial. Such a methodology can be defended only as a way to make it easier to develop meaningful generalizations about historical developments.

This approach will make use of three periods, those of the Allied Occupation (1945-52), of Rapid Economic Growth (1952-68), and of Challenge and Reappraisal (from 1968). It might be said at this point that although the use of the first period is obvious, the distinction between the second and the third periods is to some extent a matter of personal opinion. It is true that all groups have not been going through a time of reappraisal, but this has been the case often enough to warrant special attention. Nor is it yet evident that this period of reappraisal is anywhere near an end.

It also must be said in passing that the writing of contemporary history can be a hazardous, brazen, or even amusing undertaking. How much easier it is to write about an epoch long gone than about one's own times! Yet there is the consolation that the writing of contemporary history began, after all, with Thucydides, and has often flourished in the interim.[1] We must somehow be able to come to grips with the era through which we have just come, if we are to deal meaningfully with what happened long ago and also with what is yet to come.

The Period of the Occupation (1945-52)

At the end of the Pacific War in 1945 all Japanese had to respond to the new situation that had arisen after the first national defeat in their history and to the onset of the first occupation by foreign powers. There was relief that the long ordeal during wartime was over, but they knew that a new one in peacetime was about to begin. Even when they found that the Occupation forces were not bent on massive plunder and revenge, there were the hardships and the dislocations that represented the brutal aftermath of war. Somehow the nation found its way through survival and began a massive job of reconstruction. There was need not only to reconstruct the shattered cities, the ruined economy, and the torn lives of its people, but also to rebuild the very sense of identity of what it meant to be Japanese.

This was a time when the Japanese Christian community, numerically small, scattered, and indescribably weary, shared the lot of its fellow citizens. A quarter of the 1600 Protestant church buildings throughout Japan were completely destroyed, while half of all Protestant school buildings were demolished.[2] Losses were even greater for the Roman Catholic Church, because the atomic bombing of Nagasaki brought havoc to what had been the most active parish in the country.[3] But beyond the physical damage came the blows to Christians' self-esteem, since except for a few scattered individuals who had criticized the nation's war policies, most had loyally backed their country, so much so that the purge of a leading Protestant pastor was seriously considered in 1947.[4] Yet apart from the passing of a few resolutions, there were minimal changes in the churches at the time, and many of the same leaders from the wartime era continued to hold places of postwar responsibility in the churches.[5]

Hence the first task of the Christian community in Japan was to come to grips with the meaning of their nation's defeat and occupation. "All is lost except faith in God" was the text of a telegram sent from Japan to American Christian friends at this time. But as the initial postwar shock subsided, Christians in Japan found that they along with their fellow citizens were called upon to respond to a number of specific Occupation policies that became embodied in Japanese government legislation. These measures were to provide the agenda for a number of Christians for years to come.

Postwar Policies on Freedom of Religion

The Allied Powers had made it clear from the time of the Potsdam Declaration that they would seek to establish freedom of religion in Japan. Soon after the Occupation began, therefore, Japanese authorities took steps to release from prison those who had been detained there because of their religious beliefs, and removed some of the legal obstacles for certain ecclesiastical groups. But beyond such obvious abuses, most Japanese—including most of the Christian community—believed that they had been enjoying freedom of religion all along. Did not article 28 of the Meiji constitution (1889) declare that "Japanese subjects shall, within limits not prejudicial to peace and order, and not antagonistic to their duties as subjects, enjoy freedom of religious belief"? What more could Occupation require in regard to freedom of religion than what they had already?

The answers were to come in the various instructions put out by the Occupation, beginning with the Shintō Directive (1945) of SCAP (the initials for "Supreme Commander, Allied Powers" which came to stand for the entire Allied Occupation). Far from being aimed specifically at Shintō, this directive ordered that there must be separation between the government and all religious organizations, so that religious groups would be freed from any kind of governmental supervision and control and would be enabled to exist legally and acquire property in order to carry out their religious functions freely. At the same time, the state was to be prohibited from engaging in religious education or the support of any religious group whatever. These policies were to be spelled out in the constitution (promulgated 1946; came into force 1947), and implemented through the Religious Corporations Ordinance (1945), later replaced by the Religious Juridical Persons Law (1951). Even if these new policies prevented governmental favoritism to any religious group and discouraged the favoritism toward Christianity that Buddhist and Shintō leaders had feared, they made it possible for Christian groups to grow at an unprecedented rate in the immediate postwar period. The widespread introspection caused by the defeat and the emperor's "renunciation of his divinity" (1946) seemed to set the stage for a "religions boom" in postwar

Japan, including a "Christian boom" of considerable proportions. Although many who thronged the churches during the Occupation years did so out of curiosity and formed no lasting connections with Christianity, some of the students who did join the churches at this time were, in the years to come, to provide important leadership. New congregations were formed all over the country, church buildings were rebuilt or newly built, and the Christian community gained a self-confidence that it had lacked since the Meiji era. The tremendous creativity in Christian literature, art, theology, lay witness, social service, and other areas that was to flourish in the succeeding years was due in no small measure to the dynamism that was generated during the comparatively short period of the Occupation. Religious liberty in Japan was to remain a live issue, however, as was seen in the repeated attempts by the ruling Liberal Democratic party to nationalize the Yasukuni Shrine and the continuing efforts by Christians and others to block such legislation.

Another aspect of the SCAP policies on religion was the encouragement given to the return of Christian missionaries to Japan. After exploratory visits by Protestant and then Catholic church leaders made it clear that their Japanese counterparts would welcome the return of missionaries—with certain well-expressed reservations—mission boards and societies in Europe, North America, and Australia made extensive efforts to send missionaries and to raise funds for relief and reconstruction of Christian buildings. The mission groups that in these ways resumed ties with Japanese Christians with whom they had developed historic relations, for the most part decided that their personnel and funds should be used in cooperative relationships with the Japanese churches in such ways that the autonomy of the latter would be affirmed and not weakened. The methods by which Roman Catholic groups and Protestant boards set about doing this bear striking similarities to each other, even though it does not seem that there was any mutual consultation at the time. Roman Catholic missionary societies drew up "contracts" with the Japanese diocesan bishops, by which the privileges and responsibilities of both sides were stated with as much clarity as possible, and joint committees were established to implement the arrangements. Protestant mission boards achieved virtually the same result by establishing with their related Japanese Christian groups "councils of cooperation" (under various names), which were to administer programs that previously had been jointly approved. The overseas relationships of the Orthodox Church of Japan soon became complicated by cold-war politics because SCAP sought to relate this group to their Orthodox counterparts in North America and not to the government-dominated Russian Orthodox Church.[6] The specific contributions of the missionaries and the overseas relationships that were developed by various Japanese churches make, of course, a separate study. But the very presence and work of the missionaries in Japan and the churches' international ties from the Occupation period onward gave a dimension of "mission" to Japanese Christianity that was to influence much else that Christians in Japan were doing.

Postwar Policies on Education and Social Work

The policies of SCAP for education were to have almost as much significance for Christian groups as the policies toward religion. Some of the Christian schools had been founded even before the lifting of the ban against Christianity, and from the Meiji era onward had served as the most fertile ground for converts to the new faith. But until 1945 Christian schools had been hampered by such governmental directives as the Ministry of Education's "Order No. 12" (1899), which prohibited the teaching of religion or courses in religious education in all officially recognized schools, whether public or private. The ministry rescinded this order in November 1945 and about the same time sent out instructions stating that, while in the past Christian schools had "suffered from a great deal of interference and excessive oppression," this should henceforth cease.[7] But beyond the removal of such government restrictions in education, the Occupation made it clear that one of its goals was to promote education for "democracy." And what in the world was that?

The answer was to be slowly formulated and was to take much the same form as was the case with freedom of religion and social welfare. The guarantee was stated in the new constitution (1947), article 26: "All people shall have the right to receive an equal education correspondent to their ability, as provided by law." The new educational system was to be spelled out in the Fundamental Law of Education (1947) and in many other subsidiary laws, such as the Private Schools Law (1949). The precise details of the new educational system, and the difficulties it encountered from the late 1950s when the government began to increase its supervision over education, especially in conflict with the leftist-dominated Japan Teachers' Union, must be dealt with separately. What needs to be pointed out here is that the new educational system, together with the centuries-old Japanese respect and hunger for learning, the sudden increase in the school population that was brought on by the postwar baby boom, and the gradual improvement of the national economy, which provided greater resources for education—all combined to create an "education boom," in which the Christian schools were among the chief beneficiaries. The addition of three years of middle school to the program of compulsory education made high school and college education newly popular, and it was in these latter areas that the Christian schools enlarged their programs. Expanding an older Christian school was far easier than founding a new school, but new institutions such as International Christian University near Tokyo showed that the latter could be done also, although with great difficulties.

The enormous postwar expansion of the Christian schools is a story in itself. That such schools, especially the new Christian universities, gained a new respectability for the Christian faith in Japanese society and brought in numbers of new converts for the churches is beyond question. But the extent to which the Christian schools developed new philosophies of education to enable them to cope with their new situation and the long-range administrative planning to deal with the ever-increasing problems that expansion brought are other questions.

As in education, social work was another area that was deeply influenced by SCAP policies aimed at "democratization." Social work done on a family or neighborhood basis was traditional in Japan, but the care of persons to whom one was not bound by kinship or clan was an area in which Japanese Christians pioneered. In fact, some of the first orphanages in Japan, programs for the reformation of prisoners, social settlement work, and work for the blind were started by Christians.[8] Hence when SCAP and the Japanese government faced the staggering social problems of postwar Japan, there were Christians who were already acknowledged leaders in social work with experience in coping with them. Christians were major supporters of legislation to outlaw licensed prostitution, and they established rehabilitation centers for ex-prostitutes (1957). The government's decisions to take the steps for securing the minimum guarantees of a so-called welfare state posed the questions of public responsibility in ways that some Christian social workers could well understand.

As was the case in education, the form of the new social legislation enacted under the Occupation took some time to become systematized. The new constitution enunciated the people's "right to maintain the minimum standards of wholesome and cultured living" (article 25). Specific legislation took the form of the Livelihood Protection Law (1946) and other laws dealing with the welfare of children, the physically handicapped, the aged, the mentally retarded, mothers and dependent children, which all together made up the "Six Welfare Laws" to be administered by social work agencies and social case workers. The new legislation made it possible for many new social work agencies to be started during the Occupation era, when the needs were more pressing than ever, and minimum facilities for meeting these needs were all that could be afforded. Many of these new social work centers were either avowedly Christian or largely staffed with Christian personnel. It was not accidental that the proportion of Christians among social work personnel was high, for such humble work for long hours at low pay required a personal commitment that Christian faith helped to supply. To be sure, in order to fulfill their responsibilities, such social workers had to cooperate with people in the governmental and business "establishments" that made them the targets of criticism by Christian social activists in later years. While recognizing the limitations under which they had to work, Christian social workers were nevertheless able to develop patterns of responsibility and an esprit de corps that have had widespread influence.

The Search for Peace

The almost universal revulsion against war found among postwar Japanese, together with the Occupation's initial determination that Japan would never again become a military menace in East Asia, led to the drafting of the famous article 9 of the new constitution, which renounced war as a sovereign right of the nation and declared that "land, sea, and air forces, as well as other war potential, will never be maintained." But the principle of unanimity among the "Big Five" powers that had been allied in World War II, which underlay the formation of the United Nations and other postwar settlements, soon proved illusory. Confrontations between pro-Communist and pro-Western forces began in the Greek Civil War in 1946 and spread to other European countries in the following years. The North Atlantic Treaty Organization (NATO) was formed (1949) for collective Western European and American action in the face of the U.S.S.R and its Communist allies. The victory of the Chinese Communists on mainland China (1949) brought the cold war nearer Japan. And the outbreak of the Korean War (1950) thrust Japan right into the middle of a hot war, for the American Occupation forces in Japan under General Douglas MacArthur's command were committed by President Harry Truman to the Korean conflict. Because this left the Japanese islands virtually defenseless, and since Japanese Communists were threatening internal disorder in Japan in order to oppose the government's acquiescence with United States military policies, SCAP authorized the creation of Japanese military forces that were at first called the National Police Reserve (1950), then the National Safety Force (1952), and finally, the Self-Defense Forces (1954).[9] The Japanese government maintained then, and still maintains, that since such forces are for self-defense, they do not constitute the "war potential" prohibited by the constitution. Periodic defense buildups have left the numbers of the Self-Defense Forces small, but have given them the latest technology and equipment to enable them to have more firepower than the Japanese armed forces had at the height of World War II. Meanwhile, from 1950 Japan was used as a base for American military operations in Korea and elsewhere, and the United States–Japan Security Treaty that was signed at the same time as the Peace Treaty (1951) gave the United States the right to continued use of bases in Japan. American orders for procurement of war materials in Japan from the time of the Korean War provided a major boost to the nation's unsteady postwar economy.

Such swift and drastic changes in Japan's search for peace caused severe repercussions among its people, especially in the Christian community. Groups like the Quakers, who were pacifist in principle and therefore opposed to military forces of any sort, continued to maintain their convictions amid the changing societal circumstances. Others maintained that since America's disarming of Japan had not been based on idealism in the first place but on its reading of its own interests in the Pacific area, it was proper for Japanese to trade their misguided idealism for their own interests, which included the minimum needs for self-defense.[10] More liberal Christians argued that Japan should not rearm because an attack upon the country was unthinkable and would immediately earn the aggressor the opprobrium of the world community. They also argued that Japan's recent militaristic ventures had brought nothing but disaster, and that to rearm would only invite attack and more disaster. A few Christian leftists argued that military forces were proper for "peace-loving socialist nations" like the Soviet Union and China, but were not allowable for "warmongering capitalist nations" like the United States and Japan. Although some Christian peace groups were organized at the time of the Korean War and continued their activities thereafter, most Christians affirmed their support for peace and hoped that the problems of militarism would go away. In the meantime, there were many constructive programs that would increase understanding and cooperation among nations, and to these Christians and others could give their whole-hearted support.

The Period of Rapid Economic Growth (1952-68)

With the end of the Occupation (1952), most Japanese in all walks of life felt their nation was entering a new era. Many had sensed the transition earlier, for the high tide of experimentation that had characterized the earlier period of the Occupation had subsided, and the outbreak of the Korean War made SCAP think of Japan more as an ally than an enemy. The Christian boom in Japan gradually tapered off, and the growth rate for most groups slowed down considerably. It was also a different social climate in which they would be operating for the next fifteen years or so. For instead of having to react periodically to crises or to orders from governmental agencies, not only during the Occupation, but even from the Meiji era onward, Christian groups would now have the freedom to grow and develop in their own way. Even world events, which had their impact on the Christian community—of which four principal ones will be discussed presently—did not affect all Christians, and affected some only in certain ways.

It is important to see how Christians responded to this period of relatively peaceful development in their society. In the early days of the Occupation, there had been a number of specific issues that confronted Christian groups, to which fairly explicit responses were required. For instance, to secure juridical-person status for a church, or to open a new department in a university, or to start an orphanage, there had been certain specified requirements that had to be met. But in the post-Occupation era, the challenges and the opportunities were just as real, though much more diffuse. In particular, there was one growing phenomenon in Japanese society that soon came to eclipse almost all others in terms of importance, namely, the country's rapid economic development. How, indeed, were Christians to respond to that?

The Impact of Economic Growth

Beginning with the Korean War procurement orders, the nation's economy began to grow sporadically in the 1950s, but then developed at an unprecedented rate after Prime Minister Hayato Ikeda adopted the "doubling the national income" policy in 1960. During this period almost no aspect of Japanese society remained unaffected by economic growth. The Christian community in Japan received some of the benefits, but also some of the anguish, that came from the so-called Showa boom. For instance, the government encouraged people to move from agricultural areas, where there was a surplus of labor and earning a livelihood from farming became increasingly difficult, into the urban areas where developing industries could absorb almost all available labor. This touched off one of the greatest internal migrations in Japanese history, as rural areas became depopulated and the cities burgeoned with newly arrived residents. Christian groups since Meiji times had been stronger in the cities, where people felt freer from the traditional family communitarian and religious obligations and able to join a new religious group. The migration to the cities should have presented the churches with a new opportunity, but although a few groups in the Kyōdan (the United Church of Christ in Japan) and other churches experimented with what came to be known as Urban Industrial Evangelism, most of the churches were unprepared to deal with the changing situation. Some were preparing instead to undertake rural evangelism programs directed in virtually the opposite direction from the movement of population.

The new urbanization and industrialization made it possible for churches and various Christian schools and institutions to alter their programs or to develop new thrusts from the proceeds of judicious land sales. As the price of urban land continued to grow yearly, groups that were fortunate enough to have land from prewar days or to secure it in the immediate postwar period could sell it at much higher prices. But the same higher prices for urban land made it difficult for other urban churches or schools to secure land for their needs. In like manner, the opportunities for part-time employment in urban areas made it possible for pastors and other Christian workers to secure *Arbeit* (or side-work) and with that income to continue their Christian work at a minimal salary. But rising costs in urban areas made it necessary for Christian groups constantly to seek new sources of income in order to maintain the same programs. Similarly, economic development created new groups of people who enjoyed moderate affluence for the first time in their lives and who were therefore better able to support the work of churches and voluntary agencies. But there were also new "pockets of poverty," among fishermen, farmers, and coal miners in various parts of Japan, who suffered severe deprivation in the midst of general affluence and who laid strong claims on the consciences of Christians. Thus new prosperity brought its bane as well as blessing, its retrenchments as well as advances.

New Agenda Items for Christian Groups

Freed from the necessity of responding to periodic crises and, in some cases, able to benefit somewhat from improving economic conditions, Christian groups were more able during this period to develop their own program agenda. Anniversaries were one means of reasserting their ties with the past, and hence their continuing identity in the midst of change. Just as Roman

Catholics had celebrated the 400th anniversary of the coming of Saint Francis Xavier to Japan (1949), Protestants celebrated the centennial of the arrival of their first missionaries (1959). Thereafter, many Christian churches and schools observed their own centennials, which were interspersed with observances of the cultural centennials of such things as newspapers, the national educational system, the national railway system, and so on. In these ways, Christians could identify their origins in Japan with many aspects of modern Japanese culture. There were rounds of meetings of all sorts, including international gatherings in Japan such as that of the World Council on Christian Education, in Tokyo (1959), for which Japanese Christians were the hosts. And there were international gatherings overseas to which Japanese delegations were sent and from which they brought back reports. Various visiting scholars and churchmen made trips to Japan, and evangelists such as Stanley Jones, Bob Pierce, and Billy Graham staged crusades that attracted thousands of hearers. The Tokyo Olympic Games (1964) symbolized the type of contribution to international goodwill that Japan was capable of making, and the event signified for many the gradual return of Japan to full membership in the international community and the end of its "occupation mentality." This significance was not lost on members of the Christian community.

Christians also developed new program areas that had long awaited fuller expression. The growing strength of the educational system made it possible to develop programs of theological education of many sorts. There was no one single pattern here but, rather, a proliferation of schools and programs to meet different needs and to serve different denominational traditions. Concurrent with this was the expansion of theological research and writing. Not only were there translations of the writings of Western theologians such as Karl Barth and classical writers such as Thomas Aquinas, John Calvin, Martin Luther, and John Wesley, but a growing number of original theological works were being written by Japanese authors (see chap. 9, below). The same was true of the arts in general, for the works of Christian novelists, playwrights, the paintings and woodblock prints of Christian artists, the compositions of Christian composers and musicians, and the interpretive work of Japanese dance experts, made this period truly a "golden age" of Christian art and literature (see chap. 5 below).

Nor should the growing agenda of Christian projects be limited to those of professional clergy, scholars, or artists. There were hosts of voluntary lay-sponsored programs that gave expression to the concerns of laymen and women who often felt that church programs as such were too dominated by the professional clergy.

Four Overseas Developments Affecting Christianity in Japan

Given the fact that this period was relatively free of traumatic events, there were four overseas developments which had particular repercussions on certain Christian groups in Japan. The first was the crisis in Japan generated by the signing of the new United States–Japan Mutual Security Treaty in 1960, to replace the former security treaty (signed by Prime Minister Shigeru Yoshida in 1951), which was considered by many disadvantageous for Japan. Massive protests against this treaty, together with internal struggles within the ruling Liberal Democratic party, led to the calling off of President Dwight D. Eisenhower's scheduled visit to Japan, since the demonstrations against Prime Minister Nobosuke Kishi were so severe that the safety of the American president could not be guaranteed if the visit took place. Prime Minister Kishi had to resign because of this crisis and turn over the reins of government to Hayato Ikeda, who henceforth adopted a "low posture" toward international affairs. These incidents caused considerable repercussions among Protestant groups concerned with Christian witness in society. New coalitions of concerned groups were formed at this time, and the theological adequacy and practical usefulness of viewpoints that had been "imported" from Western countries in the immediate postwar period were called into question. The process by which this realignment of perspectives and coalitions took place—bearing striking similarities to the ideological fragmentation within the Japan Communist party that was to happen a little later—had important consequences for subsequent developments within the Christian community and it is an important subject in its own right.

Another important development for Christians in Japan was the calling of Vatican Council II, which Pope John XXIII announced in 1959, and which was held from 1962 to 1965. Not only was this the major event affecting Roman Catholics in Japan and elsewhere; it also had profound repercussions in Protestant and Orthodox circles. The new stresses that Catholics laid on the vernacular liturgy, Bible study, hymnology, and in general on the witness of the whole People of God led to closer ecumenical relations than had ever been previously true in Japan. Yet the aftermath of Vatican Council II saw several problem areas develop, especially in regard to birth control and the difficulties of recruiting and retaining clergy, so that Roman Catholics were unable to proceed to the renewal envisioned by the Council with the vigor that had been anticipated. A few observers were also wondering whether ecumenicity should be confined to Christians, or whether the dialogues that had been developing between Christians and people of other faiths in Japan should not also be carried much further. If such were to happen, it would be a new experience for most Japanese Christians, who have traditionally shown considerable hesitation over becoming formally involved in interfaith relationships.

Another development with important consequences was the growing rift between the Soviet Union and People's Republic of China, which began to be made public in 1963 and was at its most severe phase during the Chinese "Great Proletarian Cultural Revolution" (1966–67) and the confrontations between Soviet and Chinese troops along their lengthy common border (1969). This confrontation was significant for those leftists in Japan—including some Christians—whose ideological commitments had assumed a consensus of international Communist parties, and it opened the way for conflicts over heresy and orthodoxy similar to those following the Protestant Reformation in Europe. But the principal effect of these developments on Christians was that the new pluralism of the Japanese left was to produce a new diversity of opinions among Christian students and intellectual leaders, who now felt a new sympathy with leftist groups endeavoring to shake off the mantle of Soviet and Chinese power politics. This meant, for instance, that when the Security Treaty came up for reconsideration in the period before 1970, the repercussions for Christian groups were different from those of 1960.

A fourth international development affecting Christians in Japan was the intensification of the war in Vietnam and elsewhere in Indochina, and especially the involvement of the United States in that conflict following the Gulf of Tonkin Resolution passed by the U.S. Congress (1964). Among Japanese Christians there emerged growing criticism of the United States, which was already facing a deepening crisis in race relations, and a delegation of Japanese Christians made a special trip to the United States to make known their views on Vietnam (1965). There were also continuing criticisms of the fact that United States military bases remained in Japan and Okinawa and played a significant role in the Indochina conflict. The cooperation of Japanese government and industry in selling war materials for the conflict was given by critics as evidence of Japan's ambiguous moral stance, but the precise extent of this involvement—reported by the *Kirisuto Shimbun* to have been $6.5 billion worth of direct and indirect procurements for the war between 1965 and 1972—was not publicly known until later.[11] This meant that Christian leftists would come to focus their criticisms not only on political parties and governmental policies but also on the business dealings of corporations and on the roles of schools and churches in society. Thus the stage was set for challenging many institutions and procedures that had been more or less taken for granted in the postwar period.

The Period of Challenge and Reappraisal (from 1968)

A Period of Conflict in Schools and Churches

It is always a hazardous business to try to discern the beginning of a new era, especially when it is close to the present. But perhaps the outbreak of the Tokyo University struggle (1968) may be taken as a landmark for the onset of a period in which many of the programs and policies of the entire postwar era began to be called into question. Over the next two years university disorders spread all over Japan, as part of a worldwide phenomenon of student unrest, but in Japan with a particular focus on 1970 as the year in which the Japan–United States Mutual Security Treaty's ten-year period ended and the treaty could be renounced by either nation upon one year's notice. Thus the year 1970 provided a goal toward which leftist student groups, including many Christians, worked with an almost eschatological expectation. The particular issues on which the critics centered their attacks on the "establishments" in government, school, church, and society were to vary from the government-sponsored Universities Control Bill to various issues related to the Security Treaty, the Christian Pavilion at Expo '70, struggles over United States bases and the building of a new Tokyo airport, and disputes over student autonomy, police action, entrance examinations, or tuition raises at particular universities. The "New Left" groups that emerged from these struggles did not have overall objectives, but sought to use specific issues as means of heightening popular consciousness of the threats facing society, and thus of forming coalitions to help bring these threats to an end. Protests of Christian students against the Christian Pavilion at the Osaka World Exposition in 1970 (Expo '70) led to disruptions in Christian universities and theological seminaries and spilled over into the Kyōdan (the United Church of Christ in Japan), where the church's General Assembly and major District Assemblies were paralyzed for several years over this and related disputes. Japan's two leading Baptist churches were somewhat less involved in conflict over protests against the Baptist World Alliance meeting in Tokyo (1970). Other groups—Wesleyan Methodists, Anglicans, Lutherans—had lesser disputes on other issues.

Even though the school and church struggles had largely subsided by 1970, they left behind a trail of bitterness and polarization, and also a general Christian constituency bewildered as to how and why their churches and schools had been affected. The questioning process initiated in various Christian groups also coincided with similar questions being raised at this time in many different areas.

A Season for Reappraisals

Just as Japan's economic growth had been the major element causing social changes of all sorts in the previous period, so now some major reappraisals of this economic growth were triggered by concern over such consequences as pollution, congestion, and the depletion of natural resources. This was, to be sure, a phenomenon common to all industrialized countries, but the harmful consequences of pollution were more quickly felt in a congested country like Japan. Furthermore, the very successes of Japanese trading policies in the United States, Europe, and East Asia led to complaints against Japan in these areas. Meanwhile, leftist groups were rethinking their own positions, and the JCP began to register significant gains in membership and electoral strength on the basis of more moderate policies, distinct from both the People's Republic of China and the USSR, whose rivalry continued unabated. But for most Japanese, including the Christian community, the gradual reappraisal of America had important consequences. The image of "Christian America" was reexamined in the light of that country's continuing racial difficulties, incidents of political violence and assassinations of public figures, and involvement in Vietnam. Then came the two "Nixon shocks" in the summer of 1971, the one announcing President Richard Nixon's forthcoming visit to Peking and the other telling of measures to cope with the dollar crisis, both of which were taken without the prior consultation to which the Japanese government felt entitled. Thus the image of America as a nation whose principles and practices might serve as models for Japan was replaced by the picture of an America with continuing and unresolved problems of its own.

It is of course too soon to know how much Japan's Christian community has been affected by the general mood of reappraisal just described. But there were specific changes that Japanese Christians had to face. Overseas Roman Catholic mission groups were unable to continue sending sisters and priests and in some cases funds to Japan at the same level as in the past, with the result that Japanese Catholics were now thrown increasingly on their own resources. The same was true for many of the larger Protestant denominations in America and Europe, which faced severe problems of declining contributions in their churches. While conservative Protestant groups were less affected by cuts in finances and personnel, they began to experience some of the same concerns for Japanese "autonomy" that had affected other groups. Sometimes organizational changes seemed required, as when the Interboard Committee for Christian Work in Japan was replaced by the Japan–North America Commission on Cooperative Mission (1973), thus indicating that organization for mission was a two-way street between Japan and North America, and not a one-way thoroughfare as previously. At other times, the restoration of fellowship and cooperation among Christians was sought, as in the Kyōdan's continuing efforts toward internal reconciliation.

Japan and the World of Nations

Whatever the outcome of the various reappraisals, Japan's powerful dynamism as a nation and its growing role in the world of nations would have to be reckoned with. Partially because of their own internal problems, Christians in Japan had been slow to realize the significance of their nation's new international prominence and its implications for the future. There were Japanese businessmen traveling or residing abroad, and among them were to be found a "new diaspora" of Christians in various parts of the world. Some Japanese Christian groups, often in cooperation with overseas Christians, had been sending Japanese missionaries and Christian workers abroad. Would this be one of the signs of new mission outreach in the future? What might the small Christian community in Japan do in order to help its country's new international role to be a positive one, and not the beginnings of a new form of "imperialism" that would sow the seeds of new oppression and disaster?

Thus by 1979 the historical context of Christianity in Japan was very different from that of 1945. A country that lay prostrate after defeat in total war had recovered its strength to the point where it was a leading member of the world of nations. The small Christian community in Japan had also made a recovery from the low point of 1945, but had not achieved the rate of numerical growth that some had predicted for it. Yet Christians in various walks of life in Japan, despite the numerous problems they faced, nevertheless possessed a unique vitality that could serve well in the uncertain days ahead.

NOTES

1. R. W. Seton-Watson, as cited in Geoffrey Barraclough, *An Introduction to Contemporary History* (London: Penguin, 1967), p. 15.

2. William C. Kerr, *Japan Begins Again* (New York: Friendship Press, 1949), p. 11.

3. See Joseph L. Van Hecken, *The Catholic Church in Japan since 1959* (Tokyo: Enderle, 1963), pp. 95–96.

4. William P. Woodard, *The Allied Occupation of Japan 1945–1952 and Japanese Religions* (Leiden: E. J. Brill, 1972), p. 187.

5. Richard H. Drummond, "Catharsis in the Japanese Church," *The Christian Century* 79, no. 21 (May 23, 1962): 651–54.

6. Richard H. Drummond, *A History of Christianity in Japan* (Grand Rapids, Mich.: Wm. B. Eerdmans, 1971), pp. 357–58.

7. Woodard, *Allied Occupation,* pp. 39, 105.

8. Masao Takenaka, *Reconciliation and Renewal in Japan* (New York: Friendship Press, 1957), p. 28.

9. Albert Axelbank, *Black Star over Japan* (Tokyo: Tuttle, 1972), p. 8.

10. Masataka Kosaka, *100 Million Japanese: The Postwar Experience* (Tokyo: Kōdansha, 1972), p. 108.

11. *JCAN,* February 23, 1973, pp. 1, 6.

2

Christians and Politics in Japan: Dealing with the Nation's Experiment with "Peace and Democracy"

There are few times in history when one nation has been in a position to impress another not only with its military might but also with its national ideals. But this is precisely what happened during the American Occupation of Japan (1945–52). As Edwin O. Reischauer put it, "The American role of conqueror and reformer in postwar Japan was unique in the history of Japan or any modern nation."[1] Part of this uniqueness stems from the fact that it was probably the only military occupation of one nation by another which on the whole met with the tacit approval—and sometimes even the enthusiastic cooperation—of the vanquished.

The reasons for the Occupation's "success," if indeed success it was, have been dealt with at great length elsewhere.[2] Here we are to examine how the Occupation era launched goals for Japan's political life that were to be tested in subsequent decades. It is ironic that a military occupation established goals of "peace and democracy" that came to be accepted in one form or another by most of the Japanese population. At the beginning, many thought that the Christians of Japan would have a special role in the implementation of these goals, even though the Christians numbered less than 1 percent of the total population. Despite the fact that the Christian population did not grow as quickly as some Occupation spokesmen had hoped, the goals of peace and democracy remained for Christians thereafter important items on their political agenda.

This chapter will focus on some of the ways Christians in Japan worked on the new agenda in politics that was theirs after 1945. At times they tried to shape their country's course in accordance with these ideals, but more often they were reacting to developments within the larger society and trying to give directions on the basis of their own deeply-held convictions.

What would the small community of Christians do about the political life of the whole nation? One way to picture the developments of this period is to call to mind Japanese skiers on a slalom course, as they head on their rapid downhill course between gates, which are sets of poles in the snow with small flags on top, placed there by the racemasters to mark the left and right edges of the slalom course. Japanese Christians may be pictured as racemasters trying to place "gates" along the course of postwar Japanese history, to mark the limits—sometimes to the left but mostly to the right—beyond which they felt Japanese society should not swerve. We must be careful not to claim too much for this metaphor. The small size and limited resources of the Japanese Christian community meant that they were very restricted in the precise influence they could exert on the course their nation was taking. It could even be argued that Christians tried to mark an entirely different course from the one actually followed by Japan. But we may use this metaphor as a way of charting the role of Christians in regard to politics in contemporary Japan, during a period of unprecedently rapid social change.

The Occupation Era (1945–52):
Struggling to Form a National Consensus

If World War II was a "dark valley" through which the Japanese nation had to pass, the Occupation also presented its hazards, although they turned out to be not so bad as anticipated. Considering the upheavals of that time, the lack of food and housing, the economic and psychological hardships that followed upon the nation's first defeat in its history, the lack of political resources and power on the part of Japan's Christian community should not be surprising. Like their fellow citizens, Japan's Christians at that time were preoccupied by the overwhelming problems of survival in a country ravaged by wartime destruction, food shortages, economic stagnation, inflation, and social dislocation. Moreover, because they had for the most part cooperated thoroughly with their country's war effort, Japan's Christians also suffered from the sense of national confusion that followed defeat. In the nation's major cities, as far as the eye could see, there was utter devastation, and it meant a devastation of the spirit as well. And yet as Christians began to gather again here and there in their makeshift places of worship, or in war-damaged schools, hospitals, and social work agencies, new hope was infused into the small Christian community. And from that new spirit there came in time the ability to deal with a new agenda of political issues that the postwar political period forced upon them.

The Process of Defining Religious Liberty

One of the first political issues which Christians and others had to face in the postwar era was that of defining freedom of religion, or "religious liberty." To many Japanese it came and always remained as a surprise that they had not been enjoying religious liberty all along. For article 28 of the Meiji constitution (1889) granted Japanese subjects "freedom of religious belief," but went on to specify that this freedom would be exercised "within limits not prejudicial to peace and order, and not antagonistic to their duties as subjects."[3] The latter qualification was all-important, for in time governmental definitions of the duties of Japanese subjects came to include such things as the acceptance of various myths about the origin and nature of the Japanese state and the imperial system, state supervision of religious organizations, and obligatory participation in Shrine Shintō ceremonies. Yet many Japanese had never found these duties onerous, and some Christians were able to participate conscientiously in Shrine Shintō ceremonies.[4] But the Occupation knew that Shrine Shintō had been used as a way of promoting the spirit of Japanese militarism, and it was determined to make a change here.[5]

The Potsdam Declaration, which was the basis for Japan's surrender, contained as one of its conditions the adoption of religious freedom. Then after the establishment of the Occupation in Japan, the Civil Liberties Directive of October 4, 1945, secured the release of persons who had been imprisoned because of their religious beliefs, and the removal from office of those who had been guilty of violating the religious freedom of others. The major action taken by the Occupation in regard to religious freedom, however, was the famous "Shintō Directive" (as it came to be known) of December 15, 1945, which removed further obstacles to the implementation of the principle of religious freedom. Although this directive was originally drawn up to remove special privileges that Shintō shrines had enjoyed from the government—and hence its nickname—it was broadened in principle by the work of Lieutenant William K. Bunce, chief of the Religions Division in the Occupation's Civil Information and Education Branch. Bunce saw that in order to make religious liberty a reality for Japan, all kinds of governmental supports and favoritism for religious groups, including Buddhist and Christian groups as well as Shintō, would have to be removed. This broadened the impact of the directive to give it more of a universal scope, rather than as a vindictive measure aimed at one particular religious group.[6]

Thus far, the process of defining religious liberty had been a one-sided affair, with the initiatives being taken almost exclusively by the Occupation. But the further implementation of the principle required input from religious groups in Japan, and this was sought by Bunce and his colleagues in the Religious Division of SCAP. It was necessary for provisions to be made whereby religious organizations could become incorporated as religious juridicial persons, and hence not subject to governmental control or interference in regard to their religious affairs. This was done in the Religious Corporations Ordinance of December 1945, a hastily drafted work, which in addition to making possible the registration of legitimate religious groups also allowed resort hotels and even brothels to become registered as "religious juridical persons." The opinions of religious groups were taken into account for an expected revision of this ordinance, and in this process Japanese Buddhist and Shintō leaders were gratified to find that SCAP's Religions Division listened carefully to their views, and that their fears were unfounded that SCAP would be overly swayed by the views of Christians.

Meanwhile, the various directives of the Occupation were set into the larger framework of a new Japanese constitution, which was promulgated in November 1946 and came into effect on May 3, 1947. The constitution's article 20 guaranteed religious freedom to all citizens, regardless of their faith; articles 19 and 21 assured freedom of thought, conscience, meeting, association, speech, press, and other basic rights; article 89 set forth the principle of the separation of religion and the state. Many of the discussions and actions of religious groups in postwar Japan would hinge on the interpretation of several of these principles, which the constituition declared to be the supreme law of the land, and which increasingly became accepted by Japanese in all walks of life.

The specific implementation of religious freedom under the constitution came through the Religious Juridical Persons Law (April 3, 1951), a much-needed revision of the December 1945 Religious Corporations Ordinance. The passing of this law and its implementation over a period of years thereafter required the support of religious groups of all sorts in Japan. During the initial part of the Occupation era, there was a so-called Christian boom, but in retrospect it was as much a "religions boom," which brought new adherents to Buddhism, Shintō, and the New Religions as well. Although there was talk of a religious vacuum in postwar Japan that Christianity might hope to fill, this proved to be only partly the case, for the Occupation era was a time when many Japanese religious groups gained a new lease on life, supposedly in the aftermath of the emperor's renunciation of his divinity (January 1, 1946). In the end, the main groups to move into the religious vacuum were the New Religions from Buddhist and Shintō backgrounds, as well as Marxist groups functioning as quasi-religions.[7] Despite the fact that SCAP personnel—and General MacArthur in particular—often spoke of the need for Christianity to grow in Japan and called for "thousands of missionaries to transform the heart and soul of Japan," the actual implementation of the Occupation's policies about the separation of religion and the state was carried out by SCAP's Religions Division on the basis of strict separation of religion and politics, for which the new constitution provided.[8]

The Christian Socialists

Before the Christian churches were fully reorganized under the new constitutional provisions for the separation of religion and the state, Christian convictions about the directions in which the newly structured Japanese society was to go were expressed by prominent Christian lay persons, among whom the Christian Socialists were the most notable. This was a group whose views about Christianity and society had been formed in prewar years, when Japan's Socialist parties were organized and a large number of the country's

Socialist leaders were Christians. They had championed such causes as labor unions, rural cooperatives, and social welfare legislation, the concerns for which the Reverend Toyohiko Kagawa had attracted worldwide attention. Their prewar political activities had been severely circumscribed by governmental action, however, and it was only in the freedom of the postwar era that they could attempt to give their ideals organizational expression.

The leading Christian Socialist in governmental circles was Tetsu Katayama (1887–   ), who became the chairman of the Japan Socialist party. In the surprising aftermath of the nation's first election under the new constitution in May 1947, which gave a plurality to the Socialists, Katayama became Japan's first Socialist prime minister. At first lauded by SCAP authorities as one who might be effective in handling difficult trade union negotiations, Katayama was unable to exercise effective leadership, due to bickering among the factions in the coalition government he headed. He resigned after only nine months in office. Only later did it become clear that a principal reason for his early resignation was his fear that MacArthur would order him to restore the Japanese armed forces, a move that would have gone against all of Katayama's convictions as a Christian pacifist.[9] Even when General MacArthur, after the outbreak of the Korean War in 1950, ordered Prime Minister Shigeru Yoshida to take steps to reestablish Japan's armed forces by setting up the Self-Defense Forces, the mandate for these forces circumscribed their functions to defensive actions only. Katayama's stand had helped to plant a slalom gate against the reestablishment of conventional armed forces with an unrestricted mandate, such as has been the case with the two postwar Germanies. Pressures from the American government and from within Japan's ruling Liberal Democratic party would seek to remove such restrictions. But even though there have been serious encroachments, the "gate" established by Katayama and others still was standing in the 1980's.[10]

Even when the Japan Socialist party moved into the position of a seemingly permanent minority opposition party, there were Christian Diet members who continued to espouse the goals of the Christian Socialists. Komakichi Matsuoka, a supporter of Kagawa's principles, served as Speaker of the House of Representatives. Tamotsu Hasegawa served in the House of Representatives, and was able to build a number of social welfare institutions in Hamamatsu that embodied his unique approach to social welfare programs. Jōtaro Kawakami (1889–1965) served as chairman of the Japan Socialist party and spokesman for its more moderate wing. Kanichi Nishimura (1900–79) was elected to both houses of the Diet, and as a Kyōdan minister was later active during trips to Hanoi in the 1960s to set up mediation procedures to end the Vietnam War. Although his peacemaking efforts proved fruitless, they represented the hopes of many Japanese that the Vietnam War might be ended much sooner than was the case.

Although Katayama's political career as a Christian Socialist made early links between Christians and the Japan Socialist party in the public mind, Christians also supported the smaller socialist group, the Democratic Socialist party, as well as the ruling Liberal Democratic party. Thus Japanese Christians worked with the regular political parties of Japan, and with only the one exception of Tomio Mutō's Japan Christ party in 1976, which will be mentioned later, there were no efforts to form a separate political party for Christians.

Building a Social Christianity

The Occupation also saw the development of a number of programs among Christians, which had very different emphases and yet shared the common goal of attempting to build a Social Christianity in Japan. There were many prewar preparations for such programs, and in the particular social environment of postwar Japan many came to believe that the time was ripe for the fulfillment of their long-cherished dreams and plans. The willingness to try new approaches to social problems, the seeming failure of traditional methods, and the availability of support and encouragement from SCAP and from overseas friends seemed to promise a fertile field for experimentation. Beyond the rich diversity of programs that began or flourished at this time was the common vision that Japanese society could be made over, that human nature could be markedly improved, and that societal arrangements could be established to fit a new vision of the future, which the planners of a Social Christianity had developed. Whereas the Christian Socialists like Katayama had seemingly floundered as practical politicians, the builders of Social Christianity were preparing for more long-range goals.

Student Christian groups were one of the principal sources for the momentum of building a Social Christianity. The Gaku-Y (student branch of the YMCA) and Christian student centers that Protestants and Catholics established in postwar Japan addressed themselves to social and political questions with great seriousness. The writings of Reinhold Niebuhr were introduced to the public by Japanese scholars such as Professor Kiyoko Takeda Chō and Professor Yoshiaki Iisaka of Gakushuin University, while Paul Tillich's version of Religious Socialism was introduced by Dōshisha's Professor Masatoshi Doi and by Tillich's own visit to Japan in 1960. Anglicans stressed William Temple's concerns for a Christian society, and Roman Catholics emphasized the social thought of Saint Thomas Aquinas and the papal encyclicals, the programs of Catholic Action and the Young Christian Workers (JOC). In the postwar era when Marxist thought was freely gaining a hearing among Japanese intellectuals and when university departments of economics, philosophy, sociology, and other disciplines were becoming increasingly influenced by Marxism, Christian professors and students were forming study groups in which they were examining the Marxist critiques of modern capitalist societies. Only a few Protestants embraced Communism, however. One was the Reverend Sakae Akaiwa (1903–66) of the Kyōdan's Uehara Church in Tokyo, who in 1949 after some Communist election victories indicated his intention of joining the Japan Communist party. Akaiwa never actually did so, and Kyōdan officials dissociated the denomination from Akaiwa's declaration. Most Protestants sought to modify or counter the Marxist programs with help from the writings of Max Weber, Ernst Troeltsch, the Social Gospel movement in America, and the dialectical theologians. In general, the postwar period saw the incubation of ideas and programs by students and professors who were seeking to build a Social Christianity. The testing and modification of these theories and movements was to take place later, particularly at the time of the 1960 Mutual Security Treaty crisis.

Another group concerned for the building of a Social Christianity was the Occupational Evangelism (*shokuiki dendō*) group in the Kyōdan. Following a conference with Dr. John Bennett, professor of Christian Social Ethics at Union Theological Seminary in New York, held at Gotemba in 1951, an Occupational Evangelism Committee of the Kyōdan was formed later that year. This group worked at new methods of political action to meet the needs of the nation's industrial workers, and attempted to build up networks for action through regional Occupational Evangelism committees in the churches. To some extent their activities and goals ran parallel to those of the All Japan Socialist Christians' Frontier Union (Zen Nihon Shakaishugi Kirisutosha Zensen Dōmei) that was attempting from about 1948 to 1952 to bring a Christian voice to political and economic issues, until the group fell apart in the wake of the political campaign of its chief organizer, Professor Gan Sakakibara. The Occupational Evangelism group under different names persisted, however, and in the postwar period endeavored to advocate its own techniques of political action, although to a somewhat smaller constituency. (The Occupational Evangelism group is discussed at greater length in chap. 5, "Christian Outreach.")

A third group that shared a vision for building a Social Christianity, and which overlapped to some extent with the first two, was the Christian Peace Fellowship (Kirisutosha Heiwa no Kai). Although Christians were virtually all advocates of peace in some sense during the postwar era, the outbreak of the Korea War in 1950 and its reverberations within Japan led to the formation of the Heiwa no Kai group, which held that the preservation of peace required strenuous political action by Christians and others. At the outset the Heiwa no Kai included both absolute pacifists such as those influenced by the Quaker or Mennonite or Brethren traditions, and also "selective pacifists," who would condemn certain wars as unjust but others as regrettable necessities. Never very large, the Heiwa no Kai nevertheless provided an important training group for students and faculty and pastors who wanted to become politically active for peace causes. The 1960 Mutual Security Treaty crisis was also to become an important turning point for this group's attitudes toward political action.

Yet a fourth group—which also overlapped with the other three—comprised the direct followers of Dr. Toyohiko Kagawa (1888-1960), who in the postwar period followed his enthusiasm for causes like world federalism, trade unionism, the cooperative movement, social work institutions, and the like. Even though most Protestants were influenced to some extent by Kagawa's activities, which began in the 1920s in a busy career as social worker, writer, evangelist, and reformer, there was a peculiar contribution of Kagawa's charismatic leadership that made his followers in the postwar period a special group (see also chap. 4, "Christians and Social Work"). In postwar Japan, Kagawa's was a powerful name to be reckoned with, even though his decline in health led to a diminution of his public role up to the time of his death in 1960. After his death, Kagawa's *Complete Works* were published and many encomiums bestowed upon his memory, but the particular contributions of his activities in such a field as political action must await a future rediscoverer of his greatness.

The Role of the Apostolic Delegation

While Protestants wrestled with problems of the separation of religion and the government, Roman Catholics in Japan had a different approach to the question. Since 1919 Japan and the Vatican have had diplomatic relations, with an exchange of embassies. In Japan this has meant an Apostolic Delegation with offices in the Sanbanchō district of Tokyo to handle relations with the Japanese government. Cardinal Paolo Marella held the post of apostolic delegate from 1933 to 1949, and was the object of some criticism in the postwar period because of his alleged pro-Axis sympathies in wartime. Hence Marella purposely kept a low public profile in the postwar period, as have most of his successors.

In 1952 the status of the Delegation was changed by Pope Pius XII to an Apostolic Internunciature, and in 1966 it was elevated to Apostolic Nunciature by Pope Paul VI, the changes in terminology reflecting the Vatican's views of the appropriate status of its embassy in Japan. There continued to be ambiguities about the role of a diplomatic envoy of a religious organization. The system was useful to the Japanese government because it provided contacts with the widespread diplomatic work of the Holy See, and was useful to the Vatican because it enabled church leaders to have access to Japanese governmental agencies at an official level. The system also helped to deal with the problems of Catholic foreign missionaries from many countries, and on occasion to assist them when they encountered problems with the Japanese government. In the 1960s the Apostolic Nunciature was able to give diplomatic as well as religious status to the Christian Pavilion at Expo '70. Hence even though there were occasional discussions among both Catholics and Protestants in Japan as to whether and how the system of the nunciature should be changed, there was recognition that in the meantime the system performed functions that were too useful to be hastily relinquished.

The Era of Economic Growth (1952–68): A Nation in Search of Its Role

Although SCAP's direct influence on Japanese affairs had been waning ever since the outbreak of the Korean War (1950), the end of the Occupation in 1952 supposedly brought Japan into a new position of responsibility for its domestic and international politics. The qualification "supposedly" is included because in fact it was widely believed in Japan and abroad that the continuing legacies of the Occupation—in particular the 1947 constitution, the Security Treaty arrangements with the United States, and the nation's economic ties with world capitalism—diluted Japanese responsibility by prolonging its entanglements with the Western world and the United States in particular. Even so, the restoration of Japanese political sovereignty and the economic expansion that marked this next era of postwar Japanese history set the stage for some important developments in Japanese politics that were crucial for Japan's Christians.

Struggles over Constitutional Issues

Japan's 1947 constitution remained one important focus of political struggles and public debate. If that constitution had been forced on a powerless Japanese nation by a temporarily superior military power, as some maintained, how much should that constitution be revised after the occupying military power was gone? Thus there were major controversies over efforts to revise the constitution itself, and a number of related struggles about specific issues within the constitution.

Suggestions that the "MacArthur constitution" ought to be amended or set aside were made almost from the very time of the constitution's enactment in 1946. Matters took on a particularly urgent turn, however, when the ruling Liberal Democratic party established a commission in 1955 to study the origins and the operation of the postwar constitution. The commission held protracted meetings for several years thereafter, amid the occasional glare of publicity from public hearings and through the riots and confusion that accompanied the enactment of the New Mutual Security Treaty in 1960. When the commission finally submitted its report in 1964, it was not surprising that a majority of its members favored such constitutional changes as the strengthening of the executive at the expense of the Diet, the designation of the emperor's role as "head of state" and not merely "symbol of state," and the role of national self-defense added to temper article 9's renunciation of war and "war potential." While the commission was doing its work, Japanese Christians joined in the public debates about the constitution, generally on the side of those who argued that it was preferable to make no changes in the constitution rather than allow revisions that might weaken or remove what the constitution had to say about such crucial matters as human rights, religious freedom, and the renunciation of war. Scholars of constitutional law who joined in the public discussions included Christians such as Professor Nobushige Ukai of ICU and Professor Joseph Pittau, S.J., of Sophia University, both of whom also served subsequently as presidents of their respective institutions. Japanese church groups issued statements in support of nonrevision of the constitution, among which one of the better known is the

Kyōdan's "Statement on Preservation of the National Constitution of Japan" (1962). This statement said in part:

We are now at the stage of having respect for the democratic principles outlined in the Constitution. We have great expectation that respect for our Constitution will continue to grow. Therefore, we must give serious warning concerning anti-democratic signs that are apparent in this movement, now in progress, to amend our Constitution; further, we oppose wholeheartedly any enactment of law or policy that is aimed at destroying the spirit of this Constitution.[11]

Although suggestions that constitutional revision ought to be undertaken were made on other occasions—most notably by Prime Minister Eisaku Satō in 1965—it was generally conceded that there was at least sufficient opposition to revision of the constitution by Japan's minority political parties and by the general public to make any serious efforts at revision an occasion for stormy controversy. Christians in Japan thus supported the national consensus backing the postwar constitution.

Apart from the question of constitutional revision, there were in the postwar era a number of important controversies about constitutional issues that significantly involved Christians. Issues about remilitarization, which were said to go against article 9's renunciation of war, attracted the most attention. The status of Japan's Self-Defense Forces (SDF) seemed to be a perennial issue. Some Christians agreed with opposition political leaders that such military forces were clearly contrary to article 9, while others maintained that such forces only guaranteed self-defense, to which every nation is entitled according to the United Nations Charter. The issue of remilitarization brought many related controversies to the fore: arguments about the United States and the SDF military bases and privileges, status of United States armed forces personnel under Japanese law, visits to Japanese ports by American nuclear-powered submarines and aircraft carriers, the alleged disposition of nuclear weapons at United States bases in Japan, SDF studies of war scenarios for Japan, and the like. Nuclear testing by the United States became a major issue in 1954 due to the *Fukuryū Maru* incident, when the fallout from a United States nuclear explosion at Bikini caused the deaths of fishermen aboard the vessel *Fukuryū Maru* ("Lucky Dragon"). Many Christians also joined in the annual Hiroshima meetings on August 6, the anniversary of the dropping of the first atomic bomb, that called for the banning of nuclear weapons, especially by the United States. While he was president of Rikkyō University from 1955 to 1967, Dr. Masatoshi Matsushita regularly organized protests against nuclear testing by any nation, stressing that it was wrong to protest United States nuclear tests but to be silent about testing by Communist nations.

Another constitutional issue that frequently surfaced was the government's role in education. The Japan Teachers' Union (Nikkyōso) took the lead in opposing measures by the Ministry of Education to weaken the union by such measures as teacher-evaluation programs, the firing of teachers active in union activities, and the like. Closer to Christians' specific concerns were textbook controversies, where the Ministry of Education used its powers for the licensing of textbooks in order to insist on a more pro-militarist understanding of Japan's past and present policies. Another governmental action was the revival of February 11 as a national holiday, National Foundation Day (Kenkoku Kinenbi), the date being derived from a Shintō myth about the founding of the nation, and a reestablishment of the prewar holiday of Kigensetsu, which had been observed from 1872 as an occasion for militaristic propaganda. After the holiday was abolished by the Occupation in 1946, proposals to revive National Foundation Day began in the post-Occupation period, being enacted into law in December 1966. Thereafter many Christians refused to observe February 11 as a holiday, but held rallies critical of militaristic propaganda instead.[12]

A related issue was Christian opposition to efforts to nationalize the Yasukuni Shrine in Tokyo for the memorialization of the nation's war dead. Founded in 1869 by the Emperor Meiji, the shrine was a center for extolling militarism in the years leading up to and during World War II. Suicide pilots (*kamikaze*) during the Pacific War would say farewell to each other with the words, "We'll meet again under the cherry blossoms in Yasukuni." Although Yasukuni Shrine was stripped of state support and reestablished under a religious juridical person during the Occupation era, priests at the shrine from about 1953 encouraged the formation of the Japan Association of War Bereaved Families, in order to bring pressure for the nationalization of the shrine. Christians joined Buddhist groups, New Religions, and smaller sects of Shintō in opposing nationalization, which they feared would be a significant breach in the constitution's separation of religion and the state. Advocates of Yasukuni nationalization maintained that such a move would not endanger freedom of religion, since the shrine's activities would be defined as "nonreligious," but such an explanation seemed to fly in the face of common sense. Although there were some Christians who did not support the Anti-Yasukuni movement—some Roman Catholics and Anglicans had made their peace with shrine veneration in prewar years, interpreting it as a purely patriotic act—most Protestants supported the continuing efforts organized by the Kyōdan's Reverend Masahiro Tomura and others to oppose nationalization.[13]

The various constitutional issues served to attune Christians in Japan to their roles in the nation's politics in ways that were unheard of in prewar times. One of the first occasions when constitutional issues were severely put to the test was in connection with the conflicts over the 1960 Mutual Security Treaty.

The 1960 Security Treaty Struggle

Until 1960 major decisions about postwar Japanese politics had been made either under the abnormal circumstances of the Occupation or about matters of secondary importance in which the Japanese public showed little interest. Since the Japanese government had accepted the Postdam Declaration to bring the war to an end, it was widely held that this led to the unavoidable acceptance of the Occupation's measures, including the 1947 constitution and even the signing of the San Francisco Peace Treaty and its related Security Treaty in 1951. When both the Japanese and the American governments concluded that the 1951 Security Treaty was too favorable to America and needed to be replaced by a more equitable treaty, the debate that followed proved to be the first major occasion for public discussion about Japan's major postwar policies in both international and domestic affairs.[14]

It should be pointed out that only a small minority of Christians took strong positions in opposition to the revised Security Treaty. Those who did oppose the treaty found themselves in a temporary coalition of four quite different groups: (1) politically oriented groups, such as the Christian Peace Fellowship, that took their major cues about theories and practice from the People's Council for Preventing Revision of the Security Treaty, the "umbrella organization" formed in March 1959 to oppose the treaty; (2) pacifist groups with connections to the historic peace churches and the Fellowship of Reconciliation, who were opposed in principle to Christian participation in any form of military arrangements; (3) social action groups from the background of the Occupational Evangelism Committee of the Kyōdan, backed by a number of "progressive intellectuals" (*kakushin interi*) who had been advocating Social Christianity and who felt that on this occasion Christians needed to join with other groups in Japanese society to prevent the resurgence of militarism; (4) church-formation groups, whose main concern was the preservation of the freedom of religion guaranteed under the constitution, and who therefore opposed the treaty as a revival of the militarism that had been so oppressive toward the churches during the Pacific War.[15] The diverse backgrounds of the four antitreaty groups among Christians meant that the perspectives for Christian political action that they had developed from the time of the Occupation were now being significantly put to the test for the first time.

It should be noted, however, that most Christian groups avoided involvement in the Security Treaty crisis, and their justifications for noninvolvement created important patterns for their future attitudes toward political issues. Few Roman Catholics opposed the treaty, for a large number of Catholic missionaries from European countries who served in such capacities as parish priests did not wish to become embroiled in a quarrel between Japan and the United States, especially in view of their convictions that as long as the church had its freedom, political questions were of secondary importance. Conservative Protestant groups refrained from criticizing the new treaty, which they saw as a barrier to the spread of Communism and its antireligious policies. Lay persons' groups also became annoyed at what they considered the extreme political involvement of their pastors, which they saw as having little to do with the maintenance of corporate worship and individual piety. As the level of violence escalated in the demonstrations held around the National Diet building, the majority of Christians tended to conclude that it would be wrong to become involved on either side of the controversy, and they justified their stand by biblical, theological, and practical arguments. They seemed to receive a confirmation for their noninvolvement by the quick resolution of the Security Treaty crisis, which took place after the June 23, 1960, announcement by Premier Nobosuke Kishi that he intended to resign. Even though the Security Treaty was ratified, as the treaty supporters had wanted, opponents of the treaty could also claim that Kishi's resignation constituted a partial moral victory for them.

In the aftermath of the slowly developing and quickly resolved Security Treaty crisis, there were reconsiderations both by Christians who had opposed the Treaty and by those who had stood apart. Those Christians who were pacifists on conviction concluded that their participation in the coalition against the treaty had been used by the more radical groups, while the more conservative treaty opponents were shocked by the levels of violence adopted by the more radical groups in their opposition tactics. Social-action groups that had followed the social analysis of Reinhold Niebuhr's Christian Realism concluded that such concepts were not appropriate for the unique political situation of Japan. And most significant of all in the long range, the more radical groups, which despaired at the hesitation of the others to give their full support to the antitreaty coalition, thereafter moved toward the New Left groups that developed in the 1960s. The New Left looked forward to the next conflict against the treaty in 1970 at the conclusion of the pact's first ten years, when either Japan or the United States could renounce the treaty upon one year's notice. In the meantime, all erstwhile members of the coalition against the Security Treaty could conclude that their experiences during this crisis had changed their approaches to current political problems.

Searching for Peaceful Roles for Japan in Troubled Asia

When Hayato Ikeda as Nobosuke Kishi's successor as prime minister in 1960 announced that he would promote "Doubling the National Income" as a national policy, his statement was greeted with relief by most sectors of the Japanese public, who had been shocked by the momentary specter of anarchy that emerged from the 1960 Security Treaty crisis. For the next decade or so, divisive questions of political ideology seemed to be considered out of bounds, as Japanese spent their energies on industrial production and commercial expansion. As things turned out, Ikeda's goal of doubling the national income in ten years was unduly modest, for the average Japanese saw personal incomes double in about seven years, although higher wages were accompanied by severe inflationary prices, which partially offset the benefits.[16] Some of the economic expansion that took place at this time was due to Japan's increased access to the raw materials, the cheaper labor, and the markets of East Asia. But as the Korean War had shown and as the Vietnamese conflict was also to demonstrate, East Asia remained an area where Japan's peaceful intentions were constantly being called into question.

Japan's role as a peace-loving nation dedicated to promoting friendship with all nations was symbolized by the Tokyo Olympics in 1964, when athletes from around the world were given an all-out welcome in Tokyo. The few signs of discord that emerged were symbolic of troubles yet to come. For instance, even before the Olympic Games started, the North Korean delegation quit Tokyo in protest against the arrangements, which they said favored the South Koreans. The government of Japan had been trying for almost twelve years to work out some form of normalization with the South Korean government, and in so doing had antagonized the North Korean regime. A Japan–Republic of Korea Normalization Treaty was at last signed in June 1965, and was ratified in both countries after extensive demonstrations in opposition. Christians in both countries were among those who opposed the normalization treaty. Some conservative Christians in Korea were opposed to the treaty because they felt that their government had given too favorable terms to Japan, and some liberal Japanese Christians opposed the treaty because their government had not waited to have normalized relations with both North and South Korea at the same time. Once Japan did have connections with South Korea, Japanese investments began to pour into the country, and by 1971 Japan had replaced the United States as the major foreign investor in the Korean economy.[17] Such gains were to be at a cost, however, for Japanese actions in Korea caused bitter resentment by many Koreans. Japanese businessmen soon began to use their vast economic power in Korea in ways that caused alarm and anger. Not only that, but so-called prostitution tours of Japanese tourists to South Korea raised the ire of Christian women's groups in that country, and their protests were supported by Christian women's groups in Japan and by the National Christian Council of Japan (NCCJ).[18] The process of reconciliation between Japanese and Korean Christians was to be a long one, but it did manage to reestablish relations between neighbors who had been in an uneasy tension for many centuries.[19] When the Kyōdan's moderator, Isamu Ōmura, made a trip to Seoul in September 1965 in response to an invitation of the Korean Presbyterian Church, he discovered that there was such opposition to his speaking in that church's general assembly that his speech was delayed for several hours. The incident made such an impression on Ōmura that he frequently spoke thereafter about the need in Japan for better understanding of the position of Korean Christians.[20]

Ōmura was also deeply concerned about another East Asian problem, the Vietnam War. The Japanese public became increasingly restive about the expansion of the Vietnam conflict, and in particular about the growing United States involvement after 1965. There was a certain ambiguity about this restiveness. On the one hand, Japanese government officials publicly supported the United States role in the war, and Japanese business prospered because of the extensive United States military procurement contracts in Japan. The income realized by Japanese businesses from the Vietnamese conflict amounted to a staggering $6.5 billion between 1965 and 1972, a fact not known until the *Kirisuto Shimbun* (Christian Newspaper) brought it to light in March 1973.[21]

On the other hand, most Japanese had deep anxiety about the escalation of any war in Asia in which their country might become involved, and experienced deep revulsion against the bombing raids of United States planes in North Vietnam, which reminded older Japanese of their own experiences during United States bombing raids over Japan in World War II. Opposition political groups and some Liberal Democratic party (LDP) leaders frequently expressed their criticism of the United States role in the war. Christian groups began to issue statements of concern about Vietnam, as did the NCCJ at its general assembly in April 1965. By that summer, concern about Vietnam among Japanese Christians was running so high that a five-person ad hoc delegation was sent to the United States to speak directly to American Christians and public officials about their desires for an early end to hostilities in Vietnam. Ōmura headed this Christian Emergency Conference for Peace in Vietnam, which at the time seemed to have little influence on the course of events. The fact that the visit happened at all was more significant than any specific conversations that took place during the trip, for it caused American church leaders to recognize the inadequacy of their ordinary channels for hearing the concerns of Japanese Christians, and special occasions were planned thereafter to keep the channels of communication open to Japan. At this time also the attempts of the Reverend Kanichi Nishimura to arrange peace negotiations with North Vietnamese leaders attracted the attention of interested Americans, but these efforts also came to naught because of the opposition of United States government officials.[22]

As the United States–Japan Mutual Security Treaty headed toward the end of its ten-year term in 1970, there were increasing signs of restiveness that, despite the vast improvements in their economy which had come with "the Japanese economic miracle," many thoughtful Japanese felt that their country was not being treated as an equal by its trans-Pacific partner. When he was United States ambassador to Japan, Edwin O. Reischauer frequently spoke of "the interrupted dialogue" between the United States and Japan, and there were speculations in Tokyo that the dialogue was again being threatened with interruption. Despite its vast economic strength, Japan had not yet found its role in the world vis-à-vis the United States, or toward its East Asian neighbors. Japanese Christians had come to realize this in their own relations with American and Asian Christians. This was to become clearer in the subsequent era of reappraisals.

The Era of Reappraisals (from 1968):
Reexamining "Peace and Democracy"

Christians in Japan came to realize even before their nation's leaders that the political organization of their nation in the postwar period was up for reappraisal. Christians sensed this because the upheavals based on political ideologies, which hit the Kyōdan as the country's largest Protestant church, had their reverberations on the entire Christian community in Japan. We shall examine how this season of reappraisals came to the Kyōdan first of all, and then how other churches were affected.

The Kyōdan and the 1970 Struggles

The postwar consensus about "peace and democracy" as goals for Japanese political life was always somewhat insubstantial. While Germany, Korea, and Vietnam were all formerly unified countries that were split into two nations in the aftermath of World War II, with one nation aligned with the United States and the Western bloc and the other with the USSR and its Eastern allies, such a division of Japanese territory never took place. The split in Japan took the form of a severe polarization among its people, as the majority followed their government's alignment with the capitalist nations, while a minority hoped for a more socialist or at least a neutralist orientation. In some countries, the differing points of view might have been discussed thoroughly and some kind of consensus established. But for a variety of reasons, some of them deeply imbedded in traditional Japanese methods of decision-making, such a consensus could not be reached in Japan. The decision that did emerge was that Japan would officially be committed to the goals of peace and democracy, but that the definition and content of these terms would purposely be kept vague. Gradually there developed a majority pro-government group and a minority critical of the government, each insisting that its own interpretation of the national goals was the only correct one, and each increasingly willing to use unpeaceful and undemocratic means to secure compliance with its own policies. Since Japan had always been a unitary society, such diversity as either majority or minority would permit was allowed only insofar as it fit in with the general consensus. Hence the public goals of peace and democracy, reached after elaborate discussions and public elections, and enforced by governmental authority, were in reality unclear. But since public controls over dissident behavior have traditionally been strict, and private citizens in Japan have long been predisposed to follow the guidance of the authorities, the fragility of the national consensus was never put fully to the test.

In private and voluntary associations, however, it was another story. While all citizens are required to obey the laws and pay taxes, voluntary members of churches are free to reject the decisions of church groups and to refuse to support their churches with their gifts. The more loose and open in organization a church is, the more susceptible it is to chaos in the event of a breakdown of internal consensus. And such was precisely what happened to the Kyōdan. The internal disagreements and struggles within the Kyōdan during the era of reappraisals from 1968 mirrored the growing polarization within the larger society. The church as one of the few genuinely voluntary groups in Japanese society was therefore one of the few places where such conflicts could freely come out into the open. The bitterness of the disagreements could not be so freely expressed and acted upon in legislative forums, political parties, schools, trade unions, social welfare organizations, or businesses, for all of these organizations were responsible in one form or another to act under public authority. In a word, when members of these other groups became unruly, the leaders of these organizations had the right and the duty to call in the police to restore order, and everybody could acknowledge that right, even though they might disagree with the action. But "the separation of religion and the state" in Japan's 1947 constitution put religious groups in a completely different category in regard to the state, and most church members were reluctant to have it otherwise. This was why a denomination like the Kyōdan could become polarized in both ideology and activity and stay that way long after universities, trade unions, and political parties had gone through the same period of chaos and returned to something resembling business as usual.

At this point, however, a valid question arises: If all religious groups in postwar Japan were alike separated from state control, why was it that the Kyōdan was one of the few religious groups to become and stay paralyzed for such a long time, when other Protestant and Catholic groups remained relatively free from such chaotic developments? The answer to such a query is not easy, but one needs to recall the nature of the Kyōdan itself as a church that was founded in 1941 largely from governmental pressures, and therefore a church which in the postwar era long delayed its internal grappling with the meanings of "peace and democracy" for its own inner life as well as its external proclamation. Other churches that were more hierarchically organized, or doctrinally consistent, or institutionally or financially tied to foreign churches, or spiritually removed from the contemporary Japanese ethos could ride through a period of crisis relatively unscathed. To many churches of the Christian community throughout history, there have come times of crisis: Anabaptists met persecutions in the period following the Reformation; the Church of England experienced it during the English Civil Wars; the English Puritans were harassed after the Restoration of 1660; French Roman Catholics encountered trials during the French Revolution; and Russian Orthodox believers faced hardships after the Russian Revolution. With the onset of the 1970 struggles, crisis came to the Kyōdan.

The previous section showed how the Kyōdan discovered, somewhat to its surprise, that all was not well in its postwar developments primarily because of its relations to East Asian churches. As was mentioned, Isamu Ōmura as the Kyōdan's moderator was shocked to find out in September 1965 when he was invited to speak to a general assembly of the Korean Presbyterian Church that a large number of that assembly's commissioners were opposed to letting him bring greetings. As Ōmura and other Kyōdan leaders conscientiously wrestled with the meaning of that incident afterward, their conclusion was that the Kyōdan had never fully come to grips with its historical beginnings at the hands of Japanese state power, and hence had never confessed its complicity with state power *(kokka kenryoku)* during World War II, with all the harm that had been caused to other Christians in Asia and to Christians in Japan as well.

Therefore, when the Kyōdan held its twenty-fifth anniversary general assembly in Osaka in October 1966, its newly elected moderator, the Reverend Masahisa Suzuki, spoke to the delegates on the subject "The Kyōdan of Tomorrow," and said in part:

> When we examine the Kyōdan, its history and its present state from an eschatological viewpoint, it becomes obvious that three points must be stressed in the future. In the first instance, we must stop practising *parallelism*. One of the gravest mistakes of Japanese churches in the past was the stubbornness with which they held to parallelism in their attitude toward political trends in their own country. They were ever so careful not to touch politics! During the war this tendency was all the more conspicuous. At home and abroad Japanese Christians did not perform their bounden duty to speak out against politically inspired violence.

Suzuki's indictment of parallelism as a strenuous effort to keep affirmations about faith and about public affairs in parallel, nonintersecting columns applied also to the Kyōdan of his day. His suggestions about how "the Kyōdan of tomorrow" might do something different are instructive:

> Now the Kyōdan is fully aware of its mistake. It is trying to alter its attitude, though neither its level of interest nor its skill in utterance is everywhere fully matured. One of the most concrete expressions of its political interest was the *Statement on Defense of the Constitution*, announced at the Kyōdan's 12th General Assembly [1962]. The statement, considered in retrospect, is so bold that we are made uneasy about the Kyōdan's capabilities to back up its promises. Nevertheless, the statement holds decisive meaning for our future steps. One of the tasks of "the Kyōdan of tomorrow" is to grow into a strong church able to take a firm stance from which to speak boldly to political and governmental forces.[23]

After the general assembly, Moderator Suzuki, through the Kyōdan's Executive Committee, prepared a "Confession on the Responsibility of the United Church of Christ in Japan during World War II," which was released on Easter Sunday, March 26, 1967, and contained these statements:

> At this time we are reminded of the mistakes committed in the name of the Kyōdan during World War II. Therefore, we seek the mercy of our Lord and the forgiveness of our fellow humans. . . . Indeed, as our nation committed errors we, as a Church, sinned with her. We neglected

to perform our mission as a "watchman." Now, with deep pain in our heart, we confess this sin, seeking the forgiveness of our Lord, and from the churches and our brothers and sisters of the world, and in particular of Asian countries, and from the people of our own country. . . .[24]

Thus did the Kyōdan confess its wrongs to its Asian Christian neighbors twenty-three years after the conclusion of the Pacific War. But whatever effect it had on other countries, the "Confession" immediately became a center of controversy within the Kyōdan, not only because of procedural questions about its enactment but also because of its implied criticism of former Kyōdan leaders and members for being derelict about their Christian duties. It suddenly became evident that the Kyōdan's consensus about its own past history and current stance toward public issues and evangelism was uncertain indeed. Suzuki knew all this very well, for before becoming moderator he had been chairman of the denomination's Evangelism Committee. It is not easy to describe the various reactions within the Kyōdan to Moderator Suzuki's release of the "Confession," but they were a foretaste of even greater divisions to come. Suzuki's personal character and qualities of leadership prevented the incident from becoming a serious disruption within the church, and Suzuki's own courageous bout with cancer that ended with his death in July 1969 tended to dampen antagonisms.

But the underlying problems burst forth again on September 1-2, 1969, when, at a long bargaining meeting of dissatisfied seminary students with Kyōdan officials about the Kyōdan's endorsement of the Christian Pavilion at the Osaka World Exposition in 1970 (Expo '70), the discussion became unruly and Professor Kazō Kitamori of Tokyo Union Theological Seminary was slapped. There is no space here to go into the many details of how the conflict developed from that point on, except to indicate some of the reasons why the dispute about the Christian Pavilion became so heated.[25] The Christian Pavilion had been planned as the first major expression of a new spirit of ecumenicity, which had sprung from Vatican Council II, whereby Protestants and Catholics—and later, Orthodox also—could come together in a common witness to their faith, in the midst of a society that was over 99 percent non-Christian (see chap. 7, "Ecumenicity in Japan"). Even though the pavilion was seen by some as a commendable united witness to a non-Christian society, it was interpreted by others as the churches' sellout to a materialistic "festival of capitalism" that sought to celebrate the exploitations of postwar Japan's economic oppression of other nations rather than to denounce them with prophetic scorn. In raising questions about how the Kyōdan and the NCCJ before it had come to endorse the Christian Pavilion—the radical students and their supporters preferred the name of "problem posers" *(mondai teikisha)*—the very nature of the commitment of these church bodies to the goals of peace and democracy was called into question. In the struggles that followed, involving a strike at Tokyo Union Theological Seminary that was broken after nearly six months' duration only by the calling of the riot police to the campus, and including frequent interruptions of church meetings by struggle tactics, the problem posers' commitments to peace and democracy as guidelines for action either in church or in society were also called into question.

The period of 1968–71 was a time when campuses around the world were in turmoil, and the New Left in various countries was developing its own variety of Marxist ideology and tactics. In Japan the problem posers and their mentors were the heirs of those who had become disillusioned with the outcome of the 1960 Security Treaty struggles, and who therefore adopted more violent tactics in confronting the Establishment in the universities and in government buildings in order to demonstrate their total rejection of Japanese society's consensus about peace and democracy up to that point. For the New Left in Japan, including many of the problem posers in the Kyōdan, true peace was a goal that could only come as the final product of unremitting class struggle, and true democracy could only be achieved by direct pressure tactics on the modern state and its supporters in the universities, trade unions, churches, and the like. Such tactics would completely crush the Establishment and from its ruins allow new and authentic life to flourish. It is not hard to see why representatives of more conservative positions and the Old Left (traditional Marxists and Socialists, and even the Japan Communist party with its Stalinist outlook) were unable to come to a meeting of minds with New Left representatives. Yet even though they bear "New" in their name, New Left representatives in Japan were building on a centuries-old samurai mentality that spurned compromise of any kind with "purity" of doctrine and relished no cause better than a hopelessly lost cause.[26] Chaotic, violent, and undemocratic as their theories and tactics were, the problem posers nevertheless served to reveal the fragility of the consensus about peace and democracy either in the larger world of Japanese society or in the smaller world of the Kyōdan.

It is hard to trace the development of the problems within the Kyōdan without misleading exaggerations, so complicated did the issues become. But in essence three interim moderators of the Kyōdan after Suzuki found that it was not possible to restore either the peace or the democratic procedures of the Kyōdan through negotiations with the problem posers. A fourth moderator, the Reverend Isuke Toda (moderator 1973–78) concluded that general assemblies of the church and the national office work of the denomination could be carried on only by suspending the "democratic" procedures of the church as traditionally understood and by working out an accommodation with the problem posers in regard to the faith and order of the church, lest they disrupt church meetings which to their mind would bring harm to their cause. A number of groups within the Kyōdan despaired at the continuing confusion within the church, which they felt would mean undemocratic procedures in church order and denials of traditional Christian faith. At length the Federation of Evangelical Churches within the United Church of Christ in Japan (Nihon Kirisuto Kyōdan Fukuinshugi Kyōkai Rengō, or the Rengō for short) was begun in April 1977 as an "umbrella group," which sought to restore the Kyōdan or at least a part of it to its proper course in both polity and belief. A full discussion of the ecclesiastical and theological dimensions of the struggle between the Rengō adherents and the problem posers about the leadership of the Kyōdan and the course of its faith and conduct goes beyond the scope of this chapter about Christians and politics. But it seems clear that the future of the Kyōdan's understanding of what peace and democracy mean for the life of the church and for society at large is related to the outcome of these struggles.

While the Kyōdan was undergoing its own internal struggles, other Christian churches in Japan were affected either directly or indirectly. There were minor struggles in the Japan Evangelical Lutheran Church, the Anglican Church of Japan, the Japan Baptist Convention (or Renmei, related to the Southern Baptist Convention), the Japan Baptist Union (or Dōmei, affiliated with the American Baptist Convention), and the Japan Free Methodist Church. Yet such struggles never became as large or as significant as those of the Kyōdan. It was often said that these other churches watched developments in the Kyōdan closely and tried hard to prevent or forestall the kind of paralysis experienced there. In most cases, this meant that these churches refrained from becoming involved in political issues as the Kyōdan had done, and thereby they avoided some of the resulting antagonisms. The same was largely the case with other Protestant churches that experienced little or no turmoil in the 1968–71 period.

During the era of reappraisals, the Orthodox Church in Japan was undergoing a season of reevaluation of its own, in regard to its connections with Orthodoxy abroad. Having severed its ties with the Orthodox Patriarch of Moscow in April 1946 and affiliated itself with the Orthodox Churches of North America in January 1947—allegedly due to SCAP influence and help—the Orthodox Church in Japan continued to experience controversy about its relations with the Moscow patriarchate. In 1970 the church in Japan resumed relations with the Patriarch of Moscow, but with the understanding that it was an autocephalous, or independent, church on its own.

The Catholic Church in Japan from 1968 to 1971 experienced some internal pressures from its own form of problem posers, but on the whole managed to avoid the extremes of the Kyōdan situation. For one thing, the controversy over the Christian Pavilion at Expo '70 took on another appearance for Catholics, for that pavilion was also the diplomatic pavilion of the Holy See and for that reason was located among the pavilions of foreign governments at the fair. Although there were some Catholics who sympathized with the problem posers in their own church, most were dismayed at the intensity of the conflict over the Christian Pavilion, and hoped for future courses of action that would be less troublesome. Indeed, Catholics in Japan had already experienced sufficient turmoil in the aftermath of Vatican Council II (1962–64) with the resignations of hundreds of religious personnel and the weakening of church discipline in many areas. Therefore they had no desire to undergo another period of trauma after 1968, and avoided it largely by "bending to the storm" when necessary but then by reinstituting what seemed like reasonable controls afterward.

Court Decisions of Concern to Christians

One of the signs of the new period of reappraisals was the fact that Christians were increasingly ready, willing, and able to test out crucial issues of concern to them in the Japanese courts. While this might not be very striking for Westerners, in Japan the recourse to the courts has traditionally been a procedure of last resort, for there are many encouragements for settling legal disputes through arbitration rather than by pressing one's claims in court proceedings, which can consume a great deal of money and time. Yet when issues arose that often related to constitutional rights, some Christians were willing to seek public vindication of certain issues through the courts. And at times—as has been the case in other countries—the courts were just as eager to sidestep the issues where unpopular decisions might "rock the boat." The decisions that the courts did take, however, helped to clarify some of the issues about religious liberty and constitutional rights, which had been watched by Christians very closely since the immediate postwar period. To be sure, these court decisions brought mixed reactions among both the Japanese public in general and Christians in particular.

Some court cases were a direct outgrowth of the school struggles of the 1969–70 period. Tokyo Union Theological Seminary pressed charges against three students who had been involved in breaking into a private home in 1969 where faculty members were secretly conducting school entrance examinations. The trial was connected with the seminary's decision to call the riot police to its campus in March 1970 in order to remove the barricades that striking students had placed there in protest against seminary policies. The trial became an issue in the Kyōdan because the seminary was founded by the Kyōdan and had church-appointed members on its Board of Trustees. Furthermore, the 1973 Kyōdan general assembly voted a resolution over the heated opposition of the seminary and its supporters that called upon the seminary to withdraw its legal action against the students. The seminary did not do so, and the next Kyōdan general assembly meeting in December 1974 voted a resolution that Tokyo Union Seminary's calling the riot police was "an error."[27] In the meantime, the Tokyo High Court in October 1974 decided against the students and gave them suspended sentences.[28] There the matter has stood, with considerable animosity on all sides.

Aoyama Gakuin also had legal problems to resolve after its school struggle. At its March 1977 meeting, the Aoyama Board of Trustees decided to close the Department of Theology. This was merely a confirmation of the board's decision in 1972 to stop taking students into the theological department. That decision was taken nominally on the grounds that the department was no longer training many graduates for the pastorate of local churches, and that the continuation of the department was an unjustified expense. A more substantial reason, however, was that the Department of Theology had often been opposed to the policies of Aoyama's chancellor, Kinjiro Ōki, who since 1960 had guided the school with a powerful arm. When Department of Theology faculty accepted the transfer in 1971 of several former students of Tokyo Union Seminary who had been involved in radical activities, Chancellor Ōki vetoed the decision, and in the ensuing disputes some faculty members had to leave. Subsequently the Board of Trustees decided to close the Department of Theology, but this decision was opposed by a theological student, Naoto Umemoto, who brought suit against the university in April 1973, charging that his right to complete his theological education had been violated by the university's action. On October 9, 1977, the Tokyo Court of Appeals awarded Umemoto over 300,000 yen in damages, but did not require the university to reestablish its Department of Theology.[29]

Another court case arising from the time of school crises had far wider legal implications for the nature of the church and its pastoral ministry. This case involved the Reverend Shunichi Tanetani, a Kyōdan minister who in October 1970 sheltered and counseled two students who were fleeing from a school disturbance in which they had been involved. Tanetani urged the students to turn themselves in to the police, which they subsequently did, and the students' cases were leniently handled by both the police and their school. But Tanetani was subsequently arrested and fined 10,000 yen (then about $28) for his "criminal misdemeanor." Denying that he had done anything wrong, the pastor refused to pay the fine, and finally after five grueling years of litigation, on February 20, 1975, the Kobe Summary Court agreed to acquit Tanetani of the charges. The judge ruled that when pastoral activities serving the public welfare come in conflict with the law, such cases must be judged from "a broad and common-sense point of view," instead of always giving the protection and benefit of the law to the state.[30] This case attracted widespread attention in both legal and religious circles, and its outcome was hailed by Japanese Christians as a vindication of a humane interpretation of a pastor's duties.

A legal suit that was of great concern to the Korean Christian community of Japan and many others was that of Chong Suk Park vs. the Hitachi Corporation, the first racial discrimination suit in the history of Japanese jurisprudence. Park, a Korean born and raised in Japan, in August 1970 took and passed the employment examination for Hitachi, the mammoth Japanese electronic firm. He had used his regular Japanese name for the examination, but when he proceeded toward employment, the Hitachi Corporation withdrew its employment notification, since Park was Korean and not Japanese. Park held that this was a clear case of racial discrimination, and in December 1970 filed suit with the Yokohama District Court to seek reinstatement in employment. The Korean community rallied to his defense, and a Legal Defense Committee for Park was backed by contributions from the

Korean Christian Church in Japan, the NCCJ, and the World Council of Churches' Program to Combat Racism. The suit led to widespread boycotts of Hitachi products, and a heightened public awareness of the fact of discrimination in employment practices of Japanese corporations. After a four-year struggle, the Yokohama District Court in June 1974 ruled that Park had indeed been a victim of discrimination, and ordered Hitachi to pay Park back wages and a small solatium.[31]

The entire episode was a landmark decision for the Korean community in Japan, which for decades has experienced discrimination in many forms. During the course of the trial, Park declared:

> In the process of this trial, I have come to know the realities of the situation of my people. I have come to know how our identity is usurped by the patterns of discrimination, and I have been spurred to learn the Korean language and history. Through fellowship with my Christian brothers and sisters, the restoration of my humanity has begun, a humanity which refuses to accept humiliation any longer. I can stand tall as a Korean, living truly as a member of my race.[32]

A case dealing with religious freedom and its implications for governmental actions is the Tsu City case. In 1965 Tsu City held a ground-breaking ceremony for a new city gymnasium, at which Shintō priests performed Jichinsai, a ceremony to appease the land gods, for which they were paid 7,663 yen from city funds. A Communist assemblyman who was required to attend the ceremony subsequently filed suit with the Tsu District Court, objecting to having to participate in a religious service and having the service paid for out of public funds, in the light of the constitutional separation of religion and the state. This case took twelve years to make it to the Supreme Court, which ruled in July 1977 in a three-sentence decision that the city's holding of the ground-breaking ceremony with its Shintō ritual was not unconstitutional. However, five of the fifteen Supreme Court justices dissented from the decision, including Chief Justice Ekizo Fujibayashi, an active Mukyōkai Christian. His sixteen-page dissenting opinion surveyed the historical relationships between Shintō and the state in modern Japan, and concluded that governmental sponsorship of any religious ceremonies does indeed threaten the constitutional separation of religion and the state. Many Japanese Christians hope that the arguments behind Fujibayashi's dissenting opinion may ultimately prevail as the official decision at some future time.[33]

A final legal case to be considered here deals with a widow's objection to her husband's being granted Shintō deification. Lieutenant Takafumi Nakaya of the Self-Defense Forces was killed in a car accident while on duty in 1968. An SDF unit based in Yamaguchi and a veterans' organization requested that the Yamaguchi Gokoku Shrine ("Defense of the Motherland" Shrine) enshrine Nakaya, despite the objections of his widow, Mrs. Yasuko Nakaya. Supported in her stand by the Yamaguchi Shinai Church of the

Kyōdan to which she belongs, Mrs. Nakaya claimed in a 1973 suit that the deification of her husband, which had taken place the previous year over her objections, was a violation of the constitution's separation of religion and the state. In March 1979 the Yamaguchi District Court partially upheld Mrs. Nakaya's suit, and ordered the defendants to pay her a million-yen solatium for her mental anguish. At the same time, the court did not order the shrine to remove Lieutenant Nakaya's name from its list of deities, since "the veterans' organization is also entitled to freedom for its beliefs." Appeals were made by the SDF and the veterans' organization to higher courts, and hence the final disposition of the case is still in doubt.[34] This case has had wider implications, for the Yamaguchi Gokoku Shrine is viewed as a virtual branch of the Yasukuni Shrine in Tokyo, dedicated to the enshrinement of the war dead. Thus the issues involved are directly related to the conflicts over the nationalization of the Yasukuni Shrine, to which our attention returns in the next section.

The Conservative Wave in Japanese Society and the Churches

After the temporary excesses of the 1968–71 struggles in Japanese universities, there were signs of a new conservatism throughout the nation. Indeed, there were indications in many countries around the world that conservative viewpoints were taking a new lease on life. There was evidence of a resurgence of Japanese nationalism, which also had strong elements of militarism, aspects that had never completely disappeared even during the Occupation period.[35] Christians were made particularly aware of these new militaristic sentiments because of the intensification of efforts to nationalize Yasukuni Shrine, for in virtually every year after 1969 a bill to that effect has been introduced in the National Diet. By the mid-seventies some of the Buddhists and New Religions adherents who had joined Christians in opposing the nationalization of Yasukuni on previous occasions lost interest, and a larger share of the opposition to the bill was undertaken by Christians. With actual proposed legislation confronting them, the Christians also had to deal with a strongly organized new movement, founded in June 1976, called the Society to Respond to the War Heroes (Eirei ni Kotaeru Kai), with a former chief justice of the Supreme Court as its president and considerable support from members of the Diet.

Christians also had to deal with new waves of nationalistic fervor, which swept over their nation as a result of three successive shocks from foreign affairs. The first was the "Nixon shock" following the announcement in July 1971 of President Richard Nixon's forthcoming plans to visit Peking. In spite of the supposedly close relations between Japan and the United States, the American government did not inform Prime Minister Eisaku Satō about this very sensitive decision until minutes before the public announcement was made. The same year saw the culmination of the "trade shock" that the Nixon administration dealt Japan in United States efforts to curtail Japanese textile exports. Coupled with the declining value of the American dollar in relation to the yen, Japanese government and business leaders felt that the Nixon administration's measures were of such a nature as to jeopardize Japan's good relations with the United States. In 1973 came the "oil shock" as a result of the OPEC nations' increases in the price of oil. The resulting severe inflation in Japan underscored how precarious was the nation's dependence on foreign sources of energy, and in particular on oil from the troubled Middle East.

It is difficult to show a direct cause-and-effect relationship between the shocks that hit Japan during 1971–73 and some of the political developments that took place, but some connections certainly did exist. Christians began to pay renewed attention to the emperor system as one of the most serious political problems of Japan. The whole nation and the world still remembered the *seppuku* death of novelist Yukio Mishima in November 1970, when he called for the remilitarization of Japan under a restored emperor system. Then during 1971 the tour of Europe by the emperor and empress was given the fullest coverage in the public media.[36] Japanese politicians made repeated references to a whole cluster of symbols that were meant to evoke nationalist sentiment for the emperor. A news article reported a speech of former Prime Minister Nobusuke Kishi in Tokyo in May 1971 in this way:

Nobosuke Kishi, elder brother of former Prime Minister Satō, told a crowd of 2,000 at Kyōritsu Hall that the present Constitution should be discarded in favor of one genuinely Japanese in nature. After the speakers there urged the revision of the Constitution, using such words as *Yamato damashii* ("the Japanese spirit") and "Greater East Asia Co-Prosperity Sphere," the meeting resolved, among other things, to place the Emperor at the center of the state, promote defense efforts, and map out a truly independent Constitution.[37]

Similar statements could be quoted at length, especially from a young conservative group of politicians in the LDP called Seirankai, which made revision of the constitution one of the major planks in their political platform. Then when Lieutenant Hiroo Onoda in 1974 returned from twenty-nine years of hiding in the Philippine jungles, he was treated like a military hero despite the fact that he was connected with the killing of at least thirty Filipinos. Articles in the press praised Onoda highly for his unswerving devotion to the emperor.

How were Christians to respond to such changes in the Japanese political climate? For one thing, their responses remained largely fragmented, and related to particular issues and problems, even though persons in each interest group had much larger perspectives. The groups in Urban Industrial Mission, for instance, continued to press for industrial justice and for legislation to deal with the abuses of the industrial system.[38] Peace advocates in the churches saw their political objectives in connection with the continuing struggles to limit the size and role of the Self-Defense Forces.[39] There were Christians like Professor Yoshiaki Iisaka of Gakushuin University who became active in the World Conference on Religion and Peace, an interreligious group launched with the primary backing of President Nikkyo Niwano of Risshō Kōseikai, a Neo-Buddhist group. The WCRP held three major assemblies, in Kyoto (1970), Louvain (1974), and Princeton (1979).[40]

Another course of political action was taken by Dr. Masatoshi Matsushita, a former president of Rikkyō (Anglican) University and an unsuccessful candidate in 1975 for governor of Tokyo. Matsushita became active in the Peace Studies Academy, an interreligious group backed by the Unification Church of the Reverend Sun Myung Moon. The NCCJ was active in sponsoring a study group on Korean affairs, and in monitoring the violations of human rights by the administration of South Korea's president, Chung Hee Park.[41] Yasukuni Shrine nationalization bills were regularly opposed by Christians and others.[42] Some Christians joined in antipollution efforts, spearheaded by Professor Jun Ui of the University of Tokyo.[43] The former chancellor of Meiji Gakuin, Dr. Tomio Mutō, organized a Japan Christ party and ran unsuccessfully as its sole candidate in the fall 1976 elections for the House of Councilors.[44] The Rengō group in the Kyōdan carried out its independent inquiries about alleged human rights violations in Korea.[45] Roman Catholics at Sophia University backed a documentation center on their campus, which investigated political conditions in East Asia, particularly the martial-law situations of the Philippines and South Korea. A more militant approach was taken by Isaku Tomura, a sculptor and a Christian, who led a determined group of students, farmers, and their supporters against the construction of a new Tokyo airport at Narita in the 1970s. Although Tomura's group was unable to block the opening of the airport, it greatly increased the government's security precautions at the new facility.[46] Such were some of the varied responses by Christian individuals and groups in regard to political issues in the late 1970s.

The conservative wave that swept through Japanese society had its influence on the churches as well. During a 1978 visit to Japan, Harvey Cox noted that both Christians and Buddhists who were resolute in their search for peace tended to be more cautious in their methods of action.[47] Furthermore, conservative churches in Japan were growing much faster than the mainline denominations, and their greater reluctance to become involved in political issues had its influence. Social issues that conservatives dealt with included family breakups, juvenile delinquency, narcotics addiction, and the like, which were approached on a personal basis. Neo-Pentecostal charismatic groups began among Protestants in 1970, and by November 1972 there were even stronger Catholic charismatic groups, which met weekly at the Hatsudai Catholic Church in Tokyo. Catholic charismatics saw this development as an answer to the prayer of Pope John XXIII at the end of Vatican Council II's first session: "Renew Thy wonders in this day as by a new Pentecost."[48] Yet as some observers have pointed out, charismatic Christians tend toward neutrality or even noninvolvement in political issues. A sympathetic participant in the Second International Conference on Charismatic Renewal in the Catholic Church, which met in Dublin in June 1978, made these comments:

> While the conference was characterized by a tremendous sense of worship, joy, and manifestations of the Spirit, the socio-political attitude was at best neutral and at worst in support of the status quo. The movement is deeply conservative, reinforcing traditional structures of authority and traditional practices in the church.[49]

Apart from particular groups that participated in one form or another of political action, however, the average Protestant or Catholic church in Japan in the late 1970s was apt to be far less involved in political action than it had been in the immediate postwar years. The onrush of inflation made it harder for local churches to finance even their regular activities of worship and service, and although churches were apt to be busy with a variety of programs, study groups, bazaars, and such, political issues were less likely to intrude onto the churches' calendars. Should there be a national crisis that might precipitate a head-on confrontation of the political forces that were seeking to remold modern Japan, it might be a different matter. But for the time, churches were more often than not just as glad to be able to steer clear of political issues.

Christians and Japan's Politics: Some Concluding Observations

Looking back over the relation of the Japanese Christian community to politics in the period since 1945, we return to our opening metaphor of Japanese society as a skier on a rapid downhill course, with Christians trying to serve as gatekeepers to place "gates" to the right and the left within which Japanese society might be kept on the course for peace and democracy set for it in the postwar period. For the most part, the attitudes of Christians were not significantly different from the political views of the population as a whole. Yet even though they were a tiny minority in the nation, Christians did have a small but significant voice in speaking out about the directions being taken by the nation during this period. There are several characteristics of the relationships of Christians and politics in Japan that should be noted.

In the first place, *the direct involvement of Christians in politics was minimal*. This is especially noteworthy when it is contrasted with the active political roles of other religious groups, Sōkagakkai especially, but also Tenrikyō, the Honganji sects of Pure Land Buddhism, Sōtō Zen, Ittōen, and associations of the New Religions and Shintō groups.[50] Some of the political participation by religious groups might leave much to be desired, for "the religious vote" was courted by politicians for their own purposes, very often to counter leftist votes. Some observers said that votes based on religious considerations were really "floating votes" that varied according to particular issues or personalities of the candidates involved. Furthermore, the conduct of politics was often viewed by Japanese Christians as a rather dirty business, which was perhaps necessary but far beneath the dignity of respectable people. Above all, the "problem consciousness" *(mondai ishiki)* of most Christians about political issues was very low indeed. Apart from questions of constitutional revision and the state support of Yasukuni Shrine, there was minimal knowledge and interest among Christians about how the political issues affected them, or how their faith might have a bearing on politics. Most Christians assumed that the postwar constitution's ideals of the separation of religion and the state should be strictly followed. The implication of this was that Christians should refuse to become involved in political issues unless there was a clear threat to religious liberty or to the preservation of the constitution.

A second comment is that *Christians participated in politics mostly as individuals and not as members of a group.* To be sure, there were four postwar prime ministers who were Christian: Shigeru Yoshida (who was baptized a Catholic after his death!), Tetsu Katayama (an active Protestant layman), Ichirō Hatoyama (an inactive member of an independent Protestant church), and Masayoshi Ōhira (an inactive Protestant). Mention has been made of Matsuoka, Kawakami, and Nishimura, who were active in the Japan Socialist party, and there were those like Tokutarō Kitamura who were leaders in the Liberal Democratic party. Numbers of lay Christians and even pastors held political posts in all political parties except the Japan Communist party. The only attempt to form a Christian political party was Tomio Mutō's unsuccessful effort in 1976 to establish the Japan Christ party, and this move failed to receive solid backing from Mutō's fellow members in the Kyōdan. Catholics were mindful of the Christian Democratic parties of Western Europe, but they recognized that these were not outstanding examples of political idealism, and such efforts made little sense in the Japanese political scene. Furthermore, Christians as voters tended to reject the political stances of individual Christians when they veered too far to the left or to the right, beyond the generally accepted "gates" of Japan's slalom course. Hence, Sakae Akaiwa's 1949 announcement of his impending decision to join the Japan Communist party was censured by his church's committees. When the nominally Protestant prime ministers Ichirō Hatoyama and Masayoshi Ōhira made visits to the Ise or Yasukuni shrines, there were loud outcries of protest by Protestant spokespersons that such visits were breaches of the constitutional separation of religion and the state.

A third observation is that *Christians have tended to focus their attention on a few political issues that seemed to them of special significance.* In the immediate postwar era, the issue of religious liberty emerged as important to the religious integrity of Christians and of members of other religious groups as well, although some Christians had to learn the significance of the new practice of governmental neutrality toward all religions, which was markedly different from prewar practice. Thereafter, efforts by groups within the Liberal Democratic party to give special status to Yasukuni Shrine and to other shrines met with the continuing and determined opposition of most—but not all—Japanese Christian groups, who were at times joined by Buddhist and Marxist groups who acted on somewhat different grounds. There were some Catholics and Anglicans and a few Protestants who could support state aid for Yasukuni, but they mostly kept out of the political spotlight. A third issue on which most Christians could agree was the preservation of Japan's peace constitution, together with opposition to the revival of militarism and anti-democratic measures. But the definitions of "peace and democracy" kept changing in contemporary Japan, so that Christians differed almost as much on the issues here as did the public at large. In a sense, almost all Japanese favored the ideals of peace and democracy, but there was little agreement on what precisely these terms meant. Occasional efforts to raise the problem consciousness of Japanese Christian groups on current political issues gained little headway. Critics sometimes said that Christian groups suffered from "institutional egoism," meaning that as long as Christians were enabled by political arrangements to continue their institutional life, they were little concerned about issues affecting society.[51] Defenders of such viewpoints maintained that as long as religious liberty was observed, Christians should be free as individuals to embrace a wide variety of political programs.

A fourth comment is that *the polarization that developed among some Christian groups was symptomatic of an underlying political polarization in Japanese society as a whole.* The tension between the "problem posers" and the "evangelical churches" in the Kyōdan (and to a lesser degree between similar groups in several other Christian groups) did not involve the majority of the constituency of the Kyōdan by any means, but its implications for church life were serious. This led to the paralyzing of many church functions at the national level, and the development of local autonomy almost by default on the district or local level, even when it was unable to fulfill its responsibilities properly. Other groups in Japanese society—such as trade unions, schools and universities, corporations, and political parties—had also been affected by this paralysis in the 1968–70 period, but had been able to surmount it for the most part. The fact that the Christian churches as one of the few truly voluntary social groups in Japanese society continued to be affected by these divisions pointed to deep fissures within the nation as a whole, which had been only superficially covered up by events since 1970. Japanese society has been able since 1945 to contain the extremist groups both to the left and to the right, in the setting of a growing economy operating in relative peace and security. But if the fragile stability of Japanese economic and political life is broken in the course of events, it is likely that the polarization between left and right in Japan would break out afresh. Should this take place, many Christian observers fear that with the emperor system still intact and as the most likely focus of national sentiment in a time of crisis, the emperor would again be utilized by rightist groups to bring to power an authoritarian regime that would proceed to liquidate any threat from the left. These observers fear that although the future may not directly duplicate the slide of Japan in the 1930s into fascism, there might be heartbreaking similarities to that period at some time in the future.

As the 1980s begin, Japan's Christians could hope that the political climate would avoid crises which might undo the precarious postwar gains of peace and democracy, and plunge the nation again into authoritarianism. Christians would continue to plant their "gates" to the right and the left, in the hopes of guiding their rapidly moving society on a course heading toward progress and not to destruction.

NOTES

1. Edwin O. Reischauer, *The United States and Japan* (New York: Viking Press, 1965), p. 289. This chapter is a revision and amplification of a paper, "The Role of Christians in Japan's Postwar Experiment in 'Peace and Democracy' (1945–1975)," given by the writer to the American Society of Church History, Princeton, N.J., March 27, 1976.

2. On the Occupation of Japan, see Herbert Passin, *The Legacy of the Occupation of Japan* (New York: Columbia University Press, 1968); Kazuo Kawai, *Japan's American Interlude* (Chicago: University of Chicago Press, 1960); Edwin O. Reischauer, *The United States and Japan,* chaps. 10–12; Edwin O. Reischauer, *Japan: The Story of a Nation* (New York: Knopf, 1974), chap. 11; Helen Mears, *Mirror for Americans* (Boston: Houghton, Mifflin, 1948).

3. See James M. Phillips, "Japanese Christian Views of Religion and State in the Meiji Era," *JMB* 18, no. 1 (January 1964): 455–58.

4. Jan Swyngedouw, "The Catholic Church and Shrine Shintō," *JMB* 21, no. 10 (November 1967): 579–84 (Part 1); no. 11 (December 1967): 659–63 (Part 2).

5. On Shintō, see D. C. Holtom, *The National Faith of Japan* (New York: Dutton, 1938); D. M. Brown, *Nationalism in Japan: An Introductory Historical Analysis* (Berkeley: University of California Press, 1955); Joseph M. Kitagawa, *Religion in Japanese History* (New York: Columbia University Press, 1966); Sokyo Ono, *Shintō: The Kami Way* (Tokyo: Bridgeway Press, 1962).

6. William P. Woodard, *The Allied Occupation of Japan 1945—1952 and Japanese Religions* (Leiden: E. J. Brill, 1972), p. 69. This entire section is based on Woodard's treatment of the subject.

7. On the New Religions of Japan, see Harry Thomsen, *The New Religions of Japan* (Tokyo: Tuttle, 1963); H. Neill McFarland, *The Rush Hour of the Gods: A Study of New Religions in Japan* (New York: Macmillan, 1967); Clark Offner and Henry vanStraelen, *Modern Japanese Religions* (New York: Twayne Publishers, 1963); Akio Saki, *Shinkō* [The New Religions] (Tokyo: Aoki Shōten, 1960).

8. Woodard's *Allied Occupation* has an appendix on MacArthur's statements about the need for Christianity in postwar Japan.

9. Interview with Mr. Tetsu Katayama, Tokyo, May 12, 1975. Cf. "The Socialists in Power," in Asahi Shimbun staff, *The Pacific Rivals* (Tokyo: Weatherhill/Asahi, 1972), pp. 186–89.

10. Cf. Martin E. Weinstein, *Japan's Postwar Defense Policy, 1947-1968* (New York: Columbia University Press, 1971). Weinstein's discussion of the "Ashida Memorandum" of September 10, 1947, is significant in this connection.

11. *Policy Statements and Statistics of the United Church of Christ in Japan (Kyōdan)* (Tokyo: UCCJ, 1968), p. 10.

12. *JCAN*, Feb. 24, 1974, pp. 3-4; Feb. 10, 1978, p. 1; Feb. 24, 1978, p. 3.

13. See Toge Fujihara, "Japanese Christians Oppose the Shrine," *New World Outlook* 34, no. 4, n.s. (December 1973):29-31; William P. Woodard, "Yasukuni Shrine," *Japan Times,* April 20, 1962; "Japan Christians Begin Hunger Strike Against Yasukuni Shrine Bill," *Japan Times,* April 16, 1974; Rev. Masahiro Tomura and colleagues produced 13 volumes in Japanese: *Yasukuni Mondai* [The Yasukuni Problem] (Tokyo: Shinkyō Shuppansha, 1974-); *JCAN,* May 3, 1974, pp. 1-3.

14. This section is a revision of the writer's paper, "The 1960 Security Treaty Crisis and the Christians of Japan," prepared for the International Conference on Japanese Studies of Japan P.E.N. Club, Kyoto, Nov. 18-25, 1972, published in *Studies on Japanese Culture,* vol. II (Tokyo: The Japan P.E.N. Club, 1973).

15. George R. Packard III, *Protest in Tokyo: The Security Treaty Crisis of 1960* (Princeton, N.J.: Princeton University Press, 1966).

16. Masataka Kosaka, *100 Million Japanese: The Postwar Experience* (Tokyo: Kodansha, 1972), pp. 200-201.

17. Jon Halliday and Gavran McCormack, *Japanese Imperialism Today* (London: Penguin, 1973), p. 153.

18. *JCAN*, May 27, 1977, pp. 1-3.

19. James M. Phillips, "The Reconciliation of Japanese and Korean Christians": in Japanese, *Fukuin to Sekai* 18, no. 2 (February 1962); in English, *JCQ* 24, no. 1 (January 1963): 1-8.

20. *JCAN*, October 1, 1965, pp. 1-2.

21. *JCAN,* February 23, 1973, p. 1.

22. Interview with Rev. Kanichi Nishimura, Tokyo, March 13, 1978.

23. English text of sermon by Masahisa Suzuki, "The Kyōdan of Tomorrow," October 23, 1966 (Tokyo: mimeographed by Council of Cooperation, 1966).

24. *Policy Statements and Statistics of UCCJ*, pp. 10-11. The "Confession" is also in Gerald H. Anderson, ed., *Asian Voices in Christian Theology* (Maryknoll, N.Y.: Orbis Books, 1976), pp. 254-55.

25. James M. Phillips, "A Seminary in Transition, 1969-71," is a mimeographed chronicle of how the 1970 conflicts affected Tokyo Union Theological Seminary. There are numerous books and articles in Japanese that give details of many aspects of these struggles. In English, *JCAN* contains many news items. *JCQ* has an important theme issue on "A Decade of Dispute in the United Church of Christ in Japan," vol. 45, no. 3 (Summer 1979).

26. See Ivan Morris, *The Nobility of Failure: Tragic Heroes in the History of Japan* (New York: Holt, Rinehart and Winston, 1975), for a study of the failed-hero mentality.

27. *JCAN,* December 20, 1974, pp. 1-3.

28. *JCAN,* November 22, 1974, pp. 3-4.

29. *JCAN,* April 22, 1977, pp. 3-5; Oct. 21, 1977, pp. 2-3.

30. *JCAN,* February 28, 1975, pp. 1-2.

31. *JCAN,* July 12, 1974, p. 3.

32. *JCAN,* March 22, 1974, pp. 3-5.

33. *JCAN,* November 19, 1976, pp. 3-4; July 22, 1977, pp. 2-3.

34. *JCAN,* April 27, 1979, pp. 1-2.

35. Cf. Albert Axelbank, *Black Star over Japan: Rising Forces of Militarism* (Tokyo: Tuttle, 1972).

36. Yoshiaki Iisaka, "The Present Crisis in Religious Freedom," *JCQ* 40, no. 3 (Summer 1974): 129-37.

37. Quoted in "The Emperor System: A Panel Discussion," in *JCQ* 40, no. 3 (Summer 1974): 118-19. The news item is from *The Mainichi Daily News,* May 4, 1971.

38. See Satoshi Hirata, ed., "On the Scene: 'Reality Ministry' in Japan" (Osaka: Kansai Urban Industrial Movement, 1975), mimeographed.

39. *JCAN,* July 28, 1978, pp. 1-6.

40. Interview with Prof. Yoshiaki Iisaka, Tokyo, May 19, 1975.

41. See *Korea Communiqué,* published in Tokyo by the NCCJ's Korea Committee.

42. On Christian groups' continuing action on Yasukuni Shrine bills, see *JCAN,* August 31, 1978, pp. 1-3.

43. *Kyōdan News Letter,* June 20, 1972, pp. 1-3.

44. *JCAN,* July 22, 1977, pp. 4-5.

45. *Rengō: Voice of Renewal,* October 1977 (no. 1).

46. *JCAN,* May 13, 1977, pp. 1-2.

47. Harvey Cox, "Japan in Search of Its Soul," *Christianity and Crisis* 38, no. 14 (October 2, 1978): 225-29.

48. *JCAN,* March 24, 1978, pp. 4-5.

49. Michael Garde, "Going on from Milk to Meat," *Sojourners* 8, no. 8 (August 1978): 18.

50. Jan Swyngedouw, "Japanese Religions and Party Politics," *JMB* 32, no. 9 (October 1978): 541-49.

51. "Panel Discussion: Church and State," *Kirisutokyō Nenkan* [Christian Yearbook] (Tokyo: Kirisuto Shimbunsha, 1976), pp. 41-60.

3

Christians and Education in Japan: The Mixed Legacy of an Education Boom

Of all the chapters in this study, this one on Christians and education in contemporary Japan would seem to be about one of the great success stories. To the average Japanese or to a foreign visitor, the churches of Japan, with only a few exceptions, may not seem impressive or extraordinary, but the large number of Christian schools and their extensive student bodies would surely seem to indicate a Christian presence and impact of considerable proportions. The statistics for a year that marks an important transition time in our study would seem to bear this out (Table 1, below).

Table 1: Christian Schools and Students in Japan, 1969[1]

	Protestant		Catholic		Total	
	No.	*Students*	*No.*	*Students*	*No.*	*Students*
Universities	44	123,015	11	19,750	55	142,765
Junior Colleges	49	28,477	29	8,137	78	36,614
Senior High Schools	108	83,687	114	66,200	222	149,887
Junior High Schools	83	28,421	100	27,122	183	55,543
Elementary Schools	29	6,917	57	22,821	86	29,738
Special Schools	71	24,949	34	8,348	105	33,297
Kindergartens	976	105,188	568	102,690	1,544	207,878
Totals:	1,360	400,654	913	255,068	2,273	655,722

When one considers the Catholic population in 1969 was only 350,000 and the Protestant population 455,000, the size of the educational programs seems impressive indeed.

Realistically, however, it needs to be said that the Christian schools of Japan have been a problem area, and the statistics by themselves tell only a part of the story. Despite large campuses and burgeoning student enrollments, one does not have to probe far to find that all is not well in these Christian schools. They grew during the postwar period both in facilities and in enrollments at a phenomenal rate as a result of an education boom that swept the nation during this time, but the problems that surround these schools have also grown in proportion. We shall survey the circumstances of the Occupation era with its educational reform policies that made possible the spectacular expansion of the Christian schools, and then examine some of the difficulties that these schools began to encounter and some of the measures taken to deal with them. Finally, we shall turn to the schools' "time of troubles" in 1968–71, when the problems faced by educational institutions were so great that planning initiatives in education passed largely from the schools themselves to the government. This is an exceedingly complicated story, for with over two thousand schools involved it will not be possible to cover more than some of the main trends, and one who is not a specialist in educational matters may at times feel overwhelmed by the details. But a careful reading of the record of the Christian schools, with elements of hopefulness and of distress, will provide important insights into the entire Christian community of Japan.

The Occupation Era (1945–52):
Christian Schools and the Education Boom

The end of World War II found a number of Christian schools with lengthy histories of operation, and even though their facilities were often severely damaged and their operating funds depleted, they were in a better position to begin again in most cases than were the churches or the social work institutions. Indeed, from the time of the reintroduction of Christianity to Japan in 1859, schools had been in the forefront of Christian work there. One recalls that until 1873 there were still official signboards prohibiting the practice of Christianity, so that some of the early missionaries began their work through teaching, and in so doing prepared the way for several of the Christian schools that were to follow. Such schools in Japan have often been seen as precursors of the churches, for where Christian schools have been strong, churches subsequently also developed strength, and such was not true of churches in areas where there were no Christian schools at all.

Yet Japan's Christian schools have often been hampered in their work, despite the hopes of their founders that they might provide what would now be called "the substructure of a Christian society" in Japan. That is to say, the enthusiasm for things Western had spread so widely that non-Christians as well as Christians in Japan in the 1880s thought that Japan might soon become "a Christian nation," just like the nations of the West. Therefore, the "mission schools" as they were then called would be the best places to learn about the new culture. But the inevitable wave of reaction to Westernization and Christianity came in the 1890s, as highlighted by the Imperial Rescript on Education (*Kyōiku Chokugo*) of 1890, which sought to put some limitations on Western educational influences and to reorganize the nation's educational methods around more tradition-centered Confucian standards.[2] There was also the Ministry of Education's Order No. 12 of 1899, which banned religious instruction in all accredited schools, private as well as public, and which led to the collapse of some Christian schools and the great alteration of the programs of others.[3]

Nor was this all. In the period of rising nationalism in the 1930s, pressures were gradually brought on all schools to conform to the government's prevailing ideology through the use of prescribed textbooks and courses. Special ceremonies were established for doing reverence to the imperial portraits and other items installed in special places on school campuses, and students were required to participate in worship at Shintō shrines.[4] In 1941 the nationalization of the school system was further developed by a National School Order that transformed all elementary schools into "National Schools."[5] As the Pacific War increased in intensity, university students were called into military service, and formal instruction for those who were left was limited sometimes to one day a week, for college students and their teachers had to take their turns at factory labor.[6] The bombing raids on Japan's major cities did extensive damage to school campuses, and wartime dislocations scattered the schools' faculty members and students, alumni, and support groups. When the end of war came, the Christian schools as well as their secular counterparts had indeed reached one of the lowest ebbs in their history.

During the Occupation period the Christian schools along with others received a new lease on life through the educational reforms sponsored by the Occupation. Before turning to specific developments in the Christian schools, it is necessary to gain an understanding of the Occupation's educational reforms, which had a far-reaching impact on all of Japan's schools.

The Occupation's Reforms of the Japanese Educational System

Although the Japanese educational system had undoubtedly contributed to the strength of modern Japan from the time of the Meiji Restoration, it had also aided the growth of nationalism and militarism. Hence the American Occupation sought a major overhaul of the educational system. The stated goal of the Occupation was to "democratize" the educational system from top to bottom, in order to remove some of its objectionable features and to make it the basis for a peaceful, democratic society.

To begin with, the reforms altered the multitrack system that the prewar educational system had embodied, for that system fostered elitism in education by limiting openings to the relatively small number of students who could get onto the particular track that led to educational advancement.[7] In its place was put a single-track system, whereby each level of education prepared qualified students for the next higher level. The national system also adopted the 6-3-3-4 structure, supposedly based on American models, which meant six years of elementary school, three years of middle school or junior high, three years of high school, and four years of university. Compulsory education was increased from six to nine years of schooling. Coeducation was recognized as the common pattern for all schools, thus modifying the prewar system, which discriminated very heavily against women's education. Kindergarten (*yōchien*) was not compulsory or state-subsidized in the early postwar decades, but the popularity of kindergarten education grew apace anyway. At the university level, the old system of education seemed particularly elitist; the government had adapted the Prussian university system as its model, and by limiting the number of university students it made them a very small educational elite. The Occupation sought to modify such elitism by giving encouragement to the establishment of a large number of new universities and by vastly increasing the number of university students. Finally, the prewar educational system was felt to have been too highly centralized under the control of the Ministry of Education; this was to be modified by changing the role of the ministry to serving the universities in an advisory capacity, and to enable other groups at the prefectural, municipal, and private levels to play greater roles in the administration of educational policies.

By way of hindsight, the reader today may be astounded that the Occupation authorities thought they could encourage the development of democracy in Japanese education through such sweeping reforms, which ironically were introduced by the most undemocratic means of military and administrative fiat.[8] The very term "democracy" was subject to divergent interpretation and abuse during this period. Yet despite such formidable handicaps, some important things did take place as a result of the Occupation's educational programs. A major element here is the fact that these educational reforms were for the most part carried out with the enthusiastic support and cooperation of the educators themselves as well as their students and parents. This stood in marked contrast to the Occupation's attempts to reform business corporations and the government bureaucracy, where there was often outward feigned compliance with the Occupation's policies, accompanied by foot-dragging and efforts to undo the reform measures as soon as possible. But in the schools, reforms were generally favorably received, for they were seen to be in the best interests of schools themselves as well as for Japanese society as a whole.

The implementation of the reforms came with breathtaking speed. The year 1947 alone saw the adoption of the new constitution, the Fundamental

Law of Education, and the School Education Law. Special education for the blind and deaf was made compulsory in 1948, and in 1949 came the Private School Law.[9] The 6-3-3-4 single-track system of education was instituted from 1947, and for a while pandemonium reigned because of the shortage of school buildings, teachers, and supplies to cope with the new requirements. As with several other reforms of the Occupation period, the initial commitments to education took time to implement with adequate budgets, construction of new schools, and the training or retraining of teachers; it is amazing that so much was accomplished within a relatively short period of time. Of the system of compulsory education in elementary and middle schools we shall have less to say in this study because, as Table 1 indicates, Christian groups tended to concentrate their efforts in education at the educational levels not covered by compulsory education, that is, in the kindergartens, high schools, and universities. In fact, in the year 1971, 99.4 percent of all elementary schools and 94.8 percent of all middle schools were government-run.[10] Where Christian schools did establish elementary or middle schools, it was in the hopes of providing feeder-schools for their high schools and universities, as will be explained later.

The new educational reforms were supported by the traditional Japanese thirst for education, whetted in the postwar era by the desires of many people to make a new start after the nation's defeat in war. The implementation of the reforms was also made possible by the economic recovery of the nation, which after the onset of the Korean War in 1950 was able to provide jobs for graduates. These many factors served to fuel an education boom in postwar Japan. The most spectacular growth took place at the university level, where postwar Christian schools were most active. In 1947, just before the educational reforms, Japan had 48 institutions at the university level and 113,320 students. By 1970, a crucial year for the testing of the university system, there were 380 universities and 1,400,000 students, an increase of almost eight times the number of schools and twelve times the number of students. Education became indeed a mass commodity, as Table 2 indicates.

Table 2: Percentage of Groups Attending Schools in Japan[11]

	1915 %	1925 %	1935 %	1947 %	1955 %	1965 %	1969 %
Elementary Schools	98.5	99.4	99.6	99.8	99.8	99.8	99.8
Middle and High Schools	19.9	32.3	39.7	61.7	78.0	86.2	87.8
Universities	1.0	2.5	3.0	5.8	8.8	14.6	16.7

The growth of the university student population is most remarkable, for by the 1960s Japan was second to the United States in the percentage of young people who enter universities. Such growth would not have been possible without the accompanying economic growth of Japan during the postwar period, and also the continuing commitment to education by students and their parents, in particular by the "education-minded mothers" (kyōiku mama) who have been legendary in their efforts to enable their children to receive a good education.

Women's education also stood high on the priority list of the new educational reforms, and this goal was implemented all the way through the university level. The percentage of women enrolled in 1969 in higher education of the total age population at that level was 9.8, which was, however, much lower than the figure of 23.3 percent for men.[12] Many women in higher education were enrolled in junior colleges, which saw a remarkable growth in postwar Japan and which by 1969 enrolled 213,416 women but only 45,913 men. These junior colleges were 90.1 percent privately run, many of them by Christian groups. They have generally been more successful than their four-year counterparts in terms of financial income, in the placement of graduates, and in lack of school disturbances.

The prewar problem of too-early specialization on the part of university students was supposed to be handled by the SCAP curriculum reforms, which specified that the first two years of the university program should be devoted to courses in general education, and the last two years given to specialized studies. Universities were to vary in the ways they handled the general education courses, but often these courses were to become a bone of contention for both students and instructors, who tended to view them as interfering with specialized courses.

Finally, the Occupation-sponsored reforms attempted to diminish the centralized control of education by the Ministry of Education, and to strengthen local and prefectural roles in education. The ministry's control had been very strong at the elementary and secondary levels in the prewar system, but the postwar organization of local school boards supposedly on the American pattern did little to change the situation, and the postwar period saw in large measure a return to centralized control. At the university level, however, the ministry's authority was supposed to be diminished, but it still carried considerable weight due to its control of budgetary allocations. The ministry's supervision of private universities in the postwar period was supposedly limited to the authority to issue charters and to set standards for the curriculum and facilities at schools, but in actuality private universities found it most expedient to keep in close touch with the ministry for the smooth operation of their programs in regard to governmental regulations. The internal administration of universities was often a very confused picture, since departmental autonomy or faculty privileges sometimes made the coordination of a university's programs a difficult thing. Christian universities in particular were both to profit from and be hurt by the new administrative measures of the Ministry of Education.

Responses of Christian Schools to the Education Boom: Some Case Studies

Having surveyed the main features of the educational reforms of the Occupation era, we now turn to a consideration of how Christian schools responded to the new opportunities which were presented them, with the enthusiasm and public support that derived from the education boom of that period. Because there were so many and varied responses, it may be most helpful to describe the different types of programs that the schools developed by giving some case studies.

Modifying an Older School to Meet the New Educational Requirements: Tokyo Woman's Christian College. To someone not familiar with the Japanese educational system, it might seem a relatively simple thing to modify an older school to meet the new requirements of the educational system. In an ordinary time this would be mainly a question of securing adequate resources through a carefully calculated "cash flow" and "personnel flow" to make the transition relatively painless. But in the actual circumstances of capital-starved postwar Japan, with the shortage of adequately trained personnel and with the psychological climate that followed the surrender, the transition from one form of schooling to another was far from a simple matter. The problems may perhaps be best understood by considering how a relatively well-situated school with an excellent reputation, Tokyo Woman's Christian College (Tokyo Joshi Daigaku), founded in 1918, made the transition from a "higher normal school for women" (*joshi semmon gakkō*) under the old educational system to a "university" (*daigaku*) under the new.[13]

To begin with, curriculum requirements were different under the new system, for the older curriculum had a lock-step program whereby an entire class moved through a prescribed course of studies, but the new system made provision for varieties of courses through a system of electives and credits. Then there was the question of access to a new university program, because students who had not gone to the "higher schools" (*kōtō gakkō*) did not have a route to education at a university (*daigaku*), and there was a difficult period of readjustment. The methods of education also changed, for the older system had relied more on lectures by the teachers and rote memorization by the students, while the newer system was supposed to encourage individual study, research, and discussion methods. There was also a question of specialization, for the older system had started specialization already at the higher school level, while the newer university program required two years of general education before specialization proper began. All of this required new skills and qualifications for faculty members, who sometimes found the transition to the newer teaching methods rather difficult and time-consuming, especially in the light of the extensive demands that were already being made on teachers in the postwar period. Furthermore, each university had to reorganize itself into various departments (*gakka*), with their differing procedures. Questions of departmental and university autonomy and matters of academic freedom had to be hammered out in the context of actual problems as they arose.

If a relatively well-endowed school like Tokyo Woman's Christian College had to face such extensive changes simply to continue doing in the new system substantially what it had been doing under the old, one may imagine how much harder it would be for a school that did not have such resources, or which wanted to make substantial changes in its programs. Tokyo Woman's Christian College was fortunate in having an overseas supporting board that provided funds, teachers, and counsel from abroad, and a large number of talented and dedicated alumnae and supporters who continued to support the college from all parts of Japan. Schools that lacked such resources sometimes resorted to gaining income by enlarging their campuses and increasing the number of students. Since some private schools received most of their income from tuition fees, expansion was a favorite response of schools to the education boom. But expansion of the campus and the numbers of the student body brought a host of problems with it, in particular the lowering of standards of education and a concomitant frustration among both faculty and students. The full effects of such frustrations were not to be felt for several years, however, as many schools concluded that rapid growth was the most ready answer in boom times.

Expanding Schools by Adding New Levels of Education: Aoyama Gakuin in Tokyo. It is clear that educational institutions in postwar Japan expanded, but the rationale for such growth was not always evident. Why were older programs expanded or perhaps discontinued, and newer programs added at a particular time? Even for an insider to an institution, some of the reasons for growth patterns may remain obscure, but a case study of Aoyama Gakuin in Tokyo may indicate how one particular institution carried out postwar expansion.[14]

Founded in 1874, Aoyama Gakuin was closely related to Methodist churches in America and Japan, and underwent many vicissitudes during its development from small schools for girls and boys to a major educational institution in Tokyo's pleasant Aoyama residential district. The majority of buildings were destroyed in the 1923 Kantō earthquake, and in an air raid on Tokyo on the night of May 25, 1945, almost 80 percent of its physical facilities were lost again. Since very little instruction had taken place during the last year of the war, Aoyama Gakuin virtually had to start afresh when it reopened in April 1946 with a reorganized men's college with four departments, a women's college with two departments, a boys' high school, a girls' high school, and an elementary school. Despite the poor condition of the physical plant and the food shortages that plagued Tokyo in the immediate postwar period, all the divisions at Aoyama had five to six times the number of applicants that they could accept. The demand for places in a centrally located institution in Tokyo was so great that Aoyama could hardly grow fast enough to meet it.

The return of American Methodist missionaries to the campus in 1946 was symbolic of the reestablishment of ties with overseas Methodists and, through the new postwar Council of Cooperation, overseas funds began to arrive to meet the expansion needs of Aoyama. The SCAP educational reforms of 1947 made necessary the reorganization of the various divisions and a more democratic system of appointments for school administrators. A thorough reorganization of higher education at Aoyama Gakuin was approved by the Ministry of Education in 1949, and a department of education was added to the literature college in the following year, as well as an evening division for the university. The campus buildings had to be restored, and this was done by the construction of stucco-frame buildings from 1947, and by reinforced-concrete buildings from 1952.

Meanwhile, with a change in the law in 1950 about the incorporation of a school as an "educational juridical person," Aoyama established such a new juridical person in the following year. In the 1950s Aoyama Gakuin became the first private university organized under the postwar educational system to be authorized to grant doctors' degrees. The department of Christian studies became a department of theology in 1961. The elementary and middle schools were rebuilt, and the facilities of almost all departments were either expanded or refurbished. Aoyama Gakuin could boast that it was possible for students to enter its single-track system of education from elementary school through graduate shool, without taking any reentrance exams. With the increasing competition among students seeking to enter every level of education, Aoyama Gakuin's single-track system was a goal toward which many other private schools would strive. In such a system every school would be a "feeder-school" for the next higher level of education. All told, Aoyama's many departments and divisions made it as close to a "multiversity" as a private and Christian university could be.

Not every Christian school was in a position, however, to take advantage of the opportunities to expand into new departments and fields in the postwar era. A great deal depended upon location, access to overseas support, and leadership that would be able to capitalize on the particular opportunities that a school possessed. Expansion as an end in itself might become a serious hindrance, as later proved to be the case in the belt-tightening period when the end of the postwar baby boom caused a drop in school enrollments.

Educational Pioneering through a New Christian University: ICU. The schools already in existence in 1945 had a great advantage in being ready to participate in the postwar education boom. But they also had the disadvantage of having been around long enough to have settled into ruts in various areas, thereby lacking the public image of being pioneers in new educational programs. The Occupation era seemed to some Christians to be the right time to try new approaches to education, in particular through the starting of new schools to operate on quite different educational principles. The possibilities and hazards of such an attempt are well illustrated in the case study of International Christian University, better known as ICU.

There had been plans in the prewar era to begin a school in Japan that would be thoroughly international and Christian as well as of the highest academic level, but the plans were set aside and overseas mission boards concentrated instead on building up the mission schools then in existence.[15] After the Pacific War, the main legatee of these older hopes was ICU, started in 1949 in Mitaka, in western Tokyo, by the combined efforts of a Japanese group that secured the land of a wartime aircraft factory and an American-based group that raised operating funds for the new institution.[16] The founders of ICU launched their new venture at a time when there were many factors that favored their enterprise, but even so they had to make many adjustments in their plans because of Ministry of Education requirements, the difficulties of raising budgets, and the availability of personnel.

From the beginning, ICU was determined not to repeat what its founders considered to be the mistakes of other Christian schools in Japan, in expanding facilities and enrollments at the expense of the quality of education offered. ICU was also determined to maintain the Christian quality of its education by insisting that all full-time faculty members be "evangelical Christians," and by backing programs in Christian studies and the work of a campus church. The international dimensions were emphasized by insisting that all graduates should have facility in both the English and Japanese languages, and to that end invited foreign faculty and students to work and live on the campus in an international atmosphere. The quality of education was also to be helped by keeping a relatively small enrollment, by providing such innovations as an open-stack library, dormitories for a large proportion of the student body, a largely resident faculty, and, later, a well-equipped science hall. Courses in general education were not confined to the first two years of the university, but were to be available to students throughout their time at ICU. Sports and club activities were stressed by providing a student union building and later a superb gymnasium. Although ICU had originally contemplated beginning as a graduate school to aid the other Christian universities already in existence, government law required that it start as a four-year college. Later, ICU added graduate departments in education and public administration.

ICU's efforts in educational pioneering ran into obstacles. The requirement that all regular faculty members be Christian was criticized as lacking in academic objectivity and making it difficult for departments to secure the best-qualified personnel in some cases. Language requirements fostered resentment among students, and the international character of the university was attacked as a sign of ICU's subservience to foreign control. The open-stack library was subject to constant pilferage, and the dormitories became centers for left-wing agitation. Even the size of the campus made it difficult for ICU to raise funds because of the growing value of its land holdings. Despite such problems, students and faculty at ICU tried to deal with each of these situations as part of the cost of pioneering in new areas of education. Yet the very idealism that ICU encouraged made the university particularly vulnerable to the waves of student unrest which came in the 1960s.

The experience of ICU was in many ways in a class by itself, for other new Christian schools of the postwar period could not count on the resources available to the founders of ICU. Obirin Gakuen, for instance, was established in a western suburb of Tokyo by Yasuzō Shimizu, who hoped that it might secure the reputation and support of Oberlin College in Ohio, its namesake. But the founder's dreams were not fully realized, for Obirin was not able to secure funds or personnel from abroad in appreciable quantities, or even the fraternal recognition of Oberlin. Yet Obirin found a niche in the educational system by providing a relatively low-cost education for students who could not afford other private universities. The postwar education boom thus brought opportunities for many new schools, but only a few could aspire to the choice places at the top.

The Boom in Preschool Education: Church Kindergartens. The postwar education boom also led to a greater public interest in preschool training, and here churches were able to respond through the establishment of church kindergartens (*yōchien*). Although there were a few prewar kindergartens in Christian churches and some wartime kindergartens established by Catholic missionaries who were cut off from overseas sources of funds, the vast expansion of preschool education held in Catholic and Protestant church facilities was a largely postwar phenomenon. This seemed to be an ideal answer to the problem of underutilization of church facilities during the week. Not only could the church buildings and grounds be put to an income-producing use, but also the pastor or church member could be given some additional income as kindergarten director, and the local church was given an opportunity to make contact with neighborhood families by providing a much wanted service for their children. Sometimes church members grumbled that too much time and energy of the church was given over to kindergarten activities and that church meetings often had to be held using the low chairs for children, but in general the kindergartens were welcomed. Indeed, a number of churches probably could not have survived without them.

The Work of Christian Teachers and Students in Secular Schoools. We do not wish to leave the impression in this survey that the only Christian presence in education was to be found in the nation's "Christian schools." For one thing, there have been a number of schools that are secular in theory but with strong traditions of Christian leadership: Tsuda College for Women and the Jiyū Gakuen in Tokyo, Katei Gakkō in Hokkaidō, and Dokuritsu Gakuen in Yamagata are but a few examples. Furthermore, there have been active Christian teachers and students in a great many secular schools, and from their numbers have come able leaders for the entire Christian community. The work of Christian student organizations that involved many of these teachers and students will be discussed in Chapter 5 on "Christian Outreach." Although the impact of these persons in organizational or institutional terms may be hard to evaluate, their contributions in personal terms and in establishing patterns for others to follow are highly significant.

The Era of Economic Growth (1952–68):
The Problems of Snowballing Expansion

The growth of the Japanese economy seemed to provide golden opportunities for the expansion of private schools in Japan, including its Christian schools. As the case studies of the previous section showed, schools that became well established in the postwar era were in a position to expand greatly thereafter if they chose to do so. Sometimes there appeared to be no choice, for the economics of private schools seemed to dictate that they had to grow or die. Because the financial aspects of the growth of the schools were crucial during this era, we must first examine the financial considerations that fueled this rapid expansion of the Christian schools, and then analyze some of the problems that such growth brought in its wake.

Financing Private Education in a Period of Economic Growth

It should be noted that the course of postwar education in Japan was directly affected by the nature of the Japanese government's financial commitments to education. By 1968, for instance, some 4.8 percent of the national income was used for education at all levels, which amounted to 20.5 percent of all governmental expenditures. Of this amount, 14.4 percent was spent for junior colleges and universities, but most of these funds went for national, prefectural, or municipal universities. In other words, government funds in the postwar period down to the 1970s were channeled mostly into elementary and secondary education, and such funds as were spent for higher education were mostly granted to public institutions. And yet the vast majority of university students in Japan were educated in private universities, as Table 3 indicates.

Table 3: Percentages of Students in National, Local, and Private Schools, 1970[17]

	Kinder-gartens	Elem. Schools	Middle Schools	High Schools	Special Schools (full-time)	Technical Colleges	Junior Colleges	Univer-sities	Misc. Schools
	%	%	%	%	%	%	%	%	%
National	0.3	0.5	0.8	0.3	3.5	74.3	3.7	22.3	0.3
Local	24.2	98.9	96.3	67.0	95.1	9.5	6.2	3.7	1.4
Private	75.5	0.6	2.9	32.7	1.4	16.2	90.1	74.0	98.3

In 1940 private universities enrolled about 60 percent of the total number of students, but by 1970 the figure was 74 percent and by 1974 it was 78 percent.

Hence the expansion of university enrollments in the postwar era took place mostly in the private universities. And while national universities counted on student fees for an average of 3 percent of their expenditures, private universities needed to derive 78.5 percent of their expenses from them.[18] Hence the financial burden for paying for the postwar expansion of the universities has been vastly different for public and for private universities. Similar comparisons could be made for public and private elementary and high schools, but as they were much fewer we shall limit our analysis to the universities, for it was there that Christian educators as well as many of their secular colleagues in other private schools were to encounter the greatest difficulties during the school struggles that will be described in the next section.

The dependence of the private universities on student fees for keeping their programs going had several significant consequences. It meant, for instance, that when the universities began to face mounting deficits in the era of economic growth due to inflation and other factors, the most ready solution seemed to be to take in more students, and to build additional facilities to accommodate them. This was done in many cases without due consideration for the capacity of the school to supervise these expanded programs adequately, or to provide the necessary equipment, teaching staff, or educational standards for such instruction. A standard way to keep ahead of the cost squeeze was to erect new buildings and add new departmental programs in order to bring in more income. Under such circumstances, it was difficult to fail students for poor academic work, not only because of the school's paternalistic attitudes but also because each student failed would mean a loss in tuition income. Furthermore, private universities tried to keep the number of their full-time faculty to a minimum, in order to rely on part-time faculty members who could be hired at lower pay. Because faculty members could by law hold only one full-time teaching position, and faculty salaries seemed inadequate in view of the rises in living costs, many teachers sought additional income from part-time teaching. All of these factors put together led to a mounting sense of crisis in the universities among students and faculty alike.

Internal Problems of Christian Schools

There were other problems which Christian schools had to face, along with their private school counterparts, that were attributable only in part to financial circumstances. For one thing, private universities tended to cluster in the larger cities, where it was easier to gather both faculty and students. In 1974 fully 68.4 percent of private university students were in the ten largest cities (46.2 percent were in Tokyo alone), while only 40.3 percent of national university students were in these cities, and of that number, 11.4 percent in Tokyo. In fact, the overconcentration of students in metropolitan areas, and in Tokyo in particular, was to provide a tinderbox for conflagrations breaking out in the late 1960s.[19]

Another problem for private universities was the overconcentration of their students in the humanities and the social sciences, where classes were generally larger and instruction less personalized. By 1972 fully 64.7 percent of private university students were in these two areas, as compared with 20.8 percent in the national universities. The problem was compounded by a far higher faculty/student ratio and to more crowded conditions in private universities. In 1974 there were 31.3 students per teacher in the private universities but only 8.0 students in the national universities. The same picture of crowded conditions was true of space. Private university students had 7.3m² of building area and 29.9m² of land area, while national university students had 22.2m² of buildings and 84.3m² of land. Such statistical comparisons are always open to a measure of skepticism, but they do indicate that private universities were developing severe internal problems.

The Occupation's single-track system of education did indeed open up higher education to a much larger constituency, but in so doing it exacerbated the problem of the "examination hells" of entrance examinations for students entering a higher level of education. Table 2 indicates that a much larger percentage of every age group attended school in the postwar period than in the prewar era. This means that the postwar competition for the prestige schools was intense, and in particular for the national universities where the fees were much lower. Whereas only a relatively small proportion of the young people had experienced the "examination hells" in the prewar period, the postwar era saw this trauma affecting the masses. Pressures to pass the exams also built up in high schools, and outside activities waned for the last two years or so as students prepared for their university entrance exams. The percentage of those graduating from high schools and going on to higher education rose from 51.4 in 1960 to 85.0 in 1974. But because there were more university places later on, the percentage of those finding places rose during the same period from 57.1 to 74.2. However, there was still left behind a band of from 100,000 to 200,000 *rōnin*. Named after the masterless samurai of feudal days, *rōnin* are students who do not secure entrance to a university on their first try and therefore spend an extra year or more preparing to take the examinations again. These students were often seeking entrance at one of the top prestige schools, but if they failed at that they might settle for one of the less prestigious universities, among which the majority of the Christian schools were to be found.

The internationalization of universities was another of the goals of the Occupation's educational reforms, but during the period under consideration this goal also became problematic for Japanese universities. On the surface it seemed relatively easy to increase the international content of Japanese education by introducing more materials from abroad, putting greater stress on foreign language study, and promoting the international exchange of students and faculty. It should not be forgotten that Japanese universities had their start as institutions for the translation and study of foreign academic materials. Supposedly Christian schools had an advantage in promoting internationalism, with their foreign missionary teachers and their many overseas ties. But there were restrictions on internationalism as well. Bureaucratic regulations were often to blame. For instance, the Ministry of Education required for many years that studies abroad could not be entered on a teacher's educational dossier, nor could credits be transferred from foreign institutions. After a postwar wave of interest in the study of foreign languages and of English in particular, such enthusiasm gradually waned. Students and professors who did gain competence in foreign languages and in overseas contacts might find themselves increasingly isolated among their own colleagues.[20] Christians supposedly shared with Marxists an interest in international educational ties, but after the 1960 Mutual Security Treaty struggles less emphasis was placed on foreign scholarship and more on developing Japan's own capabilities (see chap. 2, "Christians and Politics"). Internationalism remained an exotic element in Japan, to be studied by scholars and cultivated through special tours abroad run by travel bureaus, and then left at the vestibule *(genkan)* of Japanese society upon return. In this respect Japan was at this time following the inward-turning trends of many countries, and it is remarkable that in the face of such trends there remained as much commitment to internationalism in Japan as there was.

University administration was another internal problem of higher education in Japan that particularly affected Christian schools. The Occupation reforms had sought to democratize administration within the schools and to diminish the administrative role of the Ministry of Education. The era of economic growth saw the development of many different administrative patterns in the Christian universities, but in most cases there was at least the principle of faculty control in the decision-making processes. Yet decisions were impaired by the near autonomy of some departments and by the "chair system" of faculty appointments. Even though the faculty were supposed to have the final word in internal university decisions, the demands of research and other teaching commitments made faculty members willing in many cases to delegate decisions to administrators who enjoyed long tenure. For Christian universities, as for most private schools, the necessary major decisions were carried out increasingly by administrators who made them primarily with financial considerations in mind.

For all of these reasons, there was a growing agenda of problems which were not being dealt with adequately by the universities, such as the marked decline in student/faculty contacts, the provision of adequate services for student welfare and club activities, problems of dormitory life, the lack of student participation in school decisions directly affecting the student body, the growing impersonality and alienation of campus life, and the increasing orientation of universities away from idealistic goals toward the demands of a consumer-oriented society. There never was any shortage of ideas as to how these problems might be tackled, but there was a severe lack of decision-making authority to put ideas into practice.

Into this vacuum of administrative leadership in the universities there stepped a number of organizations and ideologies. Organizations for student autonomy had their origins in prewar days, but with the mounting problems of postwar universities they were used to counter what the students considered the bad effects of faculty autonomy. The student organizations were fueled by New Left ideologies holding that the universities were hopelessly corrupted by their connections with the industrial/governmental establishment, and through them with the military, economic, and industrial policies of the United States and other capitalist nations. Disillusioned with democratic and gradualist approaches to social change, New Left groups increasingly came to rely on direct-action techniques to reach their goals. Increases in tuition charges or other student fees, questions about the autonomy of student organizations, the control of campus buildings, and the like were issues that could become the occasions for campus struggles that might mount in intensity far beyond the original provocation. But before we turn to a discussion of such campus struggles, it is necessary to note some of the signs of the times in education during the era of economic growth.

Signs of the Times: More Case Studies

Although the era under study was most noted for the expansion of school enrollments and facilities together with the growth of unsolved problems, there were other significant developments which bear mention.

Agencies for Cooperation among Christian Schools. All too often Christian schools as well as other private schools have seemed to lead a Robinson Crusoe existence, trying to survive by their own strength and ingenuity without any outside assistance. Despite the truth of such an impression, it should be noted that postwar Japan saw the reorganization and growth of agencies for cooperation among Christian schools.

Protestant schools in Japan had worked together since 1910 through the National Christian Education Association, which survived the war years and was reorganized in 1947, taking the name of the Education Association of Christian Schools in Japan in 1956 (Nihon Kirisutokyō Gakkō Kyōiku Dōmei).[21] Through its continuing programs of summer training courses, conferences for research in education, district councils, and the publication of its newsletter *Christian School Education (Kirisutokyō Gakkō Kyōiku)*, the association was able to foster mutual help among Christian schools and universities. There was also an Interboard Committee for Christian Work–Related Schools Council of institutions related to the North American mission boards and the Kyōdan; and the National Christian Council of Japan (NCCJ) had a Division of Education to carry out programs of research and service in educational matters.

Cooperation among Catholic educators took place through the Education Commission of the National Catholic Committee, as it was reorganized in 1945. One of the most important tasks it undertook was to deal with provisions of the Fundamental Law of Education (1947). That law rescinded the Imperial Rescript on Education (1890) and other regulations, which had put considerable restrictions on the operation of Catholic schools from prewar times. Nevertheless, the 1947 law made new requirements that Catholic schools found burdensome, such as making coeducation necessary in elementary and secondary schools, exempting students from paying certain fees, and prohibiting the recruitment of pupils beyond limited areas.[22] The Education Commission worked with academic experts at Sophia University and the Marianist Brothers to produce a plan adapting Catholic schools to the new law and suggesting changes in the regulations. This plan as presented to the Ministry of Education and accepted by them made these changes: any private school was allowed to accept tuition fees from parents who wanted their children to be educated in the school; Catholic schools could continue to conduct separate schools for boys and girls; and the restrictions on areas from which Catholic schools could recruit their students were removed. The tasks of coordination between Catholic schools were entrusted in 1956 to the Catholic Education Council, which carried out approximately the same functions for Catholic schools as the Kyōiku Dōmei did for Protestants. The monthly newspaper *Catholic Education (Katorikku Kyōiku)* reported on the council's functions for the schools.

With Vatican Council II (1962–65), some new directives were issued about education, especially the *Declaration on Christian Education* (1965), which had implications for Catholic schools in Japan. Although that document did not break much new ground about its subject, it did make clear some implications of the new principles of religious liberty as they apply to Catholic schools:

This sacred Synod proclaims anew . . . the Church's right freely to establish and to run schools of every kind and at every level. At the same time, the Council recalls that the exercise of this right makes a supreme contribution to freedom of conscience, the protection of parental rights, and the progress of culture itself.[23]

For Japan, this meant that Catholic schools could not insist that non-Catholic students receive religious instruction or take part in religious observances, and efforts were made to keep the schools informed of the implications of the Vatican Council's action.[24]

The Rewards of Excellence: The International University of the Sacred Heart. Christian schools that aimed at educational excellence and declined to compromise their educational standards by emphasizing expansion above achievement had to pay a price for their efforts. Their tuition fees rose so high that their schools seemed accessible only to the very wealthy. But sometimes excellence brought its own reward, and such was the case with the University of the Sacred Heart.

The Sisters of the Sacred Heart came to Japan in 1908, and in 1916 founded in Tokyo a Sacred Heart Higher Normal School *(semmon gakkō)* for women, based on the women's schools that the order had established in France and elsewhere. An air raid in World War II demolished almost all of the buildings of this school, but the order undertook the tasks of rebuilding and in 1948 opened the University of the Sacred Heart under the new educational system, with the indomitable Mother Elizabeth Britt as president. To achieve the goals of the new university, Mother Britt enlisted Japanese dignitaries and leaders of the Occupation, with General MacArthur himself the honorary chairman of the fund-raising appeal.[25] Fund-raising bazaars for the school became so elaborate that foreign embassies vied with each other for elegance, so that such efforts had to be curtailed in the 1960s. The university continued to insist on the highest standards for women's education.

A measure of public recognition for the University of the Sacred Heart came with the wedding on April 10, 1959, of a Sacred Heart alumna, Miss Michiko Shoda, and Crown Prince Akihito. Michiko Shoda had been president of the student body at Sacred Heart, and a student delegate from Japan to an international conference of schools of the Sacred Heart in Europe. The vast outpouring of publicity that accompanied this wedding gave due measure of credit to the University of the Sacred Heart, and represented one of the highest accolades given to a Christian school in the contemporary era.

Toward New Goals for Education: "The Image of the Ideal Man" (1965). The Fundamental Law of Education (1947) rescinded the Imperial Rescript on Education (1890), as we have seen, but it did not replace the older document with a clearer set of goals for the modern educational system. Older Japanese of a more conservative outlook noticed in particular the lack of moral education, and a continuing controversy ensued especially with the Japan Teachers' Union about the advisability of introducing new courses on moral education into the curricula of elementary and secondary schools. Critics of moral education feared that government-sponsored courses on moral education would reintroduce traditional and feudalistic values based on Confucianism, Bushidō, and Shintō, to the weakening of the ideals of liberal democracy and the separation of religion and the state that were among the goals of the postwar educational reforms.

After the failure of efforts to introduce moral education, the Ministry of Education tried again on a somewhat broader level, by publishing *The Image of the Ideal Person (Kitai-Sareru Ningenzō)*, which was meant to be a guide to educational goals. Between the publication of the draft copy of the report in 1965 and the revised report in 1966, no fewer than two thousand articles or comments on the draft appeared in print.[26] Although reactions of Christian educators varied, most were critical, fearing not so much the content of the report itself as the way it might be utilized to restrict the freedom of both education and religion. Comparing it with the 1890 Rescript, Professor Takeshi Takasaki of Tokyo Union Theological Seminary, later to become that school's president, wrote:

> The Imperial Rescript did not have an original purpose of restricting the freedom of the Japanese nation, but when it fell into the hands of government officials it was treated as if it were something sacred, and the people were forced to swallow it. . . . I sense a concern about political unreliability in the report.[27]

A more favorable estimate came from Chancellor Kinjirō Ōki of Aoyama Gakuin:

> To issue such a report at this time is a very courageous and meaningful act. Presently colleges and universities are regarded as places for study only, and no attention is paid to building character. . . . We Christian schools have cause to regret that the government has been forced to take an initiative we should have taken ourselves.[28]

Catholic responses to *The Image of the Ideal Person* tended to be critical, as a summary of a round-table discussion reported in the Catholic theological journal *Seiki* indicates:

> It is doubtful whether the Ministry of Education is the indicated organ to produce such a document, the contents of which could hardly do justice to man's nature unless religious factors are respected. There are certain misgivings about the potential danger of the *Report*. In the past, similar committees have made reports which then became the law. It is feared that the *Report* might be taken for an updated *Rescript on Education*. The distinction between the generally human and the specific Japanese elements in the character building of the ideal man is too hazy.[29]

Although the debate on *The Image of the Ideal Person* waxed hot and furious for a while, there was no immediate implementation of its major suggestions, for public opposition to the report was sharply critical, not only on the part of educators but also from popular newspapers and religious groups. Even the timing of the publication of the report was not conducive to a good reception, for the *Asahi Shimbun* mass-circulation newspaper ridiculed the report with an article entitled "The Image of the Ideal Politician," in reference to graft and influence peddling in the Diet, which were then receiving publicity in the press.

Not to be daunted by the generally unfavorable reception given *The Image of the Ideal Person,* a number of publications with further recommendations for conservative measures were issued by the Japan Educational Federation (Nippon Rengō Kyōikukai), an organization formed by former officials of the Ministry of Education after the Pacific War to counter the influence of the leftist-dominated Japan Teachers' Union. At the end of 1966 the Japan Educational Federation issued *A Plan for Fostering Religious Sentiments,* which pointedly went beyond *The Ideal Person* by proposing a plan for revitalizing religious sentiments in Japan, without which educational goals were said to falter. Commented the authors of the *Plan*:

> Religion is a basic element of human existence. In general education, particularly in the early stages of life, religion is a unique means to-

wards attaining human perfection. Since time immemorial, religion has been the driving force behind civilization and progress. The many facets in which religion appears in human history point to the variety of ways in which it can be incorporated in educational goals. For the last two years, the Japan Educational Federation has studied the nature of religious feeling in our country and its role in the national life. We advocate strengthening those feelings and that role; we hope that the plan which we present here may contribute to the prosperity of the country and to the happiness of the world.[30]

There were no immediate consequences of the publication of the *Plan.* Hence the entire debate about educational goals, which was launched by *The Ideal Person,* was not so much productive of immediate results as it was an indication of the malaise about educational goals and purposes that had arisen by the late 1960s, and the inability of either government authorities or private groups—including Christian educators—to do anything decisive about the problem.

Changing Patterns of Theological Education. Among the Christian schools of Japan, the theological schools have had a unique position, since they are not only centers for training the professional leadership of the churches but also institutions representing in their own work the changing relationships between the schools and the churches.[31] It may be noted in passing that the academic study of religion in public universities did not attract the widespread following in Japan that has been the case in Western countries (although chap. 8, "Biblical Studies," will describe some important contributions by scholars in the public universities, and chap. 9 will do the same for "Theology in Japan").

A number of Japan's theological schools can trace their histories back to the Meiji era, when they were founded as private boarding schools for the training of pastors. Several mission schools began theological departments, and in prewar years there were mergers and realignments of such departments. The postwar era saw the founding of many new theological schools, so that of the seventy Protestant schools listed in the 1971 *Japan Christian Yearbook*, only twelve had their origins in the prewar period.[32] With the new educational policies of the Occupation era, theological schools could be grouped in three major classes: two were accredited one-faculty universities of theology, seven were university-related departments of theology (or departments of Christian studies), and twenty-seven or so were specialized vocational schools. The difference between these various types is that the first two operated programs accredited by standards of the Ministry of Education, while the third type included schools with a wide variety of educational prerequisites, entrance requirements, curriculum standards, and teaching techniques. Government accreditation did not automatically restrict standards of excellence, for some of the nonaccredited schools were able to sponsor innovative programs of theological education.

It is significant that theological schools were able in the postwar period to develop a cooperative association among themselves not only at the national level but—far in advance of other Christian schools—also at the international level. The Japan Association for Theological Education (JATE) was formed in 1965 among schools in all three categories mentioned above, and the following year the Japanese association joined its counterparts in Korea (the Korean Association of Accredited Theological Schools—KAATS) and in Taiwan (the Commission on Theological Education in Taiwan—COTE) to form the North East Asia Association of Theological Schools (NEAATS). This was done with the encouragement and assistance of the Theological Education Fund (TEF), which was affiliated with the World Council of Churches. This cooperation led to the publication of the semiannual *Northeast Asia Journal of Theology* and to conferences of seminary personnel, which helped them keep abreast of regional and international developments.

Although there was a built-in conservatism in many theological schools because of their commitment to training clergy for denominational groups of differing confessional backgrounds, the precarious financial conditions of the theological schools, their small size, and their intense dedication to the particular tasks given them made it possible for seminaries sometimes to make educational innovations that would not have been countenanced by more traditional schools. Problems of trade unions among teachers that sometimes troubled other Christian schools rarely affected the seminaries, for their faculty were in general highly motivated to do their tasks even at substandard salaries. Close relations that developed between faculty and students and the students' involvement in the life of the churches also helped to create a good educational climate.

But the seminaries were not immune to problems, as subsequent events were to indicate. In fact, the very idealistic commitment of seminary students and faculty made them prone to school struggles, which were supposedly based on idealistic considerations. For this reason seminary struggles were to play a central role in the Christian schools' "time of troubles," to which we now turn.

The Era of Reappraisals (since 1968): Chaos and Rebuilding

The underlying tensions of Japanese society, which had been papered over by a new constitution and other postwar reforms, had never been dealt with in a thoroughgoing manner. The Christian community of Japan in particular was made aware of the underlying polarizations in Japanese political life, which affected the churches as among the only completely voluntary organizations in Japanese society (see chap. 2, "Christians and Politics in Japan"). The schools were also affected by this ongoing polarization, at the university level in particular, because, at the university, Japanese students enjoy their first real taste of freedom after years of preparation for the grueling entrance exams, and their university years also mark their last taste of freedom before facing the rigid requirements of the Japanese industrial world.[33]

The Universities' "Time of Troubles," 1968-71

Christian schools along with their secular counterparts underwent intense struggles during the 1968-71 period. The troubles were not limited to Japan, of course; universities from Paris to New York and Berkeley and Mexico City were ablaze with campus struggles during this period. While clearly influenced by the course of events abroad, Japanese university radicals had reasons of their own for dissatisfaction in the late 1960s. The immediate issue for most groups was the United States–Japan Mutual Security Treaty, which was to complete its ten-year period of validity in 1970, beyond which it might be renounced by either side upon one year's notice. Critics of the treaty maintained that 1970 would be an appropriate time not only to end the treaty but also to take a decisive "turning to the left" in Japanese politics, away from the association with the United States and the Western capitalistic nations that the treaty and its predecessor had maintained all through the postwar period.

The attack on the treaty was carried out by groups whose methods and ideologies differed from those used by groups that had opposed the treaty's ratification in 1960. Opposition to the Mutual Security Treaty ratification had been led by a relatively unified leftist opposition, including the leaders of the Japan Socialist party and the Japan Communist party, against the ruling Liberal Democratic party.[34] But in the 1960s came the fragmentation of the world Communist movement, with the USSR and the People's Republic of China locked in bitter arguments about which was the true heir of the Marxist-Leninist tradition.[35] Then in 1966 came the Great Proletarian Cultural Revolution in People's China, with its devotion to the principles of perpetual revolution. This theme was picked up by self-styled Maoists in Japan who held that true followers of Marx (especially the early Marx who was more of a humanist than he later became with the writing of *Das Kapital*) should try to crush every Establishment of modern society, including those of the "Old Left" Socialists and Communists. This New Left spawned dozens of radical student groups, but at length they came together in loose structures called Zenkyōtō (All-Campus Joint Struggle Councils, which name was also applied to the national federation of such councils). One of the basic principles of New Left action groups was that there be only the loosest kind of coordination and orders imposed from above, leaving each local group to "do its own thing," based on the particular grievances of a local campus. This made it possible for Zenkyōtō to bring together students who had many diverse sorts of grievances against the Establishment into a common program of opposition to the Security Treaty and the government supporting it.

On the campuses of Christian universities as well as those of their secular counterparts were numbers of unresolved problems that had been building up from the era of postwar expansion. Very often, however, the issue precipitating a campus struggle was not a major matter in itself but, rather, a minor concern alleged by radical groups to foreshadow or symbolize a larger nexus of problems that loomed in the background. Hence Sophia University's struggle began when a police car was brought to the campus to investigate a robbery; Meiji Gakuin erupted over the removal of some leftist signboards from the front of a university building; ICU had a prolonged struggle that began with the cancellation of a school festival that would have given publicity to various radical causes; Tokyo Union Seminary's strike began when the faculty issued a statement criticizing the behavior of students at an all-night bargaining session with a Kyōdan committee.[36] The protesting Zenkyōtō students did not think that such incidents were trivial, however, for it was their conviction that they were occasions for launching their attacks on the entrenched evils of capitalism in Japan and other countries. Their attacks were directed against the universities as the "service stations" of the capitalist establishment.[37]

Although the 1960s saw campus struggles of many different sorts, it is generally acknowledged that the major outbreak of the Japanese universities' time of troubles began with the conflict in the University of Tokyo Medical School in December 1967.[38] The place is significant, for this was the top professional department of the most prestigious university in Japan; if it could have a major outbreak of trouble, what university could remain immune? Campus struggles spread quickly throughout Japan's public and private universities, especially in the Tokyo–Yokohama and the Osaka–Kyoto areas. By June 1969 over 40 percent of all university students in Japan were unable to attend classes because of campus disorders. Zenkyōtō students cherished the hope that the university campuses—together with the few high school campuses that also had struggles—would be only the first outposts of the revolutionary struggle that in 1969–70 would sweep through Japanese society, toppling its conservative government and turning the entire nation toward the left. Hindsight might judge that such hopes were totally illusory, but at the time there was no telling what might be the outcome of a major conflagration among Japan's universities. The particular grievances that had caused the outbreak of campus struggles were only loosely related to the unfinished agenda of educational problems to which the previous section referred. The tactics and goals of the Zenkyōtō groups soon became virtually nihilistic, devoted to the overthrow of the establishment in education and society rather than to the remedying of faults. For this reason the Zenkyōtō struggles largely collapsed when the universities and other establishment targets resisted overthrow with the assistance of legislation from the National Diet and the intervention on many campuses of the riot police *(kidōtai)*, for the radical students vastly underestimated the resilience of the Establishment targets. This also helps to explain why the school struggles were ended in most places by 1970, with the educational problems that had given rise to them in the first place virtually untouched and unchanged. Even the Medical School at the University of Tokyo made no significant changes despite the nationwide chaos which that school's struggle had helped to ignite.

The appeal that the university struggles had for Christian students in the various Christian universities is not hard to understand, despite the initial shock of visitors who were unfamiliar with the background of the situation. Whatever the issue at their local campus, some idealistically-inclined Christian students were moved by the Zenkyōtō criticisms of some of the current developments of their times: the continuance of the Security Treaty, the role of the United States in Vietnam, the continuing presence of United States military bases in Japan, the visits to Japanese ports of United States nuclear-powered warships, the exploitative tactics of United States and Japanese firms in Southeast Asia, and the like. To some with a theological bent, the Zenkyōtō tactics called for the death of evil and oppressive universities, which somehow would be followed by a resurrection of groups that would truly work for the people. On many campuses Christian students formed Christian struggle groups, which sought to interpret the conflicts in terms of Christian theology, in contrast to Christian students in America at the same time who often submerged their Christian identity in secular radical movements. For this reason, radical ideology continued to have its impact on the life of the Kyōdan as the leading Protestant denomination long after the struggles had subsided in the schools.

The Ending of Campus Struggles

The ending of most of the campus disputes can be traced to the measure known as the Temporary Emergency Law for University Disturbances (in Japanese, generally known as *Daigaku Rippō*, the Universities Law). This measure was submitted to the National Diet in the spring of 1969, and despite a storm of protest from the universities and members of the Japan Socialist party, it became law in August of that year. The law threatened universities that allowed campus disorders to continue beyond a specified period with the loss of their university charters. In April 1969 the Ministry of Education also announced a change in its policy of prohibiting the entry of riot police to university campuses only if they were invited by university authorities. Instead, the police were authorized to enter campuses on their own initiative when it appeared to them that there was serious danger to life or property. These two measures made it easier for university officials to call riot police to end campus struggles, and thus not to run the risk of losing their charters. Within one year after this measure had become law, most strike-torn campuses had been entered by riot police and their academic work had been resumed somehow by university authorities.

The ending of campus struggles at Christian universities differed hardly at all from the process at their secular counterparts. At ICU a strike that had suspended university activities for several months was ended when the riot police evicted striking students from the barricaded main building, and a large fence was erected around the central campus buildings to hinder radical students from recapturing these buildings before the police could be summoned again. (On almost every campus after the entry of the riot police, a large corrugated-iron fence, soon painted by the radicals with their slogans, was to be found.) At Aoyama Gakuin riot police had to be summoned several times as the Zenkyōtō strikers continued the struggle with new issues. When Aoyama's Theological Department had the temerity subsequently to admit striking students from Tokyo Union Seminary to its own student body, the wrath of the administration was such that the Theological Department was closed down, with the explanation that it had produced too few graduates who had become pastors in its recent history and that its cost to the university was excessive. (A legal battle that arose from this Aoyama conflict is described in chap. 2, "Christians and Politics.") Sophia University had a particularly prolonged struggle, partly because the location of its campus near government buildings and transportation facilities in central Tokyo made it a valuable base from which Zenkyōtō groups could stage destructive raids. Sophia too had its incursions by the riot police and its ugly fence before its time of troubles subsided.

At Tokyo Woman's Christian College, a small group of women students aided by "outside allies" *(gaijin butai)* caused several hundreds of thousands of dollars damage on college buildings before they too were dislodged by riot police. Kwansei Gakuin University in Nishinomiya also suffered extensive damage to buildings in a struggle of particular bitterness, which had its reverberations later in the internal problems of the Kyōdan. Kantō Gakuin, a school with traditional ties to the American Baptist Convention and the Japan Baptist Union (Nihon Baputesuto Dōmei), dissolved its Theological Department after that department had become torn by ideological controversies, and a new administration moved the school closer to a secularized orientation. Tokyo Union Theological Seminary became involved in a strike that protested the Kyōdan's support of the Christian Pavilion at Expo '70, and the calling of the riot police to the seminary campus also became a continuing bone of contention in the Kyōdan. Seinan Gakuin in Fukuoka, related to the Southern Baptist Convention in the United States and the Japan Baptist Convention (Nihon Baputesuto Renmei), also saw a severe struggle in its theological department that for a period virtually depleted its student body, requiring several years to rebuild its strength and its morale. The details of the beginning, development, and ending of all of these struggles at Christian schools are indeed wearisome, and in the end there was "victory" for no one but, rather, the exhaustion of all sides after protracted struggles, followed by the gradual restoration of academic life.

Government Initiatives for University Changes

In the aftermath of the university struggles, there were various suggestions about what might be done to improve the situation. Despite the submission of scores of "reform proposals" during the school conflicts when the situations were critical, most of these proposals were quickly forgotten once the time of crisis had passed. Only in some smaller schools were there significant steps toward change that attempted to deal with the problems that had occasioned the school disorders in the first place. For the most part, the universities of Japan—public and private, Christian and secular alike—were unable to make any significant steps toward reform. Furthermore, the schools were troubled by the rapid inflation that followed the "oil shock" of 1973, and were increasingly unable to remain financially viable by their own efforts. Hence the initiatives for educational policies fell to the government by default. In particular, it was the ruling Liberal Democratic party that through the Ministry of Education began to take measures that would restructure the Japanese educational system—particularly at the university level—more to its liking. These government initiatives were given additional support by a survey of Japanese education carried out by the Organization for Economic Co-operation and Development in 1970, but the directions of government policies were based more on political than on academic considerations.[39]

The Ministry of Education had requested the Central Council for Education in July 1967 to prepare guidelines for a new educational system for the nation, which would be as it were a third major educational reform, comparable to the reforms of the Meiji era and those following the Pacific War. The council worked on its mandate through the period of intensified university disturbances, and in one sense the government's Temporary Emergency Law for University Disturbances (August 1969), to which reference was previously made, might be considered to be a part of the entire program of change. The council at last submitted its report to the Minister of Education in June 1971.[40] The guidelines of that report were subsequently followed for educational reform in the main, with modifications due mostly to shortages of funds. Fundamental to all recommendations in the report was the principle that educational planning itself was essential. And since the universities themselves were not able to undertake that planning, the national government endeavored to do so.

Public funding for private universities was one of the first issues to be dealt with, since the private universities' constant fee increases were a continuing occasion for student disorders. Until the universities' time of troubles in 1968-71, public funds for private schools had not been forthcoming, due to article 89 in the constitution, which specified: "No public money or other property shall be expended or appropriated for the use, benefit, or maintenance of any religious institution or association, or for any charitable, educational, or benevolent enterprises not under the control of public authority." This restriction was dealt with—some would say "circumvented"—by the establishment of a foundation to dispense public funds for private universities' faculty salaries according to stipulated rules. This funding program began in 1970 and soon accounted for a large portion of private universities' incomes. These private universities continued to raise their fees, and student disturbances over this were particularly severe in 1975, but they gradually subsided because without government assistance the tuition increases would have been all the greater.[41]

Along with the dispensing of funds to private schools, however, the government has also attached numerous strings, which sought to set higher standards of quality in private universities. For instance, the Ministry of Education greatly restricted the practices of private universities in collecting extra admission fees and in enrolling students far in excess of their registered capacities. The ministry did this by refusing subsidies to forty-one private universities that had engaged in such practices in fiscal 1973. Then in March 1975 the ministry sought to alleviate the concentration of universities in urban areas, and particularly in the Kantō district of Tokyo–Yokohama and the Kansai area of Kyoto–Osaka, by refusing to allow the establishment of further private universities in these areas. The ministry also made it more difficult to create new departments by raising the amount of funds that a university had to possess before it could create a new department.[42] Such measures were designed to curb the seemingly unrestricted growth of private universities, which had created such intense problems in 1968–71.

Dealing with the problem of the "examination hells" was also on the agenda of educational reform. "Examination hells" got their name from situations where ten or twenty applicants would compete in rigorous examinations for every available university opening. The Ministry of Education's University Entrance Examinations Revision Council recommended in March 1975 that a uniform scholastic achievement test be used by all national universities as a first stage in testing applicants, leaving the universities free to carry out second-stage tests of their own making.[43] Similar requirements for private universities made the entrance examinations a little more orderly, but it seems that a completely satisfactory approach to the issue is still a thing of the future.

Efforts to promote internationalization in Japanese higher education have taken many forms, for criticisms have often been leveled at Japan's universities for being too parochial in outlook. Bringing foreign students to Japan had its difficulties, for among the approximately five thousand foreign students in Japan in any one year, some 80 percent came from Asian nations and often complained that they were shunted into foreign student dormitories that were "ghettos" set apart from regular university life.[44] Christian universities pioneered in receiving foreign students to their campuses, but even there the integration of overseas students into the regular programs of the schools was often problematical. Japanese government interest in internationalization of education led instead to support for the United Nations University, and the location of its main base of operations in Japan. Some Christian educators pointed out that the government's efforts to promote internationalization in education were unrealistic, for the government's measures were not always based on actual experience with overseas students and faculty, such as Christian schools have had over the years.

A long-range problem of Japanese higher education to which the government addressed itself was that of finding an adequate number of university openings for applicants. The first postwar baby boom subsided and was followed by declining numbers in the school-age population. At the eighteen-year-old level of college entrants, the low of 1,550,000 was reached in 1976, of whom some 35 percent went on to higher education. But a Ministry of Education study indicated that the number of eighteen-year-olds would climb again to an anticipated high of 2,060,000 in 1991.[45] Instead of relying on private universities to provide the bulk of openings for these increased enrollments, as was the case in the Meiji era and again in the period right after the Pacific War, the ministry intends that the government's role should be greater, through establishing "new-style universities." The ministry founded Tsukuba University in Ibaraki Prefecture in 1973 as a prototype of what the new-style university might be. Tsukuba University, located away from metropolitan areas, is given a system of more centralized and tighter administrative control, and operates with more severe restrictions on the political activities of both faculty and students. The measures instituted at Tsukuba may give some indication of the patterns that the ministry hopes other universities will adopt henceforth.

The ministry has also worked on a "University of the Air," modeled on a similar project of Britain's BBC, for making higher education available to the masses through television broadcasts correlated with correspondence courses. Critics of the proposal have claimed that it represents another method by which the ministry seeks to control both the content and the administration of higher education.

The new measures sponsored by the Ministry of Education cover every level of education, even though the primary stress has been at the university level. There have also been proposals once again for courses in ethics and for teacher-evaluation systems, which continue to receive the sharp criticism of the Japan Teachers' Union. School textbooks are constantly being revised to meet the ministry's criteria of what is acceptable. The ministry has also tightened up the standards for kindergartens to receive government subsidies, a step on the way toward making kindergarten education compulsory. Some Christian churches have been concerned that the new kindergarten regulations would not only threaten the future of many church-sponsored kindergartens, but might also jeopardize the continuation of the churches themselves, since they are heavily dependent upon income from the kindergarten programs for their very existence.[46]

Christians and Education: Concluding Observations

Since the ramifications of the subject of education are almost endless, it is hard to know where to set the limits in this treatment of it. With the benefit of hindsight, it may be possible to make three general observations about Christians and education in contemporary Japan.

In the first place, it seems clear that the rapid expansion of Christian schools and universities in the postwar period as a response to the education boom was an advantage that was bought at a severe price. Where Christian schools insisted on high standards, there were satisfactions to compensate for the financial and administrative burdens that made this possible. But where Christian schools like so many of their secular counterparts among the private schools expanded primarily for financial reasons and with a sacrifice of educational standards, the aftermath of the schools' time of troubles in 1968-71 was apt to be bitter indeed, especially at the university level. Very often the expansion of these schools had been done in the name of "democracy," which was supposed to have been the keynote of the SCAP educational reforms, but it actually led to a weakening of democratic practices.

Second, the universities' crises in 1968-71 proved to be significant for Japanese education in general, for the campus struggles grew so intense that the government became alarmed and began a series of measures to revise the entire educational system. The fact that the government was able to take the initiative here was due to the fact that educators themselves did not take sufficient steps to provide for necessary changes. Christian schools must bear part of the onus here, along with the private schools in general, for they were not able to initiate viable reforms that might have forestalled government action.

Finally, it is still too early to make a measured judgment about the future role of Christians in Japanese education. We have seen that although the Christian schools of contemporary Japan have more pupils and better facilities than ever before, these gains have often been bought at the price of lower standards. Yet Christians have sometimes proved to be pioneers in Japanese education, and they may still find creative ways to help meet the needs not only of their own educational institutions but also of Japanese society as a whole.

NOTES

1. Source of Table 1: *Japan* (Pro Mundi Vita Study no. 34) (Bruxelles: Pro Mundi Vita, 1970), p. 41, with arithmetical errors corrected. For background materials on Christian schools in Japan, see Richard H. Drummond, *A History of Christianity in Japan* (Grand Rapids, Mich.: Wm. B. Eerdmans, 1971); Charles W. Iglehart, *A Century of Protestant Christianity in Japan* (Tokyo: Tuttle, 1959); Joseph L. Van Hecken, *The Catholic Church in Japan since 1859* (Tokyo: Enderle, 1963).

2. The text of "The Imperial Rescript on Education" (1890) is in Ryusaku Tsunoda, et al., eds., *Sources of Japanese Tradition*, 5th ed. (New York: Columbia University Press, 1964), 2:139-40.

3. Ira B. Burnell, "Order Number 12," *JCQ* 35, no. 4 (Fall 1969): 239-46.

4. Drummond, *History of Christianity in Japan,* pp. 254, 323; Jan Swyngedouw, "The Catholic Church and Shrine Shintō," *JMB* 21, no. 10 (October 1967): 579-84 (pt. 1); 21, no. 11 (December 1967): 659-63 (pt. 2).

5. Ministry of Education, *Education in Japan* (Tokyo: Government Printing Office, 1971), p. 14.

6. Interview with Prof. Yoshishige Herman Sacon, Tokyo, July 5, 1972.

7. Herbert Passin, *Society and Education in Japan* (New York: Teachers College Press, 1965), pp. 108–16.

8. These sections are based on the writer's paper, "The Development of University Education in Postwar Japan," given before the Asiatic Society of Japan, Tokyo, May 15, 1975.

9. *Education in Japan,* p. 14.

10. Ibid., p. 22.

11. Ibid., p. 16.

12. Ibid., p. 24.

13. Interview with Dean Teruko Komyo, Tokyo, July 17, 1972.

14. John W. Krummel, "Aoyama Gakuin: One Hundred Years" (mimeographed, 1974).

15. Ira J. Burnstein, "Towards a Christian University in Japan," *JCQ* 34, no. 2 (Spring 1968): 118–22; Donald P. Chandler, "A Christian University in Japan," *JCQ* 39, no. 2 (Spring 1973): 87–100.

16. Charles W. Iglehart, *International Christian University* (Tokyo: ICU, 1964).

17. Table 3 is from *Education in Japan*, p. 22.

18. "Inequitable University Fees" (editorial), *Japan Times*, March 16, 1975.

19. The statistics used for this entire section are from Mombushō [Ministry of Education], "Fuzoku Shiryō" [Attached Materials] (Tokyo: Ministry of Education, mimeographed materials on higher education, April 7, 1975).

20. James Phillips and Hiroshi Shinmi, "The Ecumenical Gap," *JCQ* 25, no. 1 (Winter 1969): 39–44.

21. This paragraph is based on mimeographed, undated memoranda from the Kyōiku Dōmei and the NCCJ.

22. Van Hecken, *The Catholic Church in Japan*, pp. 163–64.

23. Walter M. Abbott, ed., *The Documents of Vatican II* (New York: Guild Press, 1966), p. 646.

24. Peter Nemeshegyi, "Religious Freedom in Catholic Schools and Institutions," *JMB* 23, no. 1 (January–February 1969): 11–17.

25. Interview with Sisters of the Sacred Heart, Tokyo, Dec. 21, 1974.

26. Joseph J. Spae, *Christianity Encounters Japan* (Tokyo: Oriens, 1968), pp. 121–39.

27. *JCAN*, Oct. 1, 1966, pp. 1–2.

28. Ibid.

29. Spae, *Christianity Encounters Japan*, p. 126.

30. Ibid., p. 131.

31. This section is based on the writer's unpublished manuscript, "Protestant Theological Schools in Modern Japan."

32. Shoki Coe, "North East Asia (Survey of Theological Schools)," *Directory of Theological Schools and Related Institutions* (London: Theological Education Fund, 1974), pp. 208–14.

33. Passin, *Society and Education in Japan*, pp. 107–8.

34. *The Fifty Years of the Communist Party of Japan* (Tokyo: Central Committee of the CPJ, 1973), pp. 156–59.

35. See Stuart J. Dowsey, ed., *Zengakuren: Japan's Revolutionary Students* (Berkeley, Calif.: Ishi Press, 1970).

36. This section is based on the writer's "A Seminary in Transition, 1969–71" (mimeographed).

37. The name "Zenkyōtō" is here, as generally, applied to the "nonsect radical" student activists at various Japanese universities (i.e., those not belonging to a particular political or ideological "sect"), even though the precise designation of local groups varied from place to place. In general, most of the striking students adopted the tactics and the ideology of Zenkyōtō, if not the name.

38. See Dowsey, *Zengakuren*, chaps. 5ff.

39. Directorate for Scientific Affairs, Organization for Economic Co-operation and Development, *Educational Policy and Planning: Japan* (Paris: OECD, 1973).

40. English translation is *Basic Guidelines for the Reform of Education: Report of the Central Council for Education* (Tokyo: Ministry of Education, Japan, 1972).

41. "Private Universities Vexed by Tuition Hike Issue," *Asahi Evening News,* Jan. 23, 1975. Cf. Jerrold B. Burnell, "Public Funds for Private Education in Japan," *Intellect* 102, no. 2357 (April 1974): 436–39.

42. "New Rules to Open Campuses Announced," *Japan Times,* March 25, 1975.

43. "Entrance Exams for All Nat'l Universities to be Held Together," *Asahi Evening News,* March 27, 1975.

44. "On Receiving Foreign Students," *Japan Times,* April 5, 1975.

45. Ministry of Education, "Attached Materials," statistical materials.

46. See theme articles on "Kindergarten Apostolate," *JMB* 27, no. 7 (August 1973).

4

Christians and Social Work in Japan: Dilemmas of Serving Both Caesar and the Humblest of God's Children[1]

Two Scripture passages, both in the Gospel of Matthew, have posed dilemmas for Christians down through the ages. In Matt. 22:15-21 Jesus responded to a trick question as to whether or not it was right to pay taxes to Caesar with the reply, "Give to Caesar what belongs to Caesar and to God what belongs to God" (J. B. Phillips trans.). Jesus' followers were therefore to serve their earthly sovereign, but all the time remembering that their final allegiance was to their heavenly king. Then only three chapters later in the same Gospel (Matt. 25:34-40), we encounter Jesus' parable of the final judgment, where the heavenly king was seated on his throne in glory, dividing all the nations before him. To those on his right hand the king extended a gracious invitation to enter his kingdom, for he said that they had given him food and drink and clothing and shelter. When the startled group asked when they had done such things, the king replied, "I assure you that whatever you did for the humblest of my brothers you did for me" (J. B. Phillips trans.).

Here were seemingly confusing and sometimes contradictory commands: Serve Caesar, serve the humblest of God's children, but above all, serve God. The task of knowing how to relate these commands in the lives of individuals and groups has been grist for Christian ethics down through the ages. There will be no attempt here to provide even a provisional resolution of the tension involved in these commands. Rather, our task will be to examine how this tension, present in the history of Christian ethics, was dealt with by a small group of Christians of many different backgrounds in Japan during the thirty years following World War II. This is an account of how Christians in the field of social work sought to serve the humblest of God's children while at the same time serving Caesar, in order to serve God.

81

The New Circumstances of Social Work in the Occupation Period

One fact that stands out about doing social work in Japan in the immediate postwar period is that it was unavoidable. At the close of the war and during the beginning of the Occupation period, Japan was virtually prostrate, both economically and spiritually. Its cities lay in ruins. Many of its people were hungry. Its once far-flung empire was no more.[2] Of the cities of any size in the three southern islands, only Kyoto and Kanazawa were left intact. In the other major cities, over 250,000 had died in the air raids, while over 2.5 million buildings had been burned and another 150,000 were partly damaged. There were perhaps 2 million in all who had died during the war. And at the time when the nation's material resources were depleted, over 5 million people were repatriated to the main islands of Japan from the country's former colonies and conquered territories. At this time the nation experienced massive breakdowns in such public services as electricity, flood control, fire fighting, public transportation, food distribution, and the like. Since the onset of hostilities with the China incident of 1931, the repair and the replacement of equipment on the domestic front had lagged far behind, and these conditions were to become even worse with the increasing demands of the wartime economy, and then with the massive air raids. Hence when floods, typhoons, and fires swept the war-battered nation in the early postwar years, and millions of homeless or displaced persons thronged the nation's roads, bringing every imaginable problem with them, there was need for social intervention on a massive and unprecedented scale. From the standpoint of modern social work practice, it might be said that at that time about one-tenth of the entire population of Japan were potential "social work clients." Clearly the needs of the nation as a whole for social work services were greater than ever before in its history.

At the same time, the traditional methods in Japanese society for providing social welfare services in times of emergencies were inadequate under such circumstances. There was, on the one hand, the centuries-old pattern of fixing responsibility for meeting a particular case of social need on that person's *next-of-kin*. This principle had been enunciated by Prince Shōtoku (573–621) in his famous Seventeen-Article Constitution in 604, and it had worked fairly well during the relatively settled periods of Japan's history.[3] Social work had also operated under a second principle, namely, *philanthropy*. This meant that innocent victims of misfortunes were aided through the donations of charitable institutions, either Buddhist or Christian.[4] The social work institutions that existed in Japan right after the war and the legislation on the nation's lawbooks were based on these two time-honored principles. But in the face of the massive extent of postwar social needs, neither next-of-kin responsibility nor philanthropy could begin to meet the vast needs on a necessary scale. There was clearly need for immediate and extensive intervention by the Occupation and Japanese governmental authorities. Only governmental agencies could secure, coordinate, and administer the resources needed on a scale large enough to deal with the situation. This meant the establishment of an entirely new basis for social work in Japan, that of *governmental responsibility* for the livelihood of the people.[5]

But even though it came gradually to be accepted that the government should guarantee the people's basic livelihood, there was no intention of overlooking the existence of a considerable number of private social work institutions throughout the land, many of which had pioneered in various phases of social work in Japan. The contributions that Christians in particular had made to the development of social work in this country could not be ignored, and had been recognized by the government itself. Official histories of social work in Japan indicated that some of the first social welfare institutions in the modern sense had been started under the auspices of the Catholic church during the so-called "Christian Century" (1549–1638). As to the period since the Meiji era, the Japanese government in 1926 had made awards to those who had contributed most to the development of social work in the country since that time, and of the thirty-two thus selected, twenty-two were Christians. Then in the fall of 1956 when the government was asked to name the four outstanding leaders in the field of social work in Japanese history, it picked Jūji Ishii, founder of the Okayama Orphanage; Kōsuke Tomeoka, who worked in prison reform; Gumpei Yamamuro, a leader of the Salvation Army in Japan; and Takeo Iwahashi, founder of the Light House for the blind in Osaka. All four were Christians.[6]

It was only natural, then, after World War II when social needs were greater than ever before in history, that the Occupation authorities and the Japanese government turned to Christian social work leaders who already had know-how and experience in dealing with social problems. Christians served on advisory committees for the Ministry of Welfare, which worked on the drafting of new legislation and administrative procedures to deal with various social problems. Christian institutions, as weak and disorganized as many of them were in the postwar period, were often sought out as models for coping with the many problems.

Of the many Christian leaders in the field of social work in postwar Japan, perhaps the name of Dr. Toyohiko Kagawa stands out as an individual, well known abroad because of his travels in the West and from his many writings. He had been concerned with Christian social service since the age of twenty-two, when as a seminary student in Kobe he had begun to live and work among the slum dwellers of that city.[7] Some of the triumphs and trials of postwar Japanese Christian social work can be seen mirrored in Kagawa's activities at this time: he was an adviser to Prince Higashikuni's cabinet and a nominee to the House of Peers, a candidate for the Occupation's purge list, an itinerant evangelist for the Christian cause throughout Japan and abroad, and the founder of more social work enterprises than he was able to administer or find support for. In fact, Kagawa was the best known among a number of charismatic social work leaders who were rapidly to pass from the scene in the postwar period. Through the vision of such energetic pioneers, institutions such as orphanages, old peoples' homes, hospitals and sanatoria, homes for the physically and mentally handicapped, social centers, and the like had been founded throughout the country.[8] The contributions of such leaders and the institutions they founded were now to be put into the service of a much broader concept of social work than had hitherto been the case in Japan.

Indeed, accounts of how the many different Christian social work institutions from the prewar period managed to be started again in the postwar era would fill volumes. Cut off from foreign mission subsidies during the war, such Christian institutions had managed to eke out an existence on the basis of some minimal governmental assistance and various income-producing projects, but primarily through the dedication and the self-sacrifice of their workers. Even though many of these social work agencies suffered extensive damage to their facilities because of the air raids and other wartime damage, some of their personnel were able to get together again in the postwar period and make a gradual comeback with whatever resources they could muster. With relief supplies and the assistance of chaplains and returning missionaries, they began to meet some of the many requests for assistance that came their way.

Relief goods and funds from voluntary agencies abroad helped to augment the relief services that governmental channels were conducting right after the war. A number of Protestant and Catholic relief organizations began to operate during the Occupation, and their work was coordinated through the Licensed Agencies for Relief in Asia (LARA). From March 1946 to March 1952, LARA not only administered the distribution of large quantities of relief goods in Japan, but also pioneered in establishing channels for cooperation between governmental and private relief agencies, for which it was given a special commendation by the Ministry of Welfare when it wound up its five years of service.[9] A number of social service organizations continued through the three postwar decades, such as Japan Church World Service (which became the Division of Christian Service of the National Christian Council of Japan), the Central Committee of Catholic Works of Charity (the functions of which were later taken over by Caritas–Japan), the Mennonite Central Committee on Relief, and other smaller groups. Each of these organizations has written important chapters in the distribution of aid and relief supplies, the organization and supervision of social work agencies, and the raising of support from within Japan and overseas for social service projects in other parts of the world.

In the immediate postwar period, then, the first goal of social work was to meet by any available means the most pressing needs of Japanese society. And these needs were met by the combined efforts of public authorities and private voluntary agencies. The methods for coordinating these public and private efforts were a matter of concern for the Occupation and the Japanese governmental authorities from 1945 onward. The principles which were worked out, primarily during the Occupation years, gave the government a new role in social work, which was to persist through the three postwar decades.

The New Role of Government in Social Work (1945–52)

In February 1946 the Occupation authorities issued a memorandum about public relief, which contained four major principles of social welfare that were to influence social work administration and legislation thereafter. A semiofficial summary of these principles put them this way:

1. The State shall be responsible for the protection of the needy.
2. The State shall not convert this responsibility to private or semi-governmental organizations.
3. The needy shall be protected equally and without discrimination.
4. The amount of relief shall not be limited so far as it is needed for the protection of the poor. [10]

It was on the basis of these principles that the Livelihood Protection Law was enacted in October 1946. The following year saw the passing of the Child Welfare Law, the Disaster Relief Law, a complete revision of the prewar Public Health Law, the Unemployment Insurance Law, the Employment Security Law, and the Labor Standard Law. In order to implement such legislation, and other laws soon to appear on the books, it was necessary to have detailed examinations of clients' incomes and expenditures. This created the need for considerable numbers of social workers with special training and skills to carry out such duties.

Many of the new principles of social welfare were incorporated into the new Japanese constitution, which came into force on May 3, 1947. Some of its important provisions in this area were:

All people shall have the right to maintain the minimum standards of wholesome and cultured living. In all spheres of life, the State shall use its endeavors for the promotion and extension of social welfare and security, and of public health (Art. 25).

All people shall have the right and the obligation to work. Standards for wages, hours, rest and other working conditions shall be fixed by law. Children shall not be exploited (Art. 27).

No public money or other property shall be expended or appropriated for the use, benefit or maintenance of any religious institution or association, or for any charitable, educational or benevolent enterprises not under the control of public authority (Art. 89).

Since the constitution was handed down by public authority at the insistence of the Occupation, many of its provisions were not fully understood at first by the public at large. In time, however, its provisions brought about a number of far-reaching changes in Japanese society, such as in the field of social welfare.

One provision that was immediately clear, however, was the ruling based on article 89 that the subsidies which the state had formerly given to voluntary agencies would no longer be legal. Hence in the fall of 1947 the Community Chest movement was launched in Japan, modeled after the Red Feather campaigns in the United States, through which funds could be raised voluntarily to replace the former government subsidies. By degrees, many aspects of the prewar social welfare system in Japan were modified in the same way. In fact, the only function of the prewar welfare system to be continued in the postwar reforms was the work of the *minsei-iin*, unpaid district welfare commissioners. Their activities were incorporated into the new social welfare system by special legislation in 1946 and 1948.

For some time, the legal status of the voluntary social work agencies was left unclear under the new system. This was at length dealt with by legislation that provided for the establishment of "social welfare juridical persons" *(shakai fukushi hōjin)*, which were to be approved and supervised by public agencies. The Occupation reforms in social work at this point ran somewhat parallel to the reforms in education. The postwar educational system set up by the government had nevertheless kept the door open for private schools, since they could supplement the efforts of the governmental schools and also provide for new experimental methods. In similar fashion, private social work agencies were expected to supplement what the government at various levels was doing and to provide valuable testing ground for new social work methods as well.

Although it is not possible to go into the details of the social work legislation passed during the immediate postwar period, a number of its features are important to note. In the first place, it needs to be stressed that the new social welfare system of postwar Japan—except for the work of the *minsei-iin*—was operated in a completely different way from that of the prewar period. The new system was based largely on the experience of the American government in the New Deal social legislation enacted after 1933 to meet the social problems of America's Great Depression, when people had also come to realize that private welfare efforts together with piecemeal governmental programs were inadequate. Hence Japan's new social welfare system was based not on next-of-kin relations or on private philanthropy, but on the principle of social justice. Adequate standards of livelihood were supposed to be established by citizens' *rights*, not by donors' goodwill. For Christian social work agencies this meant, for instance, that their activities could no longer be understood as dispensing charity or as a means for promoting conversions. Christians would continue to offer their services on the basis of love and compassion, but with the understanding that the recipients were entitled to these services on the basis of their legal rights. The humblest of God's children must be served, but so also must Caesar. The new principles of social work would cause Christians to reexamine the theological bases on which they had been conducting social work, as well as the methods they had been using.

In the second place, it is significant that the response to the new social welfare legislation of the public at large, and of Christian social workers in particular, was overwhelmingly positive. Toyohiko Kagawa, for instance, declared that the new social welfare system was the embodiment of a Christian social conscience in national legislation. There were, of course, inadequacies in the actual operation of the system. As Christian social workers were often the first to recognize, many people "fell in between the cracks" of the various categories set up by the new legislation, and additional measures would be needed to meet their situations. Furthermore, some observers of the new social welfare system, such as the taxpayers who had to shoulder the additional tax burdens that paid for the new social services, might complain that the system was too expensive. From the side of the clients, there would be complaints that the level of benefits was entirely too low and that the system was too bureaucratically administered. But all such complaints were about the *way* the new welfare system worked. As to its basic principle, that the government should maintain minimum standards for livelihood, there was widespread public approval. Christians could understand such a principle as embodying care for the humblest of God's children, and on a scale that only Caesar could undertake.

A third observation relates to the prohibition placed by the constitution's article 89 on direct governmental support of private benevolent enterprises. If this provision had been stringently carried out, it might have meant in time the strangulation of many private social welfare agencies, due to lack of funds. This would have made the government liable for a much larger proportion of welfare services than it was prepared to deliver. Hence in social welfare, as in education, a compromise was worked out whereby public funds could be given indirectly to private agencies. In the field of education this was to be accomplished by the establishment of a semi-independent foundation that would dispense government funds to private schools according to certain legal standards. In the field of social welfare the principle of "purchase of services" came to be accepted, whereby governmental agencies would arrange to purchase certain services from private agencies for specific needs, rather than to pay for the establishment of additional governmental agencies to meet such needs. Such purchase-of-services arrangements were advantageous for national and local governments, for they were able in this way to limit their welfare expenditures wherever private agencies could do the job cheaper. There were also advantages for the private social work agencies, for these arrangements meant that they could count on governmental agencies for a large proportion of their income.

A fourth observation that can be made of the postwar social service system is that its motivation had political as well as humanitarian overtones. While it is proper to emphasize the humanitarian goals of the new social work system, it can also be stressed that one reason SCAP and the Japanese government supported such programs was in order to prevent internal disorder in the country. Nor were the Occupation and the conservative Japanese government leaders alone in this feeling. No matter what kind of government had been in power in postwar Japan, it would of necessity have had to institute a widespread social welfare program, much like the one that was set up, even though it might have operated differently in particular areas. One of the major differences in the social welfare system that Japan actually has had is the place made for privately operated social work institutions. Yet by their very nature and function these private agencies in Japan have for the most part operated as part of a national program for providing social services. Caesar was to be served, but also the humblest of God's children. This must be kept in mind as we examine some of the details of how the new social welfare system worked in practice.

Characteristic Developments in Christian Social Work under the New Social Welfare System: Some Case Studies

By the end of the Occupation in 1952 the major guidelines and implementing legislation for the new social welfare system in Japan had been established. Both the guidelines and the legislation were, of course, to be expanded and refined thereafter, but not substantially changed. For the next decade or so, Christian social work institutions primarily did two things. First of all they had to establish a new legal basis in order to operate under the new social welfare system. This generally meant the establishment of a new juridical person for their work and the modification of their activities to conform to their changed status. The second process was one of expansion. The agencies either enlarged their older facilities or founded new institutions in order to meet the greatly expanded needs for social services over the next decade or so.

The modification and expansion processes taking place in Christian institutions at this time indicated, as has been already mentioned, that Christian social workers for the most part decided to work within the new national social welfare system. This meant that they would have access to available governmental support, funding, and services, but they would also be subject to the accompanying governmental controls, supervision, and obligations. Although there were a number of areas where Christian social workers could continue to work outside of publicly supported programs —and a very few, as will be seen, decided to work entirely without governmental support—Christian social workers for the most part made either conscious or implied decisions in favor of the system. They would continue to point out its inadequacies, gaps, inequalities, and injustices. But in so doing they underscored their fundamental agreement with the goals that the system sought to promote.

It must also be pointed out that the growth of the Japanese economy from the early 1950s onward made possible the social support and the tax base for the expansion of the nation's social welfare system. Without such backing, the ideals of the social legislation from the Occupation period would have remained for the most part hollow promises. For the growth of the nation's economy not only provided through taxation the funds by which social programs could be supported, but also made possible advances in education, technology, public services, governmental programs, and the like, all of which benefited the expansion of social work along the lines mapped out for it in the new legislation.

Furthermore, it should be noted that the way the expansion of the Japanese economy took place not only brought benefits but also created a number of new social problems for the country. Industrialization brought hazards of pollution and dangers to health; urbanization increased the sense of rootlessness, which led to all sorts of social ills; the new pace of society in rapid social change undermined institutions like the family upon which social cohesion ultimately rests. The dilemmas caused by the nation's economic growth were not overlooked by social workers. Indeed, some Christians among them were the most keenly aware of the ambiguities of the situation and sought to raise some of the problems involved, even if they were unable to find completely satisfying solutions.

It is difficult to make many generalizations about the developments that took place in Christian social work in the 1950s and 1960s, for each local institution and type of work tended to develop according to its own special circumstances. In fact, each individual social worker went about his or her work with a unique set of personal assets and characteristics. (There is indeed a problem of defining precisely what "Christian" social work is, but here we shall be concentrating on the roles of Christians engaged in social work projects and institutions, leaving the ambiguities of precise definition to be unraveled at another time.) One way to gain some understanding of what took place during this period is to indicate a few of the general trends in Christian social work during this period and to illustrate them by reference to specific case studies.

The Transition from General Welfare Work to Specialized Programs: The Airinkai in Tokyo

Some Christian social work institutions did not develop according to any preconceived plans, but simply changed from welfare work of a generalized nature to the development of specialized programs, in response to specific needs as they arose.

The development of the Christian social work institution now known as the Airinkai (Neighborly Love Association), conveniently located near bus and train lines in Tokyo's Meguro Ward, did not proceed according to a specific plan. Rather, as its director, Shigeru Satō, pointed out, it was founded in 1946 as a general welfare facility to accommodate squatters who had been living in the Ueno Subway's underground pedestrian passageways.[11] A group of Christians secured the use of barracks in a former army camp for the relocation of the squatters and this location is still being used by the Airinkai. Dormitory facilities for working adults are still provided by the Airinkai, but early in the postwar period it recognized the need to establish a separate home for mothers and children *(boshi-ryō)* at a nearby location. A day nursery was subsequently opened to care for children on the compound as well as in the neighborhood. A diagnostic clinic was also opened to meet the pressing health needs of the residents and others. In order to carry out such work, the Airinkai became established as a "foundation juridical person" *(zaidan-hōjin)*, and in 1952 this was changed to a "social welfare juridical person" *(shakai fukushi hōjin)*. (Since virtually all social work institutions went through a somewhat similar process to establish a legal basis for their activities, such details will not be repeated in other case studies below.)

By 1953 the needs of the elderly occupants at the welfare home were such that a separate home for the aged was established on the grounds and, in the following year, the needs of retarded and handicapped children were met by building a separate facility for them. In time, some of the handicapped adults were able to hold daytime jobs away from Airinkai, and it seemed best to provide separate living quarters for them, in addition to the apartments for family living also being established. Director Satō emphasized that the development of new programs did not follow a master plan, but simply took place to meet specific needs as they became recognized. Providing for each new facility meant making extensive fund-raising efforts, submitting special requests to the authorities, and coordinating personnel and funds to meet the new goals. The programs at Airinkai may be considered by some to be lacking in imagination, but they are directed toward meeting pressing human needs in helpful and effective ways.

The Development of New Concepts of Social Work as Community Service: The Yokosuka Christian Community Center

There have been times when Christian social workers, on the basis of their innate abilities and their experiences with specific institutions, have been able to develop new concepts of social work as a part of the service of Christians to their communities.

The beginnings of the Yokosuka Christian Community Center (Yokosuka Kirisutokyō Shakaikan) in Taura, near the American naval base in Yokosuka, were inauspicious. As Shirō Abe, the director of the center, put it in a pamphlet, "The Shakaikan started with what is nearly a fatal handicap for community work, in that it was not established in response to the needs of the community, nor requested by community people, but was rather the response to an unexpected gift."[12] The gift was a building that had been a

Japanese Navy dance hall and then an enlisted men's club for the American Navy, which was turned over to a Christian group to be used as a community center. The Reverend and Mrs. Everett Thompson, Methodist missionaries from the United States, began the work of the center in 1948 and were able to secure the services of Shirō Abe as director from 1957. Initially providing facilities for a number of neighborhood groups to meet, the center became noted for its introduction of new social work techniques from America, especially in such fields as case work, group work, and community organization. The center was able to begin a home for mothers and children, a day nursery for preschool children and babies of working mothers, a daytime program for crippled children in the community, a clinic for outpatients, an agency for family case work counseling, and a club for the elderly (said to be one of the first such in the country).

From extensive experience with such programs and with his particular abilities and concerns, Abe was able to develop a program of integrated community services as well as to elaborate the philosophy behind such a program. Furthermore, he was able to put his ideas to work in much larger contexts. He has served as Chairman of the Japan Christian Social Work League, an association formed in 1949 to enable Christian social workers in Japan to consult on common problems and maintain liaison with overseas Christian groups. Even though it was but one of several similar denominational Christian groups concerned with social work, this league was able to raise questions about specific Christian responsibility for social work within the United Church of Christ in Japan (the Kyōdan).[13] Also, during his term as a lay member of the World Council of Churches' Central Committee, Abe was able to express some of the same concerns with Christian groups in other countries. But through all of his activities on behalf of social work throughout Japan and overseas, Abe has remained close to the work of the community center in Yokosuka. He has insisted that theories of social work must always be made to fit realities in terms of the service of Christians to their communities.

The Change from Charismatic Leadership to Institutional Management: The Konodai Home for Mothers and Children

Behind the start of most Christian social work agencies there has generally been a charismatic leader, however humble, whose vision and determination started the work. But in order to continue such programs with good management practices, the pressures to entrust the work to institutional supervision have been almost irresistible.

Some Christian social work agencies in Japan have been founded by charismatic figures of international reputation, such as Toyohiko Kagawa or Gumpei Yamamuro. But in the case of the Konodai Home for Mothers and Children in Ichikawa City about twelve kilometers east of Tokyo, the chari-matic founder was a relatively obscure American Lutheran missionary, Miss Annie Powlas.[14] Yet from her prewar experiences in the Colony of Mercy (Jiai-En), which the Lutherans operated in Kumamoto, and in Lutheran social work in Tokyo, Miss Powlas was recognized as one who knew how to run homes for mothers and children. While she was living in Ichikawa City during the Occupation period in order to help the Lutherans' Tokyo Bethany Home for Mothers and Children back on its feet, she was approached by officials of the Ichikawa City welfare office with the request that she start a similar home in their city. An abandoned army camp was made available for the work—as also at Airinkai, a number of postwar social work facilities were started in former army camps—and in the face of many obstacles, the work was started. But fortunately for Miss Powlas and her project she was soon able to entrust the direction of the home to Etsuo Tomoda, whom she had known from his work at the Kumamoto Colony of Mercy. Through the efforts of Tomoda and a dedicated board of directors, the Konodai Home was firmly established, with impressive new facilities, and this has made it possible for the home to serve its surrounding community in a number of ways. For instance, Tomoda has been able to work with Korean residents who are living in the area and who are divided into two quarreling factions, one of which supports North Korea, and the other South Korea. The friendly and efficient services that Tomoda and his colleagues at the home have provided to both sides have been respected and appreciated.

The work of the Konodai Home is almost a textbook case study in the process of "routinization of charismata" in the best sense, to which Max Weber called attention in his various writings.[15] The same would be true of many other Christian social work institutions throughout Japan. The postwar social welfare legislation provided the framework for the process of institutionalization that enabled many Christian social work agencies to grow and develop in service to their communities in many ways. But such institutions would not have been started in the first place had it not been for the charismatic leadership of devoted Christian men and women.

Trying to Serve the Community as Well as an Institution:
The Tokyo Home for the Aged

Some Christian social workers came to recognize that, while it was proper to build and manage institutional programs, there were also broader needs of people in society out beyond the institutions, whose needs could be met in part by imaginative extensions of services provided by institutions.

Work with the elderly in postwar Japan has brought to the fore the dilemma of institutionalism. The family system traditionally was so strong in Japan that there were very few institutions for the elderly in this country before 1945. And in recent years some 99 percent of the aged are living outside of institutions. Such statistics were of great concern to Noboru Hidaka, superintendent of the Tokyo Home for the Aged in Hoya, a western suburb of Tokyo.[16] One of the oldest homes for the aged in Japan, the Hoya Home was founded after the great Kantō earthquake of 1923, when numbers of homeless people were cared for by a Lutheran pastor on the grounds of the Spanish embassy in Tokyo. After several moves, the home was finally located in Hoya in 1936, where it held out during the difficult days of World War II through the determination of Miss Chima Matsunaga, its superintendent for forty years. There were difficult times in the immediate postwar years also, when the funds provided by the government through the Daily Life Security Law were far from adequate, and the home had to struggle to raise the necessary additional funds until special legislation (1968) for the elderly made the financial picture more tolerable.

But despite provisions for those in nursing homes, the vast majority of older people live at home, either by preference or by necessity. A 1970 White Paper of the Ministry of Welfare revealed that serious problems were being faced by the elderly living at home, but the institutions for the aged were doing little about them. With the help of the Hoya Home's board of directors, Hidaka analyzed the needs of the elderly living at home and concluded that they concerned nutrition, companionship, help in emergencies, and health care. He then proceeded to organize a "Meals on Wheels" program for elderly people in August 1972, the first in Japan, whereby special meals for older people are prepared at the homes for the aged or in other institutions, then distributed to the elderly at their own residences by volunteers who drop by for visits and help to arrange for any special needs that may arise. The "Meals on Wheels" program, copied from similar programs overseas, has now been widely adopted throughout Japan. Hidaka has also joined in efforts to promote other services for the aged, such as installing telephones at low cost in their homes, providing for periodic medical checkups, establishing clubs for the elderly and special facilities for hot baths and recreational gatherings, and the like.[17]

Social workers like Noboru Hidaka can take encouragement from the fact that care for the aged is no longer as tied to institutionalism as it was a few years ago. But much remains to be done in regard to the needs of the elderly. Hidaka cautions that it may be easier to recruit volunteer help for the aged, since almost all of us can imagine our own needs when we grow old. But help for people who are mentally or physically handicapped—individuals whom many members of the public would rather forget about altogether—may remain the acid test for commitment in social concern. And it is perhaps in such areas that Christians can lead the way.

The Willingness to Change Programs to Meet Changing Needs:
The Sisters of the Visitation in Kamakura

In a rapidly changing society like that of Japan, the need for some social services has diminished, but new needs are constantly arising. There have been Christian social workers who have had the willingness and

the ability to modify older programs or institutions, or to found new
ones, in order to meet the newer needs.

Since virtually all of the Roman Catholic hospitals and sanatoria and a
large number of the social work institutions have been founded and operated
by congregations of sisters, it is essential to take a closer look at how these
congregations have carried out their work. One such group is the Sisters of
the Visitation, a congregation of Japanese sisters, which began its work in
Japan in 1915. After starting a number of educational and social work projects, they followed the example of Father Joseph Flaujac, M.E.P., who had
established a number of tuberculosis sanatoria in Japan and in 1930 founded
the Sanatorium of Saint Therese of Lisieux in Kamakura.[18] The need for such
sanatoria continued through the postwar period, but with improved health
conditions and medical treatment by the 1960s, the number of patients in TB
institutions declined. During this time the work of Saint Therese became
more that of a general hospital, with particular emphasis on the needs of
elderly people.[19] Then in 1965, with the help of American naval personnel and
the support of the Kanagawa Prefectural authorities (including the governor,
an active Catholic layman), the Sisters of the Visitation established the Shi-
chirigahama Home for the Aged on a piece of property adjacent to the Saint
Therese Hospital. Support for its program comes primarily from the prefecture, which signs an annual contract with the superior general of the sisters to
specify the responsibilities of both sides.

Nor was that all. In 1970, on another piece of property near the hospital,
the sisters established the Garden of the Smallest Flower (Chiisaki Hana no
Sono), a home for severely physically and mentally handicapped children.
The founding of such a home was made possible by the widespread public
concern at that time for the needs of doubly handicapped children. Elsewhere
in Japan during this period facilities for tuberculosis patients were being converted for the use of the elderly and for handicapped children, and in Kamakura the Sisters of the Visitation had a flexibility in their work that made
possible such alterations in program and institutional management. At the
order's nearby motherhouse, Superior General Sister Romana Wakako Seki
indicated that the order is still open to further changes in the future, depending on what needs may arise and how the order feels that it can meet them.

Carrying On without Government Help:
The Aikei Gakuen in Tokyo

A few Christian agencies have been able to carry on their programs
without government support, but the problems that they have faced,
particularly in regard to financing, have been so formidable that only a
small number has been able to surmount them.

In the social work case studies mentioned thus far, the major support for
the programs has come from various government funds, in accordance with

the provisions of the postwar social welfare legislation. One question that is inevitably asked is: Would it have been possible to carry on social work under private auspices, without relying on government funds? A partial answer is provided by the work of Aikei Gakuen, a nursery school and kindergarten, which operates in Tokyo's working-class Adachi Ward.[20]

Strictly speaking, the work of Aikei Gakuen is not classed as social work, but falls, rather, into the category of educational work. There is a nursery school, a kindergarten, a children's program for after-school study hours, a youth program, and a well-baby consultation service. In the broadest sense, these educational programs are related to social work, since they have arisen directly from the social needs of the surrounding community. All of these are fee-paying services, and although the fees are very moderate, they are substantial for the mainly working-class families of the neighborhood who send their children to Aikei Gakuen. Founded in 1930 under the leadership of Miss Mildred Payne, an American Methodist missionary, the school for many years relied on subsidies from the American Methodist Board of Missions, Women's Division, but the work has become well enough established that Aikei Gakuen has been able to continue it even after foreign subsidies virtually disappeared. Most of the school's buildings are, however, still of early 1930 vintage. Although well maintained, they surely need replacing. The school thus has operated for the benefit of families with modest incomes, for whom it has represented the best chance for improving the future prospects of their children. Because it has enjoyed the enthusiastic support of its children's parents for almost two generations, as well as the cooperation of the neighborhood as a whole, the school has been able to continue financially in a day when similar enterprises have disappeared.

The charismatic spirit of the founder is still very much kept alive in the work of her successor as director, Miss Toshiko Nishida. The programs of Aikei Gakuen are clearly Christian in content, and the school has helped to start two nearby congregations of the Kyōdan. The dedicated staff members, all of whom are Christian, provide the main strength of the institution. There are fifteen staff members, one of whom is married, and they live together at the school and share two meals every day. There is very little personnel turnover at Aikei Gakuen; it was the only place visited by this writer where it was said that there were no problems in securing enough staff members. They are proud of their rugged independence and stubborn self-reliance, which have enabled the school to carry on through the years and to send its graduates into responsible positions as teachers, pastors, social workers, homemakers, office workers, and the like. The school is so well known in the community that it has no sign or nameplate of any kind on its gate.

A skeptic might point to the fact that the experience of Aikei Gakuen is unique, and in any case unrepeatable. One might also point out that while the school has enough financial support to cover its operating expenses, it lacks any visible source of capital funds for such expenses as replacing the present buildings. Securing funds in such amounts would probably mean giving up some of the rugged independence on which the school has thrived. But such doubts do not worry Toshiko Nishida. "We have a sense of mission," she explains, "and that gives us a determination to go ahead. We follow Miss Payne's example, for wherever she went, she would start work in a Christian perspective, but without forcing Christianity on anybody." Summing it up, she remarks, "Praying together, we have gone on for forty years!"

The Impact of Specialization and Professionalization in Social Work: More Case Studies

The 1960s saw a very rapid growth of the programs and the institutions that had been launched in the earlier postwar era. In the 1960-68 period alone, the number of children cared for in institutions rose 148 percent, the number of elderly in institutions rose 171 percent, and the physically handicapped in institutions grew by an astounding 269 percent.[21] No longer were the people being cared for in these institutions primarily the victims of the Pacific War—except among the elderly—as had been true in the immediate postwar period. Once established, the new social welfare system was increasingly relied on to provide services for those in society who needed them in ordinary times as well as in extraordinary ones.

From the 1960s onward the field of social work had to face the impact of two related phenomena—specialization and professionalization—which also affected many other areas of Japanese life in that period, as education, business, industry, sports, agriculture, mass communications, the professions, bureaucracies, and so on.

Specialization in social work was a natural development, arising from the very nature of the problems themselves. For instance, in 1973 the Ministry of Welfare classified "child welfare institutions" into eighteen different categories, whose functions sometimes overlapped but which were generally quite distinct in their operations. Christian institutions had often pioneered in such work and had discovered from practical experience, for instance, that the needs of blind children are different from those of deaf children, and that both are different from the needs of mentally retarded children. Some agencies had also discovered that a right "mix" of specialized social work institutions can sometimes help each other by being located near each other. The *Kombinat* in industry, which established petrochemical and machine plants alongside each other, found a counterpart in social work in the "welfare community" that placed such institutions as a hospital, a home for the aged, a nursing school, and a rehabilitation institute relatively close together, for the help that they could give one another. Rightly used, specialization could make many contributions to the field of social work.

Professionalization was the other related trend that was everywhere noticeable in the 1960s. While unskilled workers and volunteers could carry out certain tasks in social work, it became generally recognized that many of the specialized areas that had been opened up could be adequately handled only by people who were in some sense professionals with special skills to cope with particular problem areas. As in other fields of work, social workers by the 1960s came to be organized in various professional associations in order to protect their rights and interests, to promote standards for the training and licensing of their members, and in general to further their professional skills. There were times, of course, when some distinctions made between the various professional areas and the limits of responsibility set up led to some friction and not a little misunderstanding. One need not subscribe to the pessimistic adage that "every profession is a conspiracy against society" to recognize that problems could easily arise here.

In general, three factors promoted specialization and professionalization in social work in the 1960s. First of all, there were the pressures from the social workers themselves through the establishment of professional associations. The Japan Association of Social Workers was established in 1960, and it was followed by other groups in the field.[22] A second contributing factor was the formation in the 1960s of various types of citizens' groups to bring pressure for improvements in regard to particular social problems. There were special societies formed to protect maternal health, and others to fight tuberculosis, parasites, and the like. There came to be associations of parents of children who were physically handicapped, or had multiple sclerosis, cerebral palsy, and so forth. These movements became active at about the same time as the civil rights movement was gaining momentum in the United States, but their methods of functioning were quite different. Richard Halloran has pointed out that in Japan "there has been no mass movement even remotely akin to the civil rights movement in the United States."[23] Yet a third pressure for professionalization came from Japanese governmental agencies. Partly as a result of political pressures at the national and local levels, governmental agencies made increasing commitments to social welfare expenditures in the 1960s. They wanted to make sure that funds were spent wisely and effectively, and hence tended to stipulate that such programs must be drawn up and supervised by professionals.

The moves toward professionalization met a mixed reaction among Christians in social work. On the one hand, many Christians had been in the forefront of efforts to increase the standards of social work and the training of social workers. At the same time, the new divisions of responsibilities brought a certain measure of inflexibility and bureaucratization of welfare services that aroused criticism. These were also difficult times for some Christian social work agencies that had pioneered in new areas of social need with minimum budgets and inadequate facilities, only to find themselves frozen out by the higher standards introduced. It was also much harder to pioneer in new areas because of the increased costs for meeting the much higher standards required by governmental agencies and professional groups.

The implications of the new specialization and professionalization for Christian social work can be better understood by examining some additional case studies of particular institutions and social workers.

New Patterns in the Training of Social Workers:
The Role of Christian Schools' Departments of Social Work

One of the areas where Christians made particular contributions to social work was through the training of professional social workers in departments of social work in Christian schools.

Just as Christians had pioneered in social work in Japan in both the early Catholic and the Meiji eras, the first training for social workers had been provided in the Christian schools.[24] Before World War II, Meiji Gakuin, Dōshisha, and Kwansei Gakuin universities all had programs of professional training for social work, sometimes arising out of the work of their theological departments. In the postwar era other Christian universities such as Rikkyō and Sophia established departments of social work, and they were followed by other schools in various parts of the country. The Japan College of Social Work in Tokyo, with the support of the Ministry of Welfare, came to be one of the major training centers for social workers, and a number of its leading faculty members were Christians. Among private schools in the postwar era, the Christian schools were the principal ones to have departments of social work at the university or junior college level.

Through the work of such schools, future social workers became familiar not only with social work in Japan but also with such developments in other countries as case work, group work, integrated community services, community organization, counseling, and the like. Other countries' programs such as the social security system in the United States, England's national health scheme, and other aspects of social planning were studied and evaluated with an eye to their possible usefulness in Japan. The Montessori educational methods from Italy and elsewhere were studied and introduced into Japan. Indeed, many of the professional contributions to social work in postwar Japan have been related in some form to the work of the Christian schools.

Meeting the Changing Needs of Children in Modern Society:
Nozomi no Ie, Home for Children

The care of children was one area where specialization was keenly felt, particularly as children's homes changed from the care of orphans to the care of children with special needs.

Children's homes have been a major Christian contribution to Japanese society. Although there had probably been foundling homes in Japan from the time of Prince Shōtoku, an orphanage recognizable in the modern sense was first begun by Luis Almeida (1525–83), who subsequently became a Jesuit priest.[25] Orphanages were one of the first works of charity undertaken by Catholic missionaries after the reintroduction of Christianity in 1859, and this work has continued to the present. In 1973 there were some 55 Catholic children's homes, served by 22 priests, 23 brothers, and 377 sisters.[26] Japanese Protestants were also active in orphanage work, following the example of Jūji Ishii's Okayama Orphanage, founded in 1887.[27] The Japanese Christian Social Work League, for instance, could report 27 affiliated children's homes accommodating 2200 children.[28] Throughout Japan, there were in October 1972 some 520 children's homes with 30,950 children.[29]

Japanese orphanages in modern times have gone through three stages in their development.[30] Most of the orphanages founded in the Meiji era were for children who had lost their parents in natural disasters or who were mistreated. Then, in the early Shōwa era, especially after the Great Depression of 1929, orphanages were needed to take care of the many children abandoned at that time, some of whom had been ill-treated by their parents. In the post-1945 period there were large numbers of war orphans, followed by numbers of mixed-blood children fathered by American soldiers during the Occupation era. Many of these children encountered difficult problems while growing up, meeting discrimination along the way and sometimes getting into trouble with the law.[31]

The changes affecting Japan's children's homes by the 1960s as a result of specialization can be seen in the work of one such agency, the Nozomi no Ie (House of Hope), in Musashino City, a western suburb of Tokyo. The home's director, Shigenobu Yamazaki, explained how from the 1960s very few of the children assigned to the home by the city's Child Welfare Agency were actually orphans. Most of them were children of divorced parents, or from homes where a family member's illness or other circumstances made temporary care necessary. On the whole, the need for the services of children's homes has been decreasing throughout the country, but there are still needs primarily in the larger cities, where urbanization has weakened the family system. The situation is made difficult by the fact that rising land prices in urban areas have made it very difficult to establish new social work institutions. In Tokyo, only three new homes for children have been started since 1953.[32] Very few children are adopted from such homes, for in many cases a parent holds out hope of taking his or her child back, and legal complications surrounding adoptions by Japanese couples have been very difficult and discouraging.[33] Sometimes there are foster-home arrangements whereby children are taken into the homes of small shopkeepers as virtually unpaid employees.

Yamazaki believed that the religious atmosphere of a Christian children's home is of crucial importance in the development of the children. Out of thirty-nine private children's homes in metropolitan Tokyo, eighteen are Christian, eight are Buddhist, and one each is related to Tenrikyō and Seichō no Ie, two of Japan's New Religions. From 1974 Yamazaki helped to establish an informal group of Christian social workers in children's homes, for those who wanted to find ways to sustain religious worship and training in their Protestant and Catholic homes, in a time when growing pressures for secularization make such arrangements increasingly difficult. This group feels that with the changing needs of children in their homes, maintaining a Christian atmosphere should have high priority.

Finances are no longer the headache in children's homes they once were, Yamazaki indicated, for 79.4 percent of the budget of Nozomi no Ie is now provided from government sources. Yet the home must find 15.5 percent of its budget from private contributions, primarily to cover school fees for senior high school, which are only partly publicly underwritten. The major problem for children's homes, however, as for many other social work institutions, is that of finding the right number and the right kind of staff members. Because the hours that staff members must put in are long, their work difficult, and their salaries modest, the annual turnover of staff averages about 15 percent per year at Nozomi no Ie, and higher in many other homes. Hence Yamazaki felt that one of the most important contributions of Christianity toward meeting the needs of the children in these homes is to provide motivation for staff members to continue to do their work and to do it well. The rewards are those of human satisfaction, not monetary return, and such rewards may best be understood from the standpoint of faith.

Doing the Jobs No One Else Wants to Do:
The Ikuno Kodomo no Ie in Osaka

The care of mentally retarded children has long been recognized as one of the most difficult tasks of social work, in Japan or any other country. Until fairly recently, in Japan as elsewhere, families tended to hide mentally or physically retarded children, fearing that public knowledge about them might handicap the marriage and job prospects of their normal children. When institutions for the care of such children became established, there were the further difficulties of recruiting and keeping staff members who were willing to undertake the tiresome and sometimes traumatic responsibilities of caring for such children. Motivation for staff members becomes more difficult in homes for handicapped children than in orphanages for normal children. One who understands such problems well is Father Raimund W. Zinnecker, O.F.M., from his experiences in the establishment in 1973 of the Ikuno Kodomo no Ie (Ikuno Children's Home), in Osaka's Ikuno Ward.[34]

The course of specialization in social work is well illustrated by Zinnecker's earlier experiences. It all began with the Ikuno Catholic Church, which Zinnecker helped to found in 1960, in one of the poorest wards of the city, where about 30 percent of the residents were of Korean background. After the church programs, Father Zinnecker and his parish members became involved in a number of service projects in the community. From 1960 to 1969 there was the Young People's Home (Seinen no Ie), a dormitory for young working men, which had to be closed because the church was unable to give it adequate supervision and care. The parish set up the Saint Francis Gakuen, a day nursery for children ages three to six in the neighborhood, a Children's Center (Jidōkan) for ages six to eleven, and the Jordan Baby Center for children from infancy to three years. To help with the work, the parish welcomed the services of the Franciscan Sisters of the Annunciation who came to staff the first two projects and Korean sisters from Seoul who came to handle the baby center. These were services very much needed in the community, but which literally nobody else wanted to undertake. The parish's ability to handle such difficult assignments prepared it for more that was to come.

The Ikuno parish's work with children came to the attention of the Osaka city government's welfare department, which from 1970 to 1972 had been running a day-care center for mentally retarded children, ages three to six. The city asked to relocate this work to a site adjacent to the Ikuno church, where the church sold to the city the ground on which a well-built ferroconcrete building of the Ikuno Kodomo no Ie was opened for eighty-five children in 1973. The establishment of such a home was made possible by national legislation in 1947 and 1960, but the public's concern for this specialized need came to a particular focus in the 1960s. By October 1972 there were 122 such day-care centers throughout Japan, caring for 3,972 children.[35] But even if the government built scores of such facilities, they would still not be sufficient in number, since there are estimated to be one hundred or so mentally handicapped children born every day throughout Japan.[36] Proper therapy for such children takes money, time, ingenuity, and patience. Of these, the government can provide only the money. A great deal of ingenuity went into the design of the Ikuno Kodomo no Ie, and much time not only goes into the work with the children but also into counseling with their mothers. Even though the home was founded only in 1973, it has a large waiting list, and many families bring in their children for part-time consultation and therapy at the home. Parents and staff members are constantly sobered by the realization that although these handicapped children may show some improvement as a result of such care, they will never become completely normal. The determination to persevere in such work comes from a motivation that faith in Christ has helped to supply—as is seen in the Ikuno Kodomo no Ie.

Christian Social Workers in Public Institutions

The contributions of Christians to social work in Japan have not been limited to the activities of Christian institutions, for individual social workers with strong religious convictions have made their contributions in almost every sphere of social service.

It would be unfortunate if the emphasis of this report on the work of Christian social work institutions should lead to the erroneous impression that only in such places have Christians contributed to social work in Japan. In fact, there is hardly an area of social work where Christians have not left their mark. Professor Tariho Fukuda of Meiji Gakuin University's Department of Social Work has made some important observations along this line.

He has pointed out that with only a few exceptions Japanese Protestant churches have had very little involvement as organizations in social work or social action in Japan.[37] It has been a different picture with the Catholic church in Japan, which has been directly involved in social work, but as far as Japanese Protestants are concerned, the involvement has generally been through support from overseas mission boards, or from the personal work of Japanese Christian lay men and women. Even the social work of Toyohiko Kagawa was viewed by many Protestants in Japan as tangential to the main tasks of the church. Although individual Protestant pastors like Masahisa Uemura helped to sponsor particular charitable works, such activities did not find their way into his theological formulation of the doctrine of the church. In fact, the leading Protestant systematic theologian at the present time, Yoshitaka Kumano, held that, while social work was an activity to be conducted by Christian voluntary groups, it was not a part of the church's mission program and therefore not of the essence of the church.[38]

Despite the lack of encouragement from church circles, individual Christians have persistently sought to express their faith in various fields of social service. In fact, the "ministry of the laity" among Japanese Protestants has tended to be the story of lay contributions either in the field of evangelistic witness or of social service. Lay women and men have been involved in the Christian Medical Association of Japan (Ika Renmei), the Christian Mission to Lepers, various groups that work with the blind, and work in many other fields. Professor Fukuda has pointed out that Japanese society tends to esteem such people highly as professionals, but not very highly as persons of religious faith. As has so often been the case, the contributions of faith, as real as they are, have been largely hidden from the eyes of the world.

The Transition to New Forms of Social Service:
Seibo Seishien in Osaka

Financial stringencies and changing social service needs have sometimes made it necessary for Christian institutions to adopt new forms of social service, but to do it with continuing Christian commitment.

Changing from one form of social service to another has its difficulties, and the example already given of the Sisters of the Visitation in Kamakura indicated one way the problems were handled. Another example of a Catholic social work institution in transition is the Seibo Seishien in Osaka (literally, the Holy Mother Garden for Limb Treatment).

In 1941 the Daughters of Charity of Saint Vincent de Paul founded the Seibo Byōin (Holy Mother Hospital) as a general and tubercular hospital.[39] By 1965 the major part of the hospital was rebuilt at the expense of the Daughters of Charity in order to modernize its operations. But in 1968 the sisters closed the Seibo Byōin because of the decline in the number of tubercular patients and the burdensome expenses of staffing a general hospital.[40] Thereupon the order consulted with officials of both Osaka city and prefecture as to what sort of social welfare work the buildings should best be converted. Because the Daughters of Charity had experience in operating a hospital for crippled children in Wakayama and there was dire need for such a facility in Osaka, the government officials requested that the buildings be put to such a use. Agreements were worked out whereby the funds for alterations and additions to the buildings would be provided by the governmental agencies involved, the buildings themselves would be deeded to the social work juridical person of a Catholic institution for children located across the street from the hospital, and the land on which the buildings stood would remain the property of the religious juridical person. That such complicated arrangements for a transition to a new form of social service could successfully be worked out by governmental and religious groups indicates the high degree of rapport that these groups had with each other as the result of past experience.

May 1, 1970, saw the opening of the new facility, Seibo Seishien, which is primarily for the treatment of victims of cerebral palsy. Although cerebral palsy is only one of the physical handicaps that can strike children, it has been estimated that in the Osaka area alone there are some three hundred new victims of this disease every year.[41] Across the nation there were in 1972 some seventy-five such hospital-homes for children crippled from cerebral palsy and other diseases, with 8,220 patients.[42] Seibo Seishien has facilities both for children who are admitted with the attendant care of their mothers for a three-month period, and for children who are admitted without their mothers. The expenses for such treatment are underwritten by governmental funds from various levels.

In meeting what governmental authorities recognized as a pressing public need, the Daughters of Charity have nonetheless endeavored to carry out their service in a Christian spirit. As in other Catholic hospitals and institutions in many countries, management positions are increasingly being entrusted to lay persons so that religious personnel may be more directly involved with patient care. The overall management of the institution through its board of directors still resides, however, with the Daughters of Charity, and many members of the hospital staff are ardent Catholics or Protestants. The Seibo Seishien shows that it is possible for a Christian social welfare organization to change its forms of social service in response to the changing needs of society, and yet maintain its Christian commitment.

The Role of Trade Unions in Social Work

Even though unionization has brought difficulties to the administrators of social work institutions, it has also brought needed dignity and security to staff workers.

An account of the impact of specialization and professionalization on Christian social work in Japan in the 1960s would not be complete without reference to the effects of unionization in social work.

From the administrators' point of view, unionization has often seemed to compound the difficulties of running a social work institution.[43] Budgets for private social work agencies have been limited, but the demands of unionized workers for increases in pay and improvements in working conditions have often created severe strains. Social workers are often called upon to work long hours, lift heavy loads, and do volunteer work of various sorts that frequently goes far beyond union regulations. Sometimes sacrifices of this sort are requested of staff members by administrators in the name of Christian charity, and this has led to difficulties.

From the staff members' point of view, union membership has just begun to give proper security and recognition to workers who have long been deprived of them. Sometimes Christian social work institutions have made unjust demands on their staff members in the name of charity. Such has been the struggle between the demands of justice and love from Old Testament times to the present day. There are, of course, no simple solutions. Most Christian social workers would probably agree that their tasks require both love and justice from both clients and staff.

Discovering New Needs for Which Volunteers Are Required:
The Inochi no Denwa, Telephone Counseling Service

Even though some assume that only professionals and specialists can do social work, Christians and others have found that in particular areas— such as telephone counseling—volunteers are still the best ones to do the job.

With professionalization making its impact in almost every field, it has been widely assumed that only people with professional training could do social work, and that only salaried personnel could be relied on to do the job. Thus when the tasks of social work multiplied in the postwar period, the first reaction of some administrators was to hire additional workers. Obviously, budgetary considerations put severe limitations on such an approach. It has only been in certain areas that the contributions of volunteer, unpaid workers have been recognized. One such field already mentioned is care for the aged. Another is telephone counseling.

Inspired by Alan Walker's impressive Lifeline program of telephone counseling in Australia and many other countries, a small group of Christians gathered in 1971 to discuss the possibilities of starting a similar service in Japan.[44] They were told that any hope of establishing a telephone counseling service staffed by volunteers was impossible, since people in Japan wouldn't work without pay, and those with problems wouldn't speak freely over the telephone. But the experience of the Inochi no Denwa program (literally, Life Telephone, a rough equivalent of Lifeline), which they inaugurated in October 1971, has proved such assumptions wrong. Volunteer telephone counselors were recruited and they took very seriously the twenty-five training sessions necessary in order to prepare them for their tasks. Although the

Lifeline program on which it was modeled was a specifically Christian undertaking, Inochi no Denwa in Japan has operated on a secular basis, since its counselors and supporters from the beginning have been drawn from a much wider group than the Christian community alone. Yet the majority of those associated with Inochi no Denwa have been Christian, both Catholics and Protestants, and much of their initial support came from church groups of many denominations.

Once the program was under way, its sponsors discovered that the very anonymity of the telephone made people in Japan willing to confide to a sympathetic but unknown stranger what they would be very hesitant to reveal in face-to-face encounters. The Inochi no Denwa group was instrumental in launching in April 1973 the Tokyo English Life Line (TELL), an English-language counseling service. In December 1973 Inochi no Denwa was granted the status of a social work juridical person on the basis of its 270 volunteers, the first time that such recognition had been granted by the Ministry of Health and Welfare to an agency possessing neither money nor property. Such recognition was made only after very thorough checking by officials of the ministry, and after they had been convinced that because the volunteers had functioned conscientiously for two full years, the service would be sure to continue. Thus, Inochi no Denwa proved that even in a day of advanced professionalization there are still places where volunteers are wanted and needed.

Continuing to Pioneer in an Era of Rising Costs:
The Umeda Kodomo no Ie

Although the rising costs of almost everything have made it hard for Christians to continue to pioneer in new methods or with new institutions, there are cases where this has been done, when Christians have offered services people wanted badly enough.

It has already been mentioned in several connections that Christians in Japan have been noted for their pioneering efforts in social work. The three major periods in Christian church history of Japan—the early Catholic period, the Meiji era, and the post-World War II era—have all seen abundant examples of this. But the economic situation of Japan from the late 1960s onward made it very difficult for Christians to continue in their pioneering role, largely because of the high costs of land, equipment, and labor, as well as the difficulties in recruiting personnel. It seemed hard enough to keep old programs going, without thinking of new projects to undertake. But there are those who feel that Christians can still continue in their pioneering role, even in the establishment of new facilities, when three important conditions are met: (1) there is sufficient need for the new services that people are willing to pay for them; (2) there are sponsors who have an interest in underwriting the high capital expenses of the new venture; (3) there are workers who are sufficiently dedicated to the program to see it materialize. The Umeda Kodomo no

Ie (Children's Home) in Tokyo's industrial Adachi Ward demonstrates that these three conditions can still be met.

"The day of pioneering in Christian social work is not over," reflects Father Peter Heidrich, S.J., who was until his retirement a professor in Sophia University's Department of Social Work. "It's just harder now, and it requires methods different from those which were used right after the war. Also, you must have something that people are willing to pay for."[45] In the case of the Umeda day nursery, the "something" is the Montessori method of childhood education.

Maria Montessori (1870–1952) developed techniques of educational training in her work with retarded and handicapped children in Rome, and then discovered that these techniques worked even better when they were used with normal children. Use of the Montessori method spread around the world, sometimes under secular auspices, and sometimes under sponsorship of the Roman Catholic Church to which Maria Montessori herself belonged and for which she devised some particular methods of religious education. A Japan Montessori Association (JMA) was established in 1968, largely by Catholics, to promote the Montessori methodology, teacher training, and educational principles. After Sophia University established its Department of Social Work in 1965, it began a Montessori teachers' training course, through which Montessori day nurseries have been founded and staffed.

The Umeda Kodomo no Ie began as a day nursery attached to Sophia University in 1965, but it changed its registration in 1972 to a social welfare juridical person named Karashidane ("the mustard seed") for which the Catholic archbishop of Tokyo, Peter Seiichi Shirayanagi, was the chairman. The adoption of the Montessori method at Umeda was a gradual thing and was fully launched only with the completion of a new building in April 1973 that had the requisite room and equipment for the Montessori method. Plans were launched in 1974 for the construction of Akenobo Gakuen, a facility for the education of handicapped children, on a nearby piece of property. It is anticipated that both normal and handicapped children will thus have opportunities to play together and to learn from each other. The cost of erecting such new facilities is of course formidable, but with the backing of the staff trained at Sophia University's Department of Social Work, donations from companies that have employees' apartments in the area, and support from the Tokyo metropolitan government and Adachi Ward authorities, it has been possible to launch such a new program even under difficult financial conditions. Above all, it has taken the determination of a few dedicated persons who want to see the program succeed. Christians who have such a vision keep alive the tradition of pioneering in social work in Japan.

Christian Social Work in the 1970s:
Seeking a Balance between Tensions

From about 1968 many areas of Japanese life underwent a period of conflict and reappraisal. Social work did not experience traumatic crises of the sort that Japan's universities encountered, but there are indications that its day of reappraisal is drawing near and may already be at hand. The hope is entertained that the process of rethinking social work goals and methods will be a more gradual and peaceful one.

Thus far, the process of rethinking social work in Japan has been linked primarily to questions of finances. Funds for social work had been forthcoming in such increasing quantities in the later 1950s and the 1960s that, as the latter decade ended, there were predictions that funds from Japan's constantly growing economy would soon be sufficient to provide the kinds of social services about which planners had dreamed. But then came the series of celebrated "shocks." Social work was affected mostly by such economic disturbances as the oil shock, which in 1973 sent prices for oil and for almost everything else rising at unprecedented rates, and thus contributing to business slowdowns. Suddenly, the anticipated funding for social work projects was greatly diminished. Furthermore, the nation's business needs began to receive closer attention than its social needs. And with the sudden collapse of the non-Communist governments in Cambodia and South Vietnam (April and May 1975), there was some talk about the need to revise Japan's military budget upward. The needs of the humblest of God's children were suddenly in direct competition with the demands of Caesar.

Whatever the outcome of the growing debates over future priorities and funding for social work, the experiences of the 1945–79 period have placed social workers in Japan in the midst of four major areas of tension. It may be helpful to note each of these areas in order to see the framework within which particular decisions about social work have been made in the recent past and will probably continue to be made in the near future.

1. *Public support vs. private initiative:* Virtually all the case studies mentioned above have indicated a very delicate and sometimes fragile balance between public support and private initiative in social work. This was made necessary because of the nature of the postwar social welfare legislation, which made governmental agencies responsible for social welfare, but at the same time left the door open to the work of private agencies. For the conscientious Christian social worker, this tension is never finally solved, for at each step of the way he or she must consider what is the best balance between the public support necessary to carry on a particular service and the private initiative that sees such service not simply as a job to be done but as a calling to be fulfilled. This tension may be unique to Japan in a legal sense, but it is universal in a moral sense. For even in countries that give the state a monopoly of all social services, there are bound to be areas of injustice and inequality that can best be remedied not by bureaucratic administration but by personal initiatives.

2. *Pioneering endeavors vs. routine management:* There has also been a tension, or perhaps a varying change in focus, between Christian social workers' emphasis on their pioneering roles and their management of projects that are already under way. The experience of Christian social work in Japan since 1945 has sometimes been the process of moving from one need

largely met to a newer need mostly unmet. Where particular groups have shown the flexibility to terminate programs no longer needed and to begin new programs that are wanted, the proper balance between tensions has been struck. Related to this has been the desire of some Christian social workers to reach out beyond their social work institutions to provide services to people in ordinary society—such as the elderly or the handicapped—without institutionalizing them. For, while it may be true that it is harder to pioneer now than it has been at certain times in the past, it still can be done if the circumstances are right.

3. *Social service vs. social justice:* From the middle 1960s onward some Christian social workers have been made acutely aware that various more liberal or radical groups have considered their functions as overly subservient to the Establishment. The criticisms have been closest to their targets in connection with some social services for people who could be considered in a sense victims of an unjust social order—such as minority groups, or the poor or economically exploited—instead of making efforts to end the flagrant social injustices that create such victims. In such cases, social workers are left to ponder the needs of the actual persons whom they meet for social services, as well as the needs of social justice that would put an end to systems of human exploitation. Questions of social justice also strike home in regard to the managing and financing of social work institutions themselves. Labor negotiations with staff members must weigh the clients' needs for service and the staff members' need for justice. And where capital funds for social work projects have had to be raised from contributions from bicycle racing or other gambling funds, additional problems of social justice arise. There is also the issue whether or not victims of social hardship have the right to immediate attention as a matter of social justice. Furthermore, the "purchase of service" arrangements, which have enabled the majority of private social work agencies to stay in business, might be reconsidered some day as being in violation of the constitution's article 89. It may be hoped that before a denouement arrives in any of these areas, Christian social workers will have carefully reconsidered the delicate balance between service and justice.

4. *Human dignity vs. human fulfillment:* Although there are other areas of tension beyond these four that might be mentioned, this last is one that is experienced most acutely by those who are trying to recruit social workers to deal with especially difficult cases, such as those involving mentally or physically handicapped people. The demands of such work are so severe that in many cases only one or two years is considered a normal term of work, before the staff member moves on to a less demanding position. Hence the clients' needs for human dignity must somehow be matched with the staff members' needs for human fulfillment. In the midst of such quandaries, Christian social workers have often expressed the conviction that what they need from others, and their Christian friends in particular, is not so much financial support or technical advice as spiritual encouragement to continue at the job. It is at points such as this that the resources of the gospel of Christ can be most

valuable, and indeed indispensable. For Christians are the followers of a Lord who found his greatest fulfillment on a cross. And it was through his dying and rising again that a new dignity has been given to all humankind.

It may well be that Christians involved in social work in postwar Japan have in general been able to find a reasonable balance among the tensions summarized, a balance that has enabled them to do their jobs well. Although all the evidence is not yet in, it may indeed be true that Christian social workers in Japan have come to a reasonably good understanding of who they are, what their limitations are, and what their contributions can be. Their accomplishments represent one of the brightest spots in the history of Christianity in postwar Japan. For those who have done their job well, there will be the words of commendation from their heavenly king: "I assure you that whatever you did for the humblest of my brothers you did for me."

NOTES

1. This chapter contains materials given in a lecture by the writer at ICU on Oct. 15, 1974.

2. This section is based primarily on three sources: William C. Kerr, *Japan Begins Again* (New York: Friendship Press, 1949), chap. 1; Edwin O. Reischauer, *Japan: The Story of a Nation* (Tokyo: Tuttle, 1970), chap. 11; and a series of articles, "Nihon Shakai Jigyō no Ayumi" [The Course of Social Work in Japan], in *Gekkan Fukusho* [Social Welfare Monthly], 1972.

3. On Prince Shōtoku's constitution, see Wm. Theodore de Bary, ed., *Sources of Japanese Tradition,* 5th ed. (New York: Columbia University Press, 1969), 1:47-51. On Prince Shōtoku's influence on social work, see Dorothy Dessau, ed., *Glimpses of Social Work in Japan,* 2nd ed. (Tokyo: John Weatherhill, 1968), pp. 4-6.

4. Dessau, *Glimpses,* chaps. 1-3.

5. Cf. Masataka Kosaka, *100 Million Japanese: The Postwar Experience* (Tokyo: Kodansha, 1972), esp. chap. 4.

6. Masao Takenaka, *Reconciliation and Renewal in Japan* (New York: Friendship Press, 1957), p. 28.

7. Of the very extensive literature on Kagawa in English, the most influential has probably been William Axling, *Kagawa* (New York: Harper, 1946). In Japanese, one of the best analyses is Mikio Sumiya, *Kagawa Toyohiko* (Tokyo: Kyōdan Shuppanbu, 1966).

8. For example, on postwar Roman Catholic social work, at the very beginning of the Occupation period, see Paul Taguchi (now archbishop of Osaka), *The Catholic Church in Japan* (Mainichi Shimbun, 1946), pp. 32ff.

9. Ministry of Welfare (of Japan), *LARA—A Friend in Need* (Tokyo: Ministry of Welfare, 1953), esp. pp. 16, 43.

10. Seiji Matsuno, ed., *Social Welfare Services in Japan* (Tokyo: Japanese Joint Organizing Committee for 9th ICSW, 1958), pp. 39-40.

11. Interview with Mr. Shigeru Satō at Airinkai, June 4, 1974.

12. Shirō Abe, *Christianity and Social Welfare* (Yokosuka: privately printed,

1975), p. 1. This section is also based on interviews with Mr. Abe at Taura, March 4, 1973, and on other occasions, and on various printed materials he has provided the writer.

13. Shirō Abe, *Kyōkai to Shakai Jigyō: Kyōdan to Shakai Jigyō Renmei no Kankei wo Megutte* [The Church and Social Work: On the Relation between the Kyōdan and the Social Work League], (Tokyo: Naigai Kyōryoku Kai, 1969).

14. Interviews with Rev. William Billow and Mr. Etsuo Tomoda at the Konodai Boshi Hōmu, Ichikawa, April 22, 1974.

15. Weber's major essays on these themes have been brought together in Max Weber, *On Charisma and Institution Building,* ed. S. N. Eisenstadt (Chicago and London: University of Chicago Press, 1968).

16. Interview with Mr. Noboru Hidaka at the Tokyo Rōjin Hōmu [Tokyo Home for the Aged], Hoya, May 7, 1974.

17. Daisaku Maeda, "Participation in the Promotion and the Delivery of Social Welfare Systems," in *Development and Participation: Operational Implications for Social Welfare* (Tokyo: Japan National Committee of ICSW [1974]), pp. 20–21.

18. Joseph L. Van Hecken, *The Catholic Church in Japan since 1859* (Tokyo: Enderle, 1963), pp. 171, 178. See also *Japan Missionary Bulletin* 27, no. 11 (December 1973), with the theme of "Social Welfare."

19. Interviews with Mr. Kenji Arai, Sr. Beatrice Yuke Yoshida, and Superior General, Sr. Romana Wakako Seki, in Kamakura, August 18, 1974.

20. Interview with Miss Toshiko Nishida at Aikei Gakuen, Tokyo, June 17, 1974, and materials such as *Aikei Dayori* [Aikei Correspondence], which she supplied at that time.

21. Maeda, *Development and Participation,* p. 19.

22. Ibid., pp. 31ff.

23. Richard Halloran, *Japan: Images and Realities* (Tokyo: Tuttle, 1969), p. 258.

24. Interview with Prof. Tariho Fukuda at Meiji Gakuin, May 2, 1974.

25. Joseph Jennes, *A History of the Catholic Church in Japan (1549—1973),* (Tokyo: Oriens, 1973), p. 19.

26. *Japan Catholic Directory, 1975* (Tokyo: Katorikku Chūō Kyōgikai, 1975), p. 691.

27. Richard Drummond, *A History of Christianity in Japan* (Grand Rapids, Mich.: Wm. B. Eerdmans, 1971), p. 222.

28. *Japan Christian Social Work League* (pamphlet, no date, printed in Tokyo).

29. *Social Welfare Services in Japan, 1973* (Tokyo: Ministry of Health and Welfare, 1973), p. 9.

30. Interview with Mr. Shigenobu Yamazaki, Nozomi no Ie, Tokyo, May 11, 1973, and on other occasions. Mr. Yamazaki's untimely death occurred in June 1978.

31. The difficulties of twenty young men of mixed blood from the Elizabeth Saunders Home in Ōiso, Kanagawa-ken, were described in the *Asahi Evening News,* April 28, 1973. The home was also the subject of a television documentary in June 1978.

32. Yamazaki, Interview.

33. Articles on adoption laws in *Japan Times,* Jan. 3, 4, 5, 1974.

34. Interview with Fr. Raimund W. Zinnecker, O.F.M., at Ikuno Kodomo no Ie, Osaka, July 19, 1974.

35. *Social Welfare Services in Japan, 1973,* p. 9.

36. This and subsequent material from Zinnecker, Interview.

37. Fukuda, Interview.

38. Yoshitaka Kumano, *Kirisutokyō Rinri Nyūmon* [Introduction to Christian Ethics], (Tokyo: Shinkyō Shuppansha, 1960). Cf. Shirō Abe, "Service to the Needy: Church and Social Work," in *Toward the New Form of Service in Japan* (Tokyo: Japan Church World Service, 1961), pp. 29–30.

39. Interview with Mr. Minoru Maeda, business manager at Seibo Seishien, Osaka, July 20, 1974. On Catholic hospitals in Japan, see Van Hecken, *Catholic Church,* pp. 169–73. The author is also deeply indebted to Sr. Baptista of the Daughters of Charity for her corrections to the original version of this article, in her letter to the *Vox Fratrum* column of *JMB* 29, no. 11 (December 1975):684.

40. Financial problems have brought changes to many Christian social work institutions. The Ōmi Brotherhood, founded in 1920 by William Merrill Vories Hitotsuyanagi, operated a school, a hospital, and other enterprises with proceeds from the sale of the salve Mentholatum. The bankruptcy of the Ōmi Brotherhood was announced in December 1974, leaving the future of its dependent projects in doubt (*Japan Times,* December 26, 1974).

41. *Seibo Seishien* (pamphlet, ca. 1973).

42. *Social Welfare Services in Japan, 1973,* p. 9.

43. Interviews with Messrs. Lawrance Thompson and William Billow, Tokyo, June 25 and October 4, 1974.

44. Talk by Miss Ruth Hetcamp, Tokyo, June 2, 1974.

45. Interview with Fr. Peter J. Heidrich, S.J., at the Umeda Kodomo no Ie, Tokyo, April 30, 1974.

5

Christian Outreach in Japan: Searching for the Right Ways to Do a Necessary Task

The noted Swiss theologian Emil Brunner once remarked, "The church exists by mission, just as a fire exists by burning."[1] In the case of the Christian community in Japan, not only has it come into being as a result of Christian outreach but it continues to exist because of it. In this chapter we shall consider some of the forms whereby the Christian community has reached out beyond its own members to others, to witness to them in order to urge them to become Christian, to serve them in obedience to the imperatives of the faith, or to celebrate with them the entrance of the divine into human history. The term "Christian outreach" is intended to embrace activities known variously as evangelism, mission, growth, or witness. Christian outreach seeks to be true to the gospel (the evangel) and is therefore evangelism in action; it follows a pattern of sending out the good news into the world and is therefore a work of mission; it seeks growth not only in statistical terms but also in terms of depth of understanding and commitment; it continues to bear witness to the mighty acts of God in Jesus Christ. Christian outreach therefore embodies the existence of the church, "just as a fire exists by burning."

From a very practical standpoint, the Japanese Christian community must continually be doing outreach if it is to thrive or even to survive. Churches in Japan are constantly taking in new members, and yet the total number of Christians in recent years has not increased as fast as the population. The attrition rate is high among church members and inquirers in Japan, and many reasons have been advanced to indicate why: the churches are too remote from peoples' needs; congregations lack adequate leadership and support; churches make unrealistic demands on their members and fail to provide them needed pastoral guidance and social interchange; Christians are

112

too foreign in their outlook and hypocritical in their actions, and the like. Whatever the reasons for the numbers of so-called "graduate Christians" who pass in and out of the churches, Japanese Christian groups have found that they must keep up their outreach programs if they are to have modest growth, or even to maintain their same numbers.

There is another sense in which Christian outreach is an inescapable task of the churches in Japan. Japanese society has been changing so rapidly in the postwar era that one "never steps into the same river twice." The challenges that are presented to Christian faith are rapidly changing, and Christians must keep reaching out to their society if they are to have any continuous relevance to its varied circumstances.

In order to gain a general picture of the many differing programs of Christian outreach to be discussed in this chapter, we need to examine the three major types, or paradigms, for Christian outreach that were used during this period. The *Sinai type* involves church-extension programs, after the biblical example of the proclamation of the law of God to the people from Mount Sinai, which need to be repeated by the people on subsequent occasions as the congregation of the faithful grows and expands into other lands. This is a proclamation ministry, and its goal is to proclaim the law of God in ever new surroundings, where it may be heard and acted upon, and the community of the faithful expanded. A second model is the *Zion type* of outreach, which corresponds to the time when the people of Israel were at home in their own land of Zion, and when they responded to God's action, which had preceded them there. From this type come social-action programs, which are not so much the proclamation of God's will as a response in action to what God has already done for his people. A third model is the *Jubilee type,* which differs from the first two primarily because it does not assume that the actions of God and his people are to be in historical continuity with what has gone before. The Jubilee freeing of the slaves and forgiveness of debts represents the motif of liberation, which delivers people from the bondage and oppression into which they have fallen, and enables them to celebrate their new life in strikingly new ways.

The programs of outreach that we shall be surveying generally may not be identified completely with one of the foregoing paradigms as a "pure type," but are generally a mixture of them, primarily of the first two types. Furthermore, the outreach programs do not remain the same, but take on different characteristics in the three historical eras that we are to examine. The differences were due not only to changing circumstances in Japanese society, but also to altered understandings of what the essence of the gospel was when it reached out to new conditions.

The Occupation Era (1945–52): New Doors Opened to Christian Outreach

To place the achievement or at least the attempts of the Occupation era within their historical context, one must understand the anticipation that

greeted the period. This was the third time that Christianity had been introduced to Japan, and gradually a great expectation built up that comparable if
not greater Christian growth might take place in this new era. Christianity's
first introduction was during the century or so after Saint Francis Xavier's
arrival in Japan in 1549, when the Catholic church grew to a greater percentage of the entire population than has been the case since. The second period
was in the decades after 1859 when Protestant and Catholic missionaries
came to Japan to spread the faith among zealous bands of inquirers. The
third period of Christian mission (after 1945) was also set in motion by the
historical circumstances of yet another outside incursion into Japanese society, this time to the accompaniment of an Occupation army after the nation's first defeat in its long history.

There was a period of shock at the beginning of the Occupation, as mentioned in other chapters, when Christian churches, schools, and social work
institutions were so numbed by the fact of their nation's defeat and the times
of incredible hardships that followed, that Christians were not in any position to expend energy on outreach but had to concentrate merely on survival.
Yet there gradually developed among the defeated and disillusioned masses
of postwar Japan an eagerness to inquire further into ultimate questions.
This meant for many a "religions boom," and for the Christian community
in particular, a "Christian boom." People thronged to Christian churches
and institutions in the hopes of finding out something about the "god of the
Americans" that had gained victory in the war, and also about "democracy"
that somehow was supposed to be related to Christianity. Superficial though
many of these inquiries were, they established a highly significant momentum. We need to examine first of all how the traditional forms of Christian
outreach, inherited from the Meiji period, were affected by the new spirit of
outreach.

Local Church Outreach

The earliest type of Christian outreach in Japan, as in many places, was
that of the local church itself. Whether from an imposing building or more
likely from a modest edifice, local churches reached out to their communities
with the Sinai type of outreach. Christian worship services attracted newcomers, who came to join in the singing of the hymns and in hearing the
sermons of Protestant churches, or to watch the solemn celebration of the
Mass in Catholic churches. Weddings marked the happy occasions of life,
and funerals the solemn ones. Meetings for inquirers and classes in Bible
study or catechetical instruction were ready ways by which churches could
introduce their faith to others. Women's societies and young people's groups
made special contacts through friendships, and bazaars provided the
churches not only with income but also with a means of informing the neighborhood of the church's existence and programs. Kindergartens (yōchien)
were often held in church buildings during the week, and contacts were es-

tablished with the parents of the pupils. Some churches had neighborhood fellowships of believers that were modeled on the five-member organizations *(gonin-gumi)* of traditional neighborhoods. Some churches copied labor-union tactics in holding "spring and fall offensives" for evangelism, during which neighborhood visits were made to contact people who might be interested in the church. Evangelistic programs of local churches included children's meetings *(kodomokai)*, evangelistic rallies, street preaching, parades and processions through the neighborhood, musical concerts or film showings, public lectures, and so forth.[2]

Very little about these forms of church outreach was new, for in fact Christian churches in Japan, as soon as they had the freedom to do so from the Meiji era on, had carried on most of these forms of outreach, although the technology provided by the new public-address systems, movie projectors, tape recorders, and the like was somewhat updated after 1945. In most cases these church-centered programs of outreach were also pastor-centered, for the local minister or priest generally took the initiative in carrying them out and kept the control in his own hands, although with the support of lay members. Since Sinai-type outreach relies heavily on proclamation, it seemed fitting that the pastor as the one who was generally responsible for the proclamation of the gospel in the church would also perform this task in the community. This had its advantages, for Japanese social groups that are traditionally structured in hierarchical fashion would readily understand the pastor's preeminent role in a local church.[3] But the price that was paid in limiting the initiatives and the sense of responsibility by lay participants was severe in many cases. This is why alongside local church clergy-inspired programs there have been numbers of lay-sponsored Christian activities.

Lay Groups

With very few exceptions, most Japanese Christian groups have been dominated by clergy, or those who serve in the roles of clergy, whether they are mainline Protestant, Roman Catholic, conservative Protestant, Orthodox, or Non-Church Christian groups. New religious groups among Christians have often stressed the role of the laity in Christian outreach—as the Spirit of Jesus Church demonstrated in the early postwar period—but within a relatively short time such groups also became dominated by the clergy.[4] Such developments are deeply ironical, for from the time that Kanzō Uchimura and his followers in Non-Church Christianity (Mukyōkai) called attention to the dangers of clerical control in Japan, it has been the lot of his and other reform movements to fall into similar patterns of operation.

The result has been that, in Japan, lay persons in Christian churches have become restive and have established groups that would enable them to participate in Christian witness and outreach, away from the "deadening hand" of clerical control. Some of the New Religions of postwar Japan have gone much further in emphasizing lay initiatives, even though they too would often develop their own forms of bureaucratic structures that are for lay persons but nevertheless hierarchical in nature. Sōkagakkai, the largest of the New Religions, developed as a lay movement related to the Nichiren Shōshū sect. The second largest new group, Risshō Kōseikai, is also an outgrowth of Nichiren Buddhism, and operates as a lay Buddhist group in which clergy are relegated to relatively ceremonial roles. Such lay emphases among Japanese religious groups resemble similar trends among laity in America and elsewhere, and are based on a long tradition of vertically structured organizations in Japanese society.[5]

Among Christians, there have been numerous roles in which laity could serve. In addition to their participation in the institutional churches and their programs, lay persons could serve as staff members or administrators of church-related institutions such as schools, hospitals, social work agencies, and the like, as described in other chapters of this study. The laity in Japan experienced many of the same phases of service as have the "younger churches" around the world.[6] Christian teachers and social workers were able to command particular respect for their contributions, for their title *Sensei* (Teacher) was the same as the title accorded their pastors.

It was in groups committed to the Zion model of outreach in community service, however, that Christian lay persons gained particular recognition in the postwar era. Outstanding is the work of the Japan Women's Christian Temperance Union (Kyōfūkai; literally, Society for the Reform of Manners), the director of which for fifty years was Mrs. Ochimi Kubushiro (1893–1972). A leader in women's liberation long before that term was popular, Mrs. Kubushiro led many of the antiprostitution movements that finally led to national legislation in 1956 ending the system of licensed prostitution in Japan.[7] It may be symbolic that this activist woman, daughter and wife of ministers, was finally ordained a minister herself in 1966 at the age of eighty-three. The WCTU itself celebrated its ninetieth anniversary in 1976 in typically modest fashion, for its leaders stressed in their celebration speeches that their organization's work had hardly begun.[8]

Another lay movement that gained considerable momentum in the postwar period was the Laymen's Prayer Breakfasts, which began at the Osaka Christian Center in the 1950s and from there spread throughout Japan. Leading Christian businessmen in the Kansai and Kantō areas in particular kept in touch with each other through these prayer breakfasts, and contacts were made which led to other forms of Christian service. Many of these same men, for instance, were also active in the Gideons, a lay group for the widespread distribution of Christian Scriptures in hotels, hospitals, and other public places.

A more specialized group is the Christian Medical Association (Kirisuto-kyō Ika Renmei), which began in 1939 as a wartime service project, and in the postwar period greatly expanded its activities in Japan and overseas. The overseas work of Ika Renmei became better known and will be dealt with later on, but the medical-service projects within Japan were an important example of Christian lay outreach.[9]

Denominational Evangelistic Programs

Several Christian churches organized denominational evangelistic programs. Mass-meeting evangelism became part of the Japanese Protestant scene not long after its introduction from America in the late nineteenth century. The postwar period saw several variations on the original Sinai-type patterns.

In the immediate postwar era, a number of Kyōdan-related evangelistic programs were held. Dr. Toyohiko Kagawa was glad to be able to step down from his government-related posts in order to conduct evangelistic meetings throughout the country. Dr. William Axling, a longtime colleague of Kagawa, also held evangelistic meetings for large audiences in the style that he and Kagawa had used in prewar years.[10] Musical evangelism was the specialty of the Reverend Lawrence Lacour, who later collaborated with the Reverend Tomio Mutō of the Kyōdan to initiate a series of "L-type evangelism programs" ("L" stood for Lacour), which brought American pastors to Japan for several weeks or months of preaching and working with Japanese pastors.[11]

Other Protestant groups held evangelistic campaigns as well. The Southern Baptist Convention in the United States not only sent preaching missions to Japan in 1950 and 1951, but followed them with programs designed to establish new churches in every prefecture throughout the country.[12] In order to implement the plan of sending teams of a Japanese pastor and a missionary pastor working together in evangelism, the Southern Baptist Board adopted a goal of one hundred missionaries for Japan and reached that goal in 1953. These were also the years when the Evangelical Alliance Mission (TEAM) became very active with its postwar evangelistic programs, and the same was true of the Japan Evangelistic Band (JEB), which had been in Japan since 1890.[13] Pentecostal missionaries, who preferred to be called Full Gospel Missionaries, also resumed their postwar work, and one of their groups, the Far East Apostolic Mission, was very active in Nara Prefecture in tent evangelism.[14] The Spirit of Jesus Church, pentecostal in character but guarding its independence from foreign groups, began in the postwar era its evangelistic programs that led to its claim at one time to be the fastest-growing Christian group in the country.[15]

Roman Catholic groups conducted preaching missions in close connection with local churches, but generally hesitated to conduct the crusade-type mass meetings for which Protestants were noted. The role of both priests and lay persons as catechists was central in Catholic evangelistic campaigns, and schools for catechists were founded by Father Georg Gemeinder at Nanzan University in Nagoya and by Father Heinrich Honnacker in Niigata, while other schools were established in Osaka and Tokyo.[16] The preparation of catechetical materials, which have been one of the highest priorities for Catholic missionaries since the time of Saint Francis Xavier, blossomed in the postwar period, with the work of such educators as Father Hubert Cieslik,

S.J., who attempted to bridge the gap between the catechetical texts themselves and the needs for inquirers in faith.[17] Such programs for Catholic outreach—and for Protestant outreach as well—therefore had to be correlated closely with the plans of the Christian publishing houses, to which we turn next.

Christian Publishing Houses

Publications have always been an important part of Christian outreach in a country with over 99 percent literacy. There were denominational publishing companies, privately organized Christian publishing houses, and secular publishers producing materials on Christian themes. Despite the large numbers of publishers in the field, Japan's avid reading public provided a good market for them all.

The Kyōdan maintained its own publication department, which in addition to publishing hymnals also issued many books in theology, Christian education, and the like. The Lutheran churches cooperated to found Seibunsha, one of the largest Protestant publishers, with titles related not only to the Lutheran tradition but to Protestantism generally. The Japan Conservative Baptist Mission was the principal sponsor of Seisho Tosho Kankōkai (Bible Library Publishers), who undertook the ambitious project of listing all Christian publications in print in *Japan Christian Literature Review*.[18] There were similar small publishing houses for groups like the Nazarenes, the Church of Christ in Japan, Baptist denominations, the Japan Wesleyans, and others. The nature of the Japan publishing world made it possible for ad hoc church publishers to appear and then almost as quickly to disappear.

The bulk of Christian publishing houses, however, have been private companies producing materials for either Catholic or Protestant constituencies. Among the Protestants, the Kyōbunkwan has one of the longest histories, with its main offices in the Ginza area of Tokyo, in the same building where the Kyōdan offices were located for many years. Next door to the Kyōbunkwan building was the Bible House, where the Japan Bible Society produced its best-selling colloquial translation of the Bible, and other biblically related materials. The Protestant Publishing Company (Shinkyō Shuppansha) has been the major publisher of scholarly theological works and journals. The Kirisutokyō Shimbunsha was best known for the *Kirisutokyō Shimbun* [Christian Newspaper], founded by Toyohiko Kagawa, and it also published annually the *Kirisutokyō Nenkan* [Christian Yearbook] and many general religious books.[19] Faced with difficulties in distributing books in Japan's very competitive publication world, the major Protestant publishers established Nikihan [Japan Christian Publishers' Association] in the 1960s, with a common warehouse and the facilities to distribute their works efficiently to bookstores.

Catholic readers were also serviced by private publishing companies, many of which had roots in the prewar period. The Salesians were able to renew their publishing work in 1946, as their buildings had escaped the wartime bombings. The Pious Society of Saint Paul (the Paulists) also opened up again in 1946, and soon gained a reputation for their fine publications. The Franciscans of Sapporo were able to continue their publication work even during the war. Mr. Rupert Enderle, the agent of Herder in Tokyo, was able to import foreign works and to publish extensively in Japan as well. The Enderle Bookstore was located in the Yotsuya area of Tokyo, near the Chūō Shuppansha (Catholic Press Center), which coordinated many of the activities of Catholic publishers. There were also dozens of smaller Catholic publishing groups throughout the country, and individual dioceses published their own periodicals.[20]

The extensive publication work of conservative evangelical Protestants actually began in the 1950s, but their contributions may best be mentioned at this point. Starting mainly with translations of foreign religious writings, the Christian Literature Crusade (CLC) soon branched out into many fields, as did the Word of Life Press, the Baptists' Jordan Press, the Osaka Christian Bookstore, and others. A unique aspect of their approach was the development of evangelical bookstores, which served not only for the sale of their books but also as contact points for inquirers into Christianity. The establishment of such a network of bookstores, and the organization of an Evangelical Booksellers Association which produced materials for them, were steps that ran counter to the practices of secular booksellers, but by the early 1970s these moves had placed the conservative evangelical groups far ahead in their field.[21]

There is space here only to record that secular publishers also came to play an important role in the publication and distribution of Christian materials, for these publishers already had access to distribution channels that made the works of Christian authors more readily accessible to a wider public. Of course, not every writer could persuade a well-established commercial publisher like Iwanami Shōten, Toppan Press, or Hokuseido to handle his or her book, but those who could do so had access to a much wider reading public.

Student Outreach

In the postwar era, Christian student groups were reestablished or started anew, and their influence was to be felt throughout the three postwar decades. As in the other forms of Christian outreach, the ecumenical Protestant groups and the Catholic societies were the first ones to be active, and they were soon joined by conservative Protestant groups.

Among ecumenical Protestants were two main types of student outreach. There were local campus groups, which cooperated through the student department of the YMCA (Gaku-Y). Not only Christian schools had such local groups, but also national and private universities saw them organized. Their links with each other were always somewhat tenuous, but the program emphases of the World's Student Christian Federation (WSCF), active since its founding in 1895, were introduced to Japan after the Edinburgh Conference of 1910 through the visits to Japan of Dr. John R. Mott.[22] In the postwar period the study programs on the Life and Mission of the Church (LMC) in the 1950s involved Japanese students and faculty members in the thinking of the world Christian community. There were also the student centers, which represented a second type of student outreach. These were established near university campuses, some of them dating from the prewar period. The Waseda Hōshien near Waseda University, the Student Christian Fellowship in Shinanomachi, and the Lutheran Student Center near Iidabashi served Tokyo students, while the Sendai Student Center was situated near Tōhoku Gakuin, and the Seikōkai (Anglican) Student Center was adjacent to the Hokkaidō National University campus in Sapporo. Christian schools often had their own centers in connection with their chapel programs and the work of resident chaplains, as at the Southern Baptists' Seinan Gakuin in Fukuoka, Amherst House at Dōshisha in Kyoto, and Meiji Gakuin, Rikkyō University, and ICU in the Tokyo area.

Roman Catholic student outreach was organized along similar lines. There were local campus groups at Tokyo, Okayama, Kyoto, Morioka, Sapporo, and elsewhere, which through the efforts of Father Hermann Heuvers, S.J., were formed into a National Federation of Catholic University Students in the postwar era. The federation had its central bureau at Kyoto, and then it was transferred to Sophia University in Tokyo, where it could more easily keep in touch with the Students Department of the National Catholic Committee. There were also Catholic student centers, of which the most celebrated was the Veritas-Vita House in Tokyo, founded by the eminent scholar and writer Father Sōichi Iwashita (1889–1940), and reorganized in 1952 by Father Kazuo Sawada.[23]

Conservative evangelical Protestant student outreach may be said to have begun with the organization of the Kirisutosha Gakusei Kai (KGK) in 1947. The group was launched mainly through the efforts of Miss Irene Webster-Smith, affectionately known as "Sensei," who served as a staff person of the InterVarsity Christian Fellowship (IVCF) at the Ochanomizu Student Center in Tokyo. From tenuous beginnings, KGK groups spread through summer camp programs and by the 1960s were to be found on over forty campuses.[24] At first these groups existed seemingly within the shadows of the somewhat larger ecumenical student associations, but by the 1970s they were sometimes the largest Protestant groups to be found on campuses.

The significance of these various forms of student outreach can hardly be measured in terms of numbers of participants or programs carried out. For it was from these student groups in the postwar period that many of the future leaders came for both Protestant and Catholic communions. And the issues with which the students and their faculty and staff advisers wrestled were in time to become some of the major issues facing the churches themselves (see chap. 8, "Biblical Studies," and chap. 9, "Theology in Japan").

The Era of Economic Growth (1952–68):
New Forms of Christian Outreach in a Growing Economy

The five forms of Christian outreach described already were the main foundations on which other types of outreach were to be built. In most cases, the new forms we shall discuss had precedents of sorts in the prewar era and represented variations on traditional patterns of work. The new climate of freedom in postwar Japan made it possible, however, to attempt newer and bolder offshoots of the older methods. The six forms of outreach we shall discuss below give only a partial glimpse of some of the ways Christian groups attempted to reach out to the new type of society developing around them as a result of the remarkable growth of the nation's economy.

Occupational Evangelism

When a group of Kyōdan leaders gathered at the YMCA Tōzansō Center in 1950 with Dr. John C. Bennett of Union Theological Seminary in New York City, they were concerned with the Christian witness to industrial society, which Bennett and his colleague Reinhold Niebuhr were then attempting to develop in America.[25] Out of this beginning came the groups concerned with Occupational Evangelism (Shokuiki Dendō), which was the Japanese expression for what was known as "industrial evangelism" in Western countries. The center for such concerns was the Kansai district (Osaka–Kyoto), where the Kansai Labor Ministry (Kansai Rōdō Dendō) has remained active.[26] The major thrust of this group was to become involved directly with workers and their labor unions. Church leaders often recalled the response of Minoru Takano, secretary-general of the Sōhyō Labour Federation at the 1951 Tōzansō meeting, when he was asked by a minister, "What do the Labour Unions expect of Christianity?" Takano's reply was blunt and to the point, "We just want you to keep out of our way!"[27] In time, however, the triumphalist attitude of the trade unions was to diminish as the Japanese unions were unable to sustain the momentum of increasing membership that characterized the immediate postwar era. The harmful effects of industrialization were increasingly evident, and were dramatized in the coal miners' strikes in Kyūshū in the 1960s to protest the Mitsui Colliery's closing a mine and throwing the lives of its employees and their families into turmoil. Christian workers who became involved in work with the Kyūshū miners and their families gained insights that prepared them for more effective leadership elsewhere in Occupational Evangelism.

From the 1950s the rapid development of Japanese industry was accompanied by one of the largest internal migrations in the nation's history, as millions of people from farming areas moved into cities to escape the privations of rural areas and to seek jobs in the newly developed urban factories. The changed emphasis for Christian work was indicated in the change of title from "Occupational Evangelism" to "Urban Industrial Mission." It was also in the urban areas that Christian workers were to encounter flagrant cases of discrimination against the Burakumin, the so-called outcaste groups of Japanese society. The Korean Christian Church in Japan also tackled problems of discrimination, which Korean residents in Japan encountered.[28]

Christians differed among themselves as to the best ways to organize to meet the new urban problems they faced. In the Kyōdan, when denominational officials refused to participate as a church in sponsoring the Tokyo Christian Crusade (1960), they helped inaugurate instead the Kyōdan's own Ten-Year Program of Evangelism (1962–71), with the watchword *Taishitsu Kaizen* (literally, Structural Renewal). These Kyōdan leaders held that the proper organizational response to urban problems was not crusade-type meetings, but a more thorough restructuring of the churches for urban outreach. The Kyōdan adopted a "Fundamental Policy on Mission" in October 1962 to promote the ten-year program, but hopes for Structural Renewal were to flounder some six years later on the rocks of political controversy (see chap. 2, "Christians and Politics").

The 1960s saw special emphases on "development," based in part on the United Nations' designation of the 1960s as "the Development Decade." Both Protestants and Catholics were summoned to develop "a theology of development," and their efforts climaxed in the Asian Ecumenical Conference for Development, held at Tokyo's Sacred Heart University in July 1970.[29] By the time of that conference, however, it had become evident that during the Development Decade the gap between the developed and the developing countries had widened rather than narrowed, and there were calls instead for theologies of liberation, similar to those developed by black theologians in the United States and by Latin American theologians. This led to invitations from the Korean Christian Church in Japan to James Cone of Union Theological Seminary in New York to share his insights on black theology. And there was Japanese interest in the Asian Theological Conference held in Sri Lanka in January 1979 with the theme, "Asia's Struggle for Full Humanity: The Search for a Relevant Theology."

A concurrent development was recognition of the close relationship between rural and urban areas in the process of industrialization. The Christian Conference of Asia adopted the title of "Urban Rural Mission" to denote the changed emphasis. Serious questions were also being raised about the multinational corporations and their role in world affairs. The fact that during the 1960s a number of Japanese firms in effect were transformed into multinationals brought new urgency to such questions.

Hence through many changes of titles and emphases, the programs which had begun in the 1950s as Occupational Evangelism added new dimensions and perspectives in subsequent decades. There were also sharp differences of opinion about both theologies and programs among advocates of this form of Zion-type outreach.[30]

Mass-Communication Programs

Although radio and motion pictures were very much part of the prewar scene in Japan, and some initial steps were taken during the Occupation for programs of Christian outreach in this area, it was primarily with the era of economic growth after 1952 that there was a proliferation of efforts in this area, and the introduction of television to Japan in 1953 added still another medium.

Protestant ministries in mass communication have focused primarily on radio broadcasting, since work in television and movies has been more expensive and therefore spasmodic. The NCCJ's Audio-Visual Aids Commission (AVACO) was established in 1949, but its major programming began with the construction of its Christian Audio-Visual Center in Tokyo on the campus of Aoyama Gakuin in 1954. Under the leadership of its executive director, Mathew S. Ogawa, AVACO has used overseas gifts for the establishment of well-equipped studios, and rental for their use was then used to sustain broadcasts on radio such as "Friends of the Heart." When a new Mass Communications Center was opened in October 1970 adjacent to the Japan Christian Center in the Waseda district of Tokyo, income from studio rentals (and from a popular wedding hall) made AVACO's program budget largely self-sustaining.[31]

Other Protestant groups raised funds abroad for radio programs. The Japan Lutheran Hour built on the experience of Lutheran Hour broadcasts in America and Europe to produce eleven distinct programs for use throughout Japan. Far East Broadcasting was part of a network of conservative Protestant broadcasters who established transmitters throughout the Pacific area for programs to various Asian countries, including mainland China and North Korea. The Pacific Broadcasting Association in 1965 produced a number of television broadcasts, as did the Lutheran Hour in 1968, and AVACO televised an annual Christmas program. The Joint Broadcasting Committee of the Kyōdan had its special radio broadcasts, while the Seventh-day Adventists produced their own "Family Hour," "Voice of Prophecy," and "With a Light." The Japan Mission Broadcasting Evangelism broadcast its "Voice of Joy." Regional Christian groups also had programs for their own areas, such as the "Prayer for Tomorrow" of Hokkaidō Radio Evangelism and Mass Communications (HOREMCO) in Sapporo, and the Fukuoka New Life Center's "New Life Time." Films were also produced by various Protestant groups, generally for use in church programs.[32]

Roman Catholics began radio ministries in the postwar period also. The Paulists were active in Tokyo, the Salesians in Miyazaki, and local priests and bishops sponsored programs in Sendai, Nagasaki, Kyoto, and elsewhere. A more sustained effort at programming was launched by Father James Hyatt,

M.M., whose Good Shepherd Movement started in 1951 in Kyoto for parish development. By 1957 the Good Shepherd Movement had begun radio broadcasts, and its programs "Light of the Heart" and "Smile of the Sun" reached large audiences. They also started some television programming in 1964. These radio and television programs were coordinated with correspondence courses that listeners could request, and the same pattern was often used by Protestant broadcasters as well.[33] Dependent on overseas contributions, the radio programming was reorganized in 1974 under the National Committee of Bishops, and budget shortages required some curtailment of programs. Hyatt was also instrumental in persuading the national television network, NHK, to undertake religious programs as part of its public service features.[34] Hyatt also helped to produce a full-length feature film, "A Life with Meaning" (1962), which depicted the devotion of a Catholic nurse to her patients. There were also commercially directed films about Christian subjects, such as "The Bells of Nagasaki" (1950), which dealt with a Catholic doctor's A-bomb diary; "In Search of Light" (1954), on the Catholics of Madara Island; and "Maria of the Ants Village" (1958), which told of a Catholic woman who served a community of ragpickers.[35]

The impact of Christian mass-communications outreach is hard to judge. "Like cold *sake* and parents' advice, which have a delayed reaction," essayist Hideo Shibusawa told a meeting of Japanese Christian broadcasters in 1969, "Christian broadcasts should not try to force an immediate response from listeners but should look toward the cumulative effect of a series of good impressions."[36] There are many accounts of how individual lives were changed through radio or television broadcasts, but most Christian broadcasters were inclined to take Shibusawa's advice.

Crusade-Type Evangelism

Mention has already been made of evangelistic campaigns in the postwar era that reproduced patterns of prewar outreach. But the phenomenon of crusade-type mass evangelistic rallies was a product of Japan's era of economic growth after 1952. The facilities for holding such large rallies in sports auditoriums or stadiums, the mass-transit systems which made it possible to bring together such vast throngs of people, and the technical facilities for broadcasting and publicizing such events were all made possible by the period of Japan's rapid economic development. Such mass rallies differed from the denominational evangelistic programs in that they were generally sponsored by some interdenominational group, generally in cooperation with overseas leadership and financing.

The Osaka Christian Crusade (1958), conducted by Dr. Bob Pierce, launched a new era for Japan in crusade-type evangelism, for never before had evangelistic campaigns been carried out with such scope, flair, publicity, and expense. This crusade managed to enjoy rather widespread support among Osaka's Protestants. But problems arose with Pierce's Tokyo Christian Crusade (1960), for a number of Kyōdan Christians criticized the crusade as too flamboyant, expensive, and dominated by outsiders. An outgrowth of these criticisms, as we have seen, was the launching of the Kyōdan's own Ten-Year Program of Evangelism (1962–71), to counter the charge that the Kyōdan critics of the Tokyo Crusade were indifferent to evangelism. In 1967 Dr. Billy Graham led a crusade in Tokyo, and he also conducted evangelistic meetings in 1970 in connection with the Baptist World Alliance's meetings in Tokyo.[37]

There were smaller crusade-style evangelistic meetings sponsored by other foreign evangelists, and Japanese evangelists such as the Reverend Akira Hatori and the Reverend Kōji Honda were also in demand for citywide rallies throughout the country. Although there were many conservative efforts to promote such crusades in Japan, such as the Japan Congress on Evangelism (Kyoto, 1974), there were few Japanese speakers who could attract mass audiences. It is interesting to note that Catholics generally shunned crusade-type evangelism, although after Vatican Council II the way was open for Catholics to support such efforts on a local basis, and this was done in several cases in Japan.

As with mass-communications ministries, crusade-type evangelism as a product of the mass culture during Japan's rapid economic development is a difficult phenomenon to evaluate. The very fact that it was possible to hold such crusades in Japan led many groups to try this method of outreach, in the face of the staggering costs of doing so and the controversies that sometimes arose. Although the crusades reported great numbers of "decisions for Christ" from their meetings, their actual impact on Japan's Christian community seems to have been modest.

The Outreach of Christian Artists and Writers

Kaname Takado called attention to a striking fact about Christian writers in postwar Japan: "On August 15, 1945, the day that Japan faced defeat, there was not a single Christian writer in existence. The cultural soil of modern Japan did not permit the possibility of being a writer and a Christian at the same time."[38] This is remarkable, Takado went on to comment, for the large number of Japanese writers in the Meiji, Taishō, and early Shōwa eras who had temporarily embraced Christianity and then given it up was significant. When they came to face the conflict between Christian ethics and the demonic nature of modern literature, or that between a romantic view of Christianity as the background for European modernity and the needs of Japan's modernization, these earlier writers soon gave up their Christian faith.[39] The number of Christian writers and artists who appeared in the postwar period is all the more noteworthy, then, especially since for the most part they continued in their faith. For this reason, the three decades or so of postwar Japanese history may truly be characterized as a renaissance period for Christian writers and artists.

One of the first Christian writers to attract attention in the postwar period was Rinzo Shiina (1911–73), whose description of the squalor of the poor in postwar Japan in *Midnight Banquet* (1947) gained wide acclaim. Baptized in 1950 by the Kyōdan's famous pastor with leftist sympathies, the Reverend Sakae Akaiwa, Shiina continued his literary output with an autobiographical novel, *A Chance Encounter* (1952), then with *The Lovely Lady* (1955), which won the Ministry of Education Prize, and a large number of short stories, plays, and essays. Exploring such timeless themes as futility, death, freedom, and tolerance, Shiina wrote with a keen eye and a sense of humor that captivated his readers.[40]

Shūsaku Endō (1923–　), one of postwar Japan's leading novelists, was baptized a Catholic at the age of thirteen and made his debut as a writer with *White People* (1955), which won the coveted Akutagawa Prize. This was followed by *Yellow People* (1955), *The Sea and Poison* (1957), and his most celebrated work, *Silence* (1966). In most of his works Endō has wrestled with the question of how the Japanese people, who live in a nontheistic culture, can receive Christian monotheism and make it their own.[41] The haunting question raised by *Silence* is whether Christianity as introduced to Japan by Jesuit missionaries in the sixteenth century could survive the "swamp" of Japan's cultural relativism. The character of the turncoat Kichijirō, who betrayed the Jesuit missionary Father Rodrigues to the authorities on several occasions, was created by Endō to represent his own inmost weaknesses and doubts.[42] Endō subsequently dealt with the life of Jesus in *By the Dead Sea* (1973), *Life of Jesus* (1973), and *My Jesus* (1976), in all of which he maintained that the very weakness of Jesus is the basis for the power of his appeal to contemporary Japanese.

A celebrated husband-and-wife team of novelists is Shumon Miura (1926–　) and his wife Ayako Sono (1931–　). Miura was led to the Catholic faith by Endō, who was his godfather in baptism. Miura's *Ponape Island* (1956) describes the troubling of a peaceful island by a governor's oppressive policies, and the death of a missionary who stood up for the local people even though the government persecuted him for it. *The Miniature Garden* (1967), which won the Shinchō Literature Prize, describes the life of a seemingly happy middle-class family that is actually hollow at the core. Ayako Sono was already a Catholic convert and a novelist in her own right when she married Miura at the age of twenty-two. Her *Time Cut Short* (1971) deals with the ethical problems caused by mass suicides and mothers' killing their children in Okinawa in World War II, while *The Voice of Falling Leaves* (1971) describes the sacrificial death of Father Maximilian Kolbe at Auschwitz. Both works deal forthrightly with the meaning of life in the face of the death of the innocent.

Other Catholic novelists have dealt with some of the agonizing problems of life in postwar Japan. Toshio Shimao (1917–　) resigned his post as a university professor because of his wife's mental illness and went to live in her hometown on Amami-Ōshima Island. Out of this personal anguish over his wife's illness and their poverty he wrote *Out of the Depths I Cry* (1955) and *The Thorns of Death* (1960). Kunio Ogawa (1927–   ) was baptized a Catholic at the age of nineteen, spent some time wandering through Europe, and then began writing short stories with unique insight into the light of eternity purging the darkness of the human world, ruled as it is by suffering and darkness. Sawako Ariyoshi (1931–   ) wrote such best-sellers as *The River Ki* (1959) and *The Wife of Hanaoka Seishu* (1967), which portrayed the sufferings and oppression of persons trapped in traditional Japanese feudalism.

Several Protestant novelists have gained widespread recognition. Mitsuko Abe (1912–   ), the pen name of Mitsui Yamamuro, is the wife of a Kyōdan pastor in Tamagawa who began publishing novels before World War II. In the postwar period she published popular collections of short stories, such as *Not the Journey's End* (1970). Ayako Miura (1922–   ) suddenly achieved fame when her novel *The Freezing Point* (1964) won an Asahi Prize. Subsequently she has written works giving popular introductions to Christian faith and ethics, including her autobiographical *While You Have the Light* (1971). Hirō Sakata (1925–   ) won the Akutagawa Prize for her *Earthen Vessel* (1975).

Most of the novelists mentioned thus far have written plays as well. Other playwrights have been the Catholic Chikao Tanaka (1905–   ), who won the Yomiuri Literary Prize for his *Education* (1954), and the Ministry of Education's Arts Festival Prize for *The Head of Mary* (1966). Sumie Tanaka (1908–   ), baptized a Catholic in 1952, wrote *Castle Mansion* (1954) and *The Lady Gratia Hosokawa* (1959). There have also been Christian art and literary critics, such as Junichirō Sako, pastor of the Kyōdan's Naka-Shibuya Church in Tokyo and Arimasa Mori, a professor at both ICU and the Sorbonne in Paris.

Postwar Japan has also seen the work of a number of prominent Christian artists. Perhaps the best known is Sadao Watanabe (1913–   ), whose stencil prints of biblical subjects have a haunting beauty that has made his works very much in demand overseas as well as in Japan.[43] Osamu Nishizaka (1911–   ) is a painter whose oils dealing with the life of Christ have a starkness that reminds one of Rouault. In an introduction to an exhibit of his paintings, Nishizaka wrote, "I also intend to walk the same road that Jesus walked in his sufferings, from the manger to the cross."[44] Another prominent painter in oils is Tadao Tanaka (1903–   ), whose figures are etched in dark outlines, also after the fashion of Rouault, and represent biblical figures in attitudes of suffering, compassion, and contemplation, motifs that have a daily familiarity to most Japanese.[45] Such artists have had a powerful outreach to Japanese society in making Christian themes familiar to the general public in forms that are immediately understandable. Space prevents proper mention of artists who have also dealt with Christian themes through such media as flower arrangements, tray landscapes, poetry, dance, hymns, songs, and Noh theater.[46]

In sum, the writers and artists who have brought about the renaissance of

Christian art in contemporary Japan have probably had a greater impact on the general public through their Zion-type outreach than have most forms of Sinai-type outreach. Where pastors and theologians have addressed potential audiences of a few thousand, and mass evangelists have reached tens of thousands, the Christian artists have been read or seen by millions. The seeds they have sown may have a harvest in the years yet to come.

New Forms of Urban Ministries

As has been indicated, the spectacular growth of Japan's cities was one of the hallmarks of the era of the nation's rapid economic growth. While one group of Christians was addressing itself to the industrial world through the programs of Urban Industrial Mission, other Christians were focusing primarily on Sinai-type outreach to the vast new housing complexes where people lived. Although there has been a certain overlapping between these two types of ministry, the Christian pastors and lay persons engaged in "apartment-house evangelism" (*danchi dendō*) tended to stay clear of liberal economic analysis and to use traditional forms of church ministry, but forms that were modified to meet the demands of the new apartment-house dwellers. Particularly was this the case with the vast urban apartment developments, which sprouted around Japan in the late 1960s, known as "newtowns" because they were often designed as complete communities and constructed as total units, through combinations of public and private corporations.

"Newtown evangelism" harked back indeed to the model of Sinai rather than of Zion. The main effort was to establish church extensions in the new towns. Senri Newtown on the edge of Osaka was one such development, which became famous because the Osaka World Exposition (Expo '70) was located in an adjacent area. The planners of such new towns often made no provision for religious buildings in their plans; however, to avoid showing favoritism for one religious group over another, they did make provision at Senri Newtown for private groups to establish kindergartens in the new developments. This made it possible for Protestant and Catholic groups to build kindergarten structures which could also be used for worship and other religious purposes during evenings and on Sundays. Surveys of new-town dwellers revealed a high incidence of boredom, marital problems, and juvenile delinquency, and also a pervasive indifference to religious institutions. The new city-dwellers sought to keep free from community and religious responsibilities, which they had gladly left behind in rural areas. In the face of such difficulties, it is remarkable that Catholic and Protestant churches did manage to become established in Senri Newtown.[47] Similar accounts could be given for Tokyo's massive Senboku Newtown, and elsewhere.

A somewhat different approach to a newly developed urban industrial area was made by the Reverend Minoru Ishimaru, who founded the Keiyo Culture and Education Center in the midst of the Keiyo Coastal Industrial Area in

Chiba Pefecture, east of Tokyo. Ishimaru came to know the area that would be developed as a massive new industrial area, and the vicinity of the Tatsumi Housing Complex where apartments for workers' families were being built. As a Kyōdan pastor, he founded the Keiyo Chūbu Church, but at the same time also established the much larger Keiyo Culture and Education Center, which was designed as a community center and educational activities facility. At the center he established a branch of the Nippon Christian Academy,and also initiated an International Personnel Exchange Project, which took Japanese to Asian countries and brought Asians and Europeans to Japan.[48]

A Catholic parish that has developed effective programs for suburban life is the Kichijōji Catholic Church in Tokyo's western suburbs. Under the inspiring leadership of Father Teiji Yasuda, S.V.D., a parish that had been established in 1935 found itself in the era of postwar urban development occupying a strategic place in one of Tokyo's fastest-growing suburban areas. Through the postwar era the church was able to register growth each year, even though three other parishes were detached from it.[49] The church was able to do this by a very active program of parochial societies, which included a men's group, a women's organization, a young people's group, a Legion of Mary, a Vincent dePaul Society, a Marian Congregation, a Third Order of St. Francis, as well as a choir, a Sunday school, Boy Scout and Girl Scout troops, and a high school student group. The church was able to build an imposing apartment house on a portion of the land it owned, which provided not only rental income from residents who were often parishioners as well, but also space for meeting rooms on the ground floor. These meeting rooms enabled church programs to continue unabated when the sanctuary was burned in 1972. The church was also able to keep ahead of the "migration problem" of Christians who tend to lose their church ties as they move to new locations.[50]

A variation on urban ministries that developed in the era of economic growth was the Nippon Christian Academy movement. Initially this movement was started in Japan as an outgrowth of the German Evangelical academies, which proved to be highly successful centers in postwar Germany for establishing contact between groups that had become increasingly isolated because of economic and social conditions, and that were eager to explore the crucial psychological and spiritual problems that were a legacy of World War II. The state-collected church tax in West German states made it possible not only for the academy houses to become established in Germany, but also to develop overseas. The Nippon Christian Academy building in Ōiso (1963) was the first such academy house to be built in Japan, and it was followed by centers and academy groups in Kyoto, Sapporo, Chiba, Shiraoi, and elsewhere. Some of these academy groups were able to build comfortable and well-equipped centers, but in all cases provision was made for informal and friendly sessions where participants could freely come to know each other in dialogue *(Tagung)*. Companies and labor unions soon found that the academy houses were excellent places for personnel training, and church groups used them for spiritual retreats and planning meetings. The academy movement was a creative response to the problems of alienation created by urban industrial expansion.[51]

An ecumenical attempt to serve industrial workers in a particular area is the Nishijin Community Center in Kyoto, of which the Reverend Robert M. Fukada was one of the founders in 1962 and the director for the first ten years of its work. The center addressed itself to workers in the weaving industry of the Nishijin area, and also became a location for field work for seminarians from the Dōshisha School of Theology.

Another urban outreach program that represents an imaginative approach to special needs is a ministry to truck drivers. Recognizing the particular hardships of truck drivers who had to drive long distances without proper rest stops or places to relax, the Reverend Michio Imai decided in the early 1960s that instead of building a church edifice he would establish a restaurant in the town of Kakogawa; there he and his wife served inexpensive meals and provided an atmosphere of friendship for the truck drivers.[52]

In Sapporo, the Reverend Rudy Kuyten, a Kyōdan missionary, recognized a particular opportunity to meet the needs of urban dwellers by establishing his Good Hour Coffee House. Providing a relaxed atmosphere where urban shoppers, young students, salarymen on the way home from work, and others could drop in for a "cup of conversation," the coffee house is decorated with Kuyten's own woodcarvings and is served by a staff who look upon their service as a form of Christian ministry.[53]

In the 1960s, the Segregated Communities Liberation Movement (Burakumin Kaihō Undō) began to tackle some of the problems of justice for the "outcaste" groups in urban areas who have been victims of discrimination for centuries. Christian pastors and missionaries helped support this movement, which was little understood or recognized by the general public in Japan. The Kyōdan helped to sponsor the first overseas trip for publicity and study by representatives of the Burakumin community, when Mr. Kazuichi Imai and the Reverend Aimei Kanai made a trip to North America in February–March 1979.[54]

Japanese Overseas Missions

Despite its marked dependence on foreign commerce and trade throughout its modern history, Japan has seldom had completely cordial relationships with its neighbors in East Asia. During the Pacific War, the Japanese government's policies toward East Asia at their best tended to be based on opportunism and not on careful planning.[55] To some extent, Japan's Christian churches have been victims of historical circumstances, for the prewar East Asia Missions (Tōa Dendō) had been undertaken by Japanese Christians largely at the behest of governmental authorities, who had vexing religious obligations in their mandated territories and dependencies and turned to Christian groups in Japan to help fulfill them. During the Pacific War Japanese Christian pastors sometimes accompanied Japanese troops to East

Asian countries to help smooth relations between the peoples of these countries and the Japanese government. Although these well-intentioned efforts by the pastors were often resented by East Asians, there were cases where strong and continuing ties of friendship were established by the pastors. Hence even though overseas mission work before 1945 had an ambivalent legacy, there was some basis for promising mission developments in the postwar period. These may be classed under the categories of medical missions, rural leaders' training, and lay persons' work overseas.

Japanese medical missions overseas—mentioned previously in connection with lay ministries—started within the framework of the activities of the YMCA in 1938, when medical students, nurses, and doctors met to discuss their responsibility as Japanese Christians toward relieving the suffering caused by Japanese military operations in China.[56] They started their medical work in 1939, completing a Christian hospital in China in 1942, which was staffed by Christian volunteers until it was closed in 1945 by the Chinese government. In the postwar period, a group of those who had participated in the China program joined with others to form the Japan Christian Medical Association (JCMA, Ika Renmei). In 1947 this association sent health teams of Christian workers to rural areas in Japan that lacked adequate medical facilities. In 1957 the East Asia Christian Conference asked JCMA to participate in a Hong Kong meeting of Asian medical personnel. This led to the formation in 1959 of the Japan Overseas Christian Medical Cooperative Service (JOCS), which was organized to receive Asian personnel for medical study and research in Japan, and also to send Japanese medical workers to Asian countries.

In 1961 when JOCS was legally incorporated, its membership was 245, and it grew to 5460 by 1977. About half its members have been Christian, although all who join JOCS agree to support its Christian goals, and all Japanese personnel sent overseas have been Christian. During this period it sent twenty-one workers abroad and received nineteen health workers from other countries. The most illustrious of those sent abroad is Dr. Noboru Iwamura (1927–   ), who went with his wife to Nepal in 1962 for medical service and became involved in projects extending from the work of a local hospital to a Tuberculosis Prevention Program backed by the Nepal government in 1972. His book *A Hospital on the Top of a Hill* (1965) dealt with his experiences in Nepal, and Iwamura was the subject of a Japanese television documentary and widespread newspaper and magazine coverage.[57] His wife, a social worker, ran a private orphanage for Nepali children in their home.[58] Colleagues of the Iwamuras have been sent by JOCS to work in East Nepal, Indonesia, Taiwan, India, and Nigeria.

The churches of Japan began in the 1950s to send Christian mission workers overseas, following for the most part the pattern of missionaries that had been sent in past years to Japan from overseas. By 1962 there were said to be forty-three Japanese Protestant missionaries, assigned to Taiwan, Hong Kong, Laos, Thailand, Burma, Pakistan, Indonesia, Nepal, the Philippines,

Brazil, Bolivia, the United States and Canada. They were subsequently to be found in all six continents. Often these Japanese missionaries have been supported by contributions from several countries, and the East Asia Christian Conference (which later became the Christian Conference of Asia) took a continuing interest in such "third world missions," which had been developed with its help and encouragement, and set down guidelines for their sending, receiving, and support. The experience gained by Japanese Christians in sending missionaries overseas helped to create a climate in which missionaries sent to Japan from abroad could be realistically understood and accepted (see chap. 6, "Foreign Missionaries in Japan"). An outstanding theologian among Japanese workers overseas is Dr. Kosuke Koyama, author of the widely-read *Waterbuffalo Theology* (1974), as well as *No Handle on the Cross* (1977), *50 Meditations* (1979), and *Three Mile an Hour God* (1980).[59]

A number of Christian programs have focused on rural leaders' training, the most sustained effort in the postwar era being that begun in 1960, on the campus of Tsurukawa Rural Institute near Tokyo, as the South East Asia Course (SEAC). The program was launched at the invitation of the Inaugural Assembly of the East Asia Christian Conference (EACC) in Kuala Lumpur the year before, which had asked the churches in Japan to begin, with the help of the World Council of Churches, a program of rural leaders' training. The course, conducted in English, trained its participants in agricultural skills, food processing, rural life and community development, the rural church, and basic Christian beliefs. The Reverend Toshihiro "Tom" Takami became director in 1960, and in 1973 moved the program to a new location at Nishinasuno in Tochigi Prefecture, with the name Asian Rural Institute (ARI). By 1975 there were 140 graduates in seventeen Asian countries (with students from Africa also joining the program), and their contributions toward the rural areas where they served, and in service during such emergencies as floods and earthquakes, were incalculable. SEAC and ARI are examples of how Japan's lead in economic development became the occasion for an effective form of Zion-type Christian outreach.[60]

Lay work overseas during this period was not as prominent as it might have been, in view of the estimate that about 5 percent of Japanese businessmen going abroad have been Christian.[61] From time to time there were gatherings of Japanese and foreign lay persons in Japan and in East Asian countries, generally sponsored by the English-language churches of the area, with the backing of the EACC (later the CCA, Christian Conference of Asia).[62] The Catholic church kept current a list of Japanese-speaking churches and pastors in the major cities of the world, where Japanese Catholic lay persons could worship with other members of the increasing Japanese diaspora.[63]

As we conclude this survey of the forms of Christian outreach that developed during the era of economic growth, it may be noted that most of these newer programs were less directly related to the churches and other Christian institutions than was the case of the Occupation-era programs. To be sure, the crusade-type evangelistic campaigns as well as several new forms of urban mission and overseas missions aimed at church extension of the traditional type. Even so, the crusades were generally interdenominational in sponsorship and with significant outside leadership, so that their actual contributions to church growth were modest. The newer urban and overseas programs did not always make the addition of members to the church rolls their first objective. Some of the newer forms of outreach were social-action programs, such as Occupational Evangelism and its successors, which sought to make a prophetic witness to the newly developing urban and industrial areas, but not necessarily with the object of church growth.

Perhaps the changing emphasis of this period may best be understood as a gradual shift from the Sinai-type outreach, which proclaimed God's word and law in the wilderness of unevangelized Japan, to the Zion type, which responded to the mission of God which God has already undertaken in Japanese society. What was happening here was in part a subtle reevaluation of the theological significance of Japanese society itself. In oversimplified terms, Japanese society was no longer regarded primarily as a target of Christian outreach, as had been the case in the Occupation era, so much as the spiritual context within which such outreach was possible. Perhaps the Christian artists and writers captured the new mood and climate better than others, and this may explain why this period saw a renaissance of Christian art in Japan, greater than had ever taken place before. For within an era of reappraisals that began about 1968, another climate became sufficiently pervasive to make further alterations in the types of Christian outreach that would be found. The older forms of Sinai and Zion outreach would continue, to be sure, but their goals and expectations were modified in subtle ways. It is to these changes that we now turn.

The Era of Reappraisals (after 1968): What Kind of Outreach?

In the other chapters of this study we trace the changes that came over aspects of Christian work in Japan in the aftermath of the 1968 struggles in campuses and churches, and of the 1973–74 oil shock and its resulting economic dislocations. These changes had severe impact on the Christian schools, and less direct but equally significant influence on Christian social work. In this section we shall be examining how the era of reappraisals affected programs of Christian outreach.

This era saw a continuation of the two dominant models of outreach already discussed, the Sinai and the Zion types. One characteristic of this third era is the further development of the Jubilee-type outreach, about which little has been said thus far in this chapter. The Jubilee type emphasizes the spirit of liberation, which comes not as the result of historical processes, but from the direct intervention of divine power. Jubilee becomes possible when the Sinai-type outreach is failing to deal with pressing human problems of oppression and alienation; Jubilee becomes necessary when the Zion-type outreach is unable to discern the divine wrath against the status quo in the promised land itself. It should not be surprising that the Jubilee-type outreach in contemporary Japan as elsewhere takes on a liberal form and a conservative form, which at first glance seem to be diametrically opposed to each other. The liberal form is "liberation theology," which urges Christians to emulate Jesus as the opponent of all forms of oppression, injustice, and alienation, "the man for others" who was crucified by the authorities of church and state because of his dedication to the poor and the downtrodden. The conservative form of Jubilee is "the charismatic renewal" of the Holy Spirit, which stresses the immediate union of the believer with spiritual power, and release from the oppressive bonds of sickness, despair, and sin, and the identification with Jesus the anointed of God, who in the face of his own crucifixion prayed to the Father for the sending of the Holy Spirit to the world and to his disciples for their comfort and guidance.

The perceptive reader will grant readily enough that both liberation theology and charismatic renewal were distinctive groups that appeared in Japan after 1968. But there are bound to be questions as to whether it is legitimate to group them together as variant forms of a Jubilee-type outreach. What do these diametrically opposed groups have in common? As it turns out, they have a great deal more in common than an observer or even a participant in either group might notice at first glance. They share the conviction that the form of liberation which each sees as the most important part of Christian outreach is not to be the outcome of any historical process. Rather, the liberation they seek can only be the direct gift of God, as was the liberation bestowed upon the oppressed Israelites at the time of Jubilee. For both of these groups, the historical developments of Japanese capitalism *and* Communism are no longer able to provide for the most pressing need of the age. For them, the historical process has outrun its usefulness for the Japanese scene and possibly for the world as well; only the liberation process, which Jubilee will bring, can restore full meaning to life.

We need to recall that the "ideal types" of Christian outreach, which we are describing in this chapter, do not correspond entirely to what actual persons and groups believe and do. These "ideal types" are logical derivatives of programs and mindsets to which people become committed. Furthermore, the full implications of the three types of Christian outreach did not emerge immediately. Particularly is this the case with the Jubilee type in this third era. Neither the liberal nor the conservative proponents of Jubilee developed all the implications of their programs. Some of the more indirect effects of their deeds and words may not become evident for years to come. It is our present task, however, to see the emergence of this type of thinking at a particular point in history, and to note how it interacted with other types of Christian outreach already in the field. It is time, then, to analyze the actual historical record more closely.

The Kyōdan Struggles and New Concepts of Outreach

The struggles within the Kyōdan that erupted as a result of its participation in the Christian Pavilion at Expo '70 are dealt with in other chapters of this study (see chap. 2, "Christians and Politics"; chap. 3, "Education"; chap. 7, "Ecumenicity"; chap. 8, "Biblical Studies"; and chap. 9, "Theology"). Regarding Christian outreach we need to note that the Christian Pavilion was planned as a superb form of outreach, which would make an ecumenical witness of all Christian groups in Japan—Catholic, Protestant, and Orthodox—at the heart of an international exposition that heralded the place of a prosperous Japan in a new era hopefully dedicated to "Progress and Harmony for Mankind," the theme for Expo '70.

But what happened? Opposition to the Christian Pavilion within the Kyōdan rapidly created two conflicting opinions about what that pavilion represented. The "problem posers" *(mondai teikisha)* and their supporters maintained that the pavilion demonstrated the churches' support for the exposition's "celebration of capitalism" when Christians in prophetic responsibility should be denouncing capitalism and its system of exploitation that leads to oppression of the poor at home and abroad, and to militaristic measures for taking Japan and other nations down the road to destruction and war. The supporters of the pavilion, on the other hand, maintained that it was a form of Christian witness and outreach consonant with other postwar programs of evangelism, publications, mass communication, and international responsibility in the midst of the new industrial and technological mass society. After the conflict over Expo '70 got under way, the majority of Kyōdan members gave their full support neither to the claims of the problem posers nor to the Federation of Evangelical Churches in the Kyōdan (the "Rengō" group), which was organized in opposition.

Most Kyōdan pastors and church members tried to take a "mediating position," which would find elements of truth in both conflicting positions. The major trouble was that the mediating position was an increasingly difficult one to maintain either theologically or organizationally in the face of the groups that sought new patterns of faith and order to clear away the ambiguities of the past. While the mediating group hoped that the winds of controversy would somehow blow away, they gradually came to realize how difficult it would be to go from what the church was in the late 1970s to the future conditions, which the problem posers were heralding in their way, and the Rengō supporters were seeking to establish in theirs. The decision of Rengō members to hold their own ceremonies at Tokyo's Shinagawa Church in May 1979 for licensing one person and ordaining five persons to the ministry indicated the extent of their determination to establish their concepts of the church and its ministry. Moderator Toshio Ushiroku of the Kyōdan immediately announced that the Kyōdan would not recognize the validity of these ceremonies.[64] It seemed likely that the Kyōdan would continue to be polarized over conflicting views of the nature of the church and its outreach.

The fact that most other Christian groups were able to avoid the polarization that gripped the Kyōdan does not mean that they were unaffected by these developments. To be sure, the Kyōdan was not a representative microcosm of Japanese society, for the Kyōdan was more middle class, urban, and professional in its makeup than society at large, but its membership represented segments of the nation's population that were aware of the stresses and tensions of Japan as a whole, especially as a result of urban/industrial/technological developments. Other Christian bodies—Catholic, Protestant, and Orthodox—would manage to avoid the same maelstroms of polarization, but the Kyōdan itself, for better or for worse a product of modern Japanese society, was unable to avoid the divisiveness that lay just underneath the surface of the nation as a whole.

Charismatics and Neo-Pentecostals

Although they represented only a small segment of the total Christian community, the Neo-Pentecostal groups which developed in Japan in the 1970s symbolized a new approach to Christian outreach. Although there were Pentecostal groups in Japan in prewar days, and groups like the Primitive Gospel, which practiced speaking in tongues, the Neo-Pentecostals that developed in various parts of the world in the late 1960s and came to Japan in the early 1970s represented a conservative form of Jubilee-type Christian outreach. October 1972 saw the arrival of both Catholic and Protestant Neo-Pentecostal teams. The Catholics were Sisters Dorothy Chaple and Stephanie Culhane, who came to hold services in various places, especially at the Franciscan Chapel Center in Tokyo. That same month the Reverend Lester Pritchard of Team Thrust Ministries in Canada and a team of twenty members led a four-day Holy Spirit Seminar at the Yoyogi Youth Center in Tokyo, in cooperation with pastors from the Assemblies of God and other Protestant groups.[65] The Team Thrust Ministries had started in Japan in 1970 as "Japan Thrust," a Protestant body of clergy and laity, but at its 1972 seminar it moved toward closer cooperation with Catholic charismatics. A Catholic charismatic prayer meeting was organized in November 1972 at the Hatsudai Catholic Church in Tokyo, and continued to meet there regularly. Protestant charismatic groups were established in several places as Team Thrust Ministries and other Neo-Pentecostal groups continued their work.[66]

The charismatic movement in Japan was a source of both strength and divisiveness within the Christian community.[67] Phenomena similar to speaking in tongues have often been associated with indigenous Japanese religious groups, and hence are not an exclusively Christian form of worship, any more than are prayer and singing.[68] By 1977 the Neo-Pentecostal movement seemed to have reached its peak in Japan.[69] Charismatics clearly were making unique contributions to the revival of enthusiasm among the groups they influenced, as well as to a spirit of ecumenicity among those who spoke in tongues (see chap. 7, "Ecumenicity"). The Neo-Pentecostals represented another form of Jubilee-type Christian outreach, in which the continuities of past historical developments were set aside in order to celebrate the church's eschatological gifts. They believed these gifts came not by spreading the knowledge of God's law or by responding to God's work in mission, but by the direct bestowal of the Holy Spirit.

New Forms of Christian Outreach in the 1970s

Other forms of Christian outreach achieved new significance in the 1970s. The Cursillo Movement had been active among Catholics in the 1960s, and gained an even wider and more ecumenical following in the 1970s. The Movement for a Christian World gained considerable momentum in Catholic retreats by seeking to combine personal spiritual devotion and commitment to action in social causes. The Christian Family Movement and the Marriage Encounter Movement sought to further the Catholic ministry to married couples.[70]

Protestant evangelistic outreach took new forms among conservative groups. The Japan Keswick conventions for pastors brought conservative evangelical programs in the 1960s, and in June 1974 the Japan Congress on Evangelism in Kyoto sought to reach lay persons as well as pastors.[71] From 1976 a California-based organization called the Language Institute for Evangelism (LIFE) took summer deputation teams of American students to Japan in a program called Scrum Dendō (Team Evangelism).[72]

One of the difficulties encountered by Christians engaged in outreach in the 1970s was competition from the Reverend Sun Myung Moon's Unification Church (Sekai Kirisutokyō Tōitsu Shinrei Kyōkai, often known as Tōitsu Genri). The Unification Church sometimes seemed to preempt the field of evangelistic efforts with its own highly publicized and well-financed efforts. An offshoot from Protestant Christianity in Korea, the Unification Church created both friends and enemies among the Japanese public by its evangelistic methods.[73] On the campuses of Christian schools, Bible study groups were sometimes taken over by Unification Church groups, for there was considerable confusion about their identity. Even the *Kirisutokyō Nenkan (Christian Yearbook)* in 1974 listed the Unification Church as a Protestant group, but its editors deleted the group in the following year's listings. The NCCJ's Central Committee declared in January 1979 that the Unification Church was not a Christian body.[74]

Concluding Observations

This account of over three decades of Christian outreach in contemporary Japan has shown that during this period many of the forms of that outreach underwent significant changes. The Occupation era enabled the prewar forms of outreach to become reestablished, without the restraints of the previous period. The dominant patterns of the immediate postwar era were of the Sinai type, for defeat in war brought a renewed feeling that the primary task for Christians was to spread the knowledge of God's law in a land that had undergone much turmoil.

The era of economic growth that followed the outbreak of the Korean War made it possible to develop new forms of outreach that had existed only as latent possibilities before. This chapter has shown how new forms of outreach changed the climate within which outreach itself was performed, as well as the expectations which Christians had for these programs. The change from viewing one's own land as "a pre-Christian land" to seeing it as "a promised land" took many decades—even centuries—to come about in Western countries. A somewhat analagous development took place in Japan after Buddhism was introduced from abroad and gradually became indigenized.[75] Among Japanese Christians, the development of Zion-type outreach came relatively soon after the postwar renewal of Sinai-type outreach, but the former greatly expanded in the period of the nation's economic growth. In different ways there were significant shifts in the methods by which the Christian community interpreted Japanese society theologically. Christians (both Catholic and Protestant) engaged in evangelistic programs and those involved in social action responded to the changed perceptions in their own ways, but it was the writers and the artists who gave the fullest expression to the new situation.

It is of course too early to evaluate the changes brought to Japan's Christian community by the era of reappraisals. Yet it seems clear that many of Japan's Christians became convinced that they could not simply continue past forms of outreach in unaltered fashion. Now advocates of Jubilee-type outreach appeared, announcing—through seemingly contradictory programs—that there had to be discontinuity with past developments if there were to be a future of genuine liberation and hope. But the road to that future seemed to lie through continuing conflict among Christians about the fundamental nature of Christian faith and outreach.

Brunner's observation remains true that "the church exists by mission, just as a fire exists by burning." No one doubted at the close of the 1970s that the fires of Christian outreach would continue to burn in Japan. Yet a major question remained: What would the fires consume as they burned?

NOTES

1. Emil Brunner, *The Word and the World* (London: SCM Press, 1931), p. 108.

2. See Robert Lee, *Stranger in the Land: A Study of the Church in Japan* (New York: Friendship Press, 1967); *JCQ* 41, no. 3 (Summer 1975) has the theme, "The Japanese Congregation in the Mid-Seventies."

3. See Chie Nakane, *Japanese Society* (Berkeley, Calif.: University of California Press, 1972).

4. See Neil Braun, *Laity Mobilized* (Grand Rapids, Mich.: Wm. B. Eerdmans, 1971). Braun gives an over-optimistic picture of the Spirit of Jesus Church. Another study of church growth is Tetsunao Yamamori, *Church Growth in Japan* (Pasadena: William Carey Library, 1974).

5. Cf. "Power to the Laity," *Newsweek*, March 6, 1978, pp. 95–96.

6. Stephen Neill and Hans-Ruedi Weber, eds., *The Layman in Christian History* (Philadelphia: Westminster Press, 1963), pp. 337–58.

7. See *JCAN*, Nov. 10, 1972, pp. 3–4; "Nihon Kyōkai Sengo Sanjunen no Hyakunin" [One Hundred Figures from the Japanese Christian World's Thirty Postwar Years], in *Kirisutokyō Nenkan* [Christian Yearbook] (Tokyo: Kirisuto Shimbunsha, 1976), pp. 61-101. This valuable article has been used for reference purposes throughout this study; on Mrs. Kubushiro, see p. 73. *JCAN*, Oct. 27, 1972, p. 3.

8. *JCAN*, June 4, 1976, pp. 3–4; Dec. 10, 1976, p. 4.

9. John Reagan, "Overseas Christian Medical Mission," *JCQ* 44, no. 3 (Summer 1978): 142–46.

10. Leland D. Hine, *Axling: A Christian Presence in Japan* (Valley Forge, Pa.: Judson Press, 1969).

11. Interview with Kenneth Dale, Beverly Tucker, David Swain, Donald Wheeler, Len Keighley, and David Reid, at Lake Nojiri, Aug. 10, 1972.

12. Japan Baptist Mission, *Program Base Design* (Tokyo: The Japan Mission, Foreign Mission Board, SBC, 1973; privately printed), p. 69.

13. Arthur Reynolds, ed., *Japan in Review: "Japan Harvest" Anthology, 1955-1970* (Tokyo: JEMA, 1970), vol. 1, pp. 111-14.

14. Ibid., pp. 99–100.

15. Braun, *Laity Mobilized*, pp. 170–75.

16. Joseph L. Van Hecken, *The Catholic Church in Japan since 1859* (Tokyo: Enderle, 1963), pp. 260–63.

17. George A. Mueller, *The Catechetical Problem in Japan (1549—1965)* (Tokyo: Oriens, 1967), pp. 71-86.

18. Tomonobu Yanagita, *Japan Christian Literature Review* (Sendai: Seisho Tosho Kankōkai, 1958); *Supplement* (1960).

19. This study is indebted to materials published by the companies mentioned in this paragraph.

20. Van Hecken, *Catholic Church in Japan,* pp. 144–47.

21. Interview with Robert Gerry and Ken Cullen, Tokyo, Oct. 4, 1974.

22. See Ruth Rouse and Stephen C. Neill, eds., *A History of the Ecumenical Movement, 1517—1948* (Philadelphia: Westminster Press, 1954), pp. 599–612. Cf. Risto Lehtonen, "The Story of a Storm: An Ecumenical Case Study," *Study Encounter* (a WSCF publication), vol. 8, no. 1 (1972), pp. 1–18.

23. Van Hecken, *Catholic Church in Japan,* pp. 189–91.

24. Reynolds, *Japan in Review,* pp. 108–10.

25. Charles Germany, *Protestant Theologies in Modern Japan* (Tokyo: IISR Press, 1965), pp. 195–96.

26. Masahiro Tomura, "Fifteen Years of Occupational Evangelism," *Shokuden News*, May 1966 (no. 1), pp. 3–10. A helpful bibliography on industrial evangelism in many countries is Richard Poethig, ed., *Forming a Theology of Urban-Industrial Mission* (Chicago: Institute on the Church in Urban-Industrial Society, 1975).

27. Tomura, "Fifteen Years," p. 3.

28. See Satoshi Hirata, ed., *On the Scene: "Reality Ministry" in Japan* (Osaka: Kansai Urban Industrial Movement, 1975); *JCAN*, Jan. 26, 1979, p. 5.

29. The report of this conference is *Liberation, Justice, Development: Asian Ecumenical Conference for Development* (Bangkok: EACC, 1970).

30. Masao Takenaka, *Reconciliation and Renewal in Japan* (New York: Friendship Press, 1957), pp. 54ff. Cf. Masao Takenaka, *Hataraku Ningenzō wo Motomete* [Seeking the Image of Working People], (Tokyo: Shinkyō Shuppansha, 1978); *JCAN,* Jan. 26, 1979, p. 5.

31. Mathew S. Ogawa, *AVACO, 1949/1959: 10th Anniversary* (Tokyo: AVACO, 1959; privately printed).

32. *JCAN,* Dec. 25, 1968, p. 2; July 10, 1969, p. 4; William Danker letter.

33. Interview with Fr. James Hyatt, M.M., Kyoto, July 19, 1974.

34. James F. Hyatt, "Good Shepherd Movement," *JMB* 27, no. 4 (May 1973): 218-20.

35. Van Hecken, *Catholic Church in Japan*, pp. 148-53.

36. *JCAN,* July 10, 1969, p. 4.

37. *JCAN,* Jan. 15, 1962, pp. 3-4; Nov. 13, 1967, p. 3; July 31, 1970, p. 5.

38. Kaname Takado, "Postwar Japanese Christian Writers," *JCQ* 38, no. 4 (Fall 1972): 185-92. The present section is largely based on Takado's excellent article.

39. Ibid., p. 185.

40. *JCQ* 39, no. 4 (Fall 1973) has the theme, "Rinzo Shiina: Novelist, Essayist, Playwright." There is a series of 18 volumes (to date) in Japanese: *Collected Works of Modern Japanese Christian Writers* (Tokyo: Kyōbunkʻvan, 1972-).

41. Shūsaku Endō, *Silence* (English trans.; Tokyo: Tuttle, 1969). Cf. Arthur G. Kimball, *Crisis in Identity and Contemporary Japanese Novels* (Tokyo: Tuttle, 1973), pp. 179-81; Francis F. Uyttendaele, "Shūsaku Endō," *JCQ* 38, no. 4 (Fall 1972): 199-205.

42. Talk by Shūsaku Endō, Tokyo Union Church, March 28, 1971.

43. On Sadao Watanabe, see "About Our Art Work," *NEAJT,* no. 2 (March 1969), p. 155; Donald R. Purkey, "Closer to the Heart of the People," *New World Outlook* 64, no. 11 (December 1974): 25-29.

44. On Nishizaka, see "About Our Art Work," *NEAJT,* no. 3 (September 1969), p. 145.

45. On Tanaka, see "About Our Art Work," *NEAJT,* nos. 5 and 6 (September 1970/March 1971), pp. 127-28.

46. On Christian art, see Masao Takenaka, *Creation and Redemption through Japanese Art* (Tokyo: Kyōbunkwan, 1966), and *Christian Art in Asia* (Tokyo: Kyōbunkwan, 1975). On Japanese poetry, see theme issue on "Japanese Poetry and Christian Faith," *JCQ* 41, no. 4 (Fall 1975).

47. See J. Lawrence Driskill, "A Christian Ministry to a Large Scale Housing Complex: The Case of Japan's Senri Newtown" (S.T.D. dissertation at San Francisco Theological Seminary, 1969); Stanley Manierre, ed., "Danchi and Newtown," *Breakthrough* (a publication of the NCCJ's Industrial Evangelism Committee), July-October 1970.

48. The Keiyo Culture and Education Center publishes *Keiyo to Sekai* in Japanese, and *Keiyo and the World* in English.

49. Joseph Spae, "Kichijōji: A Catholic Suburban Parish," in *Christianity Encounters Japan* (Tokyo: Oriens, 1968), pp. 57-67.

50. *JMB* 27, no. 8 (September 1973) has the theme, "Migration of Catholic Population."

51. *JCAN,* Nov. 13, 1967.

52. Kyoji Buma, "A Church That Smells of Gas Fumes and Bean Soup," *JCQ* 31, no. 1 (Winter 1965): 35–39.

53. Interview with the Rev. Rudolf Kuyten, Sapporo, July 12, 1978.

54. Hirata, *Reality Ministry*, pp. 31–34; *JCAN*, April 27, 1979, p. 6.

55. Grant K. Goodman, "Japan and Southeast Asia in the Pacific War: A Case of Cultural Ambiguity," in *Studies on Japanese Culture*, vol. 2 (Tokyo: Japan P.E.N. Club, 1973).

56. JCQ 44, no. 3 (Summer 1978): 142–46.

57. "Dr. Iwamura," *The Daily Yomiuri*, June 29, 1974.

58. JOCS pamphlet, November 1973.

59. Dr. Koyama is on the faculty of Union Theological Seminary, New York.

60. Interview with the Rev. Toshihiro Takami, Nishinasuno, Jan. 12, 1975, and from pamphlets published by the Asian Rural Institute.

61. Yasuo Furuya, "The Japanese Image in South-East Asia," *JCQ* 39, no. 3 (Summer 1973): 147–49.

62. See *Laymen Abroad in Asia*, privately printed report of the Consultation on Industrial Urban Mission and Laymen Abroad, Bangkok, January 1968.

63. *Japan Catholic Directory, 1975* (Tokyo: Katorikku Chūō Kyōgikai, 1975), pp. 595–96.

64. On the disputed ordinations, see *Rengō: Voice of Renewal,* April 1979 (nos. 8, 9); *Kyōdan News Letter,* June 20, 1979 (no. 136).

65. *JCAN*, March 24, 1978, pp. 4–5.

66. Pamphlet of Team Thrust Ministries, ca. October 1973.

67. Carl C. Beck, ed., *The Contemporary Work of the Holy Spirit* (Tokyo: Hayama Missionary Seminary, 1973).

68. Patterson D. Benner, "The Universality of 'Tongues,' " *JCQ* 39, no. 2 (Spring 1973): 101–7.

69. Interviews by writer in Tokyo, July 6–Aug. 2, 1977.

70. D. Murray, "Marriage Encounter and Parish Renewal," *JMB* 30, no. 8 (September 1976): 462–66.

71. Pamphlets for "Japan Congress on Evangelism, Kyoto," June 3–7, 1974.

72. "Action Report: A Review of Conditions for Student Ministry in Japan" (Tokyo, September 1976, mimeographed).

73. Cf. Lee Seaman, "The Unification Church," *JCAN*, March 14, April 18, May 9, May 23, 1975.

74. *JCAN*, Feb. 28, 1979, p. 6.

75. See Hajime Nakamura and Philip P. Wiener, *Ways of Thinking of Eastern People: India, China, Tibet, Japan* (Honolulu: East–West Center Press, 1964).

6

Foreign Missionaries in Japan:
A Riddle with Many Attempted Answers

Reviewing the history of missionary work in Japan for a missionary conference held in 1974, Tomio Mutō, the forceful and picturesque former chancellor of Meiji Gakuin, characterized the early history of Protestant mission work in Japan in this way: "In the beginning was the missionary, and the missionary was with God, and the missionary was Japanized."[1] Beginning with this somewhat awkward paraphrase of John 1:1, Mutō went on to examine what the continuing role of missionaries might be, especially after becoming "Japanized."

The problem Mutō posed applied to all Christian groups in Japan, for Japanese Christianity, whether in its Catholic, Orthodox, or Protestant forms, is the fruit of the work of foreign missionaries. Even independent groups such as Non-Church Christianity and the Spirit of Jesus Church, which have on principle always been separate from foreign mission organization, nevertheless developed through a dialogue with Christianity as mediated by missionaries. But the dominant role of the missionary in Japan was for most groups quite a while ago, indeed "in the beginning." For most Christian churches in Japan, the umbilical cords that had once tied them to overseas mission boards and societies have been cut for some time. Although continuing to maintain their ties with the papacy, Japanese Catholics became independent of overseas mission societies in a formal way in the 1940s, when under governmental pressure the foreign ordinaries and bishops resigned and were replaced with a totally Japanese hierarchy. The Orthodox Church in Japan had in effect acted as an autocephalous, or ecclesiastically independent, church since its ties with the mother church were cut during the Russian Revolution in 1917, even though its independence was not formally acknowledged by both sides until the 1970s. And as for the older Japanese Protestant churches, their autonomous existence as congregations and as denominations began to be recognized in the 1880s, and that recognition was hastened to completion by the same Religious Organizations Law that affected the Catholics in the 1940s. Hence the Japanese Christian churches that faced the postwar period in 1945 were already mature Christian communities. Whatever their precise ecclesiastical status—in their own eyes as well as in the eyes of their overseas counterparts—the Pacific War had made the Christian churches of Japan fully independent, responsible for their own spiritual life, and no longer under the control of any foreign missionaries.

The breaking of dependence on foreign missionaries did not mean, however, that Japan's Christians did not want to have ties with overseas Christians. Even during the Pacific War when only a few foreign missionaries remained in Japan, Japanese Christians maintained their overseas ties in various ways, often at great personal cost. And after the war there were Japanese Christians who were eager to resume their connections abroad, which had generally been intimately related to the work of the missionaries. Whether in schools, churches, social work agencies, hospitals, or other areas, Japanese Christians in the postwar period prepared for the return of their foreign missionary colleagues.

Despite the best of intentions all around, the return of the missionaries to postwar Japan presented a kind of riddle to those concerned. The riddle went something like this: In a society and a church come of age, what is the role of the foreign missionary? Many answers would be attempted. The missionaries who arrived in Japan after 1945 were not starting "in the beginning," as had their forebears. There were already Japanese Christian schools, churches, and social work agencies in Japan, and to these the missionaries would come to relate, somehow, if they were to form new schools and churches on their own. Furthermore, the missionary groups that began new work in Japan after 1945 made use of the Bible and hymnals prepared by earlier Christian groups. In time the post-1945 missionaries began to encounter problems relating to the new Japanese Christian organizations which they helped to call into being similar to problems faced by earlier missionaries. So the newcomers as well as the returnees had to wrestle with the problems of the missionary's new role, what it was and how it should be carried out. The riddle might be obscured for a while by the difficult circumstances facing all Japanese in the immediate postwar period, but it was certain to emerge, sooner or later.

Christian Missionary Work in the Occupation Era

When the American Occupation of Japan began at the end of August 1945, there were already foreign missionaries at work in Japan, and they were soon joined by hosts of others. There was something deeply ironical in the fact that foreign missionaries, mostly Americans, were resuming their work under the aegis of an American military occupation. This was one element of the riddle with which almost nobody was entirely comfortable: not the Occupation authorities, not the overseas mission agencies, not the Japanese (Christian or not), and not the missionaries themselves. Despite the difficulties, however, both missionaries and the Occupation authorities settled down to the new modus vivendi.

Occupation Policies toward Missionary Activities

The official attitude of SCAP was a mixture of diverse elements. William P. Woodard has pointed out that many statements by SCAP officials initially displayed considerable favoritism toward Christian work in Japan, and to Christian missionaries in particular. For instance, General Douglas MacArthur wrote a letter (October 4, 1947) to Miss Elizabeth Whewell, an independent missionary in Gifu Prefecture, in which he said:

> As you know, religious freedom is one of the greatest boons that the Occupation has brought to Japan, and I think you equally realize the hope and belief I entertain that Japan will become Christianized. Every possible effort to that end is being made and, had I my way, I would hope for a thousand missionaries for every one that is now here.[2]

MacArthur made similar statements privately to many visitors to his office, and in a letter on official SCAP stationery, dated April 4, 1949, and reproduced in many thousands of Scripture portions distributed by the Pocket Testament League, he wrote: "This distribution of the Bible . . . has my hearty endorsement and I sincerely request any assistance the representatives of the Pocket Testament League may need in the performance of their duties."[3]

In spite of personal statements by MacArthur and other SCAP officials endorsing Christianity, official religions policy of the Occupation came from the Religions Division of the Civil Information and Education Section of SCAP, headed by Lieutenant Commander William K. Bunce. And that policy was one of strict neutrality toward all religious groups, which meant that Christian missionaries or churches were not supposed to receive any special favors. Commenting on a particular request for assistance that had come from a Sister St. Paul, Bunce wrote on January 20, 1947:

> The policy of non-assistance to missionaries is believed to be very sound, and, though apparently contradictory, is strongly consistent with the policy of strengthening Christian influence in Japan for the following reasons: (1) If the Christian movement in Japan draws support from the Occupation Forces our ultimate purpose to make Christianity permanent in Japan will be defeated at the end of the Occupation. At that time the Japanese will repudiate Christianity as a creed of

hypocrites whose proponents failed to live as Christians by accepting aid from the Occupation Forces which was not available to Japanese converts. (2) This view is supported by church leaders, including the Roman Catholic Apostolic Delegate, who wish to accept as little as possible from the Occupation Forces. They desire to present Christianity to the Japanese as a creed which needs no support from government sources anywhere. Requests for exceptions come from individuals of the rank and file as in the instant case. . . .[4]

Such a statement typified not only the views but also the actual practice of SCAP's Religions Division. It was based on the American tradition of the separation of religion and government, and it proved to be quite a new departure for Japan, where for centuries political authorities had often practiced favoritism toward particular religious groups for their own ends. In retrospect, the policies of SCAP may be seen as not unrelated to the American experience with "civil religion," whereby the government has promoted the social principles that the great majority of a nation's religious groups have shared, but without endorsing any one particular religion.[5] In any event, the SCAP policies of neutrality toward religions, later embodied in Japan's new constitution, provided during the three postwar decades a greater measure of religious freedom than Japan had ever before experienced. Although there were attempted breaches of these policies—as the chapter on politics indicates—it can be maintained that the Japanese people enjoyed a greater amount of religious freedom than did the people of most countries during this same period.

Although some overseas mission societies were initially perplexed by the ambiguities between MacArthur's endorsement of missionary work and the actual SCAP policies of religious neutrality, most of their leaders were fully prepared to operate under the latter alternative. They saw that the door was open for an unprecedented expansion of missionary work in Japan, if done on a voluntary basis. For instance, Bishop Arthur J. Moore, president of the Methodist Church Board of Missions, even before the end of hostilities with Japan had written:

We desire to return to Japan to serve, "not as overseers of their faith, but as helpers in their joy" in any area where there is need. . . . We expect an enlarging opportunity for missionary work in the days to come, growing out of a splendid past. . . . Our policy toward Japan may determine the whole future of our world mission, for it will show our capacity to rise above group loyalties to a common sense of mission in God's world.[6]

A Catholic missionary representative who saw things in much the same way was Father Patrick J. Byrne, an American Maryknoll priest who had been interned in Japan during World War II and whose radio broadcasts in both English and Japanese just before the arrival of the Occupation forces are credited with helping smooth the latter's reception in Japan. Byrne wrote to his Maryknoll superior in America, on April 26, 1946, about the future of Christian work in Japan:

Henceforth and for (every maybe but anyhow) the next twenty years, America is going to rule and remake Japan. In the remaking the Catholic Church of America has a responsibility that she has dodged in the Philippines . . . to see that this remaking by America is not on pagan lines. . . . Again, Maryknoll is *the only Catholic mission society here* [from America]. Maryknoll may not like this responsibility, but she's got it just the same; and she can't dodge it . . . though she may lessen it by getting other American religious groups over here.[7]

It should be noted that both of these statements stress the missionaries' "opportunity" or "responsibility" for restoring order and meaning in Japan after the chaos of wartime. Such goals came to be intimately related to the Occupation's goals of establishing order in conquered enemy territory, so that it would not become a threat again to America and its allies. It has never been easy to disentangle the theological, humanitarian, and political motives behind specific policies.

Japanese Christian leaders were also eager to welcome missionaries to their country under the terms of the Occupation's policies, particularly if they were missionaries from America. Writing to the Maryknoll father general in America, Roman Catholic Bishop Taguchi of Osaka commented:

I think the door of Japan is frankly open to our people to embrace our Holy Religion. . . . Therefore, our Church is now seriously asking for the messengers of Gospel of every nationality, especially of the American nationality because of the peculiar influence of the U.S.A. under the present circumstances.[8]

Meeting on August 28, 1945, the Board of Trustees of the Kyōdan adopted a similar point of view in an official statement that looked forward to the postwar period. In it the Reverend Mitsuru Tomita, the Kyōdan director (*tōrisha*), said that now after many years of repression the church would be in a position of freedom and importance in the land, but that it should not act as though "our time has come." Stating that the church's leadership had not reflected sufficiently on past events, Tomita went on to affirm the principle of the evangelism of Japan by Japanese and urged the church to make sure that missions or ecclesial structures of missionaries not be created separately from the Kyōdan.[9] Whether with enthusiasm or a sense of inevitability, Japanese church leaders awaited the return of the missionaries.

The Missionaries Return to Japan

In a sense, the first American Christians to make contact with their co-religionists in Japan during the Occupation era were Christian members of the American armed forces, and the chaplains in particular. Many chaplains sought out Japanese Christians and rendered them valuable services, especially during the period of severe hardship immediately after the war. The Christian contacts of chaplains and other military personnel were to be of particular significance for the Japanese Christian community throughout the postwar decades, and they deserve a much fuller account than can be given here. But it should not be overlooked that contacts which Occupation personnel made with Japanese Christians led to many lasting friendships, and that scores of SCAP people later returned to Japan as missionaries. Their careers came to embody some of the "riddles" of foreign missionaries in Japan.

As far as church-to-church relationships were concerned, Japanese and overseas Catholics had continued to keep in touch during the Pacific War through the Apostolic Delegate for the Vatican. Monsignor Paolo Marella remained in that post from 1933 through 1949, although his effectiveness in the postwar era is a matter of some dispute. Some Catholic missionaries from Germany and Italy, countries allied with Japan, and from neutral nations such as Switzerland, were able to stay on in Japan during the war, although under straitened circumstances. Some of those in rural areas who were cut off from overseas funds established kindergartens to support themselves, and this pattern was continued and expanded in the postwar period by many Christian groups. Father Patrick J. Byrne, the Maryknoll priest already mentioned, who had been interned in Kyoto throughout the war, was among the Catholic missionaries who had conferences with General MacArthur and reported in December 1945 that the general had told him that Catholicism had a special attraction for the Japanese people because of its solemn ceremonies.[10]

In the meantime, Protestants in Japan and overseas had gone much further toward reestablishing their contacts as a consequence of the visit in October and November 1945 of four men who represented the Foreign Mission Conference of North America and the National Council of Churches in the U.S.A.[11] The members of this "deputation of four" had all participated in a meeting with eight Japanese Christian leaders in Riverside, California, not long before the outbreak of war in 1941; and in a radio broadcast from Tokyo in September 1945 the Reverend Tsunetarō Miyakoda, the former general secretary of the National Christian Council in Japan, referred to the Riverside meeting and expressed the hope that the visit might be returned. When the group went to Japan the following month, they were the first foreigners after the war to arrive in the country in civilian dress.[12] The deputation met with leaders of the Kyōdan, with other Japanese Christians, and with people of all sorts during their visit. When they asked about the return of missionaries, the responses varied. A minister in the Kansai was quoted as saying, "It would be an excellent thing if a great number of missionaries could be sent out for rural work; a thousand missionaries in the next twenty years are needed." But a Kyoto pastor remarked, "For the present, it would be better for the missionaries not to come. Rather, send ambassadors of friendship, and food for the people of Japan." A Christian educator commented, "We all agree in welcoming the missionaries, but I doubt that the church in this country is ready to receive them. The church is disorganized, and it is not united enough to develop a missionary policy."[13] As a result of these differences of opinion, the deputation's report recommended that the American churches should send relief supplies, hymnals, and Bibles, but that they should only *study* the return of missionaries. The ambivalence toward missionaries expressed by these three persons interviewed was to persist in various forms over the next three decades, as part of the "missionary riddle."

Nevertheless, the reservations about the return of missionaries to postwar Japan were not to prevent their actual return, which resumed from 1946. A "commission of six" was formed to represent the boards of North American Protestant groups. Unlike the "deputation of four," where only one member had had missionary experience in Japan, all six members of the new commission were former Japan missionaries.[14] Serving through 1949, this group was to establish procedures for missionaries coming to Japan, to handle relief work, and to enter into liaison with SCAP, the churches, schools, women's groups, and the like.[15] They helped to make arrangements for visits by numerous individuals and groups, and from some of these visits came programs which were to have significant influence in postwar Japan. For instance, the development of Christian audio-visual and mass-communications work was a direct outgrowth of a deputation of three American audio-visual experts who arrived in Japan in February 1949.[16]

Partly through the work of the "commission of six," missionaries began arriving back in Japan. At first, because of SCAP regulations, only those were allowed to enter Japan who had some qualifications in the Japanese language and who were able to bring their own food provisions with them. The Protestant missionaries who returned found that Japan's Protestants were not of one mind as to what should be done about the Kyōdan, which had been formed in 1941 largely due to governmental pressures resulting from the enactment of the Religious Organizations Law of 1940, quite apart from whatever ecumenical hopes may have been cherished from the past. As originally constituted, the Kyōdan was a federation of denominations which kept their denominational identity through eleven "blocs" in the united church. The bloc system was officially dissolved within the first year of the Kyōdan's existence, however, upon Director Tomita's insistence that this system was inconvenient for the government's purpose of integrating religious groups in order to serve the nation's war efforts.[17] After the war, a number of these denominational groups began to meet together again to revive their fellowship and to reestablish their relations with overseas mission boards.

This in turn led to withdrawals from the Kyōdan of groups that had unwillingly joined the union church in the first place. Other groups resolved to leave when the Kyōdan decided in the postwar period to reorganize as a church united by choice, and not as a federation of denominations or a church united by governmental pressure.

The first group to withdraw from the Kyōdan was the Anglican Church of Japan (Nihon Seikōkai) in 1946 (many of the Seikōkai churches had never joined the Kyōdan in the first place); and they were followed by the Salvation Army and the Reformed Church in the same year; the Holiness groups, the Baptist Convention, Baputesuto Renmei (related to the Southern Baptist Convention in the U.S.A.), and the Lutheran Church in 1947; the Church of Christ in Japan (the Presbyterian-type Shin Nikki group) in 1951; the Baptist Union (Baputesuto Dōmei, related to the American Baptist Convention) in 1958; and various other smaller groups.[18]

The withdrawals of some denominational groups from the Kyōdan naturally had quite an impact on the work of the returning Protestant missionaries. In most cases, the missionaries related to these groups were very sensitive to the problems involved and had no desire to put pressure on the Japanese Christians to withdraw from the Kyōdan or to remain in it. What Paul Huddle has written about the Lutherans seems a fair description of what happened in most groups that withdrew:

It should be recorded that this decision to withdraw from the Kyōdan was purely Japanese, for as yet only a couple of missionaries had returned to the field, and the Board [of Foreign Missions of the United Lutheran Church in America] had purposely refrained from advising on the course to be followed, leaving the decision to the Japanese brethren. When Miller [Dr. L. S. G. Miller, the first Lutheran missionary to return to Japan, in August 1946] returned to America to retire in 1952, he reported on this action as follows: "Our Lutheran Church in Japan withdrew from the Kyōdan on their own initiative. We purposely refrained from giving them any comment or direction."[19]

Huddle added this important qualification, which was also a crucial factor in withdrawal decisions: "Yet it should also be stated that, in direct questions from the Japanese leaders, the Board had answered that the U.L.C.A. would view favorably their effort to reestablish the Lutheran Church in Japan and would give all possible financial aid."[20]

Despite the withdrawals from the Kyōdan, there were those in that church who sincerely wanted it to continue as a united Protestant church. Indeed, after all the withdrawals had taken place, the Kyōdan still contained about one-half of Japan's Protestants. The missionaries from the North American churches that were related to the groups still in the Kyōdan were—with only a few exceptions—eager to do what they could to maintain that church's unity through their own personal work and also through the policies of their mission boards. The organizational arrangements by which the work of the missionaries and the Japanese churches and other groups were to be coordinated will be discussed presently, but before any framework of organization was possible, the way had to be prepared by the personal attitudes and actions of the missionaries and the sympathetic concern of their mission boards. Dr. Tomio Mutō, quoted at the beginning of this chapter, once commented that the preservation of the Kyōdan's unity in the postwar period was made possible in part by the support of the mission boards and their missionaries. The boards were already experimenting with sending different types of missionaries, as for instance the "J-3's," generally college graduates on three year appointments, who did such effective work that many of them came back for longer assignments. Thus missionaries both old and new came to make their contributions to the Kyōdan's unity and renewal.

The return of Catholic missionaries was made possible by decisions which the Japanese Catholic hierarchy made in November 1945 and January 1946 about the postwar rehabilitation of the church. At the later meeting a committee was formed which invited the hierarchies of the United States and Australia to help with the special needs of Japan with personnel and resources. The bishops of Australia in 1947 lent fourteen of their diocesan priests to be attached for a term of five years to the dioceses of Japan, thus earning the name of "the five-year group" (*gonengumi*).[21] Father Joseph Van Hecken also records that ten religious institutes of Europe and America began to send missionaries to Japan in 1948. And then in 1949, when missionaries both Protestant and Catholic were expelled from China after the victory of the Chinese Communists, many of them were relocated in Japan.[22]

It is important to note that proportionately more of the Roman Catholic foreign missionary priests who came to Japan were able in a relatively short time to serve local Japanese parishes than was the case with their Protestant counterparts. To be sure, Catholic missionary priests often acquired greater fluency in the Japanese language, but there were theological reasons as well for their adaptability. Roman Catholic doctrines of the church and sacraments made it easier for a foreigner to serve a local parish, since the sacraments were seen as valid when performed by any properly ordained priest of any nationality. Protestant churches placed greater emphasis on the spoken word in worship, especially through sermons, and therefore required a level of linguistic competence which comparatively fewer missionaries possessed.

With the passage of time, the dependence of the Japanese Catholic bishops on missionary priests to serve their local parishes remained so high that it constituted a major problem for the indigenization of the church. In 1973 missionary priests still comprised 60 percent of the total number of Catholic priests in Japan, even though missionary sisters were by that time only 13.1 percent of all the sisters.[23] A major reason for the large proportion of missionary priests has been the shortage of Japanese candidates for the priesthood. This factor is closely related to the requirement for a celibate priesthood. Family anxiety over daughters' becoming missionary sisters has been far less, and the number of Japanese sisters has remained quite high. In spite of the chronic shortage of priests, the Japanese hierarchy has thus far been reluctant to establish a system of deacons, such as Vatican Council II provided for, partly due to the conservative and traditional outlook of most of the hierarchy.

The role of overseas personnel in the Orthodox Church of Japan was complicated in the postwar period by international tensions. Bishop Nicolai, a Japanese Orthodox bishop who had been a protopriest and was consecrated in Harbin in 1941, worked through a national synod meeting on April 3, 1946, to restore relations with the patriarchate of Moscow, which had been tenuous ever since the 1917 Russian Revolution. In fact, a synod of the Japanese Orthodox Church in 1940 had unilaterally renounced its relations with the Moscow patriarchate.[24] Bishop Nicolai's efforts in 1946 were resisted by a large part of the Orthodox church, and on April 5, 1946, an archpriest convened a new national synod, which elected him as its presiding priest. The situation of the Orthodox church during the Occupation era was made difficult by the efforts of the Soviet diplomatic corps in Tokyo to control the church headquarters and by the countervailing efforts of SCAP personnel to bring it under American influence. Indirect SCAP influence is said to have led in July 1946 to the decision of a synod which requested through SCAP that the synod of the North American bishops appoint a bishop for the Orthodox Church in Japan. In October 1946 the Orthodox Metropolitan of New York assumed jurisdiction over the Japanese Orthodox Church, and as a result a series of American bishops served the church in Japan from 1947 until 1969. After the last American bishop was replaced by a Japanese bishop, there were still two Orthodox churches in Japan which had not yet reconciled their differences in toto. The Orthodox churches in Japan have been unique, therefore, in that due to postwar political circumstances, foreign personnel have held posts at the head of the church rather than at the local level, the reverse of the ordinary Catholic and Protestant patterns.

Five Major Patterns of Japanese Christians' Relationships with Overseas Mission Groups

After the foreign missionaries had begun to return to Japan, restoring the ties between Japanese Christian groups and the overseas mission agencies, it was evident to all that the new relationships had to be regularized in some way. Even during the period of postwar privation in Japanese society, when missionaries often played a much greater role than at other times, the "missionary riddle" was never wholly out of sight. For it was not simply the ecclesiastical or organizational role of the missionary in Japan that was in question. Missionaries were symbols of the types of relationships being formed between Japanese Christian groups and overseas, for they stood at the point of intersection between the two. Quite apart from the individual personality or work of the missionary concerned, it was often his or her very presence that confronted all concerned with a riddle that brought forth all sorts of attempted answers.

Of the various relationships which evolved, five major patterns will be examined here. There were of course interesting variations of these main types, but by focusing on the predominant patterns, the issues can be put into clearer perspective.

The Predominant Roman Catholic Pattern: Diocesan Contracts

Until 1940 each major Roman Catholic foreign missionary order had its own bishop, who supervised the work of his order's members throughout Japan. But in 1940–41, due to the pressures of the Religious Organizations Law, all of the missionary bishops resigned and were replaced by Japanese "ordinaries," or bishops exercising original jurisdiction over a particular area. These Japanese bishops were all "secular" clergy, that is, they were related to the service of local parish churches and were not members of religious orders or congregations, such as the Jesuits, Franciscans, and Dominicans. In the postwar period, however, with the return of the missionary orders to Japan in large numbers, the question arose as to how these missionaries were to be related to the Japanese ordinaries, since the former system of episcopal jurisdiction was no longer in operation. Here the way was opened by the example of Monsignor Jean Alexis Chambon, who had formerly been bishop of Yokohama, and subsequently the superior of the Société des Missions Étrangéres de Paris (M.E.P., the Paris Foreign Mission Society). It is significant that it was the M.E.P. which had pioneered in the reestablishment of Catholic missions in Japan in the nineteenth century, with a virtual monopoly on Catholic mission work in Japan until 1904.[25] In the postwar era Monsignor Chambon drew up a contract of cooperation between his mission society and the bishop of Yokohama, on behalf of the M.E.P. missionaries working in that diocese. After approval by the apostolic delegate, Monsignor Marella, the contract was signed on December 10, 1947.[26] This was the first such contract, and it served as a model for virtually all the Catholic orders to follow. Although these contracts varied somewhat in content, they generally provided for the bishop to entrust a specific area or particular parishes to the care of the mission society, which supported and supervised the work of the missionaries assigned there for a specified number of years; and for all parish properties to be registered as belonging to the diocese and to revert to the diocese after the expiration of the contract.[27]

Such diocesan contracts became the major pattern for handling relations between the missionary orders and the Japanese ordinaries. To be sure, the contracts were amended periodically. Also, the contracts were not entirely original, for they embodied among other things older instructions such as those of the Sacred Congregation for the Propagation of the Faith (generally known by its Latin name of "Propaganda") dating back to December 8, 1929. It may also be noted that the contracts had secular counterparts, which were rather well understood in the postwar period. For instance, "joint ventures" in business in Japan were established by contracts between Japanese firms and overseas partners, in which each party was assigned certain responsibilities and certain privileges. Even though such secular joint-venture contracts were on the horizon in Japan in 1947, it is hard to say how much they specifically influenced the drawing up of the ecclesiastical agreements, or vice versa. In general, the diocesan contracts proved to be suitable instruments for relating the resources and needs of the groups involved in ways that provided for a balance between individual initiative and mutual responsibility. There was respect for both the past traditions and the current realities of each side.

The Predominant Protestant Pattern: Councils of Cooperation

As Protestant groups were less hierarchically organized and their relationships much less susceptible to precise definition, the predominant pattern was a "council of cooperation," such as that established by the Kyōdan, Christian schools, social work agencies, and related American mission boards. Building on the work of the "commission of six," representatives of eight Protestant churches in North America, with prewar ties to Japanese Christian groups now united in the Kyōdan, met in New York on January 9, 1947, to form a consultative structure for coordinating their work with each other and with the Kyōdan.[28] It soon became clear that the new structure would also have to relate to those Christian schools and social work agencies in Japan with which the mission boards had historic ties and were already working on problems of postwar reconstruction. The first step, then, was to coordinate the activities of the mission boards, through an Interboard Committee for Christian Work in Japan (IBC). In Japan a Council of Cooperation (CoC) was established to embrace the Kyōdan, a council of Christian schools, a federation of social work agencies, and the IBC. The CoC was to coordinate the activities of these autonomous bodies, and it did so to a remarkable extent. In 1975 the CoC's acting general secretary, the Reverend Yoichirō Saeki, looked back on the council's work since its founding in 1948:

During these twenty-seven years more than 1,100 missionaries and 8 billion yen have been sent to Japan from the North American churches through the CoC. If the cost of missionary salaries, travel and other expenses are added, the sum would come close to 20 billion yen.[29]

There were of course problems with the council-of-cooperation pattern. The North American side complained that church-to-church relationships were more difficult when filtered through such a council, while the Japanese side criticized the council's "one-way street" of personnel and programs from North America to Japan with very little moving in the opposite direction.[30] In time there would be adjustments in the pattern, and other channels between

Japan and overseas would be established, formally or informally, when the CoC's channel seemed unworkable. In retrospect it is interesting to note that the Protestant council-of-cooperation pattern was designed to embody many of the same principles that the Roman Catholic diocesan contracts provided for. Both patterns sought to recognize the common purpose and full autonomy of the Japanese and overseas partners, to assign mutual responsibilities in acceptable ways, and to provide methods for making adjustments when they were deemed necessary. It is interesting to note that, despite such parallel motivations, there does not seem to have been any consultation between Protestants and Catholics while these two patterns of relationships were being established.

An Alternative Protestant Pattern: Church Committees for Liaison

Still another method for relating the work of Protestant missionaries to the work of the Japanese Christian community has been church committees for liaison. Perhaps the best example of this pattern is to be found in the relations between the Japan Baptist Convention (Nihon Baputesuto Renmei) and the Japan Mission of the Foreign Mission Board of the Southern Baptist Convention. The Japan Baptist Convention reorganized itself after withdrawing from the Kyōdan in April 1947 and immediately set itself up as a national church, even though most of its members at that time were in the Kyūshū area. This was done at the time in order to help to keep in touch with members who moved away from Kyūshū to other parts of Japan, and it had the important consequence of doing away with a prewar "comity agreement" with the American Baptists, whereby the nation was divided into spheres of respective work.[31] The Southern Baptist missionaries' Japan Mission was reorganized the following year, and although letters were exchanged between mission board personnel and Japanese Baptist leaders, there is said to be no evidence of any written statement of formal agreement between the two groups.[32] It was decided that missionaries would relate to the Japanese church by being elected by the Japan Mission to serve as nonvoting liaison members on each convention committee. The only stipulation of this relationship was that "requests to the Board in America for funds had to be channeled through the Mission, and that funds granted had to be used as designated."[33] This system, like the two systems above, made it possible for missionaries to serve in a wide variety of capacities in the Japanese churches and their related institutions. Similar patterns of cooperation, with modifications, were worked out by Lutherans, Anglicans, American Baptists, and others.[34]

Proponents of the liaison-committee pattern of mission-church relationships point out that it affirmed the autonomy of the Japanese churches and institutions without setting up any special consultative arrangements. Critics have maintained that it led first to increased missionary influence on the Japanese church through representatives on the liaison and financial committees, and later to the stultification of missionary initiatives for independent work. Yet, as was the case with the other two patterns, it was possible to make adjustments when the need came for a clearer recognition of Japanese "selfhood" by all concerned.

The New Conservative Protestants' Pattern: Independent Missions

From the Occupation period on new groups were exercising a growing influence on mission in Japan, and they were for the most part unrelated to prewar Christian work. Some groups like the Navigators, the Evangelical Alliance Mission (TEAM), New Tribes, and the Far Eastern Gospel Crusade had their beginnings in part among SCAP personnel who caught a vision of the meaning of evangelism in Japan and wanted to carry it out after the conclusion of their military service. Finding that many of the existing mission boards were unable to send them back to Japan, they decided to establish their own mission sending agencies, which relied on freewill offerings from overseas Christians. Their basic theological stance was generally quite conservative, often reflecting a fundamentalist approach to scriptural interpretation and the work of mission. As devoted Christians, whether lay or ordained, they were eager to make a Christian witness apart from the established Japanese denominations. There was much work to be done, as the entire Christian community in Japan was a small percentage of the total population. In many cases, these missionaries tended to be strongly anti-Communist and were unable to work comfortably with Japanese Christians and other missionaries who seemed insufficiently aware of the threats which they felt that Communism, in theory and in practice, posed toward the Christian faith. Such anti-Communist attitudes were strengthened when, after the expulsion of missionaries from China following the victory of the Chinese Communists in 1949, numbers of conservative Protestant missionaries were relocated in Japan. The outbreak of the Korean War in 1950 brought a few more missionaries, but more importantly, it heightened the sense of apocalypticism among many mission groups at that time, causing some to feel that the time was approaching for the final conflict between earnest Christians and the demonic adversary.

The circumstances under which the more recent conservative missionary influx occurred made it both possible and necessary that they start at the beginning, with minimal relations to other established Christian groups. The missionaries were generally eager to engage in direct personal evangelism, and they had little patience with the vast expenditures of time by other mission groups in consultations with Japanese colleagues. The newer groups were generally suspicious of alleged theological liberalism among established Protestant churches and missions, both in Japan and overseas, and they sought to remedy the situation by emphasizing what they held was a return to the original Christian gospel. When the mission gro ps with prewar histories reestablished the Fellowship of Christian Missionaries (FCM) in the postwar period and began to publish again the *Japan Christian Quarterly,* the newer conservative groups took the lead in forming their own fellowship—first known as the Evangelical Missions Association of Japan (EMAJ) and, after a number of changes, renamed the Japan Evangelical Missionary Association (JEMA)—and founded their own publication, *The Japan Harvest*. The influx of newer conservative groups was so great that they soon outnumbered the mainline missionaries in Japan.

The principal pattern of work relationships that the conservatives established was that of independent missions which operated very much as have most missionaries in the beginnings of their work in a new area. The mission organization was the basic entity; it supervised the missionaries, administered budgets, and established its principles of operation. Wherever possible, the missionaries worked with Japanese churches and institutions that shared their denominational or confessional background.[35] Where new churches came into being as a result of their mission efforts, the major pattern was to "turn over" the work to independent Japanese groups when it was expedient. Melvin Gingerich's description of the process for Mennonites would fit most of the conservative Protestant groups:

All of the Mennonite missions in Japan are turning over congregational responsibilities to the Japanese members of their churches with the objective of eventually withdrawing their direction and support. Not only are large numbers of young people in these churches engaged in Sunday school and Summer Bible School teaching, but others also help direct the tent evangelistic campaigns, the short term Bible schools, and the summer camps. Each of the three larger groups has a Japanese pastor working with the missionaries, several congregations have Japanese pastors, and a number of others will soon be selecting their own pastors, although none of the churches are more than five years old. Students from each group are in Bible schools and seminaries preparing for leadership in their congregations. Church members' meetings, church councils, and annual church conferences, although attended by missionaries, are constantly moving in the direction of local control. The churches are encouraged to raise their own building funds, with the mission boards in no case supplying more than half of the construction costs. One missionary summarizes: "We are confident that as God blesses the work during the next five years, our hope of sharing vitally in the building of the indigenous church in this part of the Lord's vineyard will be more fully realized.[36]

There was a tendency among ecumenically minded Protestants to assume that the new conservative Protestant groups would simply repeat the patterns of the older groups as they became established for a longer period in Japan. This has been true to some extent in the 1950s—70s decades, for in the late 1960s conservatives began to face some of the same problems of "selfhood" which other groups experienced. Nevertheless, newer groups have been able to learn from the experiences of others and to meet the challenges of later historical developments differently, and thus they have been able to develop in unexpected ways. It would be a mistake to assume that the different patterns of relationships described here must necessarily be experienced in some sort of linear progression.

Japanese Christians without Direct Overseas Relationships

Since this chapter deals with missionaries, it will not describe at length the Christian groups that carry on in Japan without any missionaries at all, except to record the very important fact of their existence.

In historical sequence, mention should first be made of the Hidden Christians *(Kakure Kirishitan)*, several thousands in number, who live mainly in Kyūshū and nearby islands, but are also found in scattered places throughout Japan. They are descendants of the people converted to Catholicism by Jesuits and others during "the Christian Century" (1549—1638) and who subsequently maintained their faith in secret without any contacts with overseas Christians. After the return of the Catholic missionaries in 1859, the great majority of the Hidden Christians rejoined the Catholic church, but a minority refused to do so and have continued to practice their faith independently. To what extent their faith at the present time represents a syncretistic combination of Christian and other elements is a question that goes far beyond the scope of this chapter. It is enough to note that such a group continues to maintain its faith despite separation from foreign contacts for nearly three and a half centuries.[37]

It should also be recalled that the Non-Church Christianity (Mukyōkai) of Kanzō Uchimura (1861—1930) and his followers have left its impact on modern times. In postwar Japan, as indicated elsewhere throughout this study, Non-Church Christians have played significant roles in the nation's Christian community and also on the world scene. Although Non-Church Christians have many missionary friends, they do not on principle have any formal relationships with overseas mission bodies. The same is true for an offshoot of Mukyōkai, the Primitive Gospel Movement (Genshi Fukuin Undō), established by Ikurō Teshima (1910–73).

A number of Japanese Protestant denominations declined to have related missionaries, in order to maintain their independence. The largest is the Spirit of Jesus Church, founded by the Reverend Izuru Murai, of Pentecostal background. It will also be recalled that the Church of Christ in Japan (Nihon Kirisuto Kyōkai, nicknamed the "New Church of Christ," or Shin Nikki, because they continued to use the prewar name of their parent Presbyterian denomination) withdrew from the Kyōdan in 1951, in part to underscore their insistence on the total independence of the church.

Although these various Christian groups have declined to have formal relations with missionaries and mission agencies for different reasons, the result is the same. Doubtless such groups serve as standing challenges to the doctrines which some Christians maintain for the church, or for mission. Indeed, that may be part of their contribution to a deepened understanding of the "missionary riddle."

The Five Patterns in Theory and in Practice

An attentive reader who has followed this review of the five patterns of relationships may feel that this whole section was superfluous. Such a reader would share, in regard to questions of church government, the sentiments of Alexander Pope's couplet about civil government:

For forms of government let fools contest;
Whate'er is best administer'd is best.[38]

While it is true that some Christians did spend inordinate amounts of time during Japan's 1950s—70s era discussing such topics as "the role of the missionary," the question of proper relationships cannot be altogether avoided. Good administration may be stymied at every turn by poor structures. If patterns of relationships are not suitable, one finds oneself tripping over them all the time, and becoming distracted from more important tasks. It must be recognized that "the missionary riddle" in postwar Japan affected not only a few foreigners, but also was a reflection of the churches' understanding of their very nature and task in the world. The missionary was at times only the symbol of something else, or in Plato's metaphor, the ceiling of the cave on which other realities were projected. The symbols should therefore be examined first, in order to discern the realities that lie behind them.

If the patterns of mission relationships are in some ways important, it is worthwhile to see what the record of the postwar decades in Japan shows.

It was pointed out that the principles behind the Roman Catholic diocesan contracts and the Protestant councils of cooperation were strikingly similar, given the different polity and historical circumstances of the churches concerned. They were very similar responses to essentially the same historical challenges. Yet the two patterns are not interchangeable. After Vatican Council II, when Catholics began to get their dose of cooperative councils, and Protestants were faced with ecclesiastical contracts, it became clear that groups generally prefer to operate according to their own historical dynamics.

It was also noted in passing that the three major Protestant patterns— councils of cooperation, church committees for liaison, and independent missions—bore striking similarities to each other not only in structure, but also in actual practice. Yet again, it should not be assumed that these patterns are like interchangeable cogs in a machine. Worse yet, one should not conclude that they are three linear stages, which all groups must necessarily experience one after another, in the same order. The different patterns represent different perceptions or convictions of what and where the church is, in relation to its mission. The nuances of the patterns are by no means the same, and a careful observer should be aware of their differences and similarities.

Some readers may feel that a number of important patterns of relationships have been omitted from this analysis. They are quite right, but there are reasons for the omissions. For instance, one of the most significant omissions is the pattern whereby the Japanese church is an integral unit of a world organization, which has a headquarters abroad that issues all the important commands. Such is supposed to be the pattern of the Seventh-day Adventist churches in Japan, the Latter-Day Saints (Mormons), the Christian Scientists, the Salvation Army, and perhaps even the Roman Catholic churches. But, because of distances from the homeland—which in modern times are more psychological than geographical—such patterns generally have in actual practice been modified in Japan to operate like one of the five described above.

Finally, it has been suggested that Christian groups with no missionaries or formal overseas contacts are apt to pose a challenge to some Christians' concepts of church and mission. For that matter, they may also be a comfort to those who feel that all missionary work is abominable proselytization. Either way, it must be recognized that even though these groups may have developed in past history through dialogue with, or in reaction against, foreign missionaries, the fact is that at present they seek to do without them. However varied their reasons for rejecting missionaries and overseas ties, the fifth group is a necessary complement to the other four.

Bearing in mind such patterns of relationships for mission groups, we turn to the tasks that missionaries performed.

The Changing Roles of Foreign Missionaries in Japan

Missionaries arriving in postwar Japan generally received some orientation before proceeding to their work assignments. For those who engaged in intensive study of the Japanese language, two years of language study came to be standard, and hence the orientation process took much longer in Japan than in most parts of the world.

Orientation for Missionaries

As previously mentioned, the first missionaries to return to Japan in the postwar period had to possess some Japanese language skills and orientation before they were allowed to come. But soon newer missionaries began arriving who had no previous experience of Japan, and their orientation was at first necessarily sketchy. Both their older missionary colleagues and their Japanese co-workers were apt to be too busy to provide a carefully programmed orientation. Formalized Japanese language study had to await the organization of Japanese language schools, which several mission agencies were instrumental in establishing within a few years. In addition to language study, the process of orientation to Japanese culture and church situations was at first generally carried out for missionaries of each denomination by senior missionary colleagues. In time Japanese Christian leaders came to take on more responsibility for the orientation of new missionaries and also to share in making their work assignments.

A certain amount of mystique generally surrounded the missionary's first work assignment. He or she may have been recruited by a personnel secretary of an overseas mission agency on the basis of a "job description" of some sort. But after two years of intensive language training, quite a different picture may have emerged of the kind of work that the individual was suited for, and meanwhile the old "job description" might have been altered beyond recognition in the fast-changing society of postwar Japan.

Missionaries in Education

A most common first assignment for missionaries was to become a teacher, most likely in one of their denomination's Christian schools. Openings for teachers in postwar Japan's Christian schools were readily available; in some cases they were the first assignments open for missionaries and the easiest for foreigners to fit into, even without skill in the Japanese language. Especially with the education boom in postwar Japan, there were almost always places for foreign missionaries in the rapidly expanding school system, provided he or she was willing to teach a foreign language, in most cases English. School contacts could lead to private instruction or to English Bible classes, English-language camps, or other church-related activities. In time, as the missionary's language skills increased, it would be possible to teach other subjects in the Japanese language. There were of course many frustrations involved for missionaries with unusual or creative gifts but cramped by the demands of the classroom. Nevertheless, given the broad need for teachers of all sorts, there were in time varieties of teaching situations that would appeal to persons with different talents. And since every missionary remained to some degree a teacher throughout his or her period of service in Japan—and was generally called *sensei*, "teacher"—whatever teaching experiences one gained could generally be put to good use later on.

As the years went by, the roles of missionaries in education changed far less than in many other fields. To some extent, missionary teachers were overtaken by the demands for professionalization and specialization that affect all educators, but they found it easier to "opt out" of these demands than did their Japanese colleagues. Some missionaries developed a lifelong "love affair" with teaching, while others moved on to other tasks for which they had the necessary skills and Japanese language proficiency, though often keeping a part-time teaching assignment somewhere. Some missionaries became school administrators, an increasingly difficult role to handle after increasing financial stringencies followed by school struggles settled on the schools in the 1960s. Foreigners as such were rarely targets of radical students' attacks, but administrators were. For their part, the Christian schools were grateful for the missionaries' services, for with all their quirks the missionaries generally were hard-working and dependable. As the numbers of long-term missionaries dwindled, due to inflated costs and decreased mission giving, the schools were among the first places where new missionary service could be tried out, such as short-term contract teachers, "Volunteers in Mission" who covered many of their own expenses, and "frontier interns" on new and unconventional assignments. The Christian schools were also among the first to offer to provide "Shared Support" funds for missionaries, when their overseas support started to shrink. This, of course, meant that the missionaries no longer served as the representatives of overseas boards which provided funds for the schools but were now increasingly the recipients of the schools' favors and consequently excluded from their decision-making processes. Yet with all their problems, the roles of missionaries in education remained significant throughout the three postwar decades, bringing both missionaries and the schools a large measure of satisfaction.

Missionaries as Pastors and Evangelists

Missionaries who had the background and the willingness were sometimes assigned as pastors and evangelists, and the two roles were often very closely combined. The chronic shortage of Japanese priests for local parishes, both to found them and to staff them, has already been pointed out. Some conservative Protestant groups have seen their task in Japan primarily as that of founding new churches, which after reaching a certain size and strength were to be "turned over" to Japanese pastors, if indeed such could be found. In some cases new churches were founded by a missionary and a Japanese evangelist working together, thus speeding the eventual transition process. Transition from a missionary to a Japanese pastor has not always been smooth, however, because the work of a missionary evangelist sometimes seemed exotic to the parishioners and thus a "hard act to follow," as Japanese pastors who have undertaken such assignments have indicated. In the immediate postwar period, at the time of the Christian boom and even afterward, the process of founding new churches was seemingly easier than later when the skyrocketing prices of land and building materials required a much greater capital outlay. Serious questions were raised as to whether or not founding new churches in such a way was the best use of the personnel and resources of Japan's miniscule Christian community. Neil Braun, writing from the background of Donald McGavran's Church Growth Institute at Fuller Theological Seminary in Pasadena, California, has pointed out that the pattern of providing church buildings with resident paid pastors is not a feasible way to meet the evangelistic and pastoral needs of a country such as Japan.[39] Braun's appeals for a "laity mobilized" for evangelism rather than paid pastors, and for "house meetings" rather than church buildings, raise great expectations. Yet the experience of Japanese Christians of many backgrounds indicates that it has been extremely difficult for Christians to operate effectively in Japanese society without some minimal facilities. Even though the resolution of this problem goes far beyond the scope of this chapter, it should be noted that missionaries working as evangelists in postwar Japan were deeply affected by the issues involved.

The evangelistic work of missionaries must also be seen in connection with the evangelistic "strategies" that the various churches developed. In prewar Japan many Protestant groups had "comity" arrangements by which the nation was divided into territories for each denomination. As we have seen, Catholic groups both before and after the war had their own "comity" arrangements on a diocesan basis. But after the war, although smaller Protestant groups devised certain comity plans, the larger Protestant denominations became organized on a nationwide basis. As already mentioned, the Japan Baptist Convention took all Japan as its postwar mission field. Their plan was to place a Japanese evangelistic couple and a missionary couple in each of the country's forty-six prefectures. "The Japan Baptist Convention accomplished its part of the plan by 1960," wrote Calvin Parker, "but the Mission faltered at the half-way mark, largely because of the problem of children's schooling in the remote areas. Where this strategy was carried out, it proved effective. Missionaries and nationals working together developed churches faster than either party working separately."[40]

Roman Catholic and Protestant groups were both attracted in the immediate postwar period to widespread evangelistic work across Japan, and this meant establishing churches in rural areas where none had existed before. Father Joseph J. Spae has indicated some of the reasons why Catholic missionaries were drawn to such rural work. There was the desire to seize any opportunity to establish the church in every place, he recalled, and missionaries were often drawn to this because they were from rural areas themselves and felt more at home in such work than in the cities. Furthermore, there were appeals for help from rural residents, and it seemed that immediate success would crown the missionaries' evangelistic efforts, for cheaper land in rural areas meant it was easier to plant a church there than in the cities. And in addition, the missionaries reasoned that since so many churches were already established in the cities, and since rural evangelism had encountered increasing difficulties in the later Meiji era, this might be the right time to try again.[41] Similar views were held by Kyōdan missionaries, and a Rural Training Institute was established, initially at Hino in Tokyo's western suburbs and then moved to Tsurukawa, to prepare laity and pastors for the expected new opportunities in rural evangelism.

But the momentous boom in rural evangelism, with only a few exceptions, never came. Soon many of the small churches that had been planted in rural areas were struggling for their very survival. What had gone wrong? In the first place, as a result of conscious government policies and also of economic pressures, Japan from the 1950s saw an enormous internal migration of its population, involving perhaps some 40 million people who moved from agricultural areas into the cities. This was not an accidental or an unpredictable phenomenon. On the contrary, it was actively sponsored and encouraged by the government and anticipated by sociologists and demographic experts. Yet the Christian groups that were doing evangelistic planning, and the foreign missionaries involved in its execution, failed to take into account these developments. It was as if the churches were rushing out from the cities to the rural areas to meet the people who at the very time were rushing into the cities. There were also other factors. As for foreign missionaries, the rural areas might have been very desirable places to live, but the loneliness and isolation for missionary children and the difficulties of providing children's education made it hard for missionary families to remain away from the cities. And for those who did stay, it became all the more obvious that urban and rural mission were simply two sides of the same coin, for there has always been a close symbiotic relationship between rural areas and cities in Japanese history. No strategy for rural evangelism was adequate unless it embraced the urban scene as well.

What, then, of missionaries in urban evangelism? To begin with, we need to recall that few Protestant missionaries were involved as pastors of urban churches; Japanese pastors usually held such posts. Missionaries tended to serve in suburban areas, using "new church development" programs, which were then being widely practiced in the United States and elsewhere. In the planning and construction of massive "newtowns" of the 1960s, Protestant missionaries became active in helping to establish kindergartens, home churches, and local churches in these newly created urban housing clusters. Others served churches in smaller towns, which gradually became parts of expanding metropolitan areas. A few became active in programs known in the 1950s as Occupational Evangelism, as Urban Industrial Mission in the 1960s, and as Urban Rural Mission in the 1970s, a sequence of terms indicating the expanding understanding of the scope of mission in and to society. Ecumenical ties with the East Asia Christian Conference (later the Christian Conference of Asia) and the World Council of Churches helped to further common endeavors in the urban work of Protestants in Japan, even though by the 1970s there were only a few Protestant missionaries involved in this area.

Roman Catholic missionaries, on the other hand, became deeply involved in the planting of churches in urban areas in the immediate postwar era and, as noted earlier, in serving them afterward as parish priests. Given its hierarchical nature, the Catholic church could organize churches and assign personnel with more efficiency than could Protestants. For instance, in the Tokyo suburb of Kichijōji there is one Catholic church which serves a parish of equal size with about twice as many parishioners as that served by over twenty Protestant churches in the same area. Catholic missionaries have also been involved in a wide variety of urban centers and chaplaincies for students, workers, handicapped, and other specialized groups. By the time Vatican Council II placed additional requirements for worship services and preaching in the vernacular, the linguistic skills of the missionaries had become sufficiently developed, and there were enough language schools which were able to give adequate training for the tasks involved.

Yet, considered as a whole, the urban evangelistic and pastoral work of the Christian missionaries in Japan was an almost constantly uphill struggle in the postwar era. The urban growth of the New Religions in postwar Japan makes the Christian churches pale by comparison, and the indigenous sects had grown most often under lay leadership. Nevertheless, the missionaries laid foundations in urban work in such areas as studies of urban sociology and community organization, the significance of which the future will judge.

Missionaries in Social Work

Postwar Japan also saw many opportunities for missionaries in social work. While this refers first of all to missionaries who had special skills in group work, counseling, rehabilitation, and the like, it also embraces hospital workers and nurses, which has been a large field especially for the Roman Catholic nursing orders. With the development of an enlarged welfare system in postwar Japan (see chap. 4, "Christians and Social Work"), Christian missionaries were able to build on a long and pioneering tradition of Christian contributions in this field, dating from the Meiji era.[42] The difficulty, of course, was that no matter how highly qualified in social work skills, missionaries who lacked a thorough knowledge of the Japanese language and culture were severely handicapped in their effectiveness, and after starting work would move on to other fields. But for the qualified, areas of effective work opened up.

Missionaries in Administrative Work

A fourth major category of missionary service is administrative work. This began with the mission societies themselves, for each foreign mission group in Japan needed a number of administrators to handle such affairs as taxes, property acquisition and maintenance, legal juridical persons, finances, and so forth. If there were only two missionaries in one mission, one of them had to devote a considerable portion of his or her time to such administrative duties. The administrators' contributions were invaluable, as IBC missionaries who knew Dr. Darley Downs, and Catholics who knew Father Leopold Tibesar, can testify.

But beyond the missions themselves, missionaries served as administrators of schools, hospitals and social work institutions, student centers, and the like. Very often a missionary would begin a new program or institution and then supervise its administration until it could be turned over to a Japanese colleague.

There were three specialized areas to which missionaries in the postwar period brought new administrative and technical skills: radio-television work, publishing and bookselling, and evangelistic crusades (all are considered in more detail in chap. 5, "Christian Outreach"). These were areas of work where new techniques and equipment were being developed overseas, which missionaries could learn to use and then introduce into Japan. Furthermore, purchasing the new equipment and developing programs in Japan to make adequate use of them required funds that missionaries were able to secure through their overseas contacts. The hope here also was that when these programs were sufficiently established, they could be turned over to Japanese colleagues, provided they were not too costly for the Japanese Christian community to continue.

Preliminary Comments about the Changing Roles of Missionaries

Before we turn to developments taking place within the Japanese Christian community that affected the roles of the missionaries, we need to make some preliminary comments on how those roles had developed within the context of postwar Japanese society.

In the first place, the role of innovation in missionary work must be examined. It has been pointed out that missionaries sometimes led the way in the use of new techniques in education, evangelism, mass communications, printing, and bookselling. Some of these innovations required expensive equipment and large budgets for program operations, funds for which missions alone could provide at the time. Local churches and other organizations were established by mission groups that were able to secure pieces of property at fairly low prices in the immediate postwar era, which could later be sold for much more, thus making possible the financing and refinancing of church projects for many years thereafter. It is true that once some of these projects and properties were turned over to Japanese Christian groups, they were so costly as to be heavy burdens to operate. It has sometimes been suggested that Japanese Christian groups could have made use of the funds and the techniques in equally innovative ways. But even assuming the availability of the funds without the presence of the missionaries—which is extremely questionable—it is doubtful that innovations would have been employed to the same extent. As foreigners, the missionaries had less "face" to lose in Japanese society, and therefore their experiments could be copied when they succeeded, and forgotten when they failed. The latter option was not so readily available to Japanese Christians.

Second, it should be noted on what precarious legal status in Japan the foreign mission enterprise rested. Most of the overseas Christian workers came to Japan under the legal status of "missionary" *(senkyōshi),* a category which the laws of the United States and many other countries do not recognize. Many governments throughout Asia and Africa in the postwar era became stringent about the admission of missionaries, and the way was open for the government of Japan to do the same. For instance, one requirement that the Japanese government has made in the postwar era for maintaining the status of "missionary" is that the individual's entire financial support originate outside Japan. As missionaries became more involved in "shared-support" arrangements with the Japanese Christian community (of which more presently) it would be increasingly difficult to include them under the missionary rubric. To be sure, some Christian workers could secure legal status as "teachers," "students," "special cultural exchange persons," and the like, but this would require time-consuming changes in legal and financial arrangements. Meanwhile, there was need for some legal as well as theological reflection on the "missionary riddle."

Third, the changing roles of foreign missionaries were intertwined with worldwide discussions about the changing meaning of "mission." Different Christian groups had different views on when a "mission country" evolves to another status. Thoughtful observers were pointing out, however, that the countries of Western Christendom had become "mission countries" in actual fact, whatever the theory. In the case of Japan, despite the undoubted strengths of the Christian community, over 99 percent of its population still remained without any formal ties with the Christian faith. This is the background for the development of "selfhood" in the Japanese Christian community, to which we now turn.

Japanese "Selfhood" and Foreign Missions

We began this chapter by noting that most of the Christian groups of Japan were already fully mature in 1945, when connections with foreign mission agencies and missionaries were resumed. Yet the desolation of postwar Japan, followed by the rapid social changes in Japanese society that accompanied its economic development, temporarily set aside the problems that the missionaries' activities posed for the Japanese Christian community itself. Workable patterns of relationships were established with overseas mission groups, and the missionaries themselves began to fill a number of challenging and creative roles. Nevertheless, there was still a "missionary riddle" in the background, and it surfaced in different ways in the various Japanese Christian groups.

The Growth of "Selfhood" among Japanese Protestants

The year 1960 was a watershed for Japanese Protestants in many ways. After that time, generally following developments in the Kyōdan, Protestants had a great deal to say about "selfhood" *(shutaisei)*. Before turning to details of such developments, it is helpful to sketch the historical context.

In the immediate postwar period, Japanese Protestants relied a great deal on the Western Christian community, directly or indirectly, for restoring the understanding of their "selfhood." The morale of Japanese Christians had been so shattered by their nation's wartime defeat and postwar chaos that they looked to the Christian community overseas for a rebuilding of their self-image. It was a common experience in the immediate postwar era for missionaries to be quizzed by Japanese Christians and others when they came to Japan, as to what had gone wrong in the Japanese experience. The foreigners generally had many—not infrequently too many—answers to such queries. For the first fifteen or so postwar years, Japanese eagerly imported from Western countries, and principally from the United States, the things that they felt were necessary to rebuild their society. The importation process, however, went far beyond the mere bringing to Japan of material goods and technologies. Japan was also importing lifestyles, new ways of looking at the world, new intellectual tools for measuring its own and other societies, for understanding its past and the future. For Japanese Christians, this meant the importation of theological systems and patterns of church life from Western countries, and the details of this process are outlined in the chapters on biblical studies and theology. This meant, for instance, that if North American churches had departments of evangelism to plan church outreach and to administer new programs, the Japanese churches—no matter how small or in what different circumstances—must also have departments of evangelism to do the same. To the extent that the theologies of Barthianism or Thomism were mainstays of theological reflection among European Christians, they must be further studied in Japan. Japanese Christians were operating in similar fashion to Japanese Marxists, who were at this time importing their ideological outlook from detailed studies of Marx's writings. In this importation process, Western missionaries may have had active or passive roles, but they were certainly borne along with the tide.

The process of importing Western attitudes, techniques, and analytical frameworks continued right through the 1950s and, in a larger sense, never stopped. But the 1960 Security Treaty crisis brought important changes to Japan, as this study reveals in other chapters. The crisis revealed to many thoughtful Japanese Christians—as it did to Japanese Marxists as well—that the analytical framework which Westerners had been using to explain the changes taking place in their society was not appropriate in all respects for the Japanese scene. For Christians in Japan, a process of disillusionment set in about such matters as Reinhold Niebuhr's understanding of "Christian realism," Barth's insistence that ethics was a subdivision of dogmatics, Tillich's estimation of the role of "religious socialism," and the Neo-Thomists' confidence that their standpoint reflected "the perennial philosophy."

The cleavages in Japanese society and churches caused by the 1960 Security Treaty crisis simply could not be explained in familiar Western categories, although very few Christians fully recognized it at the time. It is fair to say that after 1960 Western theology and philosophy never had quite the same impact in Japan as they had previously. To be sure, Japanese Christians continued to read all the latest works in Western theology and philosophy, just as their secular counterparts kept abreast of Western developments in quantum physics, poetry, and biochemistry. But when a series of theological waves swept over America in the 1960s, with theologies of "the secular city" being followed by "the death of God" and "situation ethics," and then by "theology of liberation" and "political theology," Japanese Christians began to wonder what had happened in America. Had America's churches somehow lost grip on their own "selfhood"? At the same time, the churches of Germany and other Western European countries, which had given rise to serious theological reflection, seemed to be rapidly losing both their members and their creativity. What did all this have to say about the North American and European missionaries at work in Japan, in relation to the "selfhood" of Japanese Christians?

As the 1960s wore on, Americans in particular began to have doubts about some of the directions of their society, following a period of assassinations of public figures, urban and racial rioting, and the anger and division among students and the general public about America's role in the Vietnam War. Doubts that some Americans had about their nation's "selfhood" certainly had repercussions on Christian mission in Japan. As Father Joseph Spae has remarked, "From the 1880s down to the 1970s' Security Treaty crisis and perhaps later, the degree of acceptance or rejection of Christianity in Japan is related to the degree of acceptance or rejection of 'American culture.' "[43] The doubts held by Japanese Christians began to surface first in the Protestant community.

It is hard to designate precise turning points, but the Reverend Kiyoshi Ii indicated that for him a fundamental change took place in the fall of 1961 at a Kyōdan Conference on Evangelism at Yugawara.[44] Following the centennial of the arrival of the first Protestant missionaries in 1859, the Kyōdan at Yugawara embraced its "Fundamental Policy on Mission," which called for a Ten-Year Plan of Evangelism (1961–71), to be characterized by "church renewal" (taishitsu kaizen; literally, structural renewal) and "larger parish evangelism" (dendō ken dendō).[45] There is widespread disagreement among Kyōdan members as to how far the church took seriously the appeals for "structural renewal," which was a slogan borrowed from the Italian Communist party and widely used among Japanese political parties that called for "structural reform." But the intent of the "Fundamental Policy on Mission" was clear: it sought to establish the Kyōdan's mission policy resting on its own "self-reliance," without unhealthy reliance on foreign mission funds. The concept of self-reliance began to play an increasing role in the 1960s, figuring prominently in discussions during the leadership of the Reverend Isamu Ōmura (Kyōdan moderator 1964–66) and the Reverend Masahisa Suzuki (moderator 1966–69). In his stirring inaugural address as moderator in October 1966, entitled "The Kyōdan of Tomorrow," Suzuki embraced the Kyōdan's watchwords of "self-reliance" (jiritsu), "consolidation" (sōgō), and "advance" (shinten). By far the greatest emphasis was on the first principle, about which Suzuki said:

When we think together on this matter, and in particular when we think of our hopes for an ability to speak boldly about social problems of our nation, it is clear that our church ought to achieve financial independence quickly, so as not to give occasion for stumbling to our fellow citizens. They will know where the money comes from. They will easily harbor doubts about our intentions if it comes from abroad.[46]

It is important to note that the fundamental reason Suzuki advocated for the financial independence of the Kyōdan was in order to establish the church's credibility for speaking out on the nation's social issues. Even though self-reliance meant a great deal more than financial independence, Suzuki emphasized the latter as a necessary prerequisite, and concrete steps were taken to eliminate by stages the funds from overseas that went into the Kyōdan's budget.

Yet self-reliance was not the same as cries of "Missionary, go home!" then echoing through many Third World churches. To be sure, a number of highly qualified Kyōdan missionaries did leave for home in the 1964–65 period, and it was asked at the time whether there was a "missionary exodus" from Japan.[47] This was followed by the Kyōdan's calling for a moratorium on receiving any new missionaries for evangelistic work from 1969 to 1971, but this moratorium was rescinded by the Kyōdan's Standing Executive Committee after considering a number of aspects of the matter.[48] Japanese Christian leaders tended to understand the problems of missionaries of their own abroad (see chap. 5, "Christian Outreach") and hence had a better understanding of the situation facing missionaries in their own country.

In the meantime a process had been initiated from the North American mission boards represented on the Interboard Committee (IBC) to reconsider structural relations with Japan. As far back as 1967 the consultation between the North-American-based IBC and the Council of Cooperation (CoC), which coordinated Christian work in Japan, had recommended that the CoC as a separate unit should be terminated and that Japan–North America agencies should relate directly to committees of the Kyōdan on a church-to-church basis.[49] Before this issue could be resolved on the Kyōdan's part, a struggle erupted within the Kyōdan on September 1–2, 1969, over the church's endorsement of the Christian Pavilion at the Osaka International Exposition in 1970. In the conflicts that were to distract the Kyōdan for the next several years, the term "selfhood" *(shutaisei)* was used repeatedly as a slogan to denote the essential integrity and self-reliance that the Kyōdan was said to lack. Because of these turmoils, the Council of Cooperation was not restructured, but the Interboard Committee was replaced by a much broader organization called the Japan–North American Commission on Cooperative Mission (JNAC). Formed in January 1973, JNAC was organized to indicate that mission was no longer a one-way street from North America to Japan, but that Japanese Christians would henceforth be participating also in mission to North America. A concrete expression of the new emphasis on cooperation in mission was the establishment of Missionary Shared Support Contributions, whereby Christian schools and other organizations receiving missionaries agreed to provide part of their financial support, rather than accept a decline in the number of missionaries because of inflation and the budget shortages of the North American churches. Shared Support contributions amounted to about $100,000 in 1973, $200,000 in 1974, and $230,000 in 1975.[50] These actions went a long way to indicate that "selfhood" for the CoC groups did not mean the withdrawal of missionaries but, rather, the affirmation of their continued usefulness, backed by a financial commitment for their support. Such actions were especially meaningful as many overseas Protestant churches felt the need to cut mission budgets time and again in the late 1960s and the 1970s. Unless such trends could be reversed, they could mean an almost total withdrawal of mission funds and personnel.

While this section has dealt primarily with developments in the Kyōdan, there were related developments in other Protestant denominations. The Seikōkai (Anglican Church in Japan), for instance, saw the number of its missionaries decline steadily after 1960, and the process was speeded up by a reorganization process undertaken by the American Episcopal Church, which involved the termination of support for all of its missionaries in Japan.[51]

The Baptist Renmei and the Southern Baptist missionaries heard debates in the early 1960s about convention/mission relationships. While one missionary urged the mission to scrap its policy of "passive accommodation" to the Japanese church convention, another recommended the continuation of what he called "active accommodation." At length the Renmei decided to aim at total self-support by 1977 in its operating budget, 80 percent of which in 1973 came from America.[52]

The Japan Evangelical Lutheran Church was encouraged by its fellow members in the Lutheran World Federation to adopt a target of self-support by 1974, even though this meant considerable cutting of both budgets and programs.[53] The Japan Lutheran Church (Nihon Ruteru Kyōkan, or NRK), related to the Lutheran Church-Missouri Synod, found itself becoming embroiled in the internal quarrels of its American counterpart, and in order to assert its independence decided rather precipitously to become self-supporting by April 1976, even though this meant that all but four of the missionary families working with the church would have to return to America.[54]

Conservative evangelical churches and missions were less affected by discussions about "selfhood," but here also echoes of other debates could be heard. Many observers felt that for most of these churches, it was not a question of whether the subject would arise but, rather, of when and under what circumstances.

Catholics in Japan after Vatican Council II

Until late in the 1960s most of the debates about selfhood had seemingly been confined to Protestants, and Catholics looked on with dismay at the plight of their "separated brethren," toward whom they now felt a greater sympathy through the ecumenical emphases of Vatican Council II (1962–65). That council sought to give the Catholic church a new stance toward the modern world, or to use Pope John XXIII's metaphor, to open some windows to let new breezes blow through the church. And such was the case. The problem was that some of the new breezes blew trouble as well. Particularly upsetting was the "crisis in vocations" among Roman Catholic priests, sisters, and brothers, which from the late 1960s resulted in the resignations of thousands of Catholic religious around the world. This worldwide crisis affected Europe and America more than it did Japan, but its effect on Japan was severe enough. Some of the missionary orders lost up to half their personnel in Japan, and Japanese secular clergy began to resign in unprecedented numbers as well.[55] While an analysis of this "crisis in vocations" goes far beyond the scope of this study, it does demonstrate that the vocational crisis disturbed the selfhood of both missionaries and Japanese clergy.

Meanwhile, there were structural changes in the organization of the Catholic Church in Japan as a result of Vatican Council II. The "Bishops' Meeting" became the "Japan Bishops' Conference" in 1967, and the Major Superiors' Conference was also reorganized in the same year. Thereafter a number of mission institutes began to feel acutely the shortage of priests because of resignations and the decline in vocations for the priesthood. In 1973 the Superiors' Conference asked the mission institutes in Japan whether they would be able to maintain their present activities ten years hence, or not. Some forty-three replied that they would be able to continue their existing level of activities, while four said they could do so with difficulty, and twelve indicated they would find it impossible. At about the same time revisions of diocesan contracts were circulated in order to make the contracts more in keeping with the changes of Vatican II and also to reflect the changed realities of mission personnel and resources.[56] In 1967 the Major Superiors' Conference asked the Japan Bishops' Conference directly, "Are foreign missionaries still necessary in Japan?" The reply that came back is worth quoting at length:

. . . We are also told that the Church in Japan is already established, with Japanese personnel, and that therefore the presence of foreign missionaries is no longer necessary. It is true that all the Bishops are Japanese and that in the religious congregations, many of the superiors are Japanese. Even if this evolution was designed to accelerate the acculturation of the Church, it does not follow that the Church is already indigenized in this country; most of the dioceses, because still far from self-sufficient in terms of personnel, could not attain today's development and will not be able to continue the work of evangelization without the collaboration of foreign missionaries.

Missionary activity was begun in Japan about one hundred years ago, but it was only after the Second World War that the Church acquired Her present structure. Most of the mission stations are not more than twenty years old. But to implant the Faith in a non-Christian country, a continuous effort for several generations is necessary. At the present time, in a population of 108 million, only 370,000 are Catholics and everywhere there is room for real missionary activity. Our Church, without local tradition, insufficiently rooted, needs the help of foreign religious congregations and missionary institutes, and we continue to count on their collaboration. Since the end of the war, happily, we enjoy complete freedom for religious activities.[57]

It is significant that although the statement by the Japanese bishops and the decisions of the Protestant Council of Cooperation are derived from different traditions and somewhat varying circumstances, their conclusions are virtually the same.

The Missionary Riddle Revisited after Three Decades

After this survey of three decades of missionary work in Japan, we return to the riddle with which we started: In a society and a church come of age, what is the role of the foreign missionary? Let us take a look at some of the main aspects of this riddle as they appear in the light of the historical record.

In the first place, it has been seen that there is no fixed, unchangeable role of the missionary, set up in heaven or anywhere else, by which the actual performance of missionaries in the flesh can be measured. There have been many different relationships between the sending groups and the Christians of Japan under which missionaries have worked, and although there was need constantly to update these relationships, the six major patterns which were examined—including the pattern of having no missionaries at all—have continued to hold up rather well. Furthermore, there have been many different tasks to which missionaries have given themselves, and these tasks have also changed with the times. What, then, constitutes a missionary? To answer the question functionally, a missionary may be considered to be a person with some relationships to an overseas Christian community, some ties to the Christian community of Japan, and some tasks of Christian service that further the aims of both communities. Within that general framework, all sorts of possibilities could and did emerge.

Second, the reader may have noticed the writers' judgment that this historical sketch about missionary work did not need to single out many individual names of missionaries. There has been no Francis Xavier, no Albert Schweitzer, David Livingstone, Hudson Taylor, or Mother Teresa. Postwar Japan did not seem to be a place for the charismatic type of missionary, except in a few cases where new work was being started. This was an age of team workers, who were willing to work alongside others, ready to be flexible when that was called for, and putting the good of the whole group above individual fame. The writer feels that this fact is to be celebrated rather than lamented. Even though the postwar missionaries to Japan did not often inscribe their individual names in any hall of fame, and even though they did all sorts of stupid and lamentable things, on the whole they did their work well, "as servants of Christ and stewards of the mysteries of God." For after more than three decades their Japanese Christian colleagues said they would like to see more of them if possible.

And that leads to a third observation. A few people doubtless assume that the foreign missionary enterprise will go on forever, in essentially the same ways. But we have already seen how much the forms of mission changed in postwar Japan, and in the days to come they will probably change even more. It should not be forgotten that the forms of the missionary enterprise in postwar Japan have been amenable to political fortune. If political or other circumstances should change in Japan, the day might come when there are no more missionaries in that country than there are, for instance, in mainland China today. The declining financial support for foreign missionaries will also continue to take its toll. Yet the mission of the church goes on, for as long as there is a Christian church, there will be Christians engaged in mission in some form or other. What the new forms of mission may be can hardly yet be known. But it might be surmised that they will be built on the experiences, good and bad, of the missionaries of the past.

"And the missionary was Japanized," declared Tomio Mutō. And this is as it should be. Postwar Japan has witnessed many changes regarding the riddle of the missionary's role, and the future will doubtless see many more, as Christians seek to be true to their common tasks in mission.

NOTES

1. Tomio Mutō, "Address to Missionaries at 1974 Gotemba Conference," privately mimeographed.

2. William P. Woodard, *The Allied Occupation of Japan and Japanese Religions* (Leiden: E. J. Brill, 1972), p. 357.

3. Ibid., p. 359.

4. Ibid., p. 363.

5. It may be significant that one of the scholars who has forcefully called attention to the phenomenon of "civil religion" in America, Dr. Robert Bellah, was first of all a specialist in Japan studies. See his *The Broken Covenant* (New York: Seabury Press, 1975).

6. Arthur J. Moore, *Christ after Chaos: The Post-War Policy of the Methodist Church in Foreign Lands* (New York: The Methodist Church, 1944), pp. 37, 38, 43.

7. Letter of Fr. Patrick J. Byrne, M.M., to the Maryknoll Father General [Bishop James E. Walsh], June 11, 1946, in Maryknoll archives at Maryknoll, N.Y. (Byrne's italics).

8. Letter of Bishop Paul Y. Taguchi to Bishop James E. Walsh, Nov. 17, 1945, in Maryknoll archives.

9. Richard H. Drummond, *A History of Christianity in Japan* (Grand Rapids, Mich.: Wm. B. Eerdmans, 1971), p. 271.

10. Letter of Fr. Patrick J. Byrne, M.M., to Maryknoll Father General [Bishop James E. Walsh], Dec. 31, 1945, in Maryknoll archives.

11. Douglas Horton, et. al., *The Return to Japan: Report of the Christian Deputation to Japan, October–November 1945* (New York: Friendship Press, 1945).

12. Ibid., p. 6.

13. Ibid., p. 53.

14. Drummond, *History*, p. 277.

15. Arthur C. Knudten, *The Forgotten Years and Beyond, 1942—1972: Sketches in History* (Laguna Hills, Calif.: privately printed, 1972), pp. 52–53.

16. Ibid., pp. 53–54.

17. Drummond, *History*, p. 267.

18. For the impact of these withdrawals on ecumenicity, see chap. 7, "Ecumenicity in Japan."

19. B. Paul Huddle, *History of the Lutheran Church in Japan* (New York: Board of Foreign Missions of the United Lutheran Church in America, 1958), p. 219.

20. Ibid., pp. 219–20.

21. Joseph L. Van Hecken, *The Catholic Church in Japan since 1859* (Tokyo: Enderle, 1963), pp. 98–99.

22. Ibid., p. 100.

23. Andrew Sugakazu Matsumoto, ed., *Japan Catholic Directory, 1975* (Tokyo: Katorikku Chūō Kyōgikai, 1975), p. 687.

24. Drummond, *History*, pp. 356–57.

25. Van Hecken, *Catholic Church*, pp. 61ff.

26. Ibid., pp. 100–101.

27. This section is based on the contracts of the M.E.P. with the bishop of Fukuoka, and of Maryknoll with the bishop of Kyoto. The contracts are in the Maryknoll archives.

28. Drummond, *History*, pp. 278–79.

29. Yoichirō Saeki, "Historical Survey and Problem Areas in Cooperative Relationship with North America" (Tokyo: privately printed by the Council of Cooperation, Nov. 21, 1975), p. 1.

30. Ibid., pp. 2, 3.

31. *Program Base Design* (Tokyo: The Japan Mission, Foreign Mission Board, Southern Baptist Convention, 1973), p. 68.

32. Interview of the writer with Rev. Calvin Parker in Tokyo, March 15, 1972.

33. *Program Base Design*, p. 68.

34. See Oliver Bergh, "Postwar Lutheran Missionary Activities," *JCQ* 38, no. 3 (Summer 1972): 162–68; Donald Anderson, "Mission in the Seikōkai since the Pacific War: A Preliminary Study," *JCQ* 39, no. 1 (Winter 1973): 48–54; F. Calvin Parker, "Baptist Missions in Japan, 1945-1973: A Study in Relationships," *JCQ* 40, no. 1 (Winter 1974): 32–41.

35. Arthur Reynolds, ed., *Japan in Review: "Japan Harvest" Anthology, 1955—1970*, vol. 1 (Tokyo: JEMA, 1970), pp. 85, 88, 90, 100, 103.

36. Ibid., p. 103.

37. Cf. William D. Bray, "The Hidden Christians of Ikutsuki Island," *JCQ* 26, no. 2 (April 1960): 76–84. See also Kataoka Yakichi, *Kakure Kirishitan: Rekishi to Minzoku* [Hidden Christians: History and Folkways], (Tokyo: NHK Books, 1967).

38. Alexander Pope, *Essay on Man,* Ep. iii, lines 303–4.

39. Neil Braun, *Laity Mobilized: Reflections on Church Growth in Japan and Other Lands* (Grand Rapids, Mich.: Wm. B. Eerdmans, 1971).

40. *Program Base Design*, p. 69.

41. Interview of the writer with Fr. Joseph J. Spae in Tokyo, March 15, 1973.

42. Cf. Masao Takenaka, *Reconciliation and Renewal in Japan* (New York: Friendship Press, 1957), pp. 28-31; Dorothy Dessau, ed., *Glimpses of Social Work in Japan*, 2nd ed. (Tokyo: Weatherhill, 1968), chap. 2.

43. Spae interview.

44. Interview of the writer with Rev. Kiyoshi Ii in Tokyo, March 2, 1972.

45. *Policy Statements and Statistics of the United Church of Christ in Japan* (Tokyo: Kyōdan, 1968), pp. 12-14.

46. Masahisa Suzuki, "The Kyōdan of Tomorrow" [address delivered at the Kyōdan's General Assembly in Osaka, Oct. 23, 1966], privately mimeographed.

47. See Richard H. Drummond, "A Missionary 'Exodus' from Japan?" *Christian Century* 82, no. 21 (May 26, 1965): 672-74.

48. Saeki, "Historical Survey," p. 5.

49. Ibid.

50. Ibid., p. 7.

51. Anderson, "Seikōkai," p. 54.

52. Parker, "Baptists," p. 38.

53. Bergh, "Lutherans," p. 168.

54. *JCAN*, Feb. 27, 1976, p. 6.

55. See Th. Purcell, "Crisis in the Mission—in Depth," *JMB* 21, no. 11 (December 1967): 652-58.

56. J. E. McElwain, "Cooperation in the Missionary Context," *JMB* 28, no. 6 (July 1974): 355-61.

57. Ibid., pp. 362-63.

7

Ecumenicity in Japan:
A Grand Idea but an Unsteady Course

> We must count among the worst evils of our time the fact that the Churches are separated from one another to the extent that a human society scarcely exists among us, much less that holy communion of the members of Christ, which all profess by their works, but which few sincerely seek in reality.[1]

Is this a writer commenting on the state of ecumenicity in modern Japan? No, the author is John Calvin, describing the situation concerning Christian unity in his own sixteenth century, but much the same could be said about Christians in many other times and places, including Japan since 1945. No one will deny that during the postwar era Japan has seen ecumenical activities in great numbers and with considerable publicity. But the actual achievements of ecumenicity—those movements of thought and action concerned with the cooperation and reunion of Christians—in Japan still fall far short of the professed goals.

Why should this be so? Why should there be relatively little to show for the devoted and untiring efforts of so many toward cooperation and unity? One simile for explaining what has been happening is to compare ecumenicity with one of the most popular of traditional Japanese folkcraft toys, the *yajirobē*. This toy usually takes the form of a small wooden figure of a man holding an inverted-U balancing pole in his arms, and perched on a small wooden platform. As the *yajirobē* is whirled around on his pedestal, he manages to keep his precarious perch, to the amazement and delight of onlookers, both young and old. How does the *yajirobē* manage to keep standing upright as he spins around on his small perch? The answer seems to be that with his very low center of gravity, he is kept there by a balance of centrifugal and centripetal forces created by his whirling. He keeps erect as long as he stands in one place. But if anyone tries to move him—as children sometimes try to while the figure is spinning around—the *yajirobē* will immediately fall flat on his face.

To some observers, ecumenicity in modern Japan operates much like a *yajirobē*. As long as the wheels are kept spinning, there is a whirl of activity that goes round and round the same familiar points—and all is well. But if any effort is made to turn ecumenicity into a *movement*, not just to keep things standing still but to go forward, then ecumenicity—like the poor *yajirobē*—collapses in a heap.

Of course, such a comparison is an exaggeration, for there have been positive achievements over the past decades, which must be stressed in order to paint a fair picture. Nevertheless, those wishing to understand some of the advances and setbacks to ecumenicity in Japan in recent years will find it helpful to examine some of the centrifugal and centripetal forces that have been at work in the churches and in Japanese society at large.

It should be pointed out that this chapter will concentrate on a historical approach to the problems of ecumenicity, largely because of the present writer's particular emphasis. Several other fields ought to be consulted in order for one to get a broader perspective on these developments. Unfortunately, they can only be mentioned here. In particular, the work of sociologists is helpful for analyzing why some ecumenical developments have taken place and others have not. One thinks of Chie Nakane's *Japanese Society* as presenting a lucid analysis of the verticle and horizontal relationships of Japan, and their role in fostering activities of certain sorts and of preventing others altogether. Ezra Vogel's *Japan's New Middle Class* provides a valuable sociological description of the class among whom Christians of all sorts have found their most receptive hearers in modern Japan. And Richard Dore's *City Life in Japan* describes the way a particular ward district in Tokyo functions, suggesting why some projects which might be labeled "ecumenical" prove feasible and others do not. And so the list might be extended. This chapter will make indirect use of studies of this sort but will not be able to give them all the consideration they deserve.

By the use of a historical approach to the subject of ecumenicity, it becomes possible to discern three major periods through which Christians in Japan have passed since 1945. In each of these periods, the ecumenical tasks were somewhat different. We shall examine each period in turn—always bearing in mind that there are no watertight boundaries between historical periods—and attempt evaluations of particular programs and events in each period.

The Occupation Era (1945-52)

From the end of World War II in 1945 Japan found itself in a historical situation that seemed to be best characterized by the term "the postwar era."

It is difficult to determine how long this era lasted, during which the primary developments in Japanese society were shaped by the needs of the country to rebuild itself after its defeat in war and to restore the fabric of social life that had been so badly disrupted by wartime conditions. The end of the Occupation in 1952 may be taken as marking a turning point in the national consciousness that was as valid for the Christian community as for society as a whole. Within the framework of the Occupation, then, almost all Japanese had to face many of the same problems. And in regard to ecumenicity, its very nature was given a particular flavor by the circumstances of the Occupation.

The Difficulties of Postwar Japan

In a sense, Japanese were all in the same boat in the immediate postwar period. They were united in the shock that followed defeat, in the apprehension that awaited the arrival of the first occupying army in history on their soil, and then in the relief that ensued when they discovered that these occupying forces wanted to reconstruct and not to destroy their country. Among Japanese Christians, the very hardships of the first few years after the war put individuals of all different denominational backgrounds on much the same plane. They had all suffered damage to their churches, schools, and other institutions, and they had all lost members because of wartime dislocations and events.[2] They had also been mutually inconvenienced by governmental regulations during wartime and by supervision by police and others that varied from mild approbation to severe persecution. One of the Occupation's first acts was to remove the arm of the state from religious policies, and Christian groups as well as others breathed in relief. But the newly found freedom for religious groups was hampered by the severely straitened economic circumstances of the postwar era. Religious groups may have had the freedom to do many different kinds of things, but they had few resources to carry out any of them. If the Christian churches felt any kind of partnership during this period, it was a partnership of adversity.

Under such circumstances, ecumenicity was furthered by the efforts that overseas Christian groups made for relief distribution. In order to facilitate contacts with the Occupation authorities and the Ministry of Welfare of the Japanese government, the relief activities of Protestant groups under Church World Service were coordinated with those of the Church of the Brethren, the American Friends Service Committee, the Mennonites, the Lutherans, and the Roman Catholics, in an organization called the Licensed Agencies for Relief in Asia (LARA).[3] About $8 million of relief supplies came within five years, and individual friendships formed through these cooperative activities later proved significant in other areas.[4] But in general an agency like LARA, formed purely to present a united front to officialdom, did not create lasting channels of cooperation among Christians. After cash or supplies were handed over, cooperation withered.

On the other hand, the conditions of postwar Japan helped to make ecumenical cooperation among the various churches very difficult indeed. Transportation and communication were severely restricted at the time, making it easier for people who wanted to go their own way without consulting others to justify or excuse such actions. It was hard enough to manage to survive during those difficult postwar years, and there seemed to be very little energy left over to consider the needs of other groups for which one had never assumed the traditional burdens of obligation. The ethical connotations of *giri* (obligation), *gimu* (duty), and *on* (debt of gratitude) are matters of onerous importance in traditional Japanese society. Even the Christian boom of the immediate postwar period was more often than not seized upon as a chance for individual groups to gather as many new recruits as possible for their own church families or programs, without regard for others. With many small churches suddenly inundated by inquirers about Christianity, what need was there for Christians to present "a common front" to non-Christian Japanese society? Instead, the Christian boom, while it lasted, tended mainly to heighten the competition for new converts.

Attitudes toward ecumenicity varied, of course, with different groups. But some of the problems can be vividly seen by reference to the largest Protestant denomination, the Nihon Kirisuto Kyōdan, referred to in English as the United Church of Christ in Japan, or more commonly, simply the Kyōdan.

The Continuing Existence of the Kyōdan

On the face of things, it would seem that the continuing postwar existence of the Kyōdan as a united church would be a positive force for ecumenicity. This was true to some extent, but there were limiting factors at work as well. The Kyōdan had been formed from the mixed heritage of ecumenical aspiration and governmental pressure. The Kyōdan's official "Brief History" puts it this way:

Protestant Christianity in our country originated from the work of foreign missionaries who came to Japan in 1859. On February 2, 1872 (according to the old calendar), the first Protestant Church, the Nihon Kirisuto Kōkai was established in Yokohama. This church belonged to none of the denominations found in foreign countries but was, as it were, a supra-denominational church. Subsequently, however, denominations from Europe and America were transplanted to Japan, and as their mission work expanded, the number of denominations in Japan likewise suddenly increased. From a different angle at about the same time, proposals for union arose frequently among the several denominations, partly stimulated from abroad by the ecumenical movement. Finally, the opportunity arose, coincidentally occasioned by the promulgation of the Religious Organizations Law, for all the Protestant churches of the country to unite. On October 17, 1940, at a mass meeting in Tokyo of Christian laymen from all parts of Japan, a declaration of church unity was made. On the basis of this declaration, over thirty Protestant denominations achieved unity at a Founding General Assembly held at the Fumimicho Church on June 25–26, 1941. . . .[5]

Even though this "Brief History" makes but passing reference to the governmental pressures embodied in the Religious Organizations Law of 1940, these pressures gave substance to what had been an elusive ideal up to that point: unity among Japan's Protestants. Of course, several Christian groups did not want to enter the union in the first place, and many of these withdrew from the Kyōdan when governmental controls over religious bodies were removed after 1945. The Anglicans withdrew in 1946 (many Anglican churches had never joined the Kyōdan at all), and they were followed by the Salvation Army (1946), the Reformed Church (1946), the Holiness groups (1947), the Baptist Renmei, related to the Southern Baptist Convention in the U.S.A. (1947), the Lutheran Church (1947), the Church of Christ in Japan, a Presbyterian group (1951), the Baptist Dōmei, related to the American Baptist Convention (1958), and other smaller groups.[6] Yet even with all these withdrawals—which in the case of the Presbyterian, Reformed, Baptist, and Holiness groups meant the withdrawal of some but not all churches of those backgrounds—the Kyōdan still embraced over half of Japan's Protestants. At a series of postwar assemblies the majority of the Kyōdan representatives made it clear that they were determined to stay together. The "bloc system" by which the separate denominational groupings kept their identity when the Kyōdan was formed had been abolished in 1942, at least officially, much to the dismay of those groups who were not in favor of organic union at that time.[7] Despite proposals that the bloc system be revived in some form after the war, and thus constitute the Kyōdan as a federation of denominations rather than a united church, these proposals were rejected, and some denominational groups withdrew from the Kyōdan for that reason. Yet, because there was an atmosphere of mutual respect in most of these cases, the cause of ecumenicity was actually helped rather than hindered by some of the withdrawals, particularly where the groups had not wished for organic church unity in the first place.

The Kyōdan's decision to remain a united church was reinforced by the decisions of several North American mission boards, which had been related to Japan, to do their work henceforth on a cooperative basis. Prior to World War II, with a few exceptions Methodists in America had been directly related to the Methodist Church in Japan and to Methodist institutions, Presbyterians and Reformed to the work of the Nihon Kirisuto Kyōkai, Congregationalists to Kumiai churches, and so forth. But with the Kyōdan's decision to continue as a united church, seven of the North American mission boards established the Interboard Committee for Christian Work in Japan (IBC) with its headquarters in New York City. (The number of boards was to vary as churches and mission boards were reorganized in subsequent years.) A new organization was formed in Japan to correspond with the IBC, called the Council of Cooperation (CoC). The CoC was formed to coordinate the work of the Kyōdan, a schools' council, a social work federation, and IBC representatives. It is not necessary to go into the various organizational changes through which these groups went, or the problems which such cooperation entailed. It is sufficient to say that for many years the decision of North American and Japanese church leaders to work through such cooperative councils, rather than reverting to prewar denominational patterns, helped to maintain and strengthen the rather precarious unity of the Kyōdan in the postwar era.

Yet the ecumenicity that the Kyōdan embodied also involved considerable internal tensions. Many churches stayed in the Kyōdan less from a devotion to church unity than from a fear that the alternatives open to them might be worse. This was true especially for the three major denominational groups in the Kyōdan. The Kumiai churches (generally called, somewhat incorrectly, "congregational" churches because of their historic ties to American Congregational churches, despite differences in church polity) felt that while the Kyōdan might be organized *pro forma* in a presbyterian fashion, its central organs were very weak and could secure only limited voluntary acquiescence. Therefore it was a *de facto* congregational polity that prevailed in the Kyōdan, with which they had no substantial disagreement and which made it easy to disregard the central organs of the church when they chose to do so. As for the Methodist churches, it has been said that they had had such disagreeable experiences with the office of bishop in Japan that they were willing to stay in the Kyōdan in order to avoid the reestablishment of the episcopacy among them. The so-called Presbyterian-Reformed churches (which formerly had belonged to the Nihon Kirisuto Kyōkai and were therefore known as Kyū-Nikki, or "old Nikki" churches, to distinguish them from the Shin-Nikki, or "new Nikki" churches, which withdrew from the Kyōdan after the war and reorganized a new church with the old name) are said to have been willing to stay in the Kyōdan because they dreaded the revival of the factionalism and theological bickering that had plagued their previous history. As it was, the Kyū-Nikki group in the Kyōdan were to have their continuing disputes over doctrine, creedal statements, and forms of church government, but these disputes were somewhat mitigated by being carried on in a united church together with other groups who were less torn apart by such controversies.

The smaller denominational groups that stayed in the Kyōdan—Holiness, Baptist, Disciples, and others—had come to feel that the chances for Christian fellowship and cooperation afforded through the Kyōdan brought them many advantages without hindering their specific Christian witness. (One "nontheological" factor at work here was that a larger fellowship of churches made possible a wider selection of prospective spouses for young Christian men and women. But the details of this we leave to the sociologists and the loyal members of the *fujinkai* women's groups!)

Thus the Kyōdan's continuing existence as a united church had genuine significance for ecumenicity, but this fact was somewhat beclouded by the consideration that the participation of the major groups was sometimes for negative, not positive, reasons. The relationship of the Kyōdan to the other Protestant groups in postwar Japan can best be seen in the work of the National Christian Council of Japan (NCCJ).

The Reorganization of the NCCJ

The NCCJ had been founded in 1922 as an outgrowth of the mission and ecumenical movement that came into its modern focus at the World Missionary Conference at Edinburgh, Scotland, in 1910.[8] Thereafter, the NCCJ served for many years as the focus for numerous cooperative Protestant activities, even though it was not as active as its corresponding bodies in China or India. But when the Kyōdan was formed in 1941 to unite all Protestant churches, the NCCJ in its original form expired, and what remained lingered on as a commission for liaison with the government, until it too passed out of existence with the end of the Pacific War. In the postwar period, after Protestant groups began to withdraw from the Kyōdan, the NCCJ was reorganized (1948). In the years that followed, the NCCJ again became the natural group around which many projects of an ecumenical nature were to crystallize, and its contributions to ecumenicity in Japan are unquestionable. But in order to evaluate its overall contribution in this area, two important factors must be borne in mind.

In the first place, the NCCJ in the postwar era served a twofold function: it helped to coordinate activities of Christian groups within Japan, but it also served the convenience of overseas groups that needed a united Japanese Protestant council with which to work. It was sometimes difficult for these domestic and overseas functions of the NCCJ to work in harmony. For instance, when North American church groups helped to set up cooperative programs for church relief and for audio-visuals in the postwar period, they sought to relate them to an ongoing interdenominational body, and the NCCJ was just such a body. In time these two programs developed into the Christian Service Commission (which was an outgrowth of the relief operations of Church World Service, CWS) and the Audio-Visual Aids Commission (AVACO), both of which came to possess extensive staffs, programs, budgets, and facilities far overshadowing the modest operations of the NCCJ under which they supposedly worked. As CWS and AVACO were both initially capitalized primarily from overseas groups, they sometimes seemed to be in closer touch with their overseas supporters than they were with the NCCJ. Even the funds that member churches in Japan contributed to the NCCJ sometimes originated with overseas churches' support funds, and they began to decrease when overseas support in general diminished in the 1960s. When as an aftermath of the crisis concerning the Christian Pavilion at Expo '70 the NCCJ itself faced a severe financial crisis, it was fortunately able to reorganize itself in the 1970s with substantial grassroots support from Japanese sources.

A second factor to note about the work of the NCCJ is that it was not highly regarded by conservative Protestant groups because its members have been drawn from mainline Protestant churches. The ties of the NCCJ with the World Council of Churches and other ecumenical agencies only served to heighten the difficulties. When he was general secretary of the NCCJ, the Reverend John M. Nakajima wrote that ecumenical problems such as these may be deeply rooted in what he termed the Japanese "emperor-system" mentality, which means a strong sense of belonging to the group with which one is affiliated and a deep suspicion of outside connections.[9]

Protestant–Roman Catholic Relations

Ecumenicity between Protestant and Roman Catholics in Japan was not on the agenda of either group in the immediate postwar period. Although certain forms of ecumenicity embraced Catholics and Protestants in other countries in the period before Vatican Council II, such influences were very little felt in Japan.[10] There were of course individual Roman Catholics and individual Protestants who were well disposed toward each other, and some Catholic and Protestant students and faculty members who worked together, but there was very little endorsement or encouragement of such views on an official level. There had been, instead, instances of hostility between the two groups, as they sometimes saw each other as rivals or nuisances.[11] A number of elements were responsible for this.

In the first place, Protestants and Catholics differed on their interpretation of the significance of "the Christian Century" in Japan (1549–1638), the period of the phenomenal growth of the Catholic Church in Japan following the arrival of Saint Francis Xavier.[12] When it was possible for Christian missionaries to enter Japan again after 1859, the Roman Catholic missionaries saw themselves as the proud successors of the Jesuits and Franciscans of the earlier period. Even though the Protestant missionaries sympathized with many aspects of Roman Catholic work, especially with the sufferings of those persecuted or martyred, there was a tendency for Protestants to feel that some of the difficulties into which the Catholics had fallen were the result of their own mistakes, particularly in their willingness to accept the political support of Western governments in promoting missions in Japan. Most Protestants in Japan from the Meiji era on were from a "free church" background, which led them to feel that close ties with governments have always been the bane of Christian missions, especially under Catholic auspices, and that it was up to Protestants to avoid such entangling alliances as much as possible. These sentiments, however, did not prevent many Protestant missionaries in the period after 1945 from accepting favors from the American Occupation authorities in Japan, as occasion permitted. Nevertheless, such deeply ingrained suspicions of Roman Catholic mission work among Protestants were to become stronger after the victory of Communism in mainland China, to which we shall be referring in more detail shortly, when many conservative missions forced out of China relocated some of their missionaries and programs in Japan. Some of these missionaries preserved the tradition of Hudson Taylor and the China Inland Mission, where the policy had been that missionaries were not, under any condition whatever, to appeal to extraterritorial privileges or for the protection of foreign governments.[13]

In the second place, Protestants and Catholics in Japan differed on the same matters that separated them in other countries, and here we need only mention the significance of the doctrine of the church for the Japanese scene. The implications here may be seen by reference to a homely—and ultimately misleading—metaphor drawn from the field of commerce. In the mind's eye of many a Protestant believer in Japan, and in that of some Catholics as well, the Roman Catholic Church resembled nothing so much as a gigantic corporation or trading company, with its head office in Rome, its subsidiary branch offices in Tokyo and Osaka, and its retail outlets scattered throughout Japan. This mammoth enterprise was seen as engaged in the distribution of a supernatural commodity called salvation, which was dispensed with the authorization of the main office and under the supervision of its branch offices through its many local outlets by its authorized agents. Such an enterprise with international ramifications had impressive advantages, as its Catholic defenders would hasten to point out and its Protestant detractors would grudgingly admit. But there were also many disadvantages, as any Japanese with experience in international corporations would be quick to realize. Such huge enterprises lack flexibility, are unable to cater to the peculiar needs of a local market, and are not sufficiently ready to adapt the product to the desires of some eager potential customers. From a Catholic perspective, Protestant churches seemed to be so many in number, so diverse in belief, and so lacking in discipline that any acceptance of Protestant doctrines of the church would lead to sheer anarchy. It is not necessary to pursue further these ecclesiological metaphors—or rather, caricatures—to see how differing views of the nature of the church in all its aspects made any kind of ecumenical collaboration difficult at the very least and, in many cases, impossible.

Furthermore, Protestants and Catholics were often divided in their understandings of the nature of Japanese society and its religions, giving rise to different missiologies. Although ironclad generalizations must be set aside, there was a tendency among Catholics to regard many, although not all, aspects of Japanese culture and religion as part of the "precatechetical stage" for the development of Christianity in Japan.[14] Protestants, when they thought about the problem at all, were inclined to look upon the heritage of Japanese culture and religion as a somewhat dubious preparation for Christianity, toward which Christian evangelists should make both positive and negative evaluations.[15] The full extent of these disagreements, and the partial adjustment of views that became possible because of the influence of the writings of Paul Tillich and others, involves a much longer analysis than is possible here. Suffice it to say that in pre-Vatican II days such differing approaches to mission strategy vis-à-vis Japanese culture made ecumenical cooperation difficult.

To the foregoing historical and doctrinal considerations must be added a fourth factor of a practical nature. In the postwar era both Catholics and Protestants were so busy restoring the buildings and programs of churches and church-related institutions that they had little energy left over for ecumenicity. Not only that, but the very nature of the relations between the Christian groups of Japan and their overseas counterparts made ecumenical overtures difficult. We have seen how the Kyōdan related to the North American churches through the structures of the IBC and the CoC. The Baptist Renmei set out to develop its relations with the Southern Baptist Convention in the U.S.A., the Anglican Church of Japan (Seikōkai) with overseas Anglicans, Japanese Lutherans with Lutheran churches in America and Europe, the Orthodox Church with the North American Orthodox Sobor, the Baptist Dōmei with the American Baptist Convention, and so forth. All the while, Catholics in Japan were reestablishing their links with overseas Catholics, during the period after 1945, through methods remarkably comparable to those of their Protestant and Orthodox counterparts. Although there seems to have been little or no consultation between Catholics and Protestants on the nature of these overseas relations, it is surprising to see how many common elements there were in the working relationships which emerged at this time.

For Catholics in Japan the organizational problems stemmed from the decision made in the wake of the Religious Organizations Law of 1940 for all foreign ordinaries or bishops to resign and be replaced by Japanese successors.[16] Until that time each missionary society from abroad had its own bishop or superior in Japan, under whom its members worked. But when in Japan after 1945 all the bishops were Japanese and belonged to the "secular clergy" (i.e., were not members of religious orders), new organizational relationships were called for. The new modus vivendi that developed called for each foreign mission society to work out a bilateral contact with the bishop of a diocese, spelling out the working arrangements for the missionaries, programs, and funds from the society in that diocese. What this meant in the postwar era was that the Japanese bishops possessed almost all the needs for resources and personnel, while the foreign mission societies possessed nearly all the resources. Be that as it may, such arrangements led to a remarkable expansion of Catholic work in Japan in the postwar era. But very much like the working arrangements devised by their Protestant and Orthodox counterparts, these relationships put a damper for the time being on ecumenicity. To take a purely hypothetical example, it would seem likely that when the Roman Catholic bishop of Yokohama needed help in putting across a particular program in his diocese, he would be more apt to look for help and advice from the Société des Missions-Étrangères in Paris than from Japanese Protestants in Yokohama. Thus, for a wide variety of reasons, Protestant–Catholic ecumenicity in Japan amounted to very little until Vatican II.

Student Work

To return to the more specifically Protestant forms of ecumenicity, the immediate postwar era saw fruitful cooperation in the area of student work. In retrospect, the period right after 1945 now seems like a "golden age" of Christian student work in Japan, before the onset of the many problems that were to tear the movement asunder. The ranks of students at that time were swollen with returning veterans from military service, many of whom had reflected deeply about the meaning of life in modern Japan. There were also Christian teachers who returned to academic work with a deepened sense of relevance and urgency for their faith, which they communicated to their students not only in classrooms but also in personal contacts on campus, in voluntary study groups, on retreats planned by student departments of the YMCA and YWCA, or on a local, informal basis. There were groups like the Tokyo Gakuseikai which became very active and enabled students and professors of many different denominational backgrounds to get to know each other and to work together cooperatively. Some of the friendships formed in this way were to continue in many different ways later on, in church-related student organizations, in student center work, in the Christian Academy movement, in groups of Christian faculty members, in World's Student Christian Federation (WSCF) activities, in Life and Mission of the Church study programs, and elsewhere.[17]

It has often been pointed out that the ecumenical movement among the churches of the West was profoundly influenced by the friendships and loyalties to ecumenical goals that were developed through Christian student activities in such groups as the WSCF. The same could surely be said to be the case in Japan in the prewar and postwar eras. Christian students organized their own conferences and invited as their speakers men like Yoshitaka Kumano and Kazō Kitamori, and their feelings were reciprocated by the theologians' spending many hours and days helping many kinds of Christian student activities. When the luster of that "golden age" began to fade, there were strong touches of nostalgia on both sides for the enthusiastic ecumenical atmosphere that had blossomed during that time.

The Aftermath of the Communist Victory in China (1949)

As has already been suggested, the triumph of the Chinese Communists on the mainland had profound effects on Christian work in Japan, for it caused the relocation of many groups in Japan that had previously operated in

China. While many of the groups and individuals, both Roman Catholic and Protestant, brought with them a desire to work cooperatively with other Christian groups, there were others who came with decidedly noncooperative attitudes. Several new fundamentalist Protestant groups were relocated in Japan at this time, and they brought with them deep-seated suspicions about other Protestant groups, which they had carried with them from North America or Europe, but in this case their news reinforced by what they considered to be the wholly inadequate stand of liberal Protestant groups vis-à-vis the Chinese Communists. So often had the YMCA in China proved to be a breeding ground for future Communists, it was sometimes said, that it should be dubbed instead the "Young Men's Communist Association." Such missionaries were appalled at the relaxed attitudes of many Japanese Protestant groups toward Communism at that time. The newcomers encountered Japanese Protestant students and teachers studying or discussing Marxism in an academic way, showing unconcern or perhaps approval toward the current manifestations of Marxism in mainland China. And in a broader sense, the ex-China missionaries brought with them a complex combination of psychological reactions to their former experiences, which at times hindered cooperative work with other Christians in Japan. After watching the collapse of a Christian community in China under Communist pressures, they were determined to avoid what they considered the mistakes of that experience, and to bring a new type of disciplined life of faith that would not suffer the same fate as the groups of China. The Christians of Japan who had not been disciplined in the same school of adversity would simply have to change their ways, or else face the prophetic wrath of the newcomers!

Quite apart from the ideological and psychological baggage that some ex-China missionaries brought with them to Japan, there was the simple fact that the Japanese Christian community was still far too small to absorb a larger number of newcomers in relations of close personal cooperation. Hence there arose a paradox that was to trouble mission work in Japan for some time thereafter: despite the fact that Japan was over 99 percent non-Christian, and that there were more opportunities and receptiveness to the gospel than for decades previously, the Christian community of Japan (which came increasingly to feel that the primary responsibility for evangelizing Japan was theirs) seemed unable to absorb more than a limited number of foreign missionaries and funds for evangelism. The result was that many of the newcomers started out in Japan with few relationships with other Christians, either foreign or Japanese. Although this increased their evangelistic zeal in many cases—for which it is hard to express sufficient admiration—it did work against ecumenical cooperation and heightened the sense of competitiveness among Christian groups. Such competition is not wholly blameworthy, from either a theological or a practical viewpoint, but it does postpone if not avoid altogether some of the serious problems of Christian cooperation and unity that must be faced sooner or later.

The Effects of the Korean War (1950–53)

The Korean War had a number of effects on Japan and its Christian community, some of which were felt right away, and others not for some time afterward. In the former category was the fact that the war had a direct effect on the negotiations for Japan's peace treaty. That treaty was signed in San Francisco on September 8, 1951, together with the Japan–United States Security Treaty, which was signed five hours later in the same city. Because Japan was still a major base for American operations in the Korean War, these two documents were drafted in such a way as to prolong the influence of the United States in Japan after the ending of the Occupation, with all that that implied. As far as Christian work was concerned, this meant the continuation, for many years, of the patterns of Christian work that had been drafted as only temporary measures during the confusion of the Occupation period. Insofar as the non-Christian population in Japan was concerned, however, the Korean War brought them a new picture of America as a nation not wholly dedicated to the pacifist principles that it had championed in the drafting of the Japanese peace constitution, but a country that was willing to go to war to prevent the extension of Communism in the Far East. This was not actually a change in the overall foreign-policy goals of the United States toward Japan and northeast Asia.[18] But for many idealistic Japanese who had assumed that the United States was devoted to pacifism, the Korean War came as a shock. The Christian boom characteristic of postwar Japan gradually came to an end during this period, as the number of inquirers and new converts leveled off in most of the churches. From the time of Perry and Harris onward, the United States has been for many Japanese "the Christian nation" par excellence, so that the reception given Christianity in Japan and the number of converts to the faith from the Meiji era onward bears a close correlation to the improvement or worsening of United States–Japan relations. Hence when the Korean War presented the United States in a poorer light to many Japanese than they had seen it previously, there was a marked decline of Japanese interest in Christianity, the major religion of America. Not all Japanese Christians were of a pacifist persuasion, however. Some Christians were disappointed that the United States was unable to secure a military victory in Korea. When an armistice was finally signed after a military stalemate in Korea, these nonpacifist groups had their own reasons to be disillusioned about America.

Another major effect of the Korean War, which was to take longer to recognize, was the upward improvement in the Japanese economy, fueled as it was by the many American contracts for war materials and services in Japan. The "economic miracle" of Japan dates from this period, although it of course had its roots in previous eras. The improved economic situation was to have its effects on all segments of Japanese life, including the Christian churches. For instance, the growing economy not only provided more jobs and somewhat higher salaries, but also brought about a spiraling in the value of land in urban areas. Christian groups could therefore not only count on somewhat larger amounts in their offering plates, but any groups that had been able to purchase land in the immediate postwar era at low prices were thereafter able to sell such land at bonanza prices. Thus many a competitive as well as cooperative project was launched on a relatively prosperous financial basis. But the growing prosperity was also to bring a growing secularization, which for better or worse would take its toll of the "theology of the cross" and the "theology of the pain of God" that had fallen on receptive ears during the difficult postwar years. In essence, the Korean War, by helping to make economic development the major factor in Japan's national life, worked along with the signing of the peace treaty, which took effect in 1952, to bring an end to the Occupation period and the mentality of the "postwar era" that have been our major concern thus far. Christian groups were faced with an entirely new situation in mission, and this was also the case with ecumenicity.

The Era of Rapid Economic Development (1952-68)

Historical periodization is always a dubious procedure, more an analytical device than a description of reality. But there is little doubt that the next sixteen years for Japan were dominated not so much by the American presence in Japan (which continued after the end of the Occupation, but with other names and forms), but by the phenomenal growth of the Japanese economy. Japan's Gross National Product—and the GNP became a sort of secular idol during this period—stood at 3946 billion yen in 1950, the year of the outbreak of the Korean War, and was thereafter to nearly double to 7465 billion in 1954, nearly double again to 14,678 billion in 1960, and more than double to 31,044 billion yen in 1965.[19] The far-reaching effects that economic development brought to all sectors of Japanese life have been dealt with in numerous books and articles and need not be repeated here.[20] But some of the implications for ecumenicity should be noted.

Urban-Industrial Developments

The economic development of Japan during this period was mainly centered on its urban areas, and to these cities flowed one of the major population migrations of modern times, as millions of Japanese families left rural areas for new jobs and livelihood in the cities. The very numbers of the people to be reached with the Christian message in urban areas, together with the mounting costs of carrying on urban ministries, might be considered as compelling reasons for Christians to set aside competitive programs and join in ecumenical endeavors. In some cases this happened, but there were many other instances where different denominations set up competing programs in the same areas. For one thing, improved transportation in urban areas made the delineation of "comity arrangements" between different groups difficult to establish and almost impossible to maintain. A church that was located near good transportation facilities found that it could minister to people scattered over a wide metropolitan area, without regard to other churches that were active in the same district. Indeed, the very mobility of church members in such a rapidly changing social climate should have made it easier for church members to transfer their memberships when they changed residence. But local Japanese congregations were often unwilling to transfer members to other congregations, because they would lose in both statistics and income. And for their part, church members were often loathe to transfer their membership from the church of the pastor who baptized them, because of lingering loyalty and associations with the group in which they first became Christian.[21] Hence a variety of factors conspired to make the new urban mobility and prosperity as much of a hindrance as a help to ecumenical cooperation between Christians.

Nor were the churches able to mount effective campaigns to meet the new urban conditions. To be sure, several denominations had their "urban evangelism plans," but sometimes these simply meant the expenditure of overseas funds in order to secure advantageous properties in places where they could develop their own programs, in competition with other Christian groups where this proved unavoidable. There were not even agencies in existence for interdenominational church planning until a much later date, when the NCCJ launched its Urban Industrial Committee, and the East Asia Christian Council (EACC) became active in the same field. In the meantime, even a denomination like the Kyōdan, which started programs in Labor Evangelism, which came to be called Occupational Evangelism and then Urban Industrial Evangelism with consequent changes in emphasis, was able to enlist the support of only a relatively small percentage of its pastors, laypersons, congregations, and denominational resources into programs to meet the new urban challenges. Some urban-based Christian groups did grow, but rarely as fast as the cities themselves were growing. Often the churches were facing setbacks in the cities, which had been since the Meiji era the major arenas for Christian work, both Catholic and Protestant.

During this period Harvey Cox's *Secular City* became popular in the West, with its celebration of the advantages of urban life for modern Christians. But for most Christian groups in Japan, growing urbanization loomed as less a constructive opportunity than a corrosive challenge. The ending of the Christian boom and the onset of a widespread secular mentality in Japan, for instance, meant that Sunday was no longer a day set aside primarily for rest and religious activities, if indeed it had ever meant that. Christian worship had to compete with labor union meetings, PTA and neighborhood-association meetings, sports activities, department-store sales, leisure activities, and the like, all of which took their toll of church attendance and strength.

Another primarily urban phenomenon was the development of the New Religions of Japan. These were not entirely "new" groups, strictly speaking, but might be described as new buildings constructed from old bricks. These groups often developed their largest congregations in urban areas, providing sources of continuity with rural experience for many millions of people who keenly felt the dislocations of the postwar era and the loss of purpose and direction in society after the collapse of "the Imperial Way" in religion and society. Thus the so-called religious vacuum that followed the emperor's renunciation of his divinity was filled not by the Christian churches, as Christians had so fervently hoped, but by New Religions. Groups such as Tenrikyō of Shintō background, and Risshō Kōsei-Kai and Sōka Gakkai of Nichiren Buddhist background, were able to harness the new forces of urban anomie, cultural uprootedness, desires for personal advancement and security, and problems of adjustment in lifestyles in ways that greatly strengthened their movements. Christian groups were not able to capitalize on the new urban trends to anywhere near the same extent. Hence, because the new forces brought into being by rapid social change in urban areas proved so threatening, Christian groups became mainly concerned with their own institutional survival, rather than initiating programs of mission and ecumenicity together with other Christian groups.

Lay Movements

The ecumenical picture was by no means all bleak, however, as Christian lay movements were to prove. When clergy tried to get lay Christians to work together in groups dominated by clergy, they often ran into trouble. But Christian lay persons were able to gather in many different kinds of groups of their own and find there a Christian fellowship that transcended denominational barriers. A mere listing of such groups would be a lengthy one, but it should include organizations like the Gideons with their programs of distributing Bibles in hotel rooms, Laymens' Prayer Breakfasts that met in cities across the nation for prayer and Christian fellowship, YMCA and YWCA groups of many sorts, "Three Loves" groups of farm workers, special local groups for sponsoring evangelistic campaigns or community Christmas celebrations, and many more. Although pastors were sometimes active in such groups, their participation was more often by special invitation, since laypersons were not eager to have their groups dominated by a pastor, as proved to be the case in all too many church-related organizations. For this very reason, the considerable contributions made by lay movements to the cause of ecumenicity were limited by the inability of such groups to relate successfully to the pastor-dominated church structures. Indeed, pastors sometimes looked upon the activities of such lay groups with considerable suspicion, for they feared (and sometimes correctly) that the participation of laity from their congregation would lessen their support of church-sponsored activities.

Christian Education

There was a vast area of cooperative Christian work that may be called in general "Christian education," for the lack of a better rubric. In this field one may include the activities of the Japan Bible Society, the work of various church boards of Christian education, Christian publishing houses, church music groups, religious broadcasters, cooperative Sunday school activities, and the work of Christian teachers in groups like the Christian Scholars Fellowship. Common to the work of these groups was the effort for Christians to work together in order to do a better job of proclaiming the Christian message in the modern world. Sometimes the very nature of their activities brought people together in new ways, as when Japanese Christian educators came together to host the World Council of Christian Education, in Tokyo in 1959. The very magnitude of the task of Christian education in the midst of a non-Christian society would seem to make cooperation all the more necessary. And here as elsewhere, friendships were formed that led to cooperative endeavors in other fields.

But even here, centripetal forces were to be countered by centrifugal ones. The fact that many Christian educators were of a liberal persuasion made their cooperative activities suspect in the eyes of conservative Christians in Japan. Hence conservative groups developed their own tracts, their own religious education materials, their own publications, their own Bible translations. In many cases, the programs that conservatives launched in this way proved to be far stronger than the liberal activities they were intended to correct or counteract. But whatever the case, the field of Christian education was to see both pluses and minuses as far as ecumenicity was concerned.

Overseas Missions

The ecumenical movement throughout the world has been deeply indebted to the missionary movement of the nineteenth and twentieth centuries for paving the way for later ecumenical endeavors and also for providing some of the personnel and the spirit to make ecumenicity possible.[22] The same proved true in Japan in recent years, but not to the same extent. As Christian groups became better established financially, they began to send workers overseas, somewhat as some Christians had done before and during World War II. But whereas the previous mission efforts had been launched primarily with governmental support and sometimes under government direction, the more recent programs were undertaken under private auspices. Often churches or groups in Europe or North America made the funds available through which Japanese workers were sent abroad. Groups such as the Japan Christian Medical Association (Ika Renmei), however, undertook the support of overseas Japanese medical workers through their own resources. Mission efforts of this sort, even when they were sponsored by one particular denomination, nevertheless drew upon the support of Christians of many different backgrounds. And because the field was so vast and the numbers engaged so few, harmful competition rarely resulted.

Vatican II and Ecumenicity

By far the most significant event since 1945 for ecumenicity, Protestant, Catholic, or Orthodox, was the holding of Vatican Council II from October 1962 to December 1965. While the Council is still too far-reaching an event for us to be able to make a comprehensive appraisal of its effects, one may nevertheless venture a few observations. The influence of Vatican II upon ecumenicity in Japan may be seen in three moments or phases, so to speak: the personal, the doctrinal, and the practical.

As a result of Pope John XXIII's announcement in January 1959 of his intention to summon an ecumenical council, a number of new personal contacts opened up between Roman Catholics and Protestants in Japan. Although there had been informal contacts on many levels previously, the new ecumenical mood gave them recognition and encouragement. Roman Catholic priests and Protestant pastors who had lived and worked near each other for some time, but who had been going their separate ways, now came to call on each other. It sometimes happened—as a participant in such an encounter told the present writer—that the social call began with the usual exchange of pleasantries as befits Japanese courtesy. But then there came the moments of silence, and the unexpressed wishes, on both sides, that they should both have stayed home in bed! What lay behind awkwardness of this sort? Despite the new courtesies, there was still the underlying sense of mutual competition, mingled with some long-standing doubts and distrust. But beyond that, there was deep uncertainty about doctrinal matters on both sides. What was it, precisely, that the Protestant was being asked to acknowledge in the forthcoming changes in Roman Catholicism? And what approach could a Catholic priest take to the divisions and confusions within Protestantism? Until Vatican II had given some concrete answers of a doctrinal nature, there were bound to be a number of uncertainties.

The doctrinal phase of Vatican II was spread out over its four sessions.[23] Those who had hoped for too much too soon were disappointed, but so also were those who had hoped for nothing at all. The most important document as far as the Catholic churches of Japan were concerned was the Constitution on the Sacred Liturgy, issued at the end of the second session (December 1963). In time this brought noticeable changes in the liturgy of local Catholic churches in Japan, such as the use of Japanese instead of Latin in the Mass, the singing of hymns in Japanese instead of the exclusive use of Latin plainsong, and a different location for the altar and the position of the celebrant of the Eucharist. All of these changes did help other Christians to develop a new understanding of Catholic worship, if they were at all interested. And the renewed emphasis on Scripture contained in the Dogmatic Constitution on

Divine Revelation, which after delays and revisions was issued in November 1965, encouraged renewed Bible study among Catholics, thus helping to build still more bridges with their "separated brethren."

Of high importance also, although not so visible in its immediate consequences, were the doctrinal statements of Vatican II on the church, its mission in the world, and its relations to other Christians and to non-Christian religions. The documents of the third session on the Church and on Ecumenism, and of the fourth session on the Relation of the Church to Non-Christian Religions, on the Church's Missionary Activity, and on the Church in the Modern World all addressed themselves to problems that had been long-standing roadblocks between Protestants and Catholics in Japan, even in the immediate postwar era. One of the Protestant observers at Vatican II, Professor Masatoshi Doi of Dōshisha School of Theology, indicated that he could recognize in such documents a serious wrestling with the issues of the church and present-day life that Protestants could read with great profit and joy. Vatican II thus helped to give doctrinal substance to the ecumenical hopes of Christians of many communions. The third phase of Vatican II, its practical results, may be seen in the many ways in which Roman Catholics and Protestants in Japan changed their modes of operation after Vatican II. Catholic scholars in Japan joined in the project of the Japan Bible Society for a new translation of the Bible in colloquial Japanese. There was cooperation in the Week of Prayer for Christian Unity, held each January 18–25; even the posters published and the liturgical booklets issued were carefully worded so they would avoid the linguistic peculiarities of any group. There were closer approaches also to the Orthodox churches of Japan, which had been seriously divided over disputes about the role of the Patriarch of Moscow. On the local level, some Catholic priests joined pastors' associations and participated in local planning for Christian activities. Roman Catholic and Protestant lay people got together on numerous occasions for Bible study, discussion meetings, community Christmas celebrations, religious broadcasting, and the like.

The practical results of Vatican II did not extend only to Christians. Roman Catholics in Japan were also ready to join with persons of other faiths in the new era of ecumenical dialogue that was opening. Discussions and meetings were arranged with Japan's small Jewish community, and the publication of the pseudonymous Isaiah Ben-Dasan's *The Japanese and the Jews* prompted a widespread spurt of interest in Japan concerning things Jewish.[24] There were also contacts between Christians and Zen Buddhists, sparked by the publications and activities of Fathers Heinrich Dumoulin, William Johnston, and Enomiya-Lasalle. There were cooperative relationships with leaders of the New Religions. Through the friendship of Father Joseph Spae, President Nikkyō Niwano of Risshō Kōsei-kai paid a call on Pope Paul VI at the Vatican. Father Spae is also to be credited with the remarkable series of scholarly studies on Christianity and Japanese religion (many of which had appeared in article form in the *Japan Missionary Bulletin*): *Christian Corri-*

dors to Japan (1965), *Christianity Encounters Japan* (1968), *Japanese Religiosity* (1971), and *Shintō Man* (1972) and *Buddhist-Christian Empathy* (1980). Whatever scholarly or doctrinal research that will be done hereafter in regard to Christianity's approach to Japanese religion would do well to make extended use of Father Spae's corpus. Practical efforts at ecumenicity must also encounter the many personal contacts that he made during the course of his missionary work in Japan. Groups like the Japan Ecumenical Association and the Ecumenical Discussion Group in Tokyo owe their origins to his friendship and encouragement.

Were there any negative results from Vatican II? There were, and even though they were minor in relation to the positive results of the Council, it may be worthwhile to mention them. There is little doubt that Vatican II brought more far-reaching changes to the Catholic church in a short time than could be fully absorbed right away, which set in motion a period of malaise, of deep uncertainty that upset the equilibrium of some otherwise staunch Roman Catholics. If Vatican II could bring so many far-reaching changes in such a short time, what might the future hold? Others came to feel that the expectations Vatican II had aroused were not being fulfilled and that the Council had in effect not gone far enough. As an aftermath of these differing points of view, one could encounter among Catholics disappointment, or consternation, or reaction, depending on their evaluation of the Council. Because of the mood of uncertainty among Roman Catholics while their internal house was being rearranged—a mood that many Protestants encountered in their church life also and which they had come to live with somehow in one way or another—it may be said that some of the attempted reforms of Vatican II were counterproductive. That is, even though the Council had strongly promoted the engagement of the church in the modern world, the aftermath of the Council brought about such internal uncertainties within the Catholic church that the very engagement with the world that it sought to promote was hindered. Some Catholics opted out of crucial social problems of Japanese society in the 1960s. To give one prominent example, we need to go back to a crisis that was just emerging in Japan at the very time Pope John XXIII announced his intention of calling a council, in January 1959. On the minds of many Japanese at that time were the problems of the impending 1960 Security Treaty.

The 1960 Security Treaty Crisis

In a very real sense, the 1960 crisis over the United States–Japan Mutual Security Treaty presented the first major occasion for a general public debate on Japan's major postwar policies in both international and domestic affairs. Until that time, everything that Japan had done in the international sphere had been a legacy of the Occupation, and therefore had to be accepted without real debate. But the proposals for the Mutual Security Treaty, and the way they were pushed through the Diet by Premier Kishi's Liberal Democratic party, aroused a storm of nationalistic controversy in which some Christian groups soon became embroiled. Only a minority of Christians who took strong positions in opposition to the Security Treaty found themselves in a temporary coalition of four main types of groups. (1) There were politically oriented Christian groups, which followed in general the political tactics of the People's Council for Preventing Revision of the Security Treaty, an organization that came to be dominated by the opposition political parties and by the Japan Communist party in particular. (2) There were also absolute pacifist groups, rooted in the stance of the Quakers and the Mennonites, who were opposed to any participation in military arrangements whatever. (3) Another group was concerned with the search for appropriate forms of Christian social action, taking their clues from the social outlook and theology of Emil Brunner, Reinhold Niebuhr, and John C. Bennett. (4) Finally, there were church formation groups that were primarily concerned with maintaining the integrity of the churches in the face of what they considered were growing militarist encroachments.

As the struggles over the Security Treaty deepened, new kinds of "ecumenicity" began to appear between such groups of disparate backgrounds. And there was still another countervailing "ecumenicity" among the majority of Christians, who were determined *not* to become involved as religious groups in such sensitive political and ideological issues. In this latter category were to be found most Roman Catholics, together with many middle-of-the-road as well as conservative Protestant groups, whose attitudes were influenced not least by an anti-Communist stance. There were also groups who were annoyed at what they considered to be the extremist political involvement of some of the antitreaty clergy. Although there were many reasons why Catholics in Japan were unwilling to become involved in the Security Treaty controversy—the majority of Catholic priests in Japan, for instance, were overseas missionaries and thus were unwilling to become involved in issues of domestic Japanese politics—their opting out of the debates about the treaty made it easier for activist Protestant spokespersons to assume a larger leadership role in the antitreaty movement.

The most significant result of the Security Treaty crisis for ecumenicity, therefore, was that it brought about new coalitions of groups that had previously been separated by denomination, geography, and so forth. Among Protestant churches like the Kyōdan, there came to be "social action groups" (Shakai-ha) on the one hand and "church-centered groups" (Kyōkai-ha) on the other. Even the abrupt ending of the Security Treaty crisis with the announcement on June 23, 1960, of Premier Kishi's intention to resign did not resolve the polarization that was beginning to take shape in Japanese society at large, and among Christian groups in particular. The events of 1960 wrought havoc with the Protestant "ecumenical consensus" about social action, which had been hammered out in the 1940s and 1950s under the influence of the writings of Reinhold Niebuhr and others. A New Left gradually began to emerge after the 1960 crisis, which stressed the need for a "political theology" as part of a revolutionary process for society, and for which the tactics of parliamentary politics seemed a snare and a delusion. This meant that when the Security Treaty issue would emerge again just before 1970, at the end of the treaty's initial ten-year term, the struggle against the treaty would be waged on much more ideological lines than was the case in 1960. This too had profound repercussions for ecumenicity.[25]

The Ecumenicity of the World Council of Churches and of the World Denominational Fellowships

No discussion of ecumenicity in Japan would be adequate without reference to the influence of the WCC and the world denominational fellowships on the Christian community in Japan.

At the beginning, however, note must be made of a tendency among many Japanese Protestants to filter out ecumenical perspectives from the world Christian community. There is a tendency in Japan—which indeed exists in almost all countries to some extent—to isolate "ecumenical personnel" from the rest of the Japanese Christian community. Hence, if Japanese Christians become fluent in foreign languages and active in ecumenical meetings, their views are not assured of a ready acceptance at home. And documents about church conditions abroad are sometimes received with the comment that because conditions are so different in Japan there can be little or no application of these insights to the local scene. There has also been a strong emphasis on the autonomy of the Japanese Christian community—about which more will be said in a subsequent section—dating back to such figures as Kanzō Uchimura and Masahisa Uemura in the Meiji era, and this has meant that Japanese Protestants continue to study about overseas church concerns, but always at a respectful distance.[26]

Be that as it may, during the immediate postwar period there was a certain congruence between the idealism about world Christian cooperation that pervaded the WCC from the time of its organization at the Amsterdam Assembly in 1948 and the idealism that characterized the Japanese churches at the time, which emphasized the unity of a world living in peace. Even though Japanese delegates to ecumenical conferences were not as loquacious as those from other nations, they nevertheless accepted most of the principles and programs for which the WCC stood at that time. WCC study materials also received considerable attention in Japan. Because the WCC was at that time largely dominated by the churches of Europe and North America, the WCC was seen in Japan as a useful organ for learning about Western theology and programs. But a period of transition began with the WCC's New Delhi Assembly in 1961, as has been noticed in the same connection by the WCC's new general secretary, the Reverend Philip Potter.[27] At the New Delhi Assembly a number of Orthodox churches, led by the Russian Orthodox Church, joined the WCC, as did a number of churches from the Third World. In time the concerns of these churches, together with a changing international climate that was growing weary of the cold war, brought about changes in the agenda of the WCC. Some of the issues of the Third World, which had long been neglected by the Western churches—poverty, racism, war, anticolonialism— were pushed to the forefront of WCC programs. The first noticeable change as far as Japan was concerned was a result of the Geneva Conference on Church and Society (1966), which was dominated by motifs of the developing "theology of revolution."[28] The Japanese delegates to that Geneva conference were divided in their reactions to what had taken place there, and this division foreshadowed the polarization that would occur during the 1968–70 university and church struggles in Japan, in regard to the New Left student groups who were ideologically committed to the revolutionary process.

In a broader sense, the stance with which the WCC has been asssociated recently has in the eyes of some Japanese Protestants made the overall ecumenical task much harder. For instance, WCC spokespersons have at times taken a quasi-journalistic approach to crucial issues of Christian faith and life, much like the Athenians of Paul's time who "love nothing more than to tell about or listen to something new" (Acts 17:21, NAB). There has also been said to be an atmosphere of feverish politicking in such circles, which makes serious concern for substantial matters very difficult. Commenting on the fact that the membership of the Catholic church in the WCC is not to be expected within the immediate future, Cardinal John Willebrands noted: "Honesty compels one to admit that the confused situation of Catholic theology, the crisis of authority, and the attitudes that are being assumed within the field of ecclesial discipline, not only by individuals but even by entire groups, are certainly not making it easier for the Catholic Church to join the WCC."[29] The cardinal was being diplomatic in pointing only to the problems within the Catholic church, but are we amiss to read between the lines that these same difficulties exist in even greater measure in the WCC?

This is not the place to give adequate consideration to the ecumenicity of the world denominational fellowships: the Baptist World Alliance, the World Alliance of Reformed Churches, the Lutheran World Federation, the Pan Anglican Congress, and other smaller groups. Each of these groups has undertaken programs involving their constituents in Japan, with varying results. A basic question that needs to be raised about each of these bodies is this: Are their programs designed to deepen and strengthen the work of the entire Christian community in Japan and elsewhere, or are they set up to involve their constituents in Japan in world denominational programs in such ways that their relationships to fellow Christians in other denominations in Japan and elsewhere are weakened or even destroyed? Such considerations are crucial for both the mission and the unity of the Christian community in Japan.

Evangelistic Crusades

Cooperative relationships among Christian groups have been deeply influenced by joint evangelistic crusades. In the immediate postwar era

E. Stanley Jones and Lawrence Lacour were prominent in the campaigns that they conducted on behalf of a number of churches, particularly in the Kyōdan. Later there were larger citywide crusades conducted by Bob Pierce and Billy Graham, which involved a wide variety of local sponsoring groups, even though much of the financing came from overseas. And the contributions of Japanese evangelists such as Toyohiko Kagawa and Kōji Honda must not be overlooked. In order to carry out such cooperative programs, a great deal of local ecumenical effort was called forth that would not otherwise have been possible.

But here, also, there have been negative results as well. The *yajirobē* that is ecumenicity was pulled by centrifugal forces as well as by centripetal ones. Some Christians felt that highly publicized evangelistic efforts created more problems than they did opportunities. The unwillingness of evangelist Billy Graham to criticize the involvement of the United States in the Vietnam War was seen as hindering his credibility as a Christian spokesman for peace before the Japanese public. In the case of the Kyōdan, the holding of the crusades caused the denomination's Evangelism Committee to develop other types of evangelistic programs, which were thought to be ultimately more effective that crusade-type evangelism.

Theological Education

Japan has had too many theological training programs, and they are inadequately supported. Hence the theological schools have been in the forefront of promoting cooperative efforts for the improvement of their programs and for finding means of coping with the ever-growing problems they face. Spurred on by the Theological Education Fund (TEF) encouragement and offers of financial assistance, over a dozen seminaries came together to form the Japan Association for Theological Education (JATE), which thereupon became a member of the North East Asia Association of Theological Schools (NEAATS), together with similar associations of seminaries in Korea and Taiwan. These associations have sponsored various assemblies and study conferences at which theological educators have come together to discuss and work on common problems, and together they have also been publishing the *Northeast Asia Journal of Theology* as a theological voice for the region. Even though such activities were initially made possible through TEF financial grants, there are indications that most of the significant programs will continue as TEF funds are withdrawn.[30]

Despite such organizations for cooperative efforts, the seminaries were unable to deal cooperatively with a series of shocks they received from the student disturbances and church struggles that erupted after 1968. It is significant that the waves of challenge, which broke over the churches as part of the general student upheavals that Japan faced in the 1968–70 period, largely started in the seminaries. They have had widespread ramifications, and we need to look at some of their influences on ecumenicity in the next period we are to examine, the era of challenge and reappraisal.

The Era of Challenge and Reappraisal (since 1968)

There are occasionally ground swells of historical change that are so significant that they are recognized by almost everybody, even if they are hard to
analyze precisely. Such a ground swell that affected the churches—especially
the Kyōdan, the Baptist Renmei, the Baptist Dōmei, the Free Methodist
Church, and to some extent the Seikōkai—began to take place with the onset
(1968) of a series of university struggles. These soon had their repercussions
in many theological seminaries and from there spread to church districts and
local congregations. While these struggles had diverse origins, they had common elements in their raising thoroughgoing doubts about existing organizations, whether they were governments, corporations, schools, churches, or
anything else. These challenges arose because of protests against the continuing war in Vietnam, against the production and testing of nuclear weapons,
against the United States–Japan Mutual Security Treaty and its network of
bases and military preparations, against the buildups of the Japan Self-
Defense Forces and other measures interpreted as a revival of the militaristic
and imperialistic posture of prewar Japan. In the eyes of the protestors, Japan was already becoming a renewed menace to world peace and was already
exploiting people at home and abroad through its industries and its policies,
which were in close collaboration with capitalist allies in the United States,
Europe, and elsewhere. With such a conspiratorial view of history, any organization or project can become suspect. And as it turned out, the project
upon which the lightning struck was one of the major ecumenical endeavors
of modern Japan.

The Christian Pavilion at Expo '70

The idea of having a Christian Pavilion at the Osaka World Exposition
(Expo '70) originally emerged from an interdenominational group of laity in
the Osaka area, but it was in time given varying degrees of endorsement by
the National Christian Council of Japan, the Japan Ecumenical Association,
the Catholic Church in Japan, the Orthodox Church in Japan, and the
Kyōdan's General Assembly. Following the example of the joint Roman
Catholic–Protestant cooperative efforts at the Montreal World Exposition in
1967, the sponsoring group in Japan undertook this pavilion as the first major project involving Roman Catholic, Protestant—and subsequently,
Orthodox—cooperation in Japanese Christian history. Although plagued by
continuing financial problems and controversy in some of the churches, the
pavilion's organizers managed to carry out the pavilion program, which attracted 2,324,679 visitors and was judged by some to have been one of the
most significant pavilions at Expo '70.[31]
    Yet the Christian Pavilion served as a focal point for controversies that
have seriously divided the Kyōdan—and other churches, but to a far lesser
extent—from that time on. The criticisms, orginating with seminarians and

progressive pastors, were partly directed against any Christian participation in Expo '70 itself, which was seen as a ruse by the Japanese government to draw the attention of the public, by this "festival of capitalism," away from the more serious issues of the day, which were embodied in the United States-Japan Mutual Security Treaty. But criticisms were also directed against the very questionable decision-making processes by which the Christian Pavilion had been endorsed by the NCCJ and the Kyōdan. For some, the fact that the Christian Pavilion was jointly sponsored by the Holy See and therefore had a quasi-diplomatic status led to serious problems about issues of the separation of religion and society in Japan.

Indeed, the echoes of the Christian Pavilion controversy have continued to rumble, long after the close of Expo '70 and the complete dismantling of the pavilion itself. This controversy has led to serious polarization within the largest Protestant denomination in Japan, but it may be argued that such polarization would have happened around another issue—given the Kyōdan's previous background—even if the Christian Pavilion had never been undertaken. And the controversy made the advocates of ecumenicity realize that their task was no easy one, but would require greater efforts at the grass-roots level, rather than merely at the level of officialdom. The experience of building the pavilion and its program demonstrated that such grassroots support of ecumenicity was indeed present, if enthusiasm for it could only be enlisted in suitable ways.

Antiwar Activities

While the promoters of the Christian Pavilion were developing one style of ecumenicity, another style was being developed by their critics. (If this seems to be stretching the understanding of "ecumenicity," the reader is urged to refer again to the characterization of the word in the first paragraphs of this chapter.) The antiwar activists held that the issues of war and peace in East Asia and the world were more crucial than any superficial pageantry and required the support of persons of all religions, and of no religion at all. Although such groups operated with the support of only some sections of the established churches and sometimes brought about disruptions in the churches, their impact on church life and on ecumenicity was far from minimal. They drew inspiration and support from antiwar activists in many countries, as for instance from the Berrigan brothers, the Roman Catholic priests in America whose strong stands against the Vietnam War included the destruction of military conscription records. The activities of these groups in Japan caused serious divisions in Protestant churches, especially when some church leaders tried to utilize the activities of these "problem posers" toward stirring up reforms within church structures, only to find out that their anarchistic tactics played havoc with established structures of any kind. Although it is far too early to form an evaluation of these activists, it is highly probable that the future course of ecumenicity in Japan will have to take account of their activities, in one form or another.

Emphasis on Japanese Autonomy

From the 1970s onward almost all Japanese Christian denominations, from the extremely conservative Protestant groups to the larger Protestant denominations, and the Roman Catholic and Orthodox churches, have felt the ever-growing pressures toward Japanese autonomy. In a sense, these pressures have always been present in Japan, from the time of Christianity's introduction to Japan under Saint Francis Xavier and again at the time of its reintroduction in the nineteenth century. Since 1945 many people have frequently referred to the need for placing full responsibility for the control and development of Japanese Christian churches directly into the hands of Japanese Christians themselves. But although lip service was often paid to such ideals, there were numerous ways in which foreigners were able to maintain a measure of control in the immediate postwar years, due to the privations which Christians in Japan were then facing. But the nation's astounding economic growth changed these circumstances, even though Christians themselves shared only modestly in the average increase in affluence. Quite apart from economic factors, however, was the growing realization that it was unwise for Christian groups in Japan to be beholden to overseas Christians for personnel or directions, especially when the signs of the times seemed to point to unique forms of witness that only Japanese Christians could carry out in relation to their society and toward people of other nations as well.

If Japanese Christians were, in fact as well as in theory, to take charge of the future course of Christianity in their islands, then it became obvious that some new forms of ecumenical cooperation were in order. For one thing, since the Christian community was still, in terms of percentages, one of the smallest Christian communities anywhere in the world, no one denomination could hope to go it alone in witnessing to Japanese society as a whole. They ought to work together, it would appear, and share their limited resources. But it was also obvious that the resources were widely scattered. Roman Catholics had a clear lead in Christian novelists, for instance, while the larger Protestant denominations enjoyed a dominance in regard to creative Japanese theologians, and the smaller Protestant denominations excelled in enthusiasm for evangelism. The same could be said for resources of almost every sort. There was no guarantee that these limited resources would not be squandered in debilitating competitive enterprises instead of being used in cooperative fashion, but at least there was the hope that the challenges of the current era would help to clarify the issues.

Christian Dialogue with People of Other Faiths

As was mentioned in the section on Vatican II, the ecumenical dialogue of the present is going beyond the bounds of the Christian community alone and is including other religious and ideological groups as well. Indeed, some of the programs sponsored by the WCC and the new Vatican secretariats have attempted to initiate or continue such dialogues. But dialogues between the different religious communities, such as have had prominence in areas like India, for example, have not been so significant in Japan. To be sure, there have been programs for religious dialogue for some time in Japan: the NCCJ's Center for the Study of Japanese Religions, in Kyoto, in which Professor Masatoshi Doi has been prominent; the International Institute for the Study of Religion, in Tokyo, established by Professor Hideo Kishimoto and Dr. William Woodard; the Oriens Institute for Religious Research, in Tokyo, established by Father Joseph Spae; and the programs of the Japan Christian academies. But these activities have always been on the fringes of the established churches and were often of more interest and concern to overseas personnel than to Japanese Christians. There are signs that such dialogues may take on increased meaning, however, through such groups as the World Conference on Religion and Peace, which was started in Kyoto primarily through the initiative of President Nikkyō Niwano of Risshō Kōsei-kai. To be sure, whenever such groups seem to take on the functions of pressure groups, there are bound to be reactions to them and other groups formed to counter their influence. Such pressures are what keep the *yajirobē* on his perch, but they also keep him from making any forward movement.

It may be noted that the outcome of such interfaith dialogues is very much determined by which groups Christians choose to talk to: whether Zen Buddhists, or Shintō followers, or one of the New Religions, or Marxists, or Jōdo-Shunshū Buddhists, or others. If one wants to deal more with problems, with social analysis, or with the psychology of mass movements, it all depends on which partners one chooses for the interfaith dialogue.

The Charismatic Movement

Although it did not start as a movement for ecumenical cooperation, there is no doubt that the charismatic movement, which emphasizes the gifts of the Holy Spirit for the renewal of the churches, especially the gift of speaking in tongues, has definite implications for ecumenicity. Despite the fact that glossolalia has never completely died out in the Christian churches since the time of Pentecost, its appearances have often caused great suspicion, ridicule, or fear, even with the emergence of the Pentecostal denominations in the early 1900s. But the late 1960s saw the emergence in America and in Europe of a Neo-Pentecostal movement, which quickly spread through all the mainline Protestant denominations and very widely in the Roman Catholic Church as well.[32] No longer automatically ostracized by the established churches, charismatic groups in recent years have received increasing support from Christians of many backgrounds, and when they gather for meetings, it is often without regard for denominational affiliation. Although generally unwilling to become involved in social issues as such, charismatic groups have demonstrated the ability to reach and deal with narcotics addicts, on whom the rest of society—including the churches—have often turned their backs.

Charismatic groups have run into opposition in the established churches, of course, and their activities among the Japanese Christian community have often met with hostility or indifference. It does seem likely, however, that charismatic followers, together with conservative evangelical groups that carry many of the same emphases, may increasingly provide a third major form of ecumenicity, along with the Protestant-Orthodox and the Roman Catholic forms.[33] There will of course be tensions here, but it is possible that the Holy Spirit may be able to use such tensions for the renewal of the church.

Ad Hoc Ecumenical Projects

Ecumenicity in Japan may increasingly depend less on organized structures and more on ad hoc project groups, which are established only for a limited time and a particular purpose. The common project for a new colloquial Japanese translation of the Bible, for instance, has been the work of scholars enlisted by the Japan Bible Society, including a number of Roman Catholic scholars. Among conservative groups, the New Japanese Bible was also a joint project of conservative scholars of several different Protestant denominations. In Tokyo, the Inochi no Denwa, or Lifeline telephone counseling service mentioned earlier, has been a cooperative project of Protestants, Roman Catholics, and others from its very beginning. There has also been an informal group to support the work of Friendship House (community center), of which Kyōdan pastor the Reverend Reiji Takahashi is director, with broad Catholic-Protestant backing. The very enumeration of such ad hoc ecumenical projects is a lengthy task, for such groups are scattered throughout Japan. And where these projects are focused on meeting urgent human needs, and do not require large organizational overhead, they are not likely to encounter the opposition that many other ecumenical programs have. As such, they may be one of the most significant forms of ecumenicity in the days to come.

We have seen from this survey that the problem of forming "a human society" among separated Christians, to which John Calvin alluded in the sixteenth century, is still very much an issue in the twentieth. Christians in Japan since 1945 have undertaken hosts of ecumenical ventures, some of which are still active, many of which have disappeared. Indeed, one wonders whether or not all these activities have borne sufficient fruit to warrant any optimism for the future. Would the *yajirobē* that is ecumenicity continue to spin around in circles on his precarious perch, kept there by a balance of centripetal and centrifugal forces, but unable to make much forward motion?

The Vatican's Cardinal Willebrands made this generalization at the conclusion of a survey of the ecumenical scene:

The ecumenical work, and more particularly the overcoming of the doctrinal differences, are not facilitated by the general climate of the society of today and the situation of Christianity itself, exposed as it is to the violent impact of the phenomena of demythologization and secularization that have caused quite a few people to lose their doctrinal clarity and certainty. Some people are thus falling prey to fright and discouragement, while others, abandoning themselves to sentiment and to impatience, dedicate themselves to a superficial ecumenism. . . .

This sounds like more than sufficient grounds for discouragement all around, even if one does not accept all the negative premises of his analysis. But Cardinal Willebrands ends on a more positive note, and one with which we can completely concur as we conclude this survey:

The situation that we have outlined in this review therefore shows that the Spirit of Christ, the spirit of unity, is always strongly at work, and continues to inspire Christians with the desire for unity and the will to cooperate with the action of the Spirit of God. In this sense, therefore, ecumenism, far from giving reasons for preoccupation, is a source of new courage and new confidence in the midst of the present crisis.[34]

NOTES

1. John Calvin, as quoted in George H. Tavard, *Two Centuries of Ecumenism* (Notre Dame, Ind.: Mentor-Omega, 1960), p. 13.

2. A helpful study of this period is still William C. Kerr, *Japan Begins Again* (New York: Friendship Press, 1949), pp. 1-13.

3. Charles W. Iglehart, *A Century of Protestant Christianity in Japan* (Tokyo: Tuttle, 1959), p. 283.

4. Ibid., p. 300.

5. "A Brief History of the United Church of Christ in Japan" [enacted 1954], in *Policy Statements and Statistics of the United Church of Christ in Japan* (Tokyo: Kyōdan, 1968). Cf. S. Yamaya, ed., *Nihon Kirisuto Kyōdan Shi* [A History of the United Church of Christ in Japan], (Tokyo: Kyōdan, 1967).

6. Valuable discussions of these developments are contained in Yasushi Kuyama, ed., *Gendai Nihon no Kirisutokyō* [Christianity in Modern Japan], (Tokyo: Sōbunsha, 1961). Prof. Yoshimitsu Akagi gave insight for this chapter.

7. Richard H. Drummond, *A History of Christianity in Japan* (Grand Rapids, Mich.: Wm. B. Eerdmans, 1971), p. 267.

8. Ruth Rouse and Stephen C. Neill, eds., *A History of the Ecumenical Movement, 1517—1948* (Philadelphia: Westminster Press, 1954), pp. 388-89.

9. John M. Nakajima, "Ecumenical Standstill and the Japanese Mentality," *JMB* 28, no. 1 (January-February 1974): 20-28.

10. For Roman Catholic ecumenism, see Tavard, *Two Centuries of Ecumenism.*

11. See Joseph L. Van Hecken, *The Catholic Church in Japan since 1859* (Tokyo:

Herder, 1963), p. 55. On Protestant antagonisms toward Roman Catholics, see Drummond, *History*, pp. 155ff.

12. The best account is still C. R. Boxer, *The Christian Century in Japan* (Berkeley: University of California Press, 1951). For a recent appraisal of this period, see Joseph Jennes, *A History of the Catholic Church in Japan (1549—1873)* (Tokyo: Oriens, 1973), pp. 3–29.

13. Kenneth Scott Latourette, *These Sought a Country* (New York: Harper, 1950), p. 76.

14. For example, Joseph J. Spae, *Christian Corridors to Japan* (Tokyo: Oriens, 1965), pp. 133–62.

15. For instance, Tucker Callaway, *Japanese Buddhism and Christianity* (Tokyo: Shinkyō Shuppansha, 1957). A different approach is found in A. K. Reischauer, *The Nature and Truth of the Great Religions* (Tokyo: Tuttle, 1966). There have been numerous surveys of this field on a broader scale. A recent one is Owen C. Thomas, ed., *Attitudes toward Other Religions* (London: SCM, 1969).

16. See Van Hecken, *Catholic Church*, pp. 91–101.

17. Risto Lehtonen, "The Study of a Storm: An Ecumenical Case Study" [of the WSCF], in *Study Encounter* 8, no. 1 (1972).

18. Masataka Kosaka, *100 Million Japanese: The Postwar Experience* (Tokyo: Kodansha, 1972), pp. 108–9.

19. *Japan Handbook* (Tokyo: Rengo Press, 1967), p. 120. Figures are from the Finance Ministry.

20. For the impact of economic and social changes on the churches during this period, see Charles H. Germany, *The Response of the Church in Changing Japan* (New York: Friendship Press, 1967), chaps. 2 and 3.

21. Joseph J. Spae, *Catholicism in Japan* (Tokyo: IISR Press, 1964), p. 40.

22. This is well documented in Kenneth Scott Latourette, *A History of the Expansion of Christianity*; vol. 7: *Advance through Storm* (New York: Harper 1945), esp. pp. 5–38; and Stephen Neill, *Christian Missions* (London: Penguin, 1954), chap. 13.

23. For the documents and their background, see Walter M. Abbott, ed., *The Documents of Vatican II* (New York: Guild Press, 1966).

24. The English translation is Isaiah Ben-Dasan, *The Japanese and the Jews* (New York and Tokyo: Weatherhill, 1972).

25. This section is based on a paper prepared by the writer for the International Conference on Japanese Studies, November 1972, "The 1960 Security Treaty Crisis and the Christians of Japan," in *Studies on Japanese Culture*, vol. 2 (Tokyo: The Japan P.E.N. Club, 1973).

26. Hiroshi Shinmi and James M. Phillips, "The Ecumenical Gap," *Japan Christian Quarterly*, Winter 1969, pp. 39–44.

27. Philip Potter, "The Present and Future of the Ecumenical Movement," *Christian Century*, 89, no. 30 (Aug. 30, 1972): 847. This may be compared with a Roman Catholic appraisal of WCC activities: Cardinal John Willebrands, "Panorama of the Ecumenical Scene to 1971," *L'Osservatore Romano* (weekly edition in English), Nov. 16, 1972, pp. 7–8.

28. E.g., John C. Bennett, ed., *Christian Social Ethics in a Changing World* [one of the four study volumes for the 1966 Geneva Conference on Church and Society], (New York: Association Press, 1966), pp. 23–43.

29. Willebrands, "Panorama," p. 8.

30. See "The Historical Background of the Northeast Asia Association of Theological Schools," *NEAJT*, no. 1 (March 1968), pp. 132–42; also "On a Rocky Coast—Waiting for Daylight: Theological Educators on a Rough Voyage, 1971–72," *NEAJT*, no. 8 (March 1972), pp. 60–67.

31. Yoshinobu Kumazawa and Paul Pfister, *Eyes and Hands; The Discovery of Humanity: The Christian Pavilion at Expo '70* (Tokyo: Enderle, 1970), p. 32.

32. There are numerous books on the charismatic movement of Neo-Pentecostalism, of which these two general introductions are among the best: John L. Sherrill, *They Speak with Other Tongues* (New York: Pyramid Books, 1964); Kevin and Dorothy Ranaghan, *Catholic Pentecostals* (Paramus, N.J.: Deus Books, 1969).

33. This was anticipated by Lesslie Newbigin, *A Faith for This One World* (New York: Harper & Row, 1962).

34. Willebrands, "Panorama," p. 8. The writer is indebted to Fr. Raymond Renson of the Oriens Institute for calling this article to his attention.

8

Biblical Studies in Japan: Between the Ivory Tower and the Barricade

Introduction: The Bible in Japanese Christian History

"Thy word," sang the psalmist of ancient Israel, "is a lamp unto my feet, and a light unto my path." And whenever these words are read by Christians in Japan, they have a contemporary ring of truth. For the Bible has not only been a source of guidance to Christians in their services of public worship and in private devotion, but has also been a primary means of introducing the public at large to the meaning of Christian faith. It is remarkable that in a country where the total number of Christians is less than 1 percent of the population, the Bible has been a best-seller from the postwar period onward.[1] In fact, Japan's total Bible sales have ranked third in the world, surpassed only by the United States and India.[2]

To those familiar with the history of Christianity in Japan, the centrality of Bible studies and distribution should not come as a surprise. For in its Protestant form, Japanese Christianity has always been strongly based on biblical studies. Christian congregations can often trace their origins to small groups devoted to the study of Scripture. The history of the early development of Japanese Christian thought is very largely an account of the development of biblical studies.[3] From quite an early period virtually all schools and shades of biblical interpretation in Western countries found their advocates in Japan.[4] Scriptural work had a strong impact on the very forms of Protestant Christianity in Japan, after Kanzō Uchimura and his followers in Mukyōkai (Non-Church Christianity) rejected the organizational structures of Western Christendom in favor of independent Japanese groups devoted to Bible study.[5] For their part, the organized Protestant denominations from the Meiji era onward put such stress on the Scriptures that their growth was to some extent the result of widespread Bible distribution.[6] During the difficult period of militarism and the Pacific War, when government pressures against Christian groups mounted, searching the Scriptures continued to be a mainstay of the faith. There is little wonder, then, that in the postwar period the way had long been prepared for a place of continuing significance of the Bible in the life of the Japanese Christian community.

Even to a casual visitor to a Protestant church in Japan in the postwar era, the centrality of the Bible would be evident. Church members regularly brought their Bibles as well as their hymnals with them to church and followed the Scripture lessons read from the pulpit in their own Bibles. Before the preacher began his sermon, he would almost invariably announce his text, and the Bibles of church members would be kept open at the text during the sermon. Worshipers would frequently underline their Bibles and keep notes in the margins, and some would keep copious notes in a separate notebook. Sunday school classes also focused strongly on the Bible, and Sunday evening church services—where they still existed—would often be straight Bible-study sessions. Church bulletins would sometimes suggest texts for daily devotional Bible reading during the week, and the reading of Scripture commentaries was widespread among the laity as well as the clergy. In short, the amount of attention given to the Bible, and the seriousness—one is almost tempted to say the grave solemnity—with which its study is taken, often comes as quite a surprise to Western Christians visiting Japan, accustomed to a more cavalier approach to the Bible as one of those "great books" often praised but seldom read. Such stress on the Scriptures in Japan, by pastors, laity, and inquirers alike, furnishes the background for the academic studies of the Bible that are the concern of this chapter.

New Japanese Translations of the Bible

To begin with, there was a severe shortage of Bibles in postwar Japan, for many had been burned during the air raids, and the entire stock of the Japan Bible Society had been depleted. The American Bible Society responded to this need by printing and shipping 2.5 million copies of the New Testament to Japan by the end of 1947.[7] This was the JBS *bungotai* (literary) version of the Scriptures, of which the New Testament was first published in 1879 and revised in 1917, and the Old Testament published in 1887.[8] There were also republications of Catholic scriptural translations, notably Father Emile Raguet's New Testament, originally issued in 1910.[9] There was also an Orthodox Church translation of the New Testament, which was reprinted in the postwar era. It had been produced through the efforts of Bishop Nicolai, the founder of the Orthodox Church in Japan.[10] In addition, there were numbers of other translations of parts of the Bible, done in both literary and colloquial styles, which circulated both before and after the Pacific War, but we shall here focus on the widely available editions.

Because of the vast changes in the Japanese language since the period when the literary-style editions of Scripture were written, the Japan Bible Society set out in 1951 to prepare a new translation in *kōgotai* (colloquial Japanese). The New Testament committee members were Professor Shōgo Yamaya of Tokyo Union Seminary and Professor Masashi Takahashi of Dōshisha University in Kyoto, and they completed their work in 1954. The Old Testament members were Professors Senji Tsuru of Meiji Gakuin University, Giichirō Tezuka of Tokyo Union Seminary, and Toshio Endō of the Anglican Central Theological Seminary, who finished their task in 1955.[11]

It is significant to note that the members of the JBS committees did not include any scholars who were Roman Catholics, Mukyōkai, or conservative evangelicals. Each of these groups subsequently produced its own scriptural translations. The Japanese Catholic hierarchy took up the task of a new translation of the Old Testament, which was entrusted to the Franciscans and completed by them in 1959. Meanwhile, Father Federico Barbaro of the Salesians undertook a *kōgotai* translation, of which the New Testament appeared in 1953 and the complete Bible in 1964.[12] Professor Masao Sekine of the Mukyōkai published his translations of Old Testament books in a series by the Iwanami Publishing Company, beginning in 1956 with Genesis. He also collaborated with Professor Gorō Mayeda, another Mukyōkai scholar, in the translation of several Old Testament and New Testament books for a volume entitled *The Bible*, which was number 12 in a series by Chūō Kōron entitled "Great Books of the World" (1968). And a group of conservative evangelical scholars dissatisfied with the JBS *kōgotai* translation, produced the *New Japanese Bible* (Seisho: Shin Kaiyaku, 1965).

When it appeared in 1955, the JBS colloquial Bible was widely acclaimed. It received the Mainichi Newspaper Award as the Book of the Year and was recommended by the National Library Association as its selection of the year.[13] But, because it had decided limitations, and also because of archeological discoveries and continuing biblical research, the JBS decided in 1970 to start the preparation of a new translation, this one to be a common effort by a joint committee of Roman Catholic and Protestant scholars, for use by both communions. It is interesting to note, however, that the committee still contains no members of a Mukyōkai or conservative evangelical background.

The Renewal of Biblical Studies in Japan after 1945

While translation projects were moving ahead in the postwar period, scholarly work on the Scriptures was also being revived, often by the same people who were involved in the translations. It would be impossible, of course, to give anything like an adequate listing of everything done in this field, but an indication of some of the main scholars and their representative writings may be helpful.

There were, to speak very generally, four major schools of biblical studies that became active in postwar Japan, all of them having their roots in Japanese Christianity going back to the Meiji era. They may be classified as: (*a*)

Roman Catholic catechetical studies of the Scriptures; (b) Protestant church-centered studies; (c) Protestant academic studies; and (d) Protestant evangelistic studies. Bearing in mind that it is very artificial to make watertight distinctions between such categories, and that they all overlap and interpenetrate each other to some extent, we note some of the main characteristics of each group of studies.

Roman Catholic Catechetical Studies of the Scriptures

One of the major concerns of Roman Catholics in postwar Japan in regard to scriptural studies was for catechetical materials.[14] The use of the Scriptures in the Mass readings and in devotional materials was also basic, but it seems to have been in connection with catechetical materials that some of the hard problems of scriptural studies were posed. To give but one example, the lesson in the 1896 *Catholic Catechism* (Kōkyō Yōri) on the Old Testament—which was in pre-World War II days a frequent battleground between Shintō ideology and Christian doctrine—was deleted from the 1925 edition, restored in 1936, deleted again from the 1942 wartime edition, and restored again in the postwar 1947 edition.[15] There was increased concern expressed in the postwar era that the catechism needed to be brought up to date in order to reflect the changed situation of postwar Japan as well as the modifications of the Japanese language. In the 1960 catechism a number of appropriate Scripture verses were added to the answers, and these were put in colloquial Japanese. But as George Mueller has pointed out, the official Japanese catechisms have always been more sparse in their use of Scripture than was Father Deharbe's 1847 European catechism, which was the basis for the first official Japanese catechism in 1896 and for its successors down to 1960.[16]

It was, rather, in connection with what came to be commonly known as "precatechetics" that Catholic Scripture studies moved forward. At a three-day study conference of Catholic missionaries from East Asia, held in Bangkok in October 1962, the use of the idea of "three stages" by which a nonbeliever approaches the church gained widespread acceptance. These stages were: (a) *precatechesis*, a remote preparation for any person of good will, which may have very little doctrinal or scriptural content; (b) *kerygma*, the announcement of the good news of the gospel, which leads from interested friendliness toward the church to actual conversion to Christ; (c) *catechesis*, the period of instruction, which introduces the future Christian to the church, to grace, and to the sacraments. Concerning the second step, kerygma, Father Jean-Paul Labelle wrote: "A prudent, but repeated use should be made of the Holy Scriptures, especially of the New Testament. The use of Holy Scriptures should aim at presenting it as the source of Truth, not as a mere proof of the veracity or orthodoxy of our instruction."[17] Such an approach to Scripture was to open new doors for its usage in Japan by Catholics as a means of proclaiming and announcing the truth in a non-Christian society.[18]

The holding of Vatican Council II (1962–65) was to speed up and encourage these concerns. The Constitution on the Sacred Liturgy (1963) encouraged the use of vernacular languages in the Mass, and when this process began in Japan, it meant that the scriptural language used in the Mass took on a new intimacy with Japanese congregations. There were problems, too, as when Japanese Catholics winced at scriptural expressions like "the lamb of God" which seemed inelegant in the Japanese language, and when those accustomed to traditional piety found it difficult to refer to God in the familiar form *anata* (you). Vatican II's Dogmatic Constitution on Divine Revelation (1965) also had an important impact on scriptural studies in Japan, by enabling Catholic scholars to make further use of higher critical methods of Scripture study and also encouraging Catholics to work with "separated brethren" in the preparation of vernacular translations of the Scriptures. The underlying purpose here was that "easy access to sacred Scripture should be provided for all the Christian faithful."[19] This made it possible for Catholic biblical scholars to join the translation committee for a common Japanese Bible.

Renewed Roman Catholic emphases on scriptural studies meant that Catholic scholars came into closer contact and dialogue with the Protestant circles of biblical scholarship. And many Catholics were both exhilarated and depressed at what they found there, as the following sections will bear witness.

Protestant Church-centered Studies of the Scriptures

Protestants in Japan have, of course, been of many minds about the Scriptures, and some of their differences became accentuated in the postwar period. Some Protestants continued to follow Anglo-Saxon models in their insistence on continuity between the sermon and Bible study in church life, while others adopted German models of academic studies of the Scriptures, studying the Bible according to the canons of academic scholarship without direct reference to its applications for church life. Still others continued to look upon the Bible primarily for its contributions to the missionary and evangelistic tasks of Christians. Obviously, there are wide overlapping areas, as has been said, but it is important to recognize the differing emphases to be found.

The important thing about Protestant church-centered studies was that the sermon as an exposition of the Word needed to be related to the continuing study of Scripture by church groups and individuals. From the Meiji era on, leading preachers of this school of thought were also the leading Bible expositors and the leading theologians as well.[20] Theology and Bible study were auxiliary to preaching, and vice versa, and all were in the service of the church and the Christian's life of faith. Following in the footsteps of Masahisa Uemura (1858–1925) and Tokutarō Takakura (1885–1934), who had been pastors while they were seminary teachers and exegetes of Scripture, postwar church leaders such as Hidenobu Kuwada, Shirō Murata, and Yoshitaka Kumano sought to pursue the study of Scripture in the context of the life of the church.[21] This was the school of thought that was most influenced by Karl Barth's emphasis on theology as the hearing of the Word of God. The work of the church is not to develop its own wisdom but rather to hear and to be obedient to the Word, with which it is confronted in the Scriptures. Even though Barth had his critics in Japan, his influence on Protestant theological thought in the nation, including biblical studies, was thoroughgoing, both before and after World War II, although it has been pointed out that Barth's works were sometimes put to a use in Japan somewhat different from what was his original intention.[22]

In Old Testament studies, a foremost spokesman of church-centered biblical research has been Zenda Watanabe, whose writings and sermons on biblical topics, and from the Old Testament in particular, are beautifully and powerfully written and widely read.[23] He is well known for his views on the canon of Scripture, as contained in *The Doctrine of the Scriptures;* vol. 1: *The Canon of the Scriptures* (1949), and vol. 2: *Hermeneutics* (1954). He has also published two companion volumes in *A History of the Nation of Israel* (1949) and *History of Hebrew Literature* (1952), as well as *Introduction to the Pentateuch* (1949), all of which are widely used by both pastors and laity. Watanabe was also the pastor of the busy Ginza Church in downtown Tokyo, and his sermons there and elsewhere—in the present writer's opinion—would rank him among the foremost preachers of his time in any country. But it needs to be mentioned that biblical scholars are not of one mind as to the academic significance of Watanabe's works, particularly as to how far he is willing to allow critical research methods to influence his final conclusions. Watanabe has made this clear himself in his amusing metaphor of "the hanging stool." When one wants to commit suicide by hanging, one must first climb up on a stool before attaching a rope to one's neck, but then kicks away the stool. Even so, students of Scripture must make use of critical research, but when they reach their conclusions about the truth of things, they must kick such research aside and make up their minds in the light of Scripture as the canon of the church. Watanabe's academic critics are not so sure that research can be kicked aside.

Junichi Asano is another writer on Old Testament subjects who combines scholarship and lucid style. Deeply influenced by German scholarship, he has written on *Problems of Old Testament Theology* (1953), *Ethics of the Old Testament* (1947), and *Theology of the Hebrew Prophets* (1955). But his most influential writings have been those in which he describes experiences of anxiety and suffering by Old Testament writers in the light of his own personal encounters with the same problems. *Suffering and Emptiness* (1959) comments on Job, Jeremiah, "the servant of the Lord," and Ecclesiastes, as seen through the period of hardship in Japan following World War II. Twenty sermons on Jeremiah are similarly handled in *Sincerity: The Prophet Jeremiah* (1958). There are three volumes in his *Commentary on Job* (1965, 1968, 1970), which follow up his *Studies on Job* (1962). Asano also served as pastor

of the Kyōdan's Mitake Church in Tokyo and was instrumental in reorganiz-
ing the theological department of Aoyama Gakuin University after World
War II, to which were invited a number of able biblical scholars.

In connection with theological education, special attention should be given
to those who have trained several generations of theological students in their
Greek and Hebrew and who also prepared texts and reference works for their
use. Yoshishige Sacon holds a primary place here for his many years of teaching at Tokyo Union Seminary, and also for his Bible atlases, *Introduction to
New Testament Greek* (1953), *Introduction to the Greek New Testament*
(1957), and *Introduction to Hebrew* (1966), upon which countless Old Testament and New Testament students have depended.

The New Testament field in this school would include Masaichi Takemori,
a pastor at the Kichijōji Kyōdan Church and professor of New Testament,
and at one time president of Tokyo Union Seminary. His *Introduction to the
New Testament* (1958) has had wide readership, as have his translations and
writings on the Heidelberg Catechism and Calvin's works. These latter writings have helped to show the continuing relevance of older schools of biblical
interpretation. Calvin's *Commentaries* certainly lack the technical expertise
of modern critical scholarship, but they represent a wrestling with the significance of the text that is often lacking in modern commentaries.[24]

Takemori's colleague at Tokyo Union Seminary for many years was Shōgo
Yamaya, whose coming to that seminary was heralded as a blending of the
church-centered biblical studies and the academic tradition (to be examined
next). Trained in the German methods of critical scholarship in the tradition
of Ken Ishiwara, Japan's leading church historian, and Seiichi Hatano, the
country's foremost Christian philosopher of religion, Yamaya did his doctoral thesis on Paul and won recognition as the able translator (1939) of
Adolf von Harnack's *The Essence of Christianity.* Together with Shirō
Murata, another Pauline scholar in the Presbyterian–Reformed tradition,
Yamaya published *Commentaries on the New Testament: John and Acts*
(1954), and wrote *The Theology of Paul* (1950). Pauline studies are also said
to be the best parts of his masterworks. *A Brief Exposition of the New Testament Based on the Colloquial Version* (1955, co-authored with I. Takayanagi,
the first one-volume commentary on the colloquial New Testament), and the
two-volume *The Origin of Christianity* (1957–59), which has become a standard text on the subject. He also authored widely used introductory works,
such as *Introduction to the Bible* (1950), *An Introductory Explanation of the
New Testament* (1948), and *Dictionary of the New Testament* (1951). His
Theology of the New Testament (1966) was the first publication on that subject written by a Japanese scholar. Yamaya's writings combine careful scholarship and concern for the church's ministry, and thus are generally considered to be a combination of the Anglo-Saxon and German schools of biblical
research.

The other name in Pauline studies often mentioned along with Yamaya's is
Jisaburō Matsuki, professor of New Testament at Kwansei Gakuin Univer-

sity's School of Theology in Nishinomiya. His *The Apostle Paul and His Theology* (1941), *Letter to the Romans* (1966), and *New Testament Theology* (1972) are well known in Japan. Such Pauline studies, closely related to the contemporary problems of Japanese churchmanship, were to become a part of the stormy controversy which broke over the churches in the late 1960s, when—as has happened numerous times throughout the centuries of Christian history—there were attempts to drive a wedge between Jesus and Paul.

Protestant Academic Studies of the Scriptures

It is, of course, impossible to draw a neat line between "church-centered" and "academic" biblical studies, but for purposes of analysis and exposition it might be drawn in reference to two facts: the influence of the two prestigious national universities at Tokyo and Kyoto, on the one hand, and the work of Mukyōkai, on the other.

As for the attraction of the two universities, it can be said that their representative approaches to the study of religion have carried great weight in academic circles in Japan. Tokyo University (Tōdai) has had the reputation of placing strong emphasis on philology: the study of religion means the study of religious texts. Kyoto University (Kyōdai), on the other hand, has emphasized the strong connection between religious and philosophical studies.[25] And the study of philosophy at Kyoto has shown the strong influence of the Zen Buddhist philosopher Kitarō Nishida (1870–1945), best known in the West for *A Study of Good* (1911; Eng. trans., 1960). The foremost Christian member of the "Kyoto school" was Seiichi Hatano (1877–1950), whose *Time and Eternity* (1943; Eng. trans., 1963) is probably the leading Japanese work in the philosophy of religion.[26] The popular stereotype of those, including Christians, who fell under the spell of these two celebrated universities—which stereotype may or may not have any validity in particular cases—would be of scholars inclined to be earnest, dedicated, given to speculation, with attitudes of both self-importance and noblesse oblige, aloof, and somewhat indifferent toward the institutional churches. This last characteristic was very much akin to the mindset of Mukyōkai people, who had always looked askance at institutional Christianity. During the course of his career Kanzō Uchimura had gathered around him a brilliant group of Mukyōkai disciples, among whom were Toraji Tsukamoto and Tateo Kanda, both of whom were to leave their mark on biblical studies in Japan.

Since 1955 Toraji Tsukamoto has published a widely influential magazine, *The Knowledge of the Bible*, which contains well-written expositions of biblical texts as well as his own views about the Non-Church movement and lucid colloquial translations of the New Testament. His popular writings on a wide variety of subjects—Christian marriage, sin, victory over death, new life, letters to his young friends, and other subjects—went through many reprintings in the postwar era, even though some of them were written in the 1930s.

But Tsukamoto's main subject remained biblical studies, principally of the New Testament, sound in scholarship, yet written for the general public.

While Tsukamoto remained an independent writer, critic, and Mukyōkai leader, Tateo Kanda became an assistant professor at Tokyo University. The years before 1945 were difficult ones for Non-Church Christians at Tōdai, particularly when Professors Tadao Yanaihara and Shigeru Nambara had criticized the Japanese government's policies of religious nationalism. Both of these men, appropriately enough, became chancellors of Tōdai in the postwar period.[27] During the period of governmental pressure, Professor Kanda was unable to teach Christian studies directly, but did his best to train students in linguistic skills with Near Eastern languages. His *Introduction to New Testament Greek* (1956) is a standard introduction for Japanese students, and Kanda is also remembered for his translations of C. H. Dodd and Martin Dibelius, as well as his leadership in the early days of International Christian University, where he moved from his Tōdai post. From his days at Tokyo University, his extensive circle of disciples included Gorō Mayeda, who succeeded him in his academic chair there, and Masao Sekine.

Gorō Mayeda recognized from his student days at Tōdai how difficult things were there for Mukyōkai Christians like himself. He subsequently spent the years during World War II in Europe, becoming acquainted with the latest European biblical scholarship. Returning to Japan in 1950 and to Tōdai, he started his own Mukyōkai Bible study group on Sunday mornings, and began publishing his own research materials. Among these were his *Introduction to the New Testament* (1956), and *Words and the Bible* (1963). Mayeda's students included Akira Satake, Sasagu Arai, Seiichi Yagi, and Kenzō Tagawa, all of whom will presently be considered for their contributions to New Testament scholarship.[28]

Masao Sekine, another of Kanda's disciples at Tōdai, occupies a leading place in biblical studies in Japan. He began his Tokyo University studies in law before moving into philology with Kanda. Like Mayeda, he spent the wartime years in Europe, absorbing scriptural studies there, especially under Eissfeldt and Alt. When he returned to Japan in 1945, he began his own Mukyōkai Bible study group, started a monthly magazine, *Prophecy and the Gospel,* and began to publish a large number of studies, mostly in connection with the Old Testament. *The Old Testament: Its History, Literature and Thought* (1949) and *The History of Hebrew Religion and Culture* (1952) summarized much of Old Testament scholarship in Germany up to that time. *Thought and Language of Israel* (1962) includes some of his scholarly contributions to the field. Together with his disciple Yoshirō Uchida, he authored *Sociological Backgrounds of the Old Testament Religion* (1954), which examined Old Testament thought from the standpoint of Max Weber's sociological categories. He also issued a number of books on Non-Church beliefs and translations of Old Testament and New Testament books. His effort throughout has been to find "the essence of a culture" through the history of thought and also of language, thus indicating his indebtedness to both the Tōdai and the Kyōdai traditions. He has opposed the efforts of scholars like Yoshitaka

Kumano—with whom he once engaged in a scholarly debate about the doctrine of the church—to interpret the Bible primarily in theological categories. It might also be said that Sekine's long career in careful, precise Old Testament scholarship has helped to give a steadying influence to that field in the postwar period, in contrast to the turmoils that have swept through New Testament studies. Sekine's immense erudition has helped both to discourage faddism in Old Testament studies and to establish a school of Old Testament scholarship in Japan that is on a par with those in the West.[29]

The contributions of the "academic school" of scriptural studies, with its close ties with the national universities and also to the Mukyōkai tradition, cannot be denied. Yet, as the specialized academic studies multiplied and debates about the Old Testament ranged over the areas of philology, history of religion, philosophy, and sociology, there were many Japanese pastors and laity who felt that biblical studies were becoming increasingly removed from their Christian life and experience. Indeed, most sermons in Protestant churches in recent years have been based on New Testament texts, with occasional ventures into the Psalms, Genesis, or Isaiah. Hence, the riches of Old Testament scholarship in Japan rarely had any influence on preaching or daily life among Protestants. Further, New Testament studies were in confusion for reasons that will be seen presently. From the postwar period onward, one could hear with increasing frequency the complaint that biblical scholarship was becoming separated from the needs of evangelism in Japan. And to these needs another school of biblical interpretation addressed itself.

Protestant Evangelistic Studies of the Scriptures

It would be hard to do justice here to the efforts of the conservative evangelical church scholars who have sought to return biblical studies to evangelistic needs. One of the leading scholars has been Minoru Okada, professor of systematic theology at the Kōbe Reformed Theological Seminary. His *Introduction to the New Testament* (1952) and *Christianity* (1953) are brief, well-written introductions to biblical themes. He also translated into Japanese Benjamin Warfield's *Theology of the Reformation,* the *Westminster Larger Catechism* (1950), and other works. Kōsaku Nao, who has been president of the Japan Lutheran Church (related to the Missouri Synod in America) and professor of Old Testament at the Japan Lutheran Theological Seminary, has endeavored through his scriptural studies and translations (including his translation work on the New Japanese Bible) to inject new life into biblical research. Tomonobu Yanagita, who was a student of Tateo Kanda, has served as a bridge between Japanese and Western scholarship, through his *Japan Christian Literature Review* (1958; *Supplement,* 1960; both are in English), his widely sold *Christianity in Japan* (in English, 1957), the important *Study of the Petrine Letters* (1960), and his translations of F. F. Bruce's *Are the New Testament Documents Reliable?* (1959) and V. W. Johnston's *Christian Doctrine* (1959).[30]

But the work of the conservative evangelicals goes far beyond the mere publication of scholarly works. Through the mass communications ministry of preachers like Akira Hatori, the evangelistic campaigns of Kōji Honda, and the educational programs of many Christian schools, efforts have been made to put theories of biblical evangelism into practice. The evangelistic crusades of Bob Pierce and Billy Graham have given impetus to Bible distribution and study in Japan. Graham has often stated his view that he does not wish to examine higher critical studies of the Bible lest they interfere with his evangelism, and such a standpoint would be shared by many conservatives in Japan.

Indeed, the distribution of the Scriptures by conservative groups has certainly had a greater long-range impact on the Japanese public at large than have academic research articles on obscure topics. Groups like the Pocket Testament League and the Navigators have been active in distributing Scripture portions and study materials, while the Gideons have been placing New Testaments in hotel rooms, and organizations such as the New Life League and the Christian Literature Crusade have published countless tracts and leaflets for mass distribution and sale. The Bethel Bible study courses have been introduced to Japan, along with several Bible correspondence courses. Some conservative groups in Japan have experienced greater numerical growth than the traditional Christian denominations, for many of the same reasons that pertain to other countries.[31] In recent years, the worldwide charismatic movement has had some influence in Japan as well. Emphasizing the ongoing work of the Holy Spirit, it has influenced both Protestant and Roman Catholic congregations.[32] From movements such as these may come the dynamic for new appropriations of the message of the Scriptures in Japan. Bishop Stephen Neill has pointed out that an often overlooked key to the interpretation of the New Testament is to examine it from the perspectives of missionary strategy.[33]

Biblical Studies in Controversy

It is wrong to suppose that biblical studies in Japan have been carried on only through pious reflection or scholarly research. They have often been conducted amid heated controversy. To understand some of these controversies, it is helpful to review the development of biblical theology in Japan.

Many of the studies referred to above in the section on church-centered biblical scholarship were deeply influenced by the trends of biblical theology in Western countries. Karl Barth's influence was predominant in the immediate postwar period in Japan, but the works of other writers such as C. H. Dodd, Rudolf Bultmann, Oscar Cullmann, Dietrich Bonhoeffer, and Étienne Trocmé were also introduced. It was around New Testament studies that controversies principally arose in Japan, and for several reasons. It has already been pointed out that Japanese Protestant churches have been based largely on New Testament work, and on Pauline thought in particular, and hence it was inevitable that disturbances here would have repercussions about

the very selfhood of the churches. Furthermore, because it took comparatively less time to do preparatory academic work for New Testament studies,
the field came to attract some who wished to relate the New Testament to
other specialized studies that they had developed in such areas as history o
religions, Marxism, existentialism, and psychology. As has already beer
pointed out, there was no steadying influence, such as Sekine provided in Old
Testament studies, to enable a measure of group consensus and loyalty to
develop among New Testament scholars. Hence, New Testament studies became a virtual "burnt-over district" for one academic wave of controversy
after another from about 1960 on.

Since Western academic works in all fields were being carefully studied in
Japan, virtually all New Testament scholarship from the West was examined
in Japan, and controversies about the New Testament were discussed very
readily by the Japanese.[34] For instance, debates over the "theology of the
Word" in Europe were followed closely in Japan.[35] There were also Japanese
discussions of the implications of Bultmann's demythologizing program, of
the old and the "new" quest for the historical Jesus, of Hellenism and New
Testament thought, of Christology in the New Testament, of the role of Gnosis, of the Synoptic problem, and of the many varieties of Pauline studies.[36]
These discussions would take too long to summarize here, for a selected bibliography of Japanese writings on Christology alone comes to 267 items down
to 1968, with many others appearing since then.[37] But one of these scholarly
controversies stands out in recent years, namely, that between Seiichi Yagi,
who had been influenced by Bultmann, and Katsumi Takizawa, who had
studied under Barth, on the significance of Christology in the New Testament[38] (see p. 248).

Behind the many academic studies and debates, a basic controversy was in
fact brewing in Japan. The biblical theology movement in Japan to which we
have referred was almost contemporaneous with its counterpart in Western
countries, which Brevard S. Childs has depicted as rising about 1943, toward
the close of World War II, reaching the height of its development in the late
1940s and the 1950s, and then waning in the mid-1960s.[39] It has been seen how
biblical theology had its spokesmen in Japan also, in the persons of Watanabe, Kuwada, Murata, Takemori, Kitamori, and Yamaya. All of these
scholars, it is interesting to note, are also pastors in the Kyōdan, the United
Church of Christ in Japan. All except Watanabe have been faculty members
at the Kyōdan's Tokyo Union Theological Seminary. It was as if the unity of
the Kyōdan—which had been forged in 1941 partly from the desires of the
churches for unity but mostly from government pressure at the time—was to
be buttressed in the postwar period by the kind of biblical theology taught at
that seminary. Such a biblical basis for faith was stressed not only by biblical
scholars, but also by that seminary's Systematics Department, in their various ways. Hidenobu Kuwada emphasized the approach of biblical theology
in *An Outline of Christian Doctrine* (1956), Yoshitaka Kumano made it basic
in his *Dogmatics* (3 vols., 1954, 1959, 1965), Kazō Kitamori adapted it in

terms of a deeply held motif in Japanese life in *Theology of the Pain of God* (1946; Eng. trans., 1965), and its use lay behind Kitamori's *Explanation of the Confession of the Church of Christ in Japan* (1955).[40] We have seen that biblical theology was not a new and unfamiliar approach for Japanese Christians, for it was a logical outgrowth of the Anglo-Saxon tradition of biblical studies, which held that preaching and Bible study should go together in church life and that systematics and hermeneutics belong together in academic life.

There had always been those who had disagreements with biblical theology, but they were generally so involved in the programs of their own schools or churches or Mukyōkai groups that they did little more than write an occasional critical article or book to express their opposition. From the postwar period through the early 1960s, biblical theology seemed to represent the mainstream of biblical scholarship in the Protestant churches. The academic critics were written off as too ivory-towered and out of touch with the realities of church life. Vatican II had not yet opened the windows to extensive Protestant–Catholic dialogues. And the criticisms of fundamentalist groups were dismissed as so much obscurantism.

But some of the younger scholars who were being trained in the German-type academic biblical studies began to have some fundamental doubts about the presuppositions and conclusions of biblical theology. To them it appeared that the wagon of biblical studies had been hitched to the status quo in church and society, with disastrous results for all concerned. It seemed to these men that New Testament studies needed to be carried out in the broader contexts of the history of thought, sociology, history of religion, philosophy, and politics. Students who went abroad from the mid-1960s on began to absorb some of the radical activism of student and university circles in America and Europe. The important task for them became, in Marx's terms, not to try to understand the world, but to change it. As the United States became bogged down with racial problems at home and the worsening Vietnam conflict abroad, it seemed to them that the Anglo-Saxon models for society and for church life had to be set aside entirely. And what was biblical theology in Japan, asked those who had gravitated to the New Left, but an ideology for those bourgeois capitalists who were cloaking their exploitation of the poor at home and abroad with pious slogans? Such class conflicts were already to be found in the New Testament itself, it was announced, for Jesus of Nazareth had been put to death for his opposition to the status quo in state and church in his day, and his prophetic message had been blunted by a Paul who kerygmatized him as a cosmic "Christ." (Thus there was placed again a fateful wedge between Jesus and Paul, the likes of which have troubled Christians often in their pilgrimage through history.) To those who had followed the argument thus far—and of the scholars to be mentioned hereafter, only Tagawa went the whole way—it seemed that the imperative for modern-day followers of Jesus was to join with other radicals who were struggling against the Establishment.[41]

Specifically, the struggle against the Establishment in Japan began building up in the late 1960s, in a quasi-eschatological expectation of a "1970
crisis" that was predicted by the radicals for the nation when the United
States–Japan Mutual Security Treaty came to the end of its first ten years,
following which it might be renounced by either nation on one year's notice.
The student struggle, which began in the universities in a secular political
context, soon enlisted numbers of Christian college students, faculty, seminarians, and pastors in preparation for concerted attacks on the power centers of the Establishment. (It is interesting to note that orthodox Communist
party members regarded all such tactics of the New Left as "opportunism"
and "anti-communist sectarianism."[42]) The dispute spilled over into the
churches when a group of Kyōdan seminarians and pastors objected to their
church's endorsement of the Christian Pavilion at the Osaka World Exposition in 1970 as a diabolical participation in a "festival of capitalism" and
demanded that the church reverse its stand. A meeting called to discuss the
issue on September 1–2, 1969, turned into a bitter nineteen-hour disputation,
during which Professor Kazō Kitamori—long seen as a "chief ideologist" of
the Kyōdan Establishment—was slapped by some angry students. When the
Tokyo Union Theological Seminary faculty criticized those responsible for
the incident in a statement issued the following day, a small group of students
at the seminary began a student strike, which later was escalated into a barricade of the seminary's main building, lasting for six months.[43] During this
strike, and others which paralyzed a number of seminaries throughout the
country, the rationale for the strikers' actions was sometimes put in theological terms that echoed (not always accurately) the New Testament theories of
Tagawa and others. When Tokyo Union Seminary called the riot police to the
campus on March 11, 1970, to end the barricade and make possible the
reopening of classes, these actions provided additional targets for the student
strikers and their supporters. Because of the resulting internal struggles
within the Kyōdan, the denomination was not able to hold its regular General
Assembly for four years, and the Tokyo and Osaka district assemblies at
present writing are still unable to meet.

During this time of bitter controversy in the Kyōdan—while other churches
were struggling hard not to let the Kyōdan's plight become theirs also—a
large part of the ideological controversy was traceable back to conflicting
interpretations of New Testament scholarship. The New Left activists de-
nounced their critics' use of government power to throttle a prophetic protest
against the revival of fascist militarism in Japan, while their critics maintained that the New Left activists themselves were abandoning the principle
of Christian freedom by identifying the Christian faith with one particular
ideological stance. The manifold nuances of biblical theology were argued on
many sides and with much rancor. The younger New Testament scholars (to
be mentioned below) were not themselves direct participants in the conflicts
in society and in the churches, except for Tagawa, who supported the New
Left activists in his writing and lecturing. But the New Testament views of

these writers, and the methodologies they employed, had their influence on the course taken by these controversies.

We recall that all four of the scholars to be considered here were pupils in linguistic studies of Gorō Mayeda at Tokyo University. Akira Satake, a professor of New Testament at Aoyama Gakuin's Department of Theology, was for several years after graduation from Tōdai a student and chaplain at Heidelberg. He has produced several carefully wrought books of New Testament studies, written from the standpoint of "editorial history": *Church Order in John's Apocalypse* (in German, 1966), a study of Philippians (1969), and a work on Galatians (1974).[44] His study-commentaries differ from others in that he—like Abelard with his influential *Sic et Non* methodology—instead of making a choice of conflicting viewpoints in New Testament studies and then expounding the whole accordingly, carefully explains the differing views of other authors about a passage in question, thus enabling the reader to grasp what the heated conflict was all about and why it is of continuing significance. What was so startling about such a procedure? Nothing, except that like Abelard's methodology, it had never really been done before in Japan. Not a radical in the political sense at all, Satake nevertheless posed some "radical" questions that forced readers to look again at the sometimes conflicting evidence.

Sasagu Arai was Satake's colleague in New Testament at Aoyama Gakuin for a period and then returned to Tokyo University as a faculty member. He pressed forward with the sociological studies of biblical religion that Masao Sekine had done so much to develop in Japan. His Christology in *"The Gospel of the Truth": Its Position in the Ancient History of Israel* (1966) established his reputation as a creative interpreter of the Nag Hamadi writings. In *Primitive Christianity and Gnosticism* (1971), which won a cultural award and its author fame because of his refusal to accept that award, he developed at length views that he had presented in journal articles on Gnosticism. He raised the question, from the perspectives of Max Weber's sociology that every religious tradition has its own social bearer, as to what class struggle may have been in the background of the theological dispute between Christian faith and Gnosis that took place in the Corinthian church. His views here gained attention in the midst of the "1970 conflict" in Japanese society and the churches by raising timely questions as to whether a purely doctrinal interpretation is possible, or whether such doctrinal explanations are indicative of more fundamental class struggles.

The career of Seiichi Yagi is similar in many ways to those of Satake and Arai. After studying under Mayeda at Tōdai, he completed his doctoral course at Gottingen University. His first important book, *The Formation of New Testament Thought* (1965), was the starting point of the Yagi–Takizawa debate already mentioned. It was followed by *Jesus* (1966), *Christ and Jesus* (1969), *Can We Believe in Christianity?* (1970), and *Probing New Testament Thought* (1972).[45] He had long been impatient with what he considered to be the overdependence of Japanese theological thought on Occidental models, and hoped to strike out in new directions.[46] He came to the conclusion that historical Christianity made a great mistake in identifying the historical Jesus with the eternal "Christ" principle. A true synthesis of humanity and the-natural-state-of-things-as-they-are has been the goal of many religions, including—most significantly—several schools of Japanese Buddhism. Yagi's goal has been to build an academic bridge between New Testament studies and systematic theology, and in so doing he feels that he has opened the door to a much more creative dialogue between historical Christianity and other religions, Buddhism in particular. Such views would in themselves not seem radical—and Yagi has shunned the role of a political activist—were it not for the fact that they became widely influential at the time of the 1970 crisis.

A more active role in the university disputes of the 1968–70 period was taken by Kenzō Tagawa. Graduating from Tokyo University in 1958, he studied in Strasbourg under Étienne Trocmé, following that scholar's thesis about the Gospel of Mark. Trocmé distinguished the passion narratives in Mark from Mark 1–13, contending that the first thirteen chapters were the original Marcan Gospel, written against the Jerusalem church and the apostolic authorities who had kerygmatized Jesus and created thereby another religion, which Jesus himself never intended.[47] Returning to Japan, Tagawa developed this thesis of Trocmé's in several books, *A Phase in the History of Primitive Christianity* (1968), *Formation of Critical Subjects* (1971), and *Commentary on Mark,* vol. 1 (1972). Especially in his Marcan commentary, Tagawa developed the theory that the universality which Jesus opened up in his criticisms of the Establishment in church and state was perverted by primitive Christianity through the work of Paul, whereby Jesus was interpreted as a redeemer whose church transcends and therefore neglects all sorts of conditions of discrimination and exploitation. Such is the path often taken by apologists for the status quo, Tagawa held, in Paul's time and our own as well.

Yet Tagawa's elaboration of Trocmé's thesis might have remained nothing more than a purely academic struggle at International Christian University, where he taught from 1965 until his dismissal in 1970. Tagawa increasingly became a spokesman for leftist groups in the Kyōdan and other churches, for he saw the New Left as authentic heirs of the spirit of prophetic protest that ecclesiastical and political establishments since the time of Jesus and Paul have been continually trying to crush. Whether Tagawa's conversion to activism came at the time of the ICU troubles or before is open to question. But in articles he wrote for the magazine *The Finger (Yubi)*, which were later put out in book form as *Thought That Keeps Standing* (1972), and *Approaches to Thinking Action* (1972), Tagawa has maintained that he had decided on his activist role from the time he joined the church. He holds that the main task of radical Christians is to work for the "dismantling" (*kaitai*) of the church

Establishment, for it is only in that way that the radical thrust of Jesus can again be countered.[48]

It may be worthwhile to try to summarize the impact on the life of the churches in Japan of some of the above mentioned developments in biblical scholarship since about 1968. Roman Catholics have been involved in their intramural disputes about the significance of renewed scriptural studies for the life of the church, but Vatican II gave a measure of sanction for making changes that radicals felt were long overdue. The controversy that resulted has been very stormy and the Catholic Church in Japan as elsewhere has suffered a number of casualties and losses, but effort has been made to continue the debate within creative limits. For their part, conservative evangelical Protestants have grown increasingly alarmed over the doctrinal chaos and lack of what they considered evangelistic concern in mainline Protestantism. Some conservatives have concluded that it would be far better for them to withdraw from any cooperation with regular Protestant groups and carry out their evangelistic tasks by themselves, even if this leads to conflict with other Christian groups. If this should be the path ultimately taken, the loss of the conservatives' contagious zeal and corrective insights could well be more damaging to the rest of the Christian community than almost anything else.

As for mainline Protestants, the tension between church-centered scriptural studies and academic Bible studies, which has been present in Japanese Protestantism since the Meiji era, has become sufficiently acute in the Kyōdan that the unified denominational life and mission outreach of that church have been jeopardized, even though congregational and regional church activities have in some cases been strengthened. Other Protestant bodies have been anxiously waiting the outcome of the Kyōdan's difficulties. Since the Kyōdan has been built so largely on New Testament foundations, the widening breach in the interpretation of the New Testament and the church's creeds has made a renewed consensus about church life very difficult indeed. Perhaps this may lead to dismemberment of the Kyōdan, as some observers have often assumed. Or perhaps it will prove to be a time of rediscovery and renewal, as church members sort out anew their deepest convictions about the Scriptures and the Christian faith.

But the forging of a new consensus about scriptural studies, which might have profound implications for the present disturbed state of Protestant church life in Japan, will not be a matter for the churches alone to decide. There will also be crucial roles here for the societies for biblical studies in Japan. Hence it is with a consideration of their work that we shall conclude.

The Work of the Societies for Biblical Studies

The missionary elder-statesman Sam H. Franklin once made the wry comment, "Where two or three Japanese scholars are gathered together, there a *kenkyūkai* [study society] will be formed in the midst of them." Such study societies are as much a part of Japanese academic life as classroom work and scholarly research, and in recent years their roles have become increasingly important.

The oldest such group for biblical studies is the Japan Society for Old Testament Studies (Nihon Kyūgaku Gakkai), established in 1933, which has met annually on an open basis for the presentation of scholarly papers. The other associations were organized after World War II. The Japan Society for New Testament Studies (Nihon Shinyaku Gakkai), patterned after its Old Testament counterpart, has met annually since 1955 in open sessions for the reading and discussing of academic research reports. Much larger than either of these is the Japan Society for Christian Studies (Nihon Kirisutokyō Gakkai), which has held gatherings every year since 1953 and annually published reports of its meetings under the title "Theology in Japan" *(Nihon no Shingaku)*. This group has met with subsections for the various disciplines: Old Testament, New Testament, systematic theology, and church history. An examination of the papers in the various fields in each year's report would give a reader a good indication about the theological trends in each area. Another study group is the Japanese Biblical Institute (Nihon Seisho Gaku Kenkyūjō), which has met since 1948 and from 1963 has published in English an annual summary of its research projects, *Biblical Studies Annual.* The group holds monthly meetings and each year undertakes study projects on which monthly papers are read in the fields of Old Testament and New Testament, alternately. It has published an *Annual of the Japanese Biblical Institute,* with articles in European languages, from 1974.

In the case of the first three study societies mentioned, the nature of the groups has gradually changed since the early 1960s. Earlier, these societies were made up mostly of pastors, and their purpose was primarily to give help to pastors in their evangelistic efforts in the churches. But in the 1960s these societies became more academic in nature, and there has been less of a role for pastors in them, except insofar as they were at the same time professional scholars.

These study societies symbolize both the promise and the dilemma of biblical studies in Japan since 1945. They were started as a means of bridging the gap between church and academic life. But as the demands of both church programs and academic scholarship became more specialized and more detailed, the two fields tended to slip further apart. The crises in the schools and churches in 1968–70 revealed the hazards that arise from too great a separation between the two, when biblical studies seemed to be caught, as it were, between the ivory tower and the barricades. Hence efforts have been made to restore the connections between academic research and church activities, between systematic theology and biblical theology, between the life of reason and the life of faith. The perfect and unchangeable relationship between these two poles will never be found. But it is essential that the quest go on. Those who pursue it need always to recall the potent warning in Jeremiah 23:29: "Is not my word as a fire? saith the Lord; and like a hammer, that breaketh the rock in pieces?"

NOTES

1. See Tsunetarō Miyakoda, "Distribution of the Bible in Japan," *JCQ* 31, no. 2 (April 1965): 87–89.

2. Joseph Spae, *Christianity Encounters Japan* (Tokyo: Oriens, 1968), p. 240.

3. A helpful survey is Saburō Ouchi, *Kindai Nihon no Seisho Shisō* [Biblical Thought in Modern Japan] (Tokyo: Kyōdan Shuppansha, 1966).

4. See articles on the history of Old Testament studies in Japan by Masatoshi Korogi and on New Testament studies by Minoru Onumata in *Shin Seisho Daijiten* [New Bible Dictionary] (Tokyo: Kirisuto Shinbun Sha, 1971), pp. 3–23. The present writer relied on these articles throughout this chapter.

5. Cf. Raymond P. Jennings, *Jesus, Japan and Kanzō Uchimura* (Tokyo: Kyōbunkwan, 1958), and Carl Michalson, *Japanese Contributions to Christian Theology* (Philadelphia: Westminster Press, 1960), pp. 17–45. For an account by a Mukyōkai teacher, see Gorō Mayeda, "Uchimura Kanzō and His Legacy," *JCQ* 32, no. 4 (Fall 1966): 246–50. (These works are in English.)

6. Cf. Richard Drummond, *A History of Christianity in Japan* (Grand Rapids, Mich.: Wm. B. Eerdmans, 1971), pp. 166, 183, 242–43.

7. Ibid., pp. 276–77.

8. Tomonobu Yanagita, *Japan Christian Literature Review* (Sendai: Seisho Tosho Kankōkai, 1958), with *Supplement* (1960), gives valuable bibliographical information. It has been used throughout this book. (These works are in English.)

9. Cf. Bernardin Schneider, O.F.M., "Catholic Japanese Bible Translation in Japan," *JCQ* 31, no. 2 (April 1965): 74–78.

10. Interview with Rev. John Takahashi, Nov. 25, 1973.

11. Masashi Takahashi, "A Short History of Bible Translation in Japan," *JCQ* 31, no. 2 (April 1965): 74–78.

12. Schneider, "Catholic Japanese Bible Translations," pp. 83–84.

13. Miyakoda, "Distribution of the Bible," p. 88.

14. This section relies on George A. Mueller, M.M., *The Catechetical Problem in Japan, 1549—1965* (Tokyo: Oriens, 1967).

15. Ibid., pp. 63–64.

16. Ibid., pp. 132, 193.

17. Ibid., p. 158.

18. Cf. Spae, *Encounters,* pp. 99, 149, 173, 240.

19. Walter M. Abbott, ed., *The Documents of Vatican II* (New York: Guild Press, 1966), pp. 120, 125, 126.

20. Cf. Tsuneaki Katō, *Nihon no Sekkyōtachi,* vol. 1 [Preachers of Japan, vol. 1] (Tokyo: Shinkyō Shuppansha, 1972). See also Charles H. Germany, *Protestant Theologies in Modern Japan* (Tokyo: IISR Press, 1965), chap. 1.

21. Cf. Michalson, *Japanese Contributions,* chap. 2, "The Theology of Church Existence" (on Kumano).

22. Cf. Germany, *Protestant Theologies,* pp. 150–52.

23. This material is based on an interview with Dr. Zenda Watanabe, April 7, 1972, and with Dr. Yoshinobu Kumazawa, Aug. 6, 1974. The writings by Japanese authors cited in this chapter were all published in the Japanese language, unless otherwise indicated.

24. Cf. Stephen Neill, *The Interpretation of the New Testament, 1861—1961* (New York: Oxford University Press, 1966), pp. 207-8.

25. Cf. Gino K. Piovesana, S.J., *Recent Japanese Philosophical Thought, 1862—1962* (Tokyo: Enderle, 1963), chap. 7.

26. Cf. Michalson, *Japanese Contributions,* chap. 4, "The Theology of the Time of Love" (on Hatano).

27. Drummond, *History,* p. 252.

28. Interview with Prof. Gorō Mayeda, March 5, 1973.

29. This paragraph based on interviews with Prof. Kiyoshi Sacon, March 1, 1973, and Prof. Yoshinobu Kumazawa, Aug. 6, 1974.

30. See Arthur Reynolds, *Japan in Review: Japan Harvest Anthology, 1955—70,* vol. 1 (Tokyo: JEMA, 1970), also Yanagita, *Japan Christian Literature Review.*

31. See Dean M. Kelley, *Why Conservative Churches Are Growing* (1972). See also Neil Braun, *Laity Mobilized* (Grand Rapids, Mich.: Wm. B. Eerdmans, 1971).

32. See Carl C. Beck, ed., *The Contemporary Work of the Holy Spirit* (Tokyo: 14th Hayama Missionary Seminar, 1973).

33. Neill, *Interpretation of the New Testament,* pp. 272-77.

34. Ibid., chap. 6, "Re-Enter Theology."

35. See John Macquarrie, *Twentieth Century Religious Thought: The Frontiers of Philosophy and Theology, 1900—1970* (London: SCM, 1971), esp. chaps. 20 and 24.

36. For listings of books in these areas, see Onumata's article in *Shin Seisho Daijiten,* pp. 19-23.

37. Yukimaro Amagai and Yoshinobu Kumazawa, "A Selected Bibliography of Christology in Japan," *NEAJT,* no. 2 (March 1969), pp. 117-34.

38. Cf. Kenzo Tagawa, "The Yagi-Takizawa Debate," *NEAJT,* no. 2 (March 1969), pp. 41-59. Also John Barksdale, "Yagi and Takizawa," *MB* 34, nos. 1-4 (January-February, March, April, May 1970): 38f., 93f., 215f.

39. Brevard S. Childs, *Biblical Theology in Crisis* (Philadelphia: Westminster Press, 1970), esp. pt. 1, "Remembering a Past."

40. See Michalson, *Japanese Contributions,* chap. 2 (on Kumano), and chap. 3 (on Kitamori).

41. Cf. Toshikazu Takao, "An Alliance of Egoists," *JCQ* 35, no. 4 (Fall 1969): 223-33.

42. *The Fifty Years of the Communist Party of Japan* (Tokyo: Central Committee of the Communist Party of Japan, 1973), p. 192. (In English)

43. See Ian Macleod, "Whither Kyōdan?" *JCQ* 36, no. 3 (Summer 1970): 168-74.

44. Interview with Dr. Kikuo Matsunaga, July 31, 1974.

45. Cf. Toshikazu Takao, "Representative Critical Approaches to the Contemporary Japanese Situation" (on Yagi, Takizawa, and Tagawa), *JCQ* 39, no. 2 (Spring 1973): 75-86.

46. Cf. Seiichi Yagi, "The Dependence of Japanese Theology upon the Occident," *JCQ* 30, no. 4 (October 1964): 258-61.

47. Matsunaga Interview, and Takao, "Egoists" ("Representative Critical Approaches . . .").

48. Cf. Mitsuo Hori, "A Historical Survey of Radicalism in Japan," *JCQ* 37, no. 3 (Summer 1971): 165-72.

9

Theology in Japan: Toward Escape from the German Captivity

Sometimes the truth is expressed most clearly when it is written in anger. Here is Seiichi Yagi, a noted Japanese New Testament scholar, speaking his mind when he was a young man:

> Once the infant Japanese theology needed Occidental theology as its guardian. . . . Our long dependence has fostered bad habits. There are, for example, some renowned Japanese scholars who think that theology is entirely an Occidental science and that the Japanese cannot do other than learn from it. Some even publicly declared that they would not read any theological works written by Japanese. Many scholars who do not openly say so ignore Japanese theological works in fact. There is even a regrettable trend among us of being ashamed of referring to Japanese studies in the bibliography of our books. This puts us in the ironic situation that, thanks to our disregard of other Japanese works, our own writings are not read by other Japanese either! We can never hope for a healthy growth of Japanese theology under such circumstances. . . . It is therefore with good reason that the cry has recently arisen among young theologians, "Deliver Japanese theology from Germanic captivity!"[1]

There are a number of interesting points that Yagi makes in this angry statement. In the first place, he recalls the period when "the infant Japanese theology needed Occidental theology as its guardian." This was the era when, as Charles Germany pointed out in his excellent study, the early Protestant missionaries, who were mostly from the United States and the British Isles, relied on Anglo-Saxon theological models and introduced them to Japan. Among Japanese Christian leaders, English-language theological works of a

228

liberal background were used by such liberal Japanese writers as Danjō Ebina, Setsuji Ōtsuka, and Toyohiko Kagawa, while those whose background was Presbyterian-Reformed were highly esteemed by Masahisa Uemura, Tokutarō Takakura, and their followers.[2] With Takakura and his successors there was a gradual shift from Anglo-Saxon to German-language theologians. The first Japanese to write a systematic theology, Takakura was also the first major writer to make use of the works of Emil Brunner and Karl Barth, as is clear from a comment of his written in 1928:

> Because Barth is the prime mover in their [the European dialectical theologians'] activities, in order to know the tendency of the movement I have recommended him as a man whose books should be carefully read. Among them [the dialectical theologians], I myself, I believe, owe most to Brunner. At least this is true in establishing the theological foundations of evangelical faith.[3]

From this period onward, and especially after the collapse of the left-leaning Student Christian Movement in the summer of 1932, and the subsequent growth of governmental pressure, the influence of German theological scholarship was far more significant in Japan. As Yagi indicated in his article, the dominance of German scholarship (or more exactly, of German-Swiss scholarship) was so great that it tended to discourage the development of independent Japanese theological work. But this domination was bound to pass, especially when younger theologians began to cry, "Deliver Japanese theology from Germanic captivity!"

It is our thesis that in four major fields of theological writing in Japan—in church history, Christian social thought, philosophical theology, and systematic theology—roughly the same tendencies have been at work. The main items for the theological agenda for Japan were developed in the prewar period in terms of the major themes of German theology of that time, and through the use of the same academic methods. In each of these fields, we shall see how the concerns and the methods of German theology were examined by Japanese scholars in the prewar period. In the postwar period, there has been a twofold development. On the one hand, there has been a deepening and a continuation of items from the "German agenda" of theology, but at the same time there has been a broadening and a diversification of that agenda. Even when strong criticisms and rejections of the "German agenda" occurred, such writings were often based on presuppositions, antecedents, and even methodologies developed in Germany.

One parenthetical word about our handling of the subject may be in order at this point. There is bound to be a certain amount of overlap between this chapter's discussion of developments in theology, and what was said in the previous chapter about biblical studies. It should be emphasized that the two fields are intimately related; they are separated here only for the purposes of analysis.

Church History

The field of church history—sometimes called "historical theology" in Japanese as well—is perhaps the clearest example of how "the German agenda" in Japanese theology was started and how it developed. One reason for this is that the academic study of this discipline has been so greatly influenced by one major figure, Ken Ishiwara. An introduction to the career of this scholar and to his major specialized interests can also serve to introduce the entire field of developments in church history scholarship in contemporary Japan.

Ken Ishiwara and the Study of Church History

Ken Ishiwara (1882–1976) deserves to be known as "the dean of Japanese church historians," for his long and fruitful career had an enormous impact on the Christian community in Japan in many areas. He was the only Japanese Christian scholar to be decorated by the emperor for his academic writings about Christianity. A close examination of Ishiwara's career and writings may indicate how far he was able to introduce "the German agenda" of church-history scholarship to Japan, and also how far he was able to anticipate and to develop some of its major specialized areas in the country.

A graduate of the prestigious Tokyo Imperial University where he had studied under the eminent professor of philosophy Raphael von Koeber (1848–1923) and written his doctoral dissertation on the philosophy of Clement of Alexandria, Ishiwara became a faculty member of that university and a lecturer at Waseda University and Tokyo Woman's Christian College. He studied in Europe in 1921–23, where he was mainly influenced by Professor Hans von Schubert of Heidelberg University, one of the leading scholars of that day in the church history of the late Middle Ages and the Reformation period. From Schubert he gained a deepened interest in the Protestant Reformation, especially the study of Luther, which was to last throughout his life. Returning briefly to Tokyo Imperial University, he then became a professor of church history at Tōhoku Imperial University in Sendai in 1924, and it was while there that he made some of his major scholarly contributions. In 1940 he became the president of Tokyo Woman's Christian College, somewhat against his inclinations, for his main interests were in scholarship and teaching, and not administration. After World War II, when he was officially in retirement, he continued to lecture in Christian colleges in the Tokyo area and resumed the publication of his historical studies. He remained active in writing and scholarship almost to the time of his death, shortly before his ninety-fourth birthday. Ishiwara was a teacher, an inspiration, and a friend to many generations of Christian scholars in Japan.[4]

Ishiwara's writings bear the imprint of the academic historical method, which he acquired from his studies at Tokyo Imperial University and further developed during his stay in Germany. The list of his essays and books exceeds two hundred items, and while ranging across the centuries and the continents, the materials nevertheless focus on four particular areas.

The first area of Ishiwara's specialization was the Protestant Reformation and Luther studies in particular. He wrote surprisingly little about John Calvin, even though Ishiwara's denominational roots were in the Presbyterian-Reformed tradition. A second area of specialization was the early and medieval church. Besides special concentration on Augustine, Ishiwara also made detailed studies of a number of the church fathers, and his *Studies of Medieval Christianity* (1952)* is a monumental contribution in its field.[5] He was also the first chairman of the Japanese Society of Medieval Philosophy (founded in 1952, an organization composed primarily of Roman Catholic scholars), thus enhancing the stature of medieval studies in Japan. A third specialty has been the writing of surveys of the entire field of church history. His *History of Christianity* (1951) was for many years a standard text for theological students, and his *A History of Christian Thought* (1949) an often used reference work. Perhaps the long-range influence of his thought will be felt from his two-volume survey of *The Origins of Christianity* (1972) and *The Development of Christianity* (1972), which contain essays in Schubert-like style on various aspects of church history. Yet these essays are unbalanced in emphasis, for Augustine is the subject of 310 of the first volume's 570 pages, and Luther has 210 of the second volume's 600 pages, while the entire field of Christian history since the Reformation has only 100 pages.[6] His fourth specialty has been the history of Christianity in Japan, where his major work—in addition to scores of journal articles—is *Essays on the History of Japanese Christianity* (1967). Because of its particular relevance for our subject, a closer examination of this work is in order.

In *Essays*, Ishiwara places the history of Christian missions to Japan in the nineteenth century within the framework of "Oriental missions" as they were then understood. In that framework Western missionary agencies often tended to consider Christian missions in Japan merely as a subdivision of their previous work in China, and while such policies had some advantages, they also led to serious distortions. ("China booms" in the West have often led to misrepresentations of Japan.) When he comes to deal more specifically with the beginnings of Protestant Christianity in Japan, Ishiwara lays great stress on Masahisa Uemura, who was not only a leading figure in the Presbyterian-Reformed tradition that went into the United Church of Christ in Japan (the Kyōdan), but also one of his own personal mentors. Much emphasis is also placed on the first Japanese Protestant congregation in Yokohama, with whose founding Uemura was associated in 1872, which self-consciously refused to take a denominational label but on principle called itself by the ecumenical name of the Church of Christ in Japan (Nihon Kirisuto Kōkai). The ideals of *kōkaishugi* (a term that Ishiwara coined to character-

---

*Unless an English-language edition is specifically noted, all the books mentioned in this chapter are written in the Japanese language.

ize the ecumenical principles of this first nondenominational church) were soon to founder on the rocks of denominationalism, and to be countered by the Non-Churchism *(mukyōkaishugi)* of Kanzō Uchimura and his followers. Ishiwara maintains that although overwhelmed and partially superseded, *kōkaishugi* was never entirely forgotten. It remained as an inspiration of sorts for the Kyōdan's formation in 1941 when the primary force working for Protestant church unity was the Religious Organizations Law passed by the government in order to keep Christian groups under wartime control. The latter part of Ishiwara's book is concerned almost exclusively with the history of the Kyōdan. This was not simply because it was his own denomination, but because he felt that the main issues of Japanese Christianity were being hammered out in the experiences of that church. Thus, in his discussion of the history of Christianity in Japan, as in his outlines of the whole of church history, Ishiwara adopted an essay style that was similar to that of his German mentor, Schubert. While paying close attention to historical documentation, he transcended the particular events themselves in reaching for "the flow of history," and yet by laying stress on particular figures and movements he tended to minimize or omit many other movements that had been at work.

All told, it must be concluded that Ishiwara was both a pioneer and a prophet in regard to the development of church-history scholarship in Japan. All four fields on which he focused have remained areas of specialization for other Japanese church-history scholars. An examination of each of these fields will show what has happened to the "German agenda" in historical theology since Ishiwara.

Reformation Studies

In Reformation studies, Japanese scholars hardly needed Ishiwara's encouragement, for much had already been done. For instance, Shigehiko Satō, a student of Karl Holl, had published his influential book on *The Basic Thought of Luther in His Lectures on Romans* (1933, 1949 [2nd ed.], 1961 [3rd ed.]), and edited the monthly *Luther Studies* (1925–35). In the postwar period, Satō's influence could be seen in Kazō Kitamori's biography *Martin Luther* (1950) and his *Reformation Theology* (1960), and in Saburō Takahashi's *Luther's Essential Thought and Its Limitations* (1960), as well as in Chitose Kishi's *Luther's Theological Thought in His Commentary on Hebrews* (1961). In addition to the publication of translations of foreign studies of Luther, the publication of *Luther's Works* in a multi-volume series by Seibunsha, the major Lutheran publishing house in Japan, was of marked importance. A number of younger scholars, such as Yoshikazu Tokuzen, were to play significant roles in publishing this series.[7] A Luther Studies Society (Ruteru Gakkai) was established in 1970, and it has been holding annual meetings to promote Luther research, particularly in the Japan Evangelical Lutheran Church.[8]

Calvin studies have been even more thoroughly pursued in Japan, largely because of the Presbyterian-Reformed backgrounds of a number of Japanese Protestant scholars. Masahisa Uemura and Tokutarō Takakura had both encouraged the study of Calvin's *Institutes* among their followers, and the first Japanese edition of the *Institutes* appeared during 1934–39, translated by Masaki Nakayama. A new translation was undertaken by the Calvin Translation Society, founded in 1960, whose chief promoters were Masaichi Takemori, Nobuo Watanabe, and the Reformed Church missionary John Hesselink. A new translation of the *Institutes* done by Watanabe was issued in 1965, and other translations of Calvin's *Commentaries* and tracts by different translators have appeared in the same series. In addition to translations of foreign studies on Calvin, a number of significant contributions by Japanese scholars have appeared, such as Chuichi Uoki's *A Study of the History of the Christian Mind: The Spirit of Calvin's Theology* (1948), which searched in Calvin's theological ideas for clues to the fundamental nature and essence of Christianity, and Naomichi Kōdaira's *Calvin: His Life and Thought* (1963), which seeks to locate the central thrust of Calvin's theology not in dogma but in "rendering proper service to God through a rightful worship to His everlasting glory."[9] Another significant publication was the *Collected Essays on the Reformation* (1967), a group of studies on the Protestant Reformers by Japanese scholars published on the 450th anniversary of the Reformation. Appropriately enough, it took the form of a Festschrift dedicated to Ken Ishiwara for his work in pioneering Reformation studies in Japan.

Other historical figures of Protestantism were not overlooked by Japanese scholars, partly from denominational loyalty and partly from the desire to present viewpoints in Protestant theology other than those of the main Augustine-Luther-Calvin-Barth line. Wesley studies had appeared spasmodically in the prewar period, mostly in the *Theological Review* published jointly by the theological departments of two schools of Methodist background, Kwansei Gakuin and Aoyama Gakuin. Professor Yoshio Noro (1925–), a teacher of systematic theology for many years at Aoyama Gakuin and the author of *Wesley* (1963), was instrumental in founding both the Japan Wesley Translation Society in 1959 (for the publication of Wesley's *Sermons* and other works) and also the Japan Wesley Study Society in 1960 (for holding meetings about Wesley studies and publishing a journal on Wesleyan theology).[10] With the rising interest in Anabaptist studies in the West, there has been a concomitant concern in Japan, mainly led by Dr. Gan Sakakibara (1898–). Baptized in a Presbyterian church and an earnest student of political and economic thought, Sakakibara was active in the leftist Student Christian Movement, which collapsed in 1932. He then went abroad for studies in Marburg, Germany, under Professor Georg Wuensch. He remained active in the small Christian community of wartime Japan and in the postwar period served as a professor at Aoyama Gakuin University, while his wife became a socialist member of the Japanese Diet and a vice minister of justice under Premier Tetsu Katayama. Dr. Sakakibara's acquaintance with Anabaptism dated from visits to Anabaptist communities in the United States in 1960, and from then he devoted himself to making the Anabaptist heritage better known in Japan. His five volumes of Anabaptist historical studies, published by Heibonsha (1966-75), have introduced such topics as Hutterite history, Christian cooperative communities in our day, the classical age of the Anabaptist churches, and the like. Sakakibara has used some of the proceeds from the Tokyo English Center, a language institute that he founded, to support his publications and other Anabaptist activities throughout Japan.[11]

The Early and Medieval Church

Ishiwara's second area of specialization was the early and medieval church, a field in which Roman Catholic scholars in Japan have taken the lead. The basis had been laid in the prewar years through the writings of Father Sōichi Iwashita (1888-1940), who, like Ishiwara, had been introduced to medieval studies and Scholasticism by Professor Raphael von Koeber at Tokyo Imperial University. Iwashita's popular book *The Catholic Faith* (1930) as well as his more scholarly works, such as *Studies in the History of Medieval Philosophical Thought* (1942), won widespread interest among students and intellectuals, although he became best known for his humble service as a chaplain in a leprosarium during the latter years of his life. His disciple was Yoshihiko Yoshimitsu (1904-45), a Catholic layman and professor at Tokyo University, whose *Collected Works* (4 vols., 1945-52) helped to establish Thomism as a major philosophical option in Japan.[12] This tradition was carried on by Masao Matsumoto (1910-   ), a professor at Keio University, who as an ardent Catholic layman became "the unofficial spokesman for Catholicism and Thomism in Japan."[13] A successor of Ken Ishiwara as chairman of the Japanese Society of Medieval Philosophy, Matsumoto helped to encourage the society's annual publication, *Studies in Medieval Thought* (from 1959), and to make his own contributions in *Studies in the Logic of Being* (1944), *A Perspective for the Century—At the Threshold of* Philosophia Perennis (1950), and his magnum opus, *Problems of Ontology: Studies in Scholasticism* (1967). Through his academic writings and also through a number of study associations, Matsumoto helped to encourage young Catholic scholars to consider Thomism not as a relic from the past, but as a contemporary option for modern persons, in the midst of intensive dialogue with other options such as Marxism. We shall encounter Matsumoto's work again in this chapter when we discuss Neo-Thomism's contributions to systematic theology.

Although studies in Scholasticism flourished in the postwar era, there was also research on other aspects of the medieval and early church periods. Toratorō Shimomura wrote on *St. Francis of Assisi* (1965), while Toru Ingu produced *A Study of Anselm* (1951), and Nobuhisa Nagasawa published *A*

Study of the Philosophy of St. Augustine (1960). There have also been studies of such figures as Saint Bonaventura, Origen, Clement of Alexandria, Ignatius of Antioch, and others.

Church History Surveys

The third field in which Ishiwara pioneered, the writing of surveys of the entire field of church history, has not been sufficiently followed up. There have been no studies written in Japanese to supersede his *History of Christianity* (1951). Instead, theological students and others have had to rely on translations of Western church-history surveys by von Loewenisch, von Schubert, Latourette, Lortz, and Cairns, all of which have their limitations for use in Japan. It is perhaps significant that there has not yet arisen a Japanese church historian who could exceed Ishiwara's mastery of the total field of church history.

History of Christianity in Japan

Ishiwara's writings in the field of Japanese Christianity have been followed by only a few comprehensive studies, though there are many works on particular individuals or problems. Antei Hiyane's *History of Christianity in Japan* (1949), like his *History of Religions in Japan* (1951), is useful as a compendium of names and dates, but it lacks an overall analytical framework. The most comprehensive one-volume survey of the field was provided by Richard H. Drummond's English-language *History of Christianity in Japan* (1971). A much shorter work, written from a very conservative standpoint, is Tomonobu Yanagita's *A Short History of Christianity in Japan* (1957), published in both English and Japanese.

In the postwar period a number of surveys of Catholic and Protestant work in Japan were prepared by missionaries, primarily for introducing the field to their new colleagues, such as Johannes Laures's, *The Catholic Church in Japan* (1954), Charles Iglehart's *A Century of Protestant Christianity in Japan* (1959), and Joseph Jennes's *A History of the Catholic Church in Japan (1549—1873)* (1959, 1973 [2nd ed.]), with its sequel by Joseph L. Van Hecken, *The Catholic Church in Japan since 1859* (1963).

There have been many scholarly surveys of particular periods. They include Arimichi Ebisawa's *Studies of "Kirishitan" History* (1942) and the collection of essays in the periodical *Kirishitan Studies* (from 1943). In addition to biographies of such leading figures from the early Catholic period as Francis Xavier, João Rodrigues, Paulo Miki, and Ukon Takayama, there have been numerous listings of martyrs from particular areas, to preserve the names and memories of those who suffered for their faith. The entire early Catholic period suddenly became popular in Japan and abroad after the publication of Shūsaku Endō's novel *Silence* (1966; Eng. trans., 1969), the gripping account of the inner turmoil of a Christian apostate. Studies of

Christian groups from the nineteenth century on proliferate. There are studies of Kanzō Uchimura, founder of Non-Church Christianity, by Masao Sekine, Gorō Mayeda, and Kōkichi Kurosaki, but the writings of Uchimura himself continue to be best-sellers and provide the most direct access to the thought of this remarkable man. The most valuable introduction to Japanese Protestant leaders from a theological perspective is Yoshitaka Kumano's *A History of Japanese Christian Theological Thought* (1968), a compilation of articles that originally appeared in the journal *Gospel and World*. There are individual studies of such figures as Masahisa Uemura, Gumpei Yamamuro, Hiromichi Kozaki, Jō Niishima, Toyohiko Kagawa, and many others.

In the modern period, histories of particular Japanese denominations and commemorative histories of individual schools and local churches are almost without number, but are of unequal value. Particular reference should be made, however, to the tape-recorded discussions and other materials in Yasushi Kuyama, ed., *Christianity in Contemporary Japan* (1961), which were most useful for the present study. Significant historical research materials are also to be found in Tsunetarō Miyakoda's *Materials for a Study of Christianity in Modern Japan* (1967), Yoshio Yoshimura's *Modern Theology and Mission* in Japan (1964), and Saburō Ozawa's *Study of the History of Japanese Protestantism* (1964). The contributions of research centers such as Dōshisha University's Research Institute on Christianity in Japan, Sophia University's *Monumenta Nipponica* center, Tokyo Union Theological Seminary's Research Society on the History of Japanese Christianity, and ICU's Research Center on Christianity in Japan will all be important for future academic work in this field.[14]

Specialized Historical Monographs

The vast majority of Ishiwara's historical writings, like those of Japanese scholars generally, are monographs about particular subjects, which provide the basic materials for later studies of a more general nature. While the entire field is too vast to survey here, certain works have had widespread popularity and influence. Hideo Ōki's *Ethical Thought of Puritanism* (1966) and *Puritanism* (1968) helped to draw attention to a tradition that has had a powerful impact on the West, and on Japan as well. Toshio Satō's *Modern Theology* (1964) provided a survey of theological trends, mostly in Germany, from the nineteenth century on. Hiroshi Omiya's *Forsyth* (1965) examined the English theologian who was "a Barthian before Barth." Kō Yūki, a pastor with interests in liturgy, hymnody, and poetry, was the ideal person to introduce *Pascal* (1960). Enkichi Kan, and Anglican scholar (about whom, more presently), wrote on *Berdyaev* (1966). Yoshinobu Kumazawa, whom we shall also be encountering again in systematic theology, authored *Modern Discourse on Christianity* (1964). Jirō Ishii's *A Study of Schleiermacher* (1948) deals with a writer little studied thus far in Japan, while Chō Ōtani's *The Concept of Reality and Truth in Kierkegaard* (1963) is but one of numerous studies of the Danish writer, whose works have appeared in many Japanese translations.

The list of specialized historical monographs could be extended indefinitely, but must be curtailed here for lack of space. It may be worthwhile, though, to note areas of historical research that have been comparatively neglected in Japan. For instance, American church history has received little attention, despite the fact that Japan's Christian history from the Meiji era on has been intimately connected with that of the American churches. There have also been very few studies in Japan on Christianity in Asia, or in other Third World areas. (Steps to deal with this omission may have started with the Christian Conference of Asia's series in progress, entitled "Christianity in Asia," written by scholars from the respective Asian countries.) Furthermore, topics such as church-state relations, Christian liturgies, the history of Christian ethics and social thought, the sociology of knowledge, and the like, have not yet been adequately dealt with in Japan. Yet, to mention omissions is to indicate how broadly and deeply the field of historical theology has grown since the "German agenda" was introduced by pioneers like Ishiwara.

The Role of Church History: Some Preliminary Comments

With all that has been done in church history, however, the total impact of this discipline on the life of the Christian community in Japan has been modest. One reason for this is that historical theology has served so often as a handmaiden to systematic theology. While more will be said about this in the section on systematic theology, it may be pointed out here that historical research has been carried out largely to serve existing church structures and theological systems. To some extent this happened as the result of the "German agenda," which sometimes carried the assumption that the historical and theological experiences of German Christianity represented a norm by which other Christian groups are to be measured. Thus it could be assumed that for Protestants of a Barthian persuasion, there was a standard "orthodox line" running from Paul through Augustine, Luther, and Calvin to Barth. The Catholic agenda was not of German origin, but a similar "orthodox line" for them, before Vatican Council II, would run from the early church through Augustine, Thomism, Trent, and Vatican I, to Neo-Thomism. (Vatican II made some alterations in this viewpoint, however.) For either Protestants or Catholics who thought this way—to oversimplify the matter greatly—the lines of past historical developments converged in present orthodoxy. This meant that the really important task of theology was to master the present-day orthodox system, for which church history provided an interesting but less important introduction.

If this was the situation in church history, scholars of Christian ethics and social thought encountered quite a different set of circumstances.

Christian Ethics and Social Thought

For all their difficulties, church historians at least knew they were in a field that had an acknowledged (though minor) place among the theological disciplines. But this was seldom the case with scholars in the field of Christian ethics and social thought. They worked in such areas as sociology, philosophy, ethics, economics, or perhaps politics, and their contributions to theology were not always acknowledged or appreciated. For strict Barthians, ethics was a subdivision of dogmatic theology, and that was that. Other theologians may have been more sympathetic to some of the viewpoints from social thought, but could not fit them into the traditional categories of biblical, historical, systematic, or practical theology.

On the other hand, Christians concerned about ethical issues were frequently involved in action groups for social change. Such action groups had not been allowed in pre-1945 Japan, after all, with the secret police around to keep an eye on things. It was easy, then, in the postwar period for these people to be dismissed as unreflective activists by those engaged in "pure" theological scholarship. It was not easy for people involved in social issues to keep commuting between action and reflection, but those who did so were able to make significant contributions. Such a person was Mikio Sumiya.

Mikio Sumiya and Social Thought

The work of Mikio Sumiya (1916–), a professor of economics at the University of Tokyo, illustrates a number of the basic approaches that have been made by Christians to social issues in contemporary Japan. In terms of the development of theology in the postwar period, his career indicates what happened to the "German agenda" when it was reintroduced to Japan in the field of social studies.

In the 1920s sociological studies in Japanese universities were already based mostly on German scholarship. They were studies of particular social institutions, such as agricultural groups, the family system, and the like. There were times when Japanese scholars could study Marxist thought freely, and in fact the academic study of Marx was introduced to Japan by Hiromichi Kozaki (1856–1938), a Christian pastor and professor in both Kyoto and Tokyo.[15] Modern Japanese theological liberalism was to a large extent influenced by Marxism, and most of the founders of the socialist movement in Japan were initially Christians.[16] But from the 1930s, with the growth of militaristic nationalism in Japan, Marxist thought became increasingly proscribed by the government, and one of the casualties in the Christian community was the leftist-oriented Student Christian Movement, disbanded by the YMCA leaders after a stormy session at Gotemba in the summer of 1932.[17] With Marxist studies prohibited for sociology, Japanese scholars turned increasingly to the works of Max Weber. Hisao Ōtsuka (1907–), in the University of Tokyo's Sociology Department, was chiefly responsible for introducing Weber's ideas and encouraging the publication of his writings in Japan. Ōtsuka's own major work was *Reformation and Modern Society* (1948), which traced the influence of Protestantism in modern European history after the Weberian fashion. In the chapter on "Biblical Studies," it was pointed out how Weber's theories also influenced Professor Masao Sekine in his studies of the history of Israel.

When the restrictions on the study of Marx were removed after 1945, Japanese academic life was virtually flooded with Marxist scholarship in all fields of the humanities and social studies. While Christian scholars such as Sumiya paid careful attention to Marxist thought, they put renewed emphasis on Weber's works, for clearly Weber provided an alternative way of interpreting the role in human history of such nonmaterialistic factors as religion. Put in its simplest terms, Marxists interpreted the fundamental changes in human history as based on the changing factors of production, and from them, political, social, and religious ideas are understood only as reflections of the basic economic conditions. Weber, on the other hand, in his celebrated essay on *The Protestant Ethic and the Spirit of Capitalism,* indicated how the tables could be turned on the Marxist analysis, by attempting to demonstrate that religious ideas, in the form of Puritan developments of Calvinism, had been a major catalyst in the development of capitalism, and not the other way around. The "gospel of Weber" was enthusiastically embraced by Christian apologists in Japan in their dialogues with Marxism. Sumiya and his colleagues maintained that in this way there could be a fruitful coalition between the insights of socialist thought and Christian theology.

Sumiya developed some of his dominant theses about Japanese society in his major publications, *Christianity and Modern Japan* (1962) and *Japanese Society and Christianity* (1954), both of which are collections of his articles and addresses. In the first place, Sumiya evaluated very highly the critical posture taken by early Meiji Christianity toward such institutions of Japanese society as the family system, the emperor system, the feudal system, and the agricultural system of that time, as working against fundamental Christian and human values. In the later Meiji era, however, Christians began to compromise with Japanese culture in order to achieve a measure of social acceptance, and consequently the social concern of Christians began to wane.[18] Second, Sumiya explained more precisely the reasons for Christianity's failure to challenge some of the basic institutions of Japanese society from the later Meiji period. His thesis was that because the Christian churches became almost exclusively concerned with students, intelligentsia, and the middle classes, they lost touch with the workers, the farmers, and the leaders of Japanese society. As he puts it in a memorable sentence, "The churches used to be active in the countryside, but then they moved to the city, never to return." Instead of challenging the emperor system *(tennōsei),* the churches went along with it and supported it, thus losing their cutting edge in Japanese society.[19]

In regard to industrialization, the vertical structure of feudal society was taken over by capitalist leaders in the Meiji period, which served to minimize social dislocation but also increased instances of injustice. Again, Christianity began by being critical of such a process, but gradually accommodated to it, for the most part.[20] Thus Christianity gradually retired from the field of social issues and tended to concentrate more on social work, where it achieved some remarkable successes and gained widespread recognition.[21] In the post-1945 era, according to Sumiya, there has been a repetition of some of the same mistakes from the past. There was a Christian boom through which new people came to the churches in unprecedented numbers. But the churches were not able to meet the expectations of these people because, instead of challenging the basic presuppositions of Japanese social structure, the churches accommodated to the prevailing mores, just as they had done in the late Meiji period, and as a result they again lost their vital contact with Japanese society.[22]

Sumiya's views on Japanese society were widely disseminated through religious and secular publications, through student conferences and church associations. His active service as a resource person for church committees and student gatherings made his reflections on these matters perhaps better known than those of any other scholar of social thought at that time. But in Japan such ideas are often best developed in the context of small study groups of like-minded friends. In the postwar period an important study group to which Sumiya belonged was the All Japan Socialist Christian's Frontier Union (Zen Nihon Shakai Kirisutōkyo Zensen Dōmei). This group was organized by Professor Gan Sakakibara of Aoyama Gakuin University (who was previously mentioned in connection with his Anabaptist studies of a later period). The Frontier Union published a newsletter, *Christ and Society* (ca. 1951–55), and counted among its members Takenosuke Miyamoto of Tokyo Union Theological Seminary, Kanō Yamamoto of Kantō Gakuin University, Jotarō Kawakami of the Japan Socialist party, Sam H. Franklin of Tokyo Union Seminary, and Mrs. Chiyo Sakakibara, who, as we saw, was a Diet member and a vice minister of justice.[23] The group's newsletter carried articles with such provocative titles as "The Mission of the Japan Socialist Party," for the Frontier Union was indeed formed as a kind of Christian auxiliary of the JSP.[24] Members of the group tended to believe that the country's socialist political activities might somehow prove to be the catalysts of the new society in Japan. Such hopes were largely frustrated, as were the hopes of those Christians who supported the conservatives in what came to be the Liberal Democratic party. When the Frontier Union was used to promote Gan Sakakibara's own political campaign for office, some of its members resented it and the group gradually disbanded. Yet the group had helped to shape the social thought of its members, and thus continued to exert indirect influence long after its dissolution.

Before turning to later developments in social thought among Japanese Christians, it is important to indicate some of the contributions that foreign scholars made in Christian ethics in the immediate postwar period.

Contributions of Foreign Scholars in Christian Ethics

In the immediate postwar period, there was very little to challenge the dominant role of Karl Barth's theology in Japan, or of the Barthian views that Christian ethics was a subdivision of dogmatics. A few criticisms began to be heard, however, first of all through the writings of Reinhold Niebuhr and Paul Tillich.[25] Of Tillich's influence more will be said later in connection with his visit to Japan in 1960. As for Niebuhr, the differences between his views on ethics and social issues and those of Barth were analyzed by Tetsutarō Ariga (1899–   ), professor of Christian studies at Kyoto University. A few of Niebuhr's books began to appear in Japanese translation, but since his prose—loaded as it is with irony and subtle allusions of all sorts—is extraordinarily difficult to put into Japanese, it was very hard for his introducers to explain his thought clearly to Japanese readers. That difficulty, combined with the fact that Niebuhr never visited Japan, somewhat restricted his influence on postwar Japanese Christian thought.

The first major Western theologian to spend a significant amount of time in postwar Japan was Emil Brunner, who visited the country for three months in 1949 on a lecture tour, and then from 1953 to 1955 was a professor at International Christian University. Brunner was already known by most Japanese Christians as the one who had been involved in a celebrated controversy with Karl Barth over natural law. It was generally felt that, although Brunner had made many good points during the course of that controversy, Barth had gained the upper hand.[26] A rather unsettling omen of Brunner's visit was the intention that he announced for his stay in Japan:

What Japanese Christianity lacks is an interpretation of Christianity to the intellectual of this age. By that I mean an interpretation in terms of the Christian's questions about life, including problems such as ethics, culture, education, and so forth.[27]

The assumption of these lines seems to be that Japanese Christians never addressed such issues. Hence, in spite of many fine contacts and impressions that Brunner made during his time in Japan, his stay was a rather unhappy one and was concluded far sooner than had been originally anticipated on either side. The continuing admiration that many Japanese Christians had for Barth rankled in Brunner, as did the unwillingness of members of the Kyōdan to share Brunner's high esteem for Non-Church Christianity (Mukyōkai) as embodying the principles of churchmanship most suitable for Japan.[28] Hideo Ōki has concluded that if Brunner had come to Japan about a decade later, his reception might have been a much happier one, for in that period Japanese Christians were developing a greater appreciation for the approach that Brunner took toward the church and social problems.[29]

Mention should also be made of the visit in 1958 of Eduard Heimann of the New School of Social Research in New York City. His lectures gave encouragement to those engaged in Occupational Evangelism.[30]

Another challenge to the dominance of Barthianism in Japan came from none other than Karl Barth himself, whose views and activities in Germany and Switzerland gradually became better understood in postwar Japan. It is curious that Barth's courageous stand with the Confessing Church in Germany against Hitler's policies through the 1934 Barmen Declaration was not given wide publicity in Japan. Some Japanese Christian scholars such as Gorō Mayeda were in Europe at that time and sent word of these developments in Germany back to their friends in Japan. But publicizing this news in Japan at a time when the government was becoming increasingly suspicious about the patriotic reliability of its Christian citizens did not seem to be a good course.[31] It was only in postwar Japan that the Barmen phase of Barth's career became better known, as well as his own "correction" of his previous views on eschatology that seemed to make ethical questions irrelevant.[32] Nevertheless, a popular book of selections of his writings on ethics from his *Church Dogmatics* was edited by Masahisa Suzuki and published in four volumes as *Christian Ethics* (1954–55).

Still another challenge to the dominance of Barthianism came from the 1950 Gotemba Conference, which was held with Professor John C. Bennett of Union Theological Seminary in New York City as the main speaker. Isamu Ōmura (1901–   ), the pastor of the Kyōdan's Asagaya Church in Tokyo and later to become a Kyōdan moderator and chairman of the NCCJ, explained that one of the reasons the Gotemba Conference was so influential was that it represented "the initial coming together within Japanese Christianity of the theologians of the church, who traditionally emphasized dogmatics, and the Christian scholars of society, who traditionally emphasized social problems."[33] As it turned out, the coming together of these two groups was to be short-lived. Yet during that time President Hidenobu Kuwada of Tokyo Union Seminary was led to take a new interest in the social role and responsibility of the Christian church.[34] At that seminary Professor Sam Franklin began to teach a course in Christian social ethics, which was a new field for Tokyo Union. Furthermore, the leadership of the Kyōdan was sufficiently moved by the new concern which Kuwada and other leaders were expressing about current social issues that it established in 1952 a Social Problems Committee, which Kuwada called "a significant step in the United Church in Japan."[35] We shall take up other evaluations of this move later on.

Taken as a whole, foreign scholars who visited Japan or whose works were read in Japan did not replace the main Barthian tendencies of Protestantism in regard to social issues, but they did manage to give encouragement to the diversity emerging among Japanese Christians.

The Growth of Diversity in Christian Social Thought

Insofar as there had been a consensus about social issues among Japanese Protestants, at least in the Tokyo area, it was one represented by the views of Mikio Sumiya and his fellow members of the Frontier Union. The first major departure from such a consensus came from Sumiya's own pastor, the Reverend Sakae Akaiwa (1903–66), of the Kyōdan's Uehara Church in Tokyo.[36] From early in his career, as a student of Takakura, Akaiwa had wavered between the influence of Karl Marx and Karl Barth, "the two Karls" who seemed to describe different aspects of the condition of people in Japanese society at that time. After he became a pastor, Akaiwa endeavored to follow Barth as thoroughly as possible. But by 1952 he began to feel that Barth had been wrong, and under the influence of Bultmann moved toward a relative, historical interpretation of Christianity in contrast to what he felt was Barth's absolutist position. He caused quite a sensation in 1949 when, after the Communist party of Japan had won thirty-five seats in an election to the House of Representatives, Akaiwa announced his intention of joining that party. Even though he never actually took the step, he was widely criticized in Kyōdan circles for his statement.

Akaiwa's religious views were increasingly influenced by his leftist political commitments, as is seen in his *Exodus from Christianity* (1964). In that book Akaiwa stated that the beginning of trouble came when the followers of Jesus of Nazareth began to confess him as the cosmic "Christ," thus beginning a new organized religion of "Christianity," which was far removed from the social passion of Jesus himself. Such statements brought charges of heresy from some of Akaiwa's Kyōdan colleagues, but the church Committee on Faith and Order, which subsequently investigated the charges of heresy, was content to indicate that Akaiwa's statements in this regard were his own views and not those of the Kyōdan as a whole. Having said this, they did not seek to remove him from the ministerial orders of the Kyōdan. Akaiwa continued to serve as pastor of the Uehara Church until his untimely death in 1966. His influence was passed on mainly through those followers of his who subsequently became "problem posers" for the Kyōdan in the late 1960s, as mentioned earlier. Akaiwa himself continued to explore the nature of faith in Jesus on the boundary lines of the Christian community, and is even alleged to have once told a group of startled hearers, "I am Jesus."[37]

Protestants in the Kansai area (the environs of Kyoto and Osaka) had long taken a view of social problems different from the Protestants of Kantō (Tokyo and Yokohama districts). The Student Christian Movement of the late 1920s had been comparatively influential in the Kansai, as had been the movements of Kagawa and his followers in social programs related to labor unions, cooperatives, urban slum clearance, and the like. In Kansai there was more emphasis on the need for concrete programs to give practical demonstration of Christian social concerns. The emphasis of the Dōshisha School of Theology had traditionally been along this line. The concepts of socialist democracy were welcome among Kansai groups, but instead of following the Kantō Protestants' efforts to examine the theoretical basis of such a movement, Kansai people were more interested in encouraging community centers, labor-union action groups, and the like. Many of these activities were given official Kyōdan sanction when, as has been pointed out, the Kyōdan created a Social Problems Committee (Shakai Mondai Semmon Iinkai) in 1952 in the aftermath of the Gotemba Conference with John Bennett. In retrospect, Sumiya felt that this move to bureaucratize what had been a living movement in the church led to a rapid decline in its vitality. He held that the

Kyōdan's action demonstrated the transition from charisma to bureaucracy described by Max Weber.

Roman Catholics did not lag behind Protestants in their desire to create groups for Christian social thought and action. Thomist thought continued to provide the basis for Catholic social action and reflection, and Japanese copies of Pope Leo XIII's *Rerum Novarum* (1891) were widely studied by Catholics and others. Of particular concern in the postwar period was the Catholic church's teaching, expressed in several encyclicals of Pope Pius XII as well as by other church leaders, that Communism was inimical to Christian faith and social practice. At this time in France and Italy there were severe conflicts between Catholics and resurgent Communists over political power, and hence it was natural that Catholic missionaries in Japan from these countries, and most of their colleagues, would share the same concerns. Some of the responses made by Catholics in Japan to such social concerns were also patterned on overseas models. The movement known as Jeunes Ouvrières Chrétiennes (JOC, or Young Christian Workers) began in France, but there were soon JOC branches in local parishes in Japan, which flourished for a while in the 1950s and then declined in importance.[38] Centers for Catholic workers were also founded in the hopes of establishing a nationwide Catholic workers' league.[39] Catholic Action groups also were active through the Legion of Mary, which was introduced to Japan by Australian priests in 1948, and by the Action of Mary (Actio Mariae), founded in Sapporo in 1953 primarily for young people.[40] An outgrowth of the JOC movement was the establishment of the Catholic Study Center on Social Problems (Katorikku Shakai Mondai Kenkyūjō), founded by Father Jean Murgue, M.E.P., in Kitakyūshū and subsequently moved by him to Tokyo, along with the publication he edited, *Shakai Kankei to Ningen* [People and Social Relationships].[41] In sum, Catholics involved in social thought and action came to have their own groups, which operated in quite different ways and with other presuppositions than did those of Protestants.

There were also conservative Protestant groups with social concerns. Even though they tended to have a sectarian outlook, which made them shy away from taking stands on public issues, they did support freedom of religion, opposed the nationalization of Yasukuni Shrine, and often were strongly anti-Communist. They did not share the socialist views of many Kyōdan Protestants, and had no interest in an authoritative tradition of social thought such as the Catholics possessed. Their social thought was not systematically articulated, but they did have strong views on Christian personal ethics. Some groups expressed their social concerns by working to help former prisoners, to care for juvenile delinquents, to assist the elderly, to rehabilitate former prostitutes, and the like. Their concrete experiences in these areas led to a direct kind of social awareness about specific social problems.

Thus, by the end of the 1950s it was clear that there were several diverse Christian viewpoints on social issues, with varying presuppositions and methods of action. The liberal Protestants like Sumiya were no longer the only Christians who spoke out on current problems. Soon people with Sumiya's outlook were to receive new reinforcements, but also to face new challenges.

Christian Progressive Intellectuals

For the decade and a half from 1960 to 1975 the lot of scholars in Christian ethics and social thought was inseparably bound up with economic and political events of the period, as well as with the general social climate. The Christian boom of the immediate postwar period had long since cooled, and with it some of the enthusiasm for social issues among church people. The major churches, both Protestant and Catholic, had given their blessing to the study of social problems and to certain types of social action. The Kyōdan, for instance, had committees working on these concerns, and even a research institute to investigate issues affecting the church's mission. There was never enough money to do things properly, it was recognized, but at least the programs were started.

Many Christians thought that the efforts of conservatives to change the new Japanese constitution would present the first major challenge for those concerned with social issues. During this period the constitution was not amended to alter or remove article 9, which renounced war, despite many proposals to that effect. Instead, the government decided to develop the Self-Defense Forces in the shadow of article 9, so to speak, with the justification that since they were only for self-defense they did not constitute "land, sea, and air forces, as well as other war potential," which that article prohibited.

There were other issues, however, related to the revival of militarism and conservatism in Japan, which did bring social ferment. These were the struggles between the Ministry of Education and the Japan Teachers' Union over teacher rating and moral education (1957–58), protests against nuclear testing (from 1954), and the defeat of the Police Duties Bill (1958). As these social issues emerged, a social scientist who was also a Christian, such as Mikio Sumiya, found himself increasingly identified with a group of "progressive intellectuals," with whom he served on church committees, speakers' forums, and other such occasions. Of Kyōdan background, they had mostly studied in America where they absorbed the insights of Reinhold Niebuhr and became fluent in English. They agreed with the Barthian critique of liberal Protestantism, but found the Barthians' lack of concern for social issues inadequate in view of the rapid social changes taking place in their country and its growing involvement in world affairs. All made careful studies of Marx, but also made use of Weber's critique of Marx.

Among the Christian progressive intellectuals was Nobushige Ukai (1925–), a professor of constitutional law and onetime president of ICU. Also at ICU was Kiyoko Takeda Chō (1917–), professor of Christian ethics, a careful analyst of the emperor system, and the author of the classic study *Indigenization and Compromise* (1967). Very active in international work, she was an active member of the WCC's Central Committee. Yoshiaki Iisaka (1925–), a professor of political science at Gakushuin University, was the author of numerous studies on politics, such as *Modern Political Science* (1957) and *Resistance to Authority* (1959). Masao Takenaka (1925–), professor of Christian social ethics at Dōshisha University School of Theology, was involved in urban industrial issues, indigenous Christian art, and Christian dialogue with other religions and worldviews. He has written *The Community of True Humanity* (1962) and *The Modern World and the Church* (1970), as well as the English-language *Reconciliation and Renewal in Japan* (1957, 1967 [2nd ed.]).

When the struggle developed over the 1960 United States–Japan Mutual Security Treaty, the Christian progressive intellectuals were opposed to the treaty, along with a large number of progressive groups that joined a coalition to protest what were felt to be the undemocratic methods used by Premier Kishi and the Liberal Democratic party to ratify the treaty.[42] They supported the peaceful protests against the treaty, but rejected the use of violent methods. Nevertheless, the aftermath of that unsuccessful campaign to block the Security Treaty led to the gradual rejection, by many Japanese Christian students, of the Christian realism approach of Reinhold Niebuhr's writings as being inappropriate to the Japanese scene.[43]

Meanwhile, a number of scholars in theological seminaries also took up the analysis of modern social issues. Toshio Satō (1923–), professor of modern theology at Tokyo Union Seminary and onetime president of that school, sought to establish theological bases for Christian approaches to modern issues in such works as *Modern Theology* (1964), *Christianity and Modern Culture* (1964), and *Protestantism and Modern Times* (1970). At the same seminary, Sam H. Franklin (1902–), professor of Christian social ethics, wrote the first survey of Japanese social problems from the perspective of Christian social ethics, *Outline of Christian Social Ethics* (Jap. and Eng., 1964). Franklin's TUTS colleague in Christian ethics and later president of the seminary, Hideo Ōki (1928–), published an expansion of his own doctoral dissertation under Reinhold Niebuhr, *The Ethical Thought of Puritanism* (1966), and its sequel, *Puritanism* (1968), as well as works on eschatology and its relation to ethics.[44]

By the time of the eruption of New Left activism in the 1969–70 Kyōdan struggles over the Security Treaty and the Christian Pavilion at Expo '70, the Christian progressive intellectuals and their seminary colleagues were in positions of administrative authority in their schools. Ukai and Satō were presidents of their institutions, Chō and Takenaka served as deans, and all the rest were prominent faculty members. Hence in the eyes of the New Left—who in the meantime had moved much further to the left than their mentors—the progressive intellectuals represented the Establishment and were targets for sharp attacks. This was bitter medicine indeed for the professors, since they had for the most part been close sympathizers with the student opponents of the Security Treaty in 1960, and had long been looked to for guidance about social issues. So traumatic was this later period of encounter with the New Left that many of these progressive scholars have published very little on ethics and social thought since 1970, except on specialized topics. Similar ideological struggles with the New Left had comparable effects, for example, on Roman Catholic scholars at Sophia University in Tokyo and on Baptist professors at Seinan Gakuin in Fukuoka. By the late 1970s the field of Christian ethics and social thought was just beginning to emerge from the period of relative silence that had engulfed it during the 1969–70 upheavals.

Philosophical Theology

The field of philosophical theology has also been under the sway of the "German agenda," but the course of its deliverance from the "Germanic captivity" has been quite different from the other fields we are studying. For one thing, the study of philosophical theology has taken place almost entirely within the world of university scholars, and hence rather far removed from the conflicts that have swept through Japanese society and the churches from time to time. In addition, the philosophical world in Japan has been deeply influenced at every point by Buddhism, of which the career and influence of Kitarō Nishida (1870–1945) may be seen as exemplary. Nishida's successors at Kyoto, Hajime Tanabe (1885–1962) and Keiji Nishitani (1900–   ) also had considerable influence on the development of philosophical thought in Japan. The questions raised by these thinkers with Buddhist backgrounds led to roads where German maps were inadequate.

The outstanding prewar Christian scholar in this field was Seiichi Hatano (1877–1950), a professor of the study of religion at Kyoto University from 1917 to 1937. His masterwork is *Time and Eternity* (1943; Eng. trans., 1963). In that work he summarized the then current views of Western philosophers on the concept of time.[45] Indeed, it is possible to read this major work of Hatano's without realizing that it was written by a Japanese, for the context of the work is clearly that of European philosophical thought. Hatano's work represents an important stage of assimilation of Western philosophical categories, for after him it would be possible for Japanese scholars to deal with their own tradition more creatively.

Tetsutarō Ariga (1889–   ), Hatano's successor at Kyoto University, pursued theological themes in a philosophical framework in *Symbolical Theology* (1946) and *The Problem of Ontology in Christian Thought* (1969). Takenosuke Miyamoto (1905–   ), a professor at Tokyo Union Seminary and later president of Tokyo Woman's Christian College, wrote *Philosophy as Symbol* (1948) and edited *The Dialogue between Philosophy and Theology* (1967). It is perhaps significant that the writing careers of both Ariga and Miyamoto were curtailed when these men became college presidents. Kazuo Mutō (1913–   ), a professor of philosophy at Kyoto University, became the leading writer in the field, with his *Philosophy of Religion* (1955) and *Between Theology and Philosophy of Religion* (1961). Mutō was very much in dialogue with the tradition of Buddhist thought in Japan, although like Hatano he was primarily a specialist in Western philosophy.

The "Yagi–Takizawa debate" of the 1960s opened up new vistas for philosophical theology, even though they started with what seemed like a classic example of German-type scholarship, a discussion between followers of Bultmann and Barth.[46] Seiichi Yagi (1932–) wrote *The Formation of New Testament Thought* (1963) as a disciple of Bultmann, but also as one who wanted to go beyond his mentor. Whereas Bultmann's analysis started with the kerygma as the early church's proclamation about salvation in Christ, Yagi tried to go further by analyzing three different types of "salvation thought" in the New Testament. "Type A" sees salvation happening through history, "Type B" through a Divine Being, and "Type C" through love. He then describes the development of Pauline and Johannine concepts of salvation in relation to these three types. Yagi's book caused quite a stir in the scholarly world and was widely reviewed. An older scholar who examined it appreciatively and yet critically was Katsumi Takizawa (1909–), professor of religious philosophy and systematic theology at Kyūshū University, who as a student years before had been recommended by his teacher, Kitarō Nishida, to study under Karl Barth in Switzerland. The lasting influence that Barth exerted is seen in Takizawa's careful reply to Yagi, *The Biblical Jesus and Modern Thought* (1965).

Although the debate between Yagi and Takizawa may have started as one between the methodologies of Bultmann and Barth, it soon went far beyond that. Takizawa was willing to grant that there were three types of "salvation thought" in the New Testament, but asserted that what was important was to understand the fundamental basis behind all three of them, which Takizawa explained in terms of the biblical word *Emmanuel*, "God with us." All the pages of the New Testament show this one ontological truth, he maintained. Takizawa based his interpretation here on the approach he had developed in a previous book, *Buddhism and Christianity* (1964), in which he had argued with a Buddhist scholar about the uniqueness of the Christian's faith in God, as contrasted with the Buddhist experience of enlightenment through Buddha. The Yagi–Takizawa debate continued, with Yagi replying in *Biblical Christ and Existence* (1967), and with journal articles thereafter. Both Yagi and Takizawa substantially modified their positions as a result of their debate and, in so doing, the agenda they set for philosophical theology went far beyond the Barth–Bultmann "German agenda" with which they had started. Buddhist thought had been a catalyst in the evolution of their own positions.[47]

Systematic Theology

Perhaps more than the three fields surveyed thus far, systematic theology reveals the difficult and sometimes painful process that Seiichi Yagi called "delivering Japanese theology from Germanic captivity." In no other area were the initial ties to Germany so strong, the process of separation so difficult, and the road strewn with so many problems.

We begin, then, with a consideration of the school of dialectical theology—which by this time had come to mean primarily, but not exclusively, theology along the line of Karl Barth—that was the mainstream of Protestant theology in Japan in the immediate postwar period.

Dialectical Theology's Continuing Strength in Postwar Japan

It is only necessary to recall the conditions of postwar Japanese society to understand why dialectical theology continued to exercise such a deep influence on the Protestant community. After the collapse not only of the nation's military power but also of the people's morale, there was a determined desire to set aside what had led the Japanese astray and to seek out the foundations for a new society. On both scores, dialectical theology seemed to have much to commend it. We may also note in passing that dialectical thought was popular in the immediate postwar years beyond the circle of Japanese Christian thought. Professor Hajime Tanabe (1885–1962), Nishida's successor as professor of philosophy at Kyoto University, indicated in *The Dialectic of Christianity* (1948) his appreciation for dialectical thought, especially in Karl Barth's theology.[48]

Among Christian theologies, other theological traditions seemed to have fared worse under the blows of the wartime period than dialectical theology. Protestant theological liberalism was discredited in the eyes of many, for it had not proved strong enough to withstand the syncretistic pressures that had absorbed and enlisted the churches and their members in supporting militarism and authoritarianism. The same might be said of natural theology, for it had tried to provide a bridge between nature and grace, but across that bridge in wartime there traveled some of the lower elements of human nature in the wrong direction, so that grace seemed to be lowered rather than nature uplifted. Traditions of personal piety, which on principle avoided social issues, were also in disfavor with many, for in the attempt to escape from involvement in a sinful world, there was not the power to halt deterioration in society or—and this was what hurt—in the churches.

Although wartime Japan had seen no Confessing Church such as that in Germany, which had issued the Barmen Declaration, there were Christian groups that had got into trouble with the government. These were the Holiness groups, the Seventh-day Adventists, some Anglicans, Mukyōkai or Non-Church Christians, Salvation Army leaders, and some Presbyterian-Reformed pastors. However, the reasons for which the government had made life difficult for these groups or individuals were generally nontheological ones: they were suspected of being agents for hostile governments or having ties with foreign groups that seemed to put Japanese into a subservient position. Sometimes these groups were harassed because of their theological beliefs about eschatology, for instance, but their views were apt to be of a particularist sort and not widely shared by the Christian community. Thus these groups were not in a position to give theological leadership in the postwar period on the basis of the troubles they had had with the government in wartime.

The theological tradition among Protestants that survived the war with relatively greater strength than others was dialectical theology, especially in its form of Japanese Barthianism. In the 1930s after the social activism of liberal Protestants was suppressed because it clashed with the rising currents of nationalism, Japanese Barthianism appealed to Protestants because it was able to sustain faith without bringing it into conflict with patriotism. As Yoshinobu Kumazawa has pointed out, "Barthian theology and nationalism flourished together in Japan, and interestingly, there was no resistance movement among Christians who held this theological position during the war."[49] Yet by adhering to Barthianism, pastors managed to keep the semblance of congregational life going in some churches, in spite of the incredibly difficult wartime conditions. The Barthian theological teachers had managed to keep some kind of theological education going, although toward the end of the war it was precious little. Above all, the Barthians had managed to keep their morale intact, for the difficulties of wartime and even their nation's defeat did not cancel out any of their theological convictions, since these convictions were seen to transcend such difficulties. After the war, they were in a position to continue to provide theological leadership for the Protestant community. We begin, then, by considering the Japanese dialectical theologians who represented the mainstream of Protestant theology in the postwar period: Yoshitaka Kumano, Hidenobu Kuwada, and the principal Japanese Barthians.

Yoshitaka Kumano: From Dialectical Theology to a Japanese Dogmatics. Yoshitaka Kumano (1899–) was one of the first Japanese scholars to write an extensive introduction to dialectical theology in Japan, and his subsequent work as a theologian indicates some of the principal developments in the entire field. A native of Tokyo, Kumano graduated from Waseda University and Tokyo Theological Seminary, and after brief pastorates in Tokyo and Hakodate he joined the faculty of the seminary in 1934. He also became pastor of the Musashino Church in Tokyo, a church in the Presbyterian-Reformed tradition which was somewhat reluctantly joined with the Kyōdan, and at which his wife served as associate pastor. The major story of Kumano's life is that of his theological scholarship.

Kumano's earliest work of importance was *Outline of Dialectical Theology* (1932), which served as an introduction to both Barth and Brunner. This book pointed out how dialectical theology had developed in opposition to the principles of liberal Protestant theology, which was held to have demonstrated its bankruptcy in the years during and following World War I. The knowledge of God does not come from human experience, the dialectical theologians insisted, but solely through God's own revelation of himself in the Scriptures, which the church apprehends by faith.

In the following year Kumano's *Eschatology and the Philosophy of History* (1933) appeared, in which he dealt forthrightly with ethics, considered a problem area by the dialectical theologians. Liberal theology had made a great deal of the human faculties of conscience and moral will, but Kumano insisted that the ground of ethics was to be found instead in the experience of faith and an appropriation of God's lordship in eschatological perspective. These two early books of Kumano's, along with Kuwada's two prewar volumes (to be considered below), were to exercise lasting influence on the Japanese theological world.

In the postwar period Kumano published two widely read introductions to Christianity, *Outline of Christianity* (1947) and *Essentials of Christianity* (1949). The first dealt with the doctrine of faith and with dogmatics. The second volume took up the themes of the gospels: reconciliation, justification, and sanctification. In a sense, these two volumes were to serve as prolegomena to Kumano's dogmatics. In them, he stated the contrasts between *analogia entis* and *analogia fidei,* and his rejection of any kind of natural theology, convictions he echoed from Barth and which were to serve him in the construction of his own dogmatics.[50]

The appearance of Kumano's *Dogmatics* (3 vols., 1954–65) clearly marked a major milestone in contemporary Japan's theological development.[51] As Kumano himself pointed out in another connection, there had been many theological writings in Japan up until that time, but no systematic theology written by a Japanese.[52] This was because the writing of a systematic theology is possible only after the existence of a "school of theologians" who are able over an extended period of time to reflect upon the one universal Christian tradition in the light of their own nation's experience. In Kumano's case, this tradition was started primarily by Masahisa Uemura, Kumano's teacher in the Tokyo Shingakusha, and carried on to a certain extent by Uemura's successor as head of that school, Tokutarō Takakura (with whom, incidentally, Kumano had significant differences of opinion). In carrying that tradition further with the writing of a dogmatics, Kumano relied heavily on Barth's *Church Dogmatics,* even in its structural outline. After the prolegomena, Kumano takes up the doctrine of God, where the concept of the Trinity is used for the outline, with the subjects of creation, salvation, and redemption. Volume 2 is completely given over to the doctrine of creation, and indeed Kumano's style becomes increasingly Barthian as he works through the movement from creation as an original act of God to the concept of continuing creation, and to the doctrine of the human being, human freedom, responsibility before the Creator, and the fall. Then comes the law, in both the Old and the New Testaments. Thus far, Kumano has in the main reproduced Barth's outline, with frequent reference to Calvin, and yet throughout continuing the tradition of Uemura's theology.[53] (As an indication of how far

Kumano follows the style of Barth and other German-language writers, the footnotes for one page of his text at one place take up five and a half pages!) Volume 3 deals with the doctrine of reconciliation. The task of reconciliation takes place through the meeting of God and man in Emmanuel.[54] (Kumano's understanding of "Emmanuel" is more biblically oriented than that of Tatsumi Takizawa in philosophical theology.) It is here that Kumano's distinctive understanding of the church emerges, to the extent that Michalson has characterized his work as "the theology of church existence." Over against the liberal Protestants, Kumano emphasizes that the church and not human experience is the fundamental factor in the continuity of the Christian faith; against the Mukyōkai group he emphasizes the importance of the historicity of the church; and against the Roman Catholics he affirms that the church must be based solely on the Scriptures. He makes use of Cullmann's *Christ and Time* to indicate that the church is in some sense the continuation of Christ's incarnation.[55] Kumano brings his discussion of the church to a climax in his treatment of mission, wherein the church finds both its historical and its eschatological tasks.[56]

It is interesting to note that although Kumano relied on Western theological writers throughout his *Dogmatics*, his analysis in volume 3 takes place more within the context of the Japanese religious situation. He has been influenced by the Kyoto philosophers Nishida and Tanabe, by Mukyōkai authors such as Uchimura and Sekine, and also by the Roman Catholic philosopher Yoshihiko Yoshimitsu.[57] Mention has already been made of Kumano's important contribution to historical theology, *A History of Japanese Christian Theological Thought* (1968). Kumano did a very un-Barthian thing to write a separate volume on ethics, largely because he felt it was needed at the time. Kumano's own odyssey as a dogmatic theologian shows how through use of the "German agenda" for theology he has sought to advance the theological tradition of dialectical thought in his own country in order to meet the particular religious conditions of the Japanese church.

Hidenobu Kuwada: Theology in the Service of Church and Society. For many in Japan the name of Hidenobu Kuwada (1895–1975) will always be inseparably associated with that of Yoshitaka Kumano, because the two scholars from the Presbyterian–Reformed tradition worked together closely throughout their long careers in promoting the academic study of dialectical theology and in carrying out its consequences in the life of the Kyōdan as the largest Protestant body in the nation. Born in Kagawa Prefecture, Kuwada was graduated from Tokyo's Meiji Gakuin (1917), Auburn Theological Seminary in New York (B.D., 1921), and Harvard Divinity School (S.T.M., 1922). After ordination in America he returned to Japan to a theological post in Meiji Gakuin's Theological Department in 1923. For the next forty-four years he was involved in seminary education, first at Meiji Gakuin and the Japan Theological School (Nihon Shingakkō) and its successor institutions which finally were merged into what became Tokyo Union Theological Seminary (Tokyo Shingaku Daigaku: literally, Tokyo University of Theology). From 1945 until his retirement in 1967 he was the president of the seminary under its various names, and in that capacity had widespread influence on the entire shape of postwar Protestant theological education in Japan. As Tokyo Union Seminary has been the largest of the Kyōdan's theological schools and, with its predecessors, has trained about half of that denomination's pastors, its influence is widely felt throughout the Christian community of the nation.

Kuwada's first major writings, *The Essence of Christianity* (1932) and *Dialectical Theology* (1933), in many ways parallel the early works by Kumano, and indeed the latter volume was published the year following Kumano's *Outline of Dialectical Theology*. In various ways Kuwada's works amplified and strengthened the teachings of Kumano. Kuwada did not hesitate to declare, "I am a follower of the Kumano line."[58] But where Kumano's strength lay in his ability to write trenchant and penetrating theological analysis, Kuwada was a master at synthesizing varying viewpoints and in stating them in forthright and clear fashion. He did not waver from the mainline of dialectical theology, but constantly endeavored to interpret that viewpoint in relation to current problems in church and in society. His *Introduction to Christian Theology* (1941), published not long before Pearl Harbor, became a rallying point for the small Japanese Protestant community as it underwent the trials of a society engulfed in a losing war. Its critics said that it turned the eyes of its readers away from immediate and pressing problems of society, but its admirers maintained that it enabled Christians to deepen a faith that had power to transcend transient crises. The book continued to be reprinted in the postwar era as one of the most widely read introductions available to theological students.

Mention has already been made of how Kuwada was moved by the 1950 Gotemba Conference with John C. Bennett to give greater emphasis to the social role and responsibility of the churches in Japan, of Tokyo Union Seminary, and of Kyōdan committees.[59] Kuwada also took seriously his ecumenical responsibilities: he served as a member of the World Council of Church's Central Committee in 1955 and was the principal founder of the Japan Association for Theological Education (JATE) in 1966, the national association affiliated with the North East Asia Association of Theological Schools (NEAATS).[60] Since ecumenical efforts of this sort generally aroused little interest in Japan, Kuwada's support of what he recognized as essential for the future of the churches and theological schools made such programs possible. His service in numerous Kyōdan committees and interchurch groups was a concrete expression of his concern for the life of the church. Although he never served as a regular pastor of a church, as a seminary president Kuwada was instrumental in the placement of scores of pastors and took a continuing interest in their welfare and activities. As editor of *The Dictionary of Christianity* (1963), his commanding influence made it possible to put together such a work of major scholarship. When a reception was held in Tokyo at the end of 1974 (shortly before Kuwada's final illness and death) to celebrate the publication of the first volume in a seven-volume series of *The Complete Works of Hidenobu Kuwada* (1974–   ), the gathering represented one of the greatest possible cross-sections of Protestant scholars and church leaders in Japan, almost all of whom had been personally influenced by Kuwada in one form or another. It can easily be said that the theological climate of postwar Japanese Protestantism was influenced by the thought, the leadership, and the personality of Kuwada more than by any other.

The Japanese Barthians. If dialectical theology, particularly in its Barthian form, was the major current of the Kyōdan, it also had its influence in other Christian bodies as well, and this was due in no small measure to the role of several influential Japanese Barthians, of whom only two will be mentioned in this connection.

Enkichi Kan (1895–72) was a student of Seiichi Hatano at Kyoto University, did graduate study at Harvard and Cambridge, became an Anglican priest, and taught Christian studies at the Anglicans' Rikkyō University in Tokyo (from 1923 to 1971). Kan had at first been a follower of liberal Protestantism and published a book on *The Theory of the Socialization of Christianity* (1932), which consisted in large part of translations of sections from Bishop Charles Gore's *Christ and Society* (1928).[61] At an executive committee meeting of the World's Student Christian Federation in Europe in 1934, as he recalled, "Visser't Hooft opened my eyes to Barth."[62] He made a "180-degree turn" in his orientation and subsequently, under Visser't Hooft's continuing influence and friendship, became more and more attached to the Barthian viewpoint, even though he had initially sided with Brunner in their famous controversy. Kan reflected his Barthian viewpoint in a series of articles and books, including *Contemporary Philosophy of Religion* (1939), *Theology of Barth* (1939), *Christianity in Transition* (1941), and his major work, *Reason and Revelation* (1953).

Charles Germany has speculated that if Kan had been able to return from Europe with a Barthian basis for Christian social ethics before the collapse of the Japanese SCM at its Tozansō meeting in July 1932, he might have been able to give more enduring theological foundations to the SCM, which he had helped to found and steer on its course of social concern. In this way the SCM might have managed to survive both the folly of the leftists and the restrictions of the rightists that led to its demise. But even though Germany's thesis is an attractive one, it is not widely held by Japanese scholars, who feel that Kan's Barthianism was the result of his ability to recognize and interpret a major theological figure to the Japanese scene, but doubt that he would have been able single-handedly to bring about a major synthesis between Barthianism and social action, which took place nowhere else in the world at that time.[63] Along with the tenacity of Kan's Barthian views—which he maintained long after most of his theological colleagues were inclined to different perspectives—Kan's influence in the Seikōkai, the Anglican Church of Japan, is of crucial significance. The Barthian influence extended beyond the Presbyterian–Reformed tradition in Japan.

Similarly, the work of Kanō Yamamoto (1909–   ) indicates the influence that Barthianism exercised in the Japan Baptist Federation (Baputesuto Dō-mei, related to the American Baptist Convention), and also in academic theological groups in Japan. A Kyōdan pastor, Yamamoto's standpoint can be characterized as "consistent Barthianism," articulated in numerous articles, books, and symposia. His most influential work is probably *Ethical Thought of Dialectical Theology* (1961). Yamamoto's Barthianism also influenced many students in the Tokyo Shingakkō and later in the Kantō Gakuin University Theological Department in Yokohama, which trained prospective ministers for the Japan Baptist Union. As the chairman of the Japan Society for Christian Studies (Nihon Kirisutokyō Gakkai), which has held annual meetings since 1953, he exerted continuing theological leadership.

Echoing Hebrews 11:32, we can say that time would fail us to tell of all the Barthian influences that have been active in Japanese Protestantism, although not all of them have been as consistent and as persistent as those already mentioned. Keiji Ogawa (1927–   ) studied directly under Barth and went on to teach Christian studies at Tokyo Woman's Christian College. Set-surō Ōsaki (1933–   ) did a doctoral dissertation at Göttingen entitled "The Teaching of Predestination in Karl Barth" (1966). Already mentioned for his biblical scholarship, Zenda Watanabe (1885–1978) demonstrated in his later writings the thorough influence of a Barthianism that enabled him to move from his earlier biblicism.[64] Yoshiki Terazono's thesis at Bonn in 1971 was on the Christology of Barth, and Mitsumasa So-Ueda at Göttingen in 1973 wrote on the anthropology of Barth. In the Lutheran churches of Japan, a cordial welcome was extended to Barthian theology by its principal postwar leader, Chitose Kishi (1898–   ), a president of the Japan Lutheran Theological Seminary and a translator of one of Barth's books. Also at the Lutheran Seminary was Masayoshi Yoshinaga (1925–   ), author of *Barthian Theology and Its Characteristics* (1972). At ICU, the chaplain and professor of religious studies, Yasuo Furuya, was for many years a strong advocate of Barthianism.

Dialectical theology clearly represented the dominant theological influence among Japanese Christians in the postwar period, and several important characteristics of this school should be noted at this point. In the first place, the Barthian form of dialectical theology was dominant in Japan in both the prewar and the postwar eras. Charles Germany mentions Kan's observation that even by 1934 Japanese theologians could no longer use the general term *benshōhōteki shingaku* (dialectical theology) or *kiki no shingaku* (crisis theology), but had to stipulate whether they were referring to Barth, Gogarten, Bultmann, or Brunner.[65] As has been mentioned, even Emil Brunner's visit and subsequent two-year residence in Japan were unable to shake the Barthian dominance and, if anything, may have deepened it. There are doubtless many reasons for the triumph of Barth's position in Japan, though it has been largely mystifying to Western thinkers, including Barth himself.[66] There were "nontheological factors" at work, of course, such as the fact that when Japanese Marxists, for instance, were devouring the many volumes of Marx's works with their customary diligence, it was of great importance that Japanese Protestants could point to the many volumes of the *Kirkliche Dogmatik* that revealed the "German agenda" of *their* mentor. Furthermore, it is significant that Barth's writings often appeared in Japanese translation sooner than they did in English or in any other language. These works had an influence not only on Christians but on Japanese Buddhist scholars as well. A fundamental reason for the Barthian hegemony was that, as theology, it did present systematic, detailed, and very convincing answers for problems that Japanese theologians were asking at the time. With the coming of the Pacific War, and in its crushing aftermath, Japanese Christians were asking: What is faith? What meaning does the Bible have for moderns? What does the Christian faith have to say about such vexing problems as personality, time, and history? To these questions and many others, Barth's theology seemed to have clear and detailed answers. Both the form and the content of his vast works seemed to be marvelously appropriate to the spiritual needs of a nation in turmoil.

In the second place, it should be noted that the Barthian theology was presented in a peculiarly Japanese form. This is why the term "dialectical theology" has generally been used in this section, despite the unavoidable ambiguity of that term noticed by Kan as far back as 1934. Barth's resistance to Hitler at the time of the Barmen Declaration was not widely publicized or discussed among scholars in Japan, as noted earlier, for such resistance to the government would have been highly embarrassing on the Japanese scene at that time. This indicates that the Japanese "dialectical theologians" did not copy Barth servilely but adapted what they found in his works—as we have seen in Kumano's case, for instance—to meet the particular needs of the Japanese churches. Even in the postwar period, when there were no governmental pressures on Christian groups, Japanese "dialectical theology" was not exclusively Barthian, but had a number of components of the Japanese Christian tradition clearly embedded in it. Kumano's *Dogmatics* clearly is in the line of his teacher, Uemura, but the concerns of Japanese Protestantism have by Kumano been articulated in a thoroughly Barthian manner. As Michalson so clearly noted in his analysis—to which Kumano gave his hearty approval—Kumano's *Dogmatics* is not a mere repetition of Barthian categories, but a creative reshaping and rearrangement in keeping with the tradition he sought to continue and with the needs he sought to address.[67] To some extent, Japanese Barthianism might be better characterized as "Uemuraism," except that Uemura is not considered an original or a systematic theologian.[68] Yet the concerns for well-ordered church life, for systematic statement of the universal Christian faith, devotion to the ministry and preaching of the church—themes Barth so clearly emphasized—had been promoted beforehand in Japan by Uemura.

Third, whatever its shortcomings, Japanese dialectical theology served the Japanese Protestant community extraordinarily well during the time of its ascendancy. The very weaknesses that many Western observers ascribe to

Barthianism actually served as strong points in Japan. For instance, Barthianism was understood to have little sympathy—whether this accurately represents Barth's own position or not is, for the moment, beside the point—with Christianity's dialogue with other religions or with its concern for "relevance" to current social problems. A Western observer such as Notto R. Thelle has concluded that "the captivating influence of Barthianism in Japan seemed to isolate Christian theology for many years and to prevent it from engaging in a living dialogue with its spiritual environment."[69] But most Japanese Protestants did not see things in such a light. They held that the narrowing of focus that Barthianism encouraged proved to be a source of great vitality and self-identity for them during a time of unprecedented social change. Instead of spreading themselves thin with dozens of different dialogues with religions or with scores of social concerns in a frantic effort to be "relevant" to their changing society, Japanese Barthians were able to concentrate conscientiously on a few important concerns, and to do so tolerably well. Charles Germany reported that Toyohiko Kagawa had complained about the theology of Tokutarō Takakura, who first introduced the study of Barth in Japan: "The cause of social disinterest in Japan is Scottish theology as introduced by Takakura. Takakura was strongly opposed to me."[70] But as things worked out in postwar Japan, the Barthians might plead, if Japanese Protestants had for the most part followed Kagawa's summons to "relevance" for a great number of the changing social needs for their society, they would probably have become too overextended to be at all effective in the contemporary period. As it was, Japanese dialectical theology taught Japan's Protestants to do fewer things and to do them well, rather than undertake a multitude of tasks and squander their energies in frustration and impotence.

Finally, it must be said that the dominance of dialectical theology made it possible to develop variations on a common theme. Even though some of these variations did in time develop into opposing points of view, it can be plausibly argued that they would not have developed the way they did had it not been for the common elements of dialectical theology. As things worked out in Japan's three postwar decades, the dominance of dialectical theology during at least the first half of this period made it possible for a number of thinkers in various fields to undertake their respective variations, and still for the time being exist under the Barthian umbrella without having to venture out into the sun's scorching heat and take on all the perplexing problems of systematic theology for themselves.[71] It is to some of these variations that we turn our attention in the following section.

Dialectical Theology's Uneasy "Fellow Travelers"

To a certain degree, the Japanese Barthian form of dialectical theology performed for Japanese Protestant theology the function that Hegelian philosophy carried out for nineteenth-century Western philosophers. There were, roughly speaking, three possible attitudes toward a massive synthesis such as Barthianism or Hegelianism: *(a)* one could agree with it, and attempt to work out its implications for other fields; *(b)* one could both agree and disagree with it, attempting to affirm parts of the synthesis while denying other parts; *(c)* one could disagree with it, and propose alternatives. What one could not do was to ignore it. In the coverage of systematic theology we dealt with the first of these three attitudes toward dialectical theology, the position of the Barthians who very much agreed with it (pp. 254–57). Later (pp. 264–68) we shall examine the views of the third group, who rejected dialectical theology outright. Now we shall deal with scholars who may be characterized as dialectical theology's uneasy "fellow travelers," thinkers who found that they could accept much of the Barthian synthesis, and indeed went a long way toward articulating what that synthesis might mean in various fields. But at the back of their minds was often a nagging suspicion that something was wrongheaded about the whole enterprise of dialectical theology, at least in its Japanese Barthian form. They were not ready to challenge the entire synthesis of dialectical theology, however—at least not at first. They preferred to take shelter under its umbrella while developing their own alternative emphases. Some of them remained half-way Barthians, while others in time emerged as sworn opponents of the entire Barthian undertaking. Their various views merit careful examination.

Kazō Kitamori. Kazō Kitamori (1916–   ) stands in a class by himself, and for good reasons. He does not fit neatly into schools of theology, or even into denominational traditions. There is a sense in which he operates on a different wavelength from his fellows.

Born in Kumamoto, Kitamori, from straitened personal circumstances, early became familiar with the motif of pain as one of the realities of the human condition. Graduating from Kyoto University, he was deeply influenced by the philosopher Hajime Tanabe (1885–1962), who sought a Buddhist-type synthesis of opposites, a unity out of duality. Baptized in the Lutheran faith of his mother, Kitamori went to seminary and acquired his Doctor of Letters from Kyoto University. He was one of two Lutheran pastors who remained within the Kyōdan after the Pacific War, when other Lutherans withdrew to reestablish the Japan Evangelical Lutheran Church. He became a professor of systematic theology at Tokyo Union Theological Seminary and served concurrently as pastor of the Kyōdan's Chitose Funabashi Church. His most celebrated book, *Theology of the Pain of God* (1946; Eng. trans., 1965), was written during World War II and published at the war's end. It became a best-seller, running through many editions in Japanese, and was translated into English, German, Spanish, and Italian. Kitamori has been characterized as the one Japanese theologian who has "citizenship in world theology," for his work has been critically reviewed by such Western theologians as Carl Michalson and Jürgen Moltmann. Although he has written over twenty books, many of them collections of essays and speeches, most of his writings are expansions of his earlier insights into "the pain of God."

According to Kitamori, "the pain of God" is not only a fundamental category for the understanding of biblical faith—he finds such pain in places like Jeremiah 31:20, obscured by the RSV's rendering, "My heart yearns . . ."—but also provides a key to the understanding of the history of Christian theology. For pain is the category whereby God's wrath toward sinful people is reconciled with his love for them. Thereby Kitamori seeks to overcome the one-sided interpretations both of liberal Protestantism, which focus too much on God's love, and also of Barthian theology, which put too much stress on God as "wholly Other." Thus Kitamori became one of the first Japanese theologians to read Barth in a critical yet constructive fashion. In a sense, he helped to blaze the trail for other "fellow travelers" uneasy with the Barthian form of dialectical theology.

Kitamori's theology played a crucial role in postwar developments of the Kyōdan, that church born of the mixed legacy of two factors. While one of its sources was the ideal of ecumenical Japanese Protestantism (Ishiwara's *kō-kaishugi*), the other was the powerful political pressure of the Religious Organizations Law of 1940, which sought to bring the Christian groups of the country under closer governmental surveillance and control. After the Pacific War the Religious Organizations Law was rescinded, and Protestants were no longer obliged to remain in one church. When Presbyterian–Reformed groups threatened to withdraw in major numbers in the same way that other denominational groups had done, this posed a serious threat to the continued existence of the Kyōdan as a united church. Because the main objection of the Presbyterian–Reformed group was that the Kyōdan was not a creedal church, a group was commissioned by the Kyōdan to draw up a confession of faith, and Kitamori was the main theologian active in the task. The Confession of Faith drawn up by Kitamori and his colleagues was adopted by the Kyōdan in 1954. It is essentially an introduction to some basic Christian beliefs in the form of a preface to the Apostles' Creed. Kitamori subsequently wrote *A Commentary on the Confession of Faith of the Kyōdan* (1955) to explain the new creed. His explanation was very important for the process whereby the churches came to accept the creed, for he did not represent one of the three major groups that remained in the Kyōdan—Methodist, Presbyterian–Reformed, and Congregational—but, rather, a Lutheran position, which was insignificant in numbers but articulate in explanation. Kitamori's concept of "the pain of God" as embracing different types of Christian faith was also a constitutive element in his approach to the nature of the Kyōdan as a united church and to its creed.

There is little wonder that the Kyōdan is said to have carried on in the postwar era under "Kitamori theology." Nor is it any wonder that Kitamori himself became a target of the New Left radicals who, after 1968, sought radical change in the Kyōdan. But that is a story for another place. What is crucial to recognize here is the role that Kitamori played, both in his academic writings and in his practical churchmanship, in trying to move Japanese theology beyond the categories of Japanese Barthianism. His writings were appreciative of Barth and the Barthians, but he sought to transcend their limitations in ways that would be more appropriate to the Japanese scene.[72]

The Dōshisha Theologians. Theologians at the Dōshisha School of Theology in Kyoto were also uneasy with Japanese dialectical theology. They stood in the long tradition of liberal Protestantism and had received many of their guidelines from such thinkers as Setsuji Ōtsuka (1887—   ), who was for many years the chancellor of the university and one of its most influential Christian thinkers.[73] Social activism through involvement in various types of social work and community programs characterized the Dōshisha theologians, who were somewhat less than enthusiastic when the waves of Japanese Barthianism engulfed the nation's Protestant community in the 1930s. To be sure, Dōshisha theologians did not reject Barth and Japanese dialectical theology outright, but tended to place these contributions in dogmatics alongside those of other writers, and in this way foreshadowed the theological pluralism to come.

Since it is difficult to single out from a theological community like that of Dōshisha all of its significant spokesmen, two alone must suffice. Masatoshi Doi (1907–   ) may be said to represent the continuing concern at Dōshisha for creative dialogues with other religions. It is not surprising that he found a basis for such dialogues in the thought of Paul Tillich. Doi's book *Tillich* (1960) is a standard introduction for Japanese readers. Tillich's visit to Japan in 1960 led to his memorable encounters with Japanese Buddhist scholars, Professor Masao Abe in particular, and to his celebrated reflections in *Christianity and the Encounter of the World Religions* (1963). Doi was instrumental in furthering such dialogues with other religious groups in Japan, especially through his post as director of the National Christian Council's Center for the Study of Japanese Religions in Kyoto, and editor of its English-language bulletin, *Japanese Religions.* Doi also served as a Protestant observer at Vatican Council II, involving him in the Protestant–Catholic dialogues that were the fruit of those sessions. Would a thinker with the background and experiences of Doi neglect the writings of Karl Barth? Far from it! "I have the *Kirkliche Dogmatik* on my shelves," he once told a scholarly colloquium, "and I consult it from time to time, but more as one consults an encyclopedia."[74] His comment implies that using Barth as a major guide to religion today is quite another matter.

Doi's colleague at Dōshisha, Masao Takenaka, has already been mentioned in connection with his contributions in the field of Christian ethics. Takenaka also has been active in encouraging Christians to enter into dialogue with disciplines and worldviews other than their own. To this end he has been an active participant in the Urban Industrial Mission programs of the East Asia Christian Conference (which became the Christian Conference of Asia) and a founder of the Kansai Seminar House with its dialogue programs modeled on the work of the German evangelical academy houses. Takenaka has also been active in the study of indigenous Christian art and in Christian dialogues with persons of other faiths and ideologies. In all of these areas, Takenaka has been concerned to push theology out beyond the narrow bounds established for it by the Barthian agenda. As a "fellow traveler" uneasy with dialectical theology, he did not reject it out of hand. He simply has sought to go beyond it.

The Socialist Christians. Reference has already been made to the Socialist Christians who sought to develop new bases for Christian social concern in postwar Japan, particularly through the abortive Socialist Christians' Frontier Union (Zen Nihon Shakaishugi Kirisutosha Zensen Dōmei), which gathered under Gan Sakakibara's leadership from about 1951 to 1955 in the Tokyo area. It is significant that many who started out in this group were Barthians insofar as their theological orientation was concerned, but they sought to supplement this with insights drawn from Marxism and other quarters. It was from this circle, if not from this Frontier Union in particular, that some of the translators of Barth's works issued. Masahisa Suzuki (1912–69) was one of Barth's first translators, but elsewhere in this study we have seen his other contributions as pastor, church leader, and Kyōdan moderator. Yoshio Inoue (1907–), who also translated some of Barth's works, taught German at Tokyo Union Seminary and elsewhere, and has been active in the work of the Christian Peace Fellowship. It is symptomatic that some of the men who were most familiar with Barth's thought through their translations of his writings into Japanese should in their careers endeavor to combine Barthian insights with concerns for social issues, which in time took them far beyond the positions mapped out by the Japanese Barthians. The controversial career of the Reverend Sakae Akaiwa, to which we have referred earlier, was merely an extreme instance of this.

Confessional Theologies. Confessional theologies in Japan also flourished (albeit in some cases uneasily) as "fellow travelers" with Japanese dialectical theology. The sustained study of the theology of Luther in the various Lutheran churches (but not exclusively), of Calvin among the Presbyterian-Reformed groups, and of Wesley in Methodist-background churches made it possible for postwar Japanese Christians to affirm their continuity with confessional Protestant traditions, as we saw in the discussion of church-history studies. Insofar as Barth aligned himself with the Protestant Reformers, there was no direct conflict with the study of such classical theologians. At the same time, the older confessional traditions were a forceful reminder that Christian theology had its agenda long before the dialectical theologians came to dominate the Protestant scene.

Visits of Foreign Theologians. The uneasy tensions about Japanese dialectical theology were further revealed by the visits of foreign theologians from 1960 on. Of the many overseas theological scholars who made short visits to Japan, a number had a particular impact on Japan and its theological community. This list does not include Karl Barth himself, who was invited to Japan several times, in particular after his trip to the United States in 1962.

What influence the personal visit of the man who declared "I am not a Barthian" might have had on Japanese Barthianism is purely conjectural, as he never visited Japan.

Mention has already been made of the visits of Emil Brunner, Eduard Heimann, John Bennett, and Paul Tillich to Japan. Another important visitor was the veteran Dutch missiologist Hendrik Kraemer, who during his extensive 1962 lecture tour in Japan stressed the need for lay theology and for a theological encounter with other religions and ideologies. His visit was said to have led to some changed program emphases along these lines in the Kyōdan. D. T. Niles of the East Asia Christian Conference made an extended visit to Japan in 1966 when he addressed the twenty-fifth anniversary Kyōdan general assembly. Throughout his trip, he urged his Japanese audiences to become more aware of the role of Asian churches and theologies on the world scene. Fritz Buri, professor of theology at Basel University, spent a sabbatical year at ICU (1968–69), during which he pressed further Tillich's concern for a deepened Christian dialogue with Buddhism.[75] Jürgen Moltmann from Tübingen University gave a series of lectures in Japan in 1973 after his *Theology of Hope* (Ger. 1965; Jap. trans., 1967) had been widely received in that country, and shortly after the publication in German of his *Crucified God* (1973). Although he had referred in his writings to Kazō Kitamori's use of "the pain of God" as resembling in some sense his own usage of "the crucified God," Moltmann concluded from a personal discussion with Kitamori during this visit that the two men had different things in mind even though they used similar words. Moltmann is reported to have said afterward that he positively misunderstood Kitamori's *Theology of the Pain of God.*[76] In the summer of 1978 Harvey Cox of Harvard Divinity School was in Japan for a conference of religious leaders on peace issues. His book *Turning East: The Promise and Peril of the New Orientalism* (1977) dealt with the impact of Eastern religions on the American scene.

On the whole, foreign theologians who visited Japan had the opportunity to deepen and reinforce whatever influence their writings may have had. To some extent they were able to broaden the horizons of those influenced by dialectical theology, in such directions as Christian social ethics and dialogue with other religions. Of far greater importance for the Japanese scene was the work of Japanese translators and introducers of foreign theological works, for their efforts made it possible for the wider Christian community in Japan to appropriate what was being said by theologians abroad.

The Bultmannian Theologians. We come at last to the development of Bultmannian theology in Japan, for its followers began as "uneasy fellow travelers" with Japanese dialectical theology and then moved in other directions. Hideyasu Nakagawa (1908–   ), who worked in New Testament studies and published *A Study of the Letter to the Hebrews* (1958), followed the lead of Rudolf Bultmann further in his *Faith and History* (1967), where he sought to develop a hermeneutical approach to theology.[77] (Nakagawa became president of ICU.) Yoshio Yoshimura (1910–   ), a translator of Barth's *Romans,* held that Bultmann's approach to theology was the necessary complement to the Barthian program and developed this theme in *Contemporary Theology and Christian Mission in Japan* (1964). A younger theologian who had studied existentialist theology under Carl Michalson at Drew and who made most of the arrangements for Michalson's stay in Japan, out of which his excellent study of Japanese theology came, is Yoshio Noro (1925–   ), a professor of systematic theology at Aoyama Gakuin University and then at Rikkyō University. Noro was also the author of *Existentialist Theology* (1964) and *Existentialist Theology and Ethics* (1970). Reflecting on these works later, Noro commented that the program of existentialist theology, whether developed along the lines of Bultmann or of others, is very difficult for Japanese Christians to accept, despite its somewhat superficial resemblances to Zen Buddhist ontology.[78] Noro put his hopes, instead, on "awakened theologians," former Barthians or at least Barthian "fellow travelers" who were concerned about the need for Christian dialogue both with the Japanese tradition and with current social issues.

Yoshinobu Kumazawa (1929–   ), professor of systematic theology at Tokyo Union Theological Seminary, is another former Barthian who was deeply influenced by Bultmann. His published books that bear the fruit of this impact are *Bultmann* (1962, 1965 [2nd ed.]), *Modern Discourse on Christianity* (1964), and *Theology and Church for Tomorrow* (1974).[79] Kumazawa also became embroiled in the Kyōdan's controversy over the Christian Pavilion at Expo '70, for he and Kitamori were the two TUTS faculty members on the theme committee for that pavilion. During the course of that controversy, Kumazawa became famous as the "even though theologian," for he argued that the Christian churches ought to support a Christian pavilion in a secular fair, "even though" there were problems connected with it.[80] Also, Kumazawa's involvement in ecumenical affairs of the WCC and the EACC (later the CCA), his work with religious television programs on the national NHK network, and his involvement with the church's outreach to Asian countries through the TUTS Asian Institute for Ecumenical Mission embody the very kind of dialogue between Christian theology and culture that his Bultmannian background had encouraged.

The influence of Bultmann's theology was also seen in the Yagi–Takizawa debates, described previously, which had their impact on biblical studies and philosophical theology as well as on systematics.

The work of the Japanese followers of Bultmann, then, constituted the first major departure from the predominance of Barthian dialectical theology in postwar Japan. Far from being a direct rebellion against the Barthian position, this development was a gradual broadening of, and then estrangement from, that position. In time, some of the Bultmannian "fellow travelers" became avowed opponents of Japanese Barthianism. While this was taking place, completely separate theological traditions were gaining strength to offer challenges to dialectical theology on its own ground.

Other Voices, Other Rooms

It is important to distinguish between the "fellow travelers" with Japanese Barthianism described above and the "other voices" to be discussed here. Japanese Barthianism's "fellow travelers" were able to find a considerable measure of agreement with the fundamental tenets of dialectical theology, even though they went on to develop other emphases of their own. But other theological standpoints were developed on their own bases, and sought on principle to stand apart from the leading currents of Japanese dialectical theology. Broadly speaking, these standpoints were three: Neo-Thomism, conservative evangelical theologies, and Mukyōkai theologies.

Neo-Thomism. In connection with church-history studies, it was pointed out that Neo-Thomists consciously endeavored to make the philosophical and theological position of Thomas Aquinas—as developed by Jacques Maritain, Étienne Gilson, and others—a major intellectual option for the modern world. This was not an easy task in Japan, for the great majority of Catholics were of a conservative outlook, and no matter how much they venerated Aquinas, they saw dialogues with modern intellectual currents as threatening to faith. It must not be forgotten that Catholicism was reintroduced to Japan under the pontificate of Pope Pius IX, the author of the *Syllabus of Errors* and the convenor of Vatican Council I. Furthermore, Catholic mission work in the nineteenth century was initiated in Japan by the Paris Foreign Mission Society (M.E.P.), which sometimes looked upon the French Revolution and all its works as anathema. The encouragement given by Pius IX to Thomistic studies, and which Leo XIII furthered through his encyclical *Aeterni patris* (1879), was intended to defend the Catholic faith, and not to further its dialogue with the world. Sophia University was founded by the Jesuits in 1908 as the first Catholic university in Japan almost fifty years after Protestants had started their universities, by which time Japan had already become a major world power.[81] Thomism was for Japanese Catholics like Sōichi Iwashita and Yoshihiko Yoshimitsu a ready-made suit of armor to be quickly and unquestioningly donned in the interests of sheer survival. In time, European missionaries in Japan were able to supply some of the necessary updating of Thomism, and in this the long and productive careers of Fathers Joseph Roggendorf (1908–   ) and Heinrich Dumoulin (1905–   ) at Sophia University were notable.

Most of the Neo-Thomist scholarship in Japan, however, was of a very conservative nature. A representative work is *Philosophy of Law: Natural Law* (1966) by Kotarō Tanaka (1890–1974), a Roman Catholic lay scholar, who played a highly important role as chief justice of the nation's Supreme Court, and later was a justice in the International Court of Justice at The Hague. Tanaka found the categories of natural law readily available as guides to the positive law of the nations. This viewpoint was widely influential, but was also criticized as being too conservative and too accommodating to the status quo of Japanese society.

Another tendency among Neo-Thomists was represented by Masao Matsumoto (1910–), already mentioned for contributions to the study of Western medieval thought.[82] Matsumoto's efforts to broaden the outlook of Neo-Thomism are outlined in a collection of essays produced from 1942 to 1967, *An Era of Theology and Philosophy* (1968). In the volume he explains how, before Vatican Council II, Catholics saw the main threats to the faith as modernism and anticlericalism, that is, rebellions from within the Catholic fold that made it difficult for the church to present a united front to the problems of the modern world. But from the time of Pope John XXIII and Vatican Council II, the Catholic church was turned outward toward the world, and the enterprise of theology itself came to be seen more in terms of the church's mission to the world.[83] Matsumoto held that his version of Neo-Thomist dialogue with the world was vindicated by Vatican II, but such efforts in pre-Vatican II days as his travels to the Soviet Union and to the People's Republic of China in order to participate in living dialogues with Communists were viewed at the time with the deepest suspicion by high-ranking Japanese ecclesiastics. On the other hand, Matsumoto's participation in ecumenical dialogues with Protestants—he was himself a convert from Anglicanism—met with more appreciation in his own church and was encouraged by Hans Küng's comparison of the doctrine of justification by faith as taught by the Council of Trent and in the writings of Karl Barth. Matsumoto's work for ecumenicity was also given approbation by Vatican II.

Despite its growing strength, Neo-Thomism did not become a fully indigenous Japanese systematic theology. Throughout the postwar era, Neo-Thomism remained a largely exotic and foreign importation, much more so than the Japanese Protestants' dialectical theology, which was grafted onto the Uemura–Takakura tradition. By the time theological pluralism arrived in Japan, Neo-Thomism had to compete with all the other brands of theologies, both Catholic and Protestant, for a hearing. This is not to say that its role in Japan, especially among Japanese Catholics, has been without significance. It does suggest that its major time has not yet arrived.

Conservative Evangelical Theologians. Conservative evangelicals made yet another effort to stand on foundations quite different from Japanese dialectical theology, to which they were in most ways closer than to the Neo-Thomists. For many conservative Protestants, Barthianism represented a fatal compromise with liberal Protestantism, which was neither true to the spirit of the gospel nor conducive to the establishment of a biblical church in Japan. Although many conservative groups were willing to rely for the most part on translated theological materials from the West, there were two major representative evangelical thinkers who strove to provide indigenous Japanese materials for evangelical theology, one based on a Wesleyan and Arminian foundation, the other on a Calvinist tradition.

The Reverend Tsugio Tsutada (1906–71) was a leader in the Wesleyan Holiness groups in Japan, a founder of the Immanuel Church and editor of its newsletter, and also a leader in the Japan Protestant Convention (JPC) and the Japan Evangelical Association (JEA), which sought to unite the efforts of Japanese and overseas conservative evangelical groups. Tsutada wrote *Life Sanctified* (1954), an extended commentary on Wesley's doctrine of perfection, but also intended as a doctrinal and systematic basis for the Holiness movement in Japan. He oversaw the translation of R. S. Nicholson's *Notes on True Holiness* (1959) and prepared an outline of John Wesley's sermons in *The Epworth Flow* (1958).[84] His *Life of the Covenant* (1962) is a summary of his doctrinal position.[85]

Minoru Okada (1903–), principal of the Kōbe Reformed Seminary and the leading theologian of the Japanese Christian Reformed Church, attempted to establish similar theological bases for evangelicals on Calvinistic grounds. His *Christianity* (1953) and *The Christian* (1953) were written as companion volumes to introduce a mature Christian inquirer to the theological basis of the faith. Okada translated into Japanese some of the Western creeds and catechetical materials, such as the *Westminster Larger Catechism* (1950), but his major work was *Introduction to the Study of the Reformed Creeds* (1962), in which he dealt with doctrinal materials in the Calvin-Warfield-Machen line of development.[86] In all of this, he forthrightly proposed what he called "evangelical theism" as an alternative to the Uemura-Takakura-Kumano-Kuwada line of dialectical theology.

It is doubtful, however, whether the writings of either Tsutada or Okada provided conservative evangelicals with comprehensive theological alternatives to the mainstream of dialectical theology, or whether they had much influence on the Japanese Christian community beyond the conservative groups themselves. Conservative evangelicals performed significant work in the postwar years in reaching groups and individuals that other Christians were unable to contact. Although conservatives lagged in the writing of systematic theology, perhaps foundations were laid for productive work in the future.

Mukyōkai Theologians. Mukyōkai writers also took their stand on theological bases other than dialectical theology. Kanzō Uchimura, the founder of Non-Church Christianity, had been opposed in principle to the traditional ecclesiology of Western churches, and he endeavored to establish his own fellowships on an entirely different doctrine of the church, one that lacked organization, fixed membership, clergy, creeds, and sacraments. It is therefore not surprising that Uchimura's disciples were not at all in agreement with the doctrine of the church found in the dialectical theologians. Hence, for the most part, they developed their own approach to systematics, however much they kept in touch with the main currents of Western theology. Because the main focus of Non-Church groups has always been Bible study, it is hard to classify many of their writings as systematic theology. Yet even in the writers encountered in the chapter on biblical studies, such as Masao Sekine (1912–) and Gorō Mayeda (1914–80), there are doctrinal statements that cross the threshold of systematic formulation.

It is in the work of Kōkichi Kurosaki (1886–1970) that one encounters the beginnings of a systematic articulation of Mukyōkai theology. After working with Kanzō Uchimura, he went to Europe (1922-25) where he studied under Harnack, Holl, Deissmann, Heim, and others, doing research in theology and Bible. Along with his younger contemporary, Mayeda, he helped to make Mukyōkai known overseas. In time he developed connections with Mennonite scholars that reflected common concerns for simplicity of church structures and for a Christian pacifist witness.[87]

Pacifism was also a major theme in the career of Tadao Yanaihara (1893-1961), another of Uchimura's followers, who became a professor of economics at Tokyo Imperial University, and whose criticisms of the Sino-Japanese War in 1937 led to his dismissal from that post. When he returned to the University of Tokyo after the war to become its chancellor, he sought to express his convictions in clearly written and widely circulated volumes. Apart from his writings on biblical themes, his *Introduction to Christianity* (1952) outlines his view of Mukyōkai, in the words of Tomonobu Yanagita, "as the climax of the history of Christianity, and as the most radical and yet logical result of the Protestant doctrine of justification by faith." His *Marxism and Christianity* (1947) was a blistering critique of Marxism, which also included the charge that existing Christianity had become panic-stricken in the face of Marxist attacks. *Japan's Future* (1953), a series of lectures given in a prophetic mood, warned of the collapse of Japan unless the country heeded divine warnings.[88]

Yanaihara's colleague and close friend at the University of Tokyo and also a postwar chancellor of that institution was Shigeru Nambara (1889-1974), who like Yanaihara endured much anguish during World War II because of his pacifist convictions. A professor of political science whose academic magnum opus was a study of Fichte's political philosophy, Nambara wrote *The State and Religion* (1952), a work sometimes described as the most thorough written by a Japanese author on the Christian understanding of the state. Running the whole gamut of philosophical and theological views of the state, Nambara criticized Aquinas's approach to the state and came down himself closer to the Protestant Reformers.[89] He pursued the significance of politics further in *Culture and the State* (1957) and in its sequel, *Contemporary Politics and Thought* (1957). His *Collected Works* (10 vols., 1973) provide insights into pacifism, Christian theology, democracy, and social responsibility for a new postwar generation in Japan for whom these ideas had gained a measure of respectability and popularity.

There were, then, at least three groups of "other voices" whose theological writings shared little or no common ground with the Japanese dialectical theologians and their "uneasy fellow travelers": the Catholic Neo-Thomists, the conservative evangelical Protestants, and the Mukyōkai writers. Each of these groups primarily sought to meet the needs of its own circle, but in so doing, each also addressed a much wider audience. Of these three, the Neo-Thomists and the conservative Protestants enjoyed only modest influence, while that of the Mukyōkai scholars'was, by comparison, substantial. The work of all three groups contributed to some extent to the theological pluralism that gradually pervaded the Japanese scene from the 1960s on. The significance of that pluralism is even better understood if we look at some of the factors that contributed to the further decline of the predominance of dialectical theology.

The Emergence of Theological Pluralism

Dialectical theology in Japan hardly lost its predominance in one day, to be superseded on the next by theological pluralism. The shift was a gradual one; as early as 1945 there were signs of restlessness with the prevailing Barthian mood. It was not until the 1960s, however, that theological pluralism arrived unmistakably on the Japanese scene. Several major sources contributed to the changed situation.

Although it is hard to date the developments precisely, by the 1960s the plurality of theologies in Europe and America had become a recognized fact in Japan. The followers of Bultmann were of many different minds by this time, in the West as well as in Japan. The post-Bultmannians in Japan took up the concerns of their Western counterparts for a "new hermeneutic," whereby theology was seen no longer as a discrete discipline but, rather, a method practiced by reflecting on conduct in conjunction with the social sciences and other subjects. The writings of Dietrich Bonhoeffer were by now very popular in Japan, and his comments on "religionless Christianity" struck many familiar notes among Japanese readers. There were also scholars who followed the writings of Gogarten, Ebeling, Fuchs, and Pannenberg, and Roman Catholic theologians such as Küng and Rahner. Biblical scholars such as von Rad, Bornkamm, Jeremias, and Kasemann all had insights to contribute, while the writings of Robinson and Fletcher also aroused interest in Japan.

Perhaps it was the publication of Harvey Cox's *Secular City* (1965) that marked a watershed between a positive appraisal of American theological currents and increasing skepticism about what was to follow. Cox's views on urbanization struck responsive notes in rapidly urbanizing Japan, even though his views on secularization seemed more important to Buddhists in Japan than Christians.[90] Thereafter, some of the problems and views that seemed unique to America—"death of God" theology, black theology, liberation theology, political theology—were all read in Japan but with questions about their relevance to the Japanese scene.

Once Vatican Council II helped to make Catholics and Protestants somewhat more open to each other, Japanese Protestants began to read Küng, Schillebeeckx, and, above all, Rahner, with new appreciation. At the same time, Catholics in Japan began examining the bewildering variety of Protestant theological thought. Neo-Thomism was no longer the "perennial philosophy" or theology for Catholics, but simply one option among many.[91] While it is still too early to judge the long-run results of the new ecumenical era in theology, it seems clear that there have been changes that make the return to the status quo ante highly unlikely, even though some Protestants and Catholics alike might fervently desire it.

Disillusionment with America in the 1960s also had a major influence on theology. The series of assassinations of public figures, the urban crises and racial tensions between blacks and whites, and the growing anger over America's role in Vietnam—all provoked a reevaluation of the extent to which American "norms" in any field might be valid for other nations. Because German society was also to some extent plagued with similar problems of university struggles, urban violence, and guerrilla terrorism, German scholars could no longer speak with unflinching self-confidence. America's problems came to a head with the Watergate experience, which demonstrated that when constitutional processes are honored, even a president can be forced to resign. As these events unfolded, Japanese theologians who had depended on Western mentors were hard pressed indeed. Many concluded that the task of constructing theology in Japanese terms was more urgent than before. Japanese society shared many of the same problems as Western societies—crowded cities, pollution, government scandals, inflation, student unrest—but there was the necessity to face these problems in suitably Japanese ways. The very pluralism of Western theologies showed that theological diversity in Japan was not only possible but also conceivably commendable.

The problems of Western society had their Japanese counterparts in the university and church struggles that swept over Japan from the late 1960s. These struggles came from the raising of fundamental questions about the directions of Japanese and Western societies from the end of World War II. A New Left emerged in Japan, as in Western countries, to condemn the postwar decades as an era of neo-colonialist and neo-imperialist exploitation. They held that, in this dismal period, the universities and seminaries and churches had served as obedient followers of Japan's "military-industrial-governmental complex," in close alliance with American capitalism and militarism. The struggles that came to a focus over the United States–Japan Mutual Security Treaty and the Christian Pavilion at Expo '70 actually revealed a deeper conflict that ran throughout Japanese society. It affected theological formulation by calling into question theological systems that could be interpreted as mere justifications of the capitalist status quo in Japan and elsewhere.

All these factors, whether joyfully or painfully, at least unavoidably helped to bring about the emergence of genuine theological pluralism. Such a pluralism had been hinted at from the beginning of the postwar era, but it came into unmistakable existence after the ferment of the late 1960s had done its work. For some, this was a liberating time, in which the limitations imposed by Japanese dialectical theology could at last be set aside. There were now numerous alternative theological viewpoints, if not systems, and it was no longer possible to regulate the claims among them, as had theoretically been the case in the heyday of dialectical theology. For other Christians in Japan, however, the new age of pluralism in theology was a dismal time indeed. Confusion and disorder now reigned in place of the "theological consensus" of yesteryear. Christians were often forced to deal with a diversity that was to them very uncomfortable. As one theologian put it succinctly: "We live in a time of confusion, without mentors."[92]

Whether the new situation of theological pluralism will prove to be a boon or a bane seems still uncertain to most Japanese Christians. But for those like Seiichi Yagi, who in 1964 had sounded the earnest appeal, "Deliver Japanese theology from Germanic captivity!" the deliverance that actually took place within the following decade proved to be far different from what anyone had anticipated.

NOTES

1. Seiichi Yagi, "The Dependence of Japanese Theology upon the Occident," *JCQ* 30, no. 4 (Fall 1964): 259. Also quoted in Joseph C. Spae, *Christianity Encounters Japan* (Tokyo: Oriens, 1968), p. 201. It has been said that the young theologian who first pleaded for the deliverance of Japanese theology from Germanic capitivity was Professor Hideo Ōki of Tokyo Union Seminary. Be that as it may, this chapter will refer to Yagi as the source of the quotation.

2. Charles H. Germany, *Protestant Theologies in Modern Japan* (Tokyo: IISR Press, 1965), chaps. 1, 2, 4. Germany's book has helped the writer of this chapter a great deal.

3. Ibid., p. 121.

4. The present writer wishes to express his indebtedness to the late Dr. Ken Ishiwara, not only for his very helpful interviews of Nov. 18, 1974, and Jan. 20, 1975, but also for his encouragement and advice about the present project. Thanks are also due to Mr. Teruo Kuribayashi, a TUTS student, who assisted the writer greatly in the present project in 1974-75, especially in connection with the study of, and interviews with, Messrs. Ishiwara, Sumiya, Sakakibara, Kumano, Iisaka, and Matsumoto.

5. It is impossible to deal with all the writings of Ishiwara and other scholars mentioned in this chapter; we can only mention some of their most representative and influential works.

6. When these figures were pointed out to him by the present writer, Dr. Ishiwara with characteristic modesty and humor replied, "I'm sorry about that!"

7. Yoshikazu Tokuzen, "Luther Studies in Japan," *NEAJT*, no. 1 (March 1968): 110-17.

8. Interview with Prof. Yoshikazu Tokuzen, Tokyo, Sept. 25, 1974.

9. Akira Demura, "Calvin Studies in Japan," *NEAJT*, no. 1 (March 1968): 118-25.

10. John W. Krummel, "Wesley Studies in Japan," *NEAJT*, no. 2 (March 1969): 135-40.

11. Gan Sakakibara, "My Pilgrimage to Anabaptism," *Mennonite Life* (March 1973), pp. 12-15; also, interview with Dr. Gan Sakakibara, Tokyo, Jan. 20, 1975.

12. Ryosuke Inagaki, "Scholastic Studies in Japan: A survey," *NEAJT*, no. 4 (March 1970), 55-65. Cf. Gino K. Piovesana, S.J., *Recent Japanese Philosophical Thought, 1862-1962* (Tokyo: Enderle, 1963), pp. 222-23.

13. Inagaki, "Scholastic Studies," p. 57; also, interview with Prof. Masao Matsumoto, Tokyo, Feb. 17, 1975.

14. See also the Bibliographical Notes in the present book.

15. Hiromichi Kozaki, *Reminiscences of Seventy Years* (Tokyo: Christian Literature Society, 1932), pp. 359-60. Cf. Germany, *Protestant Theologies*, p. 14.

16. Charles Iglehart, *A Century of Protestant Christianity in Japan* (Tokyo: Tuttle, 1959), p. 105.

17. Ibid., p. 206. Germany, *Protestant Theologies*, p. 80.

18. Mikio Sumiya, "On the Transmission of the Gospel to the Japanese," *Gendai Nihon to Kirisutokyō* [Modern Japan and Christianity] (Tokyo: Shinkyō Shuppansha, 1962).

19. Sumiya, "Evangelism in Modern Japan," *Gendai Nihon*.

20. Sumiya, "The Challenge of Industrial Society to Christianity," *Gendai Nihon*.

21. Sumiya, "The Church's Responsibility in Modern Japan," *Gendai Nihon*. Cf. also chap. 4, above, "Christians and Social Work in Japan."

22. Sumiya, "Modern Japan and the Christian Churches," *Gendai Nihon*.

23. Interview with Dr. Gan Sakakibara, Tokyo, Jan. 20, 1975.

24. *Kirisuto to Shakai* [Christ and Society] 4, nos. 8, 9 (Sept. 1, 1954): 3-4. The Frontier Union is mentioned in Germany, *Protestant Theologies*, p. 197, but with an incorrect title.

25. Germany, *Protestant Theologies*, pp. 189ff.

26. Interviews with Drs. Ken Ishiwara and Mikio Sumiya.

27. *JCQ* 20, no. 1 (Winter 1954): 15.

28. I. John Hesselink, "Emil Brunner in Japan," *JCQ* 33, no. 2 (Spring 1967): 112-14.

29. Hideo Ōki, *Barunnā* [Brunner] (Tokyo: Shinkyō Shuppansha, 1962).

30. Richard H. Drummond, *A History of Christianity in Japan* (Grand Rapids, Mich.: Wm. B. Eerdmans, 1971), p. 287; Interview with Dr. Sam H. Franklin, Tokyo, March 19, 1973; Yasushi Kuyama, ed., *Gendai Nihon to Kirisutokyō* [Christianity in Contemporary Japan] (Tokyo: Sōbunsha, 1961), pp. 191-95.

31. Interview with Prof. Gorō Maeda (which he preferred to spell "Mayeda"), Tokyo, March 5, 1973.

32. Germany, *Protestant Theologies*, pp. 192-95.

33. Ibid., p. 196.

34. Ibid. Dr. Hidenobu Kuwada confirmed this in an interview, Tokyo, April 3, 1972.

35. Germany, *Protestant Theologies*, p. 198.

36. Interview with Prof. Mikio Sumiya, Tokyo, June 18, 1974.

37. Interview with Prof. Yoshinobu Kumazawa, Tokyo, April 6, 1972.

38. The experience of the Ikuno Catholic Church in Osaka seems typical at this point. Interview with Fr. Raimund Zinnecker, Osaka, July 19, 1974.

39. Joseph L. Van Hecken, *The Catholic Church in Japan since 1859* (Tokyo: Enderle, 1963), p. 184.

40. Ibid., p. 267.

41. Interview with Fr. Raymond Renson, Tokyo, Jan. 18, 1975.

42. George R. Packard, *Protest in Tokyo: The Security Treaty Crisis of 1960* (Princeton, N.J.: Princeton University Press, 1966).

43. See chap. 2 above, "Christians and Politics in Japan." Cf. James M. Phillips, "The 1960 Security Treaty Crisis and the Christians of Japan," in *Studies on Japanese Culture,* vol. 2 (Tokyo: The Japan P.E.N. Club, 1973).

44. For this section, the writer is indebted to Yoshinobu Kumazawa, "Japan: Where Theology Seeks to Integrate Text and Context," in Gerald H. Anderson, ed., *Asian Voices in Christian Theology* (Maryknoll, N.Y.: Orbis Books, 1976), pp. 179–208. Cf. Kanō Yamamoto, "Theology in Japan: Main Trends of Our Time," *JCQ* 32, no. 1 (Winter 1966): 37–47.

45. Prof. Seiichi Hatano's library was presented to Tokyo Union Theological Seminary, and the present writer for many years made use of copies of leading Western books in theology and philosophy from this collection. Cf. Piovesana, *Philosophical Thought*, pp. 123–31. Cf. also Carl Michalson, *Japanese Contributions to Christian Theology* (Philadelphia: Westminster Press, 1960), chap. 4, "The Theology of the Time of Love," on Hatano.

46. On the Yagi-Takizawa debate, see Kumazawa, in Anderson, *Asian Voices*, pp. 195–96; Kenzō Tagawa, "The Yagi-Takizawa Debate," *NEAJT*, no. 2 (March 1969), pp. 41–59; John Barksdale, "Yagi and Takizawa: Bultmann vs. Barth in Japan," *JMB* 24, nos. 1, 2, 3, 4 (January/February, March, April, May 1970).

47. See Katsumi Takizawa, "Zen Buddhism and Christianity in Contemporary Japan," *NEAJT*, no. 4 (March 1970), pp. 106–21.

48. Cf. Piovesana, *Philosophical Thought*, pp. 152–54. The writer is indebted to David Swain for calling attention to this material.

49. Kumazawa, in Anderson, *Asian Voices,* p. 189. The writer is indebted to Gerald Anderson for pointing out the importance of this observation.

50. Yoshitaka Kumano, *Kirisutokyō no Honshitsu* [Essentials of Christianity] (Tokyo: Shinkyō Shuppansha, 1947), preface, pp. 70, 189, 219.

51. Cf. Michalson, *Japanese Contributions*, chap. 2, "The Theology of Church Existence," on Kumano.

52. Yoshitaka Kumano, "A Review and Prospect of Theology in Japan," *NEAJT*, no. 4 (March 1970), p. 66.

53. Yoshitaka Kumano, *Kyōgigaku* [Dogmatics], 3 vols. (Tokyo: Shinkyō Shuppansha, 1954–65), vol. 2 (1959), pp. 3, 87, 325.

54. Ibid., vol. 3 (1965), p. 36.

55. Ibid., p. 289.

56. Ibid., p. 510.

57. Article on "Yoshitaka Kumano" in "One Hundred Figures from Japanese Christianity's Thirty Postwar Years," *Kirisutokyō Nenkan, 1976* [Christian Yearbook, 1976] (Tokyo: Kirisuto Shimbunsha, 1975), p. 74.

58. Interview with Dr. Hidenobu Kuwada, Tokyo, April 3, 1972.

59. See pp. 23, 121, 242, above, and Germany, *Protestant Theologies*, pp. 197–98.

60. Jong Sung Rhee and James M. Phillips, "The Historical Background of the Northeast Asia Association of Theological Schools," *NEAJT*, no. 1 (March 1968): 132–42.

61. Germany, *Protestant Theologies*, p. 62. Article on "Enkichi Kan," in "One Hundred Figures," pp. 71–72.

62. Germany, *Protestant Theologies*, p. 129.

63. The conclusion about Kan's influence is based on interviews with Profs. Yoshitaka Kumano, Yoshio Noro, and Yoshinobu Kumazawa. Cf. also Masayoshi Yoshinaga, "Barthian Theology and Prof. Enkichi Kan," *Shinkyō* [Protestantism] (periodical of Shinkyō Shuppansha, Tokyo), no. 9 (1973), pp. 7–11.

64. Kumazawa, in Anderson, *Asian Voices*, pp. 192–93. Cf. Yasuo Furuya, "The Influence of Barth on Present-Day Theological Thought in Japan," *JCQ* 30, no. 4 (Fall 1964): 262–67.

65. Germany, *Protestant Theologies*, p. 138.

66. In a discussion at the Barth residence in Basel, April 1964, Karl Barth said to the present writer, with a good-natured laugh, "So you're from Japan! Tell me, why do they take my theology so seriously in Japan?"

67. Michalson, *Japanese Contributions*, pp. 62–72.

68. Cf. Yoshitaka Kumano, "Review and Prospect," p. 66.

69. Notto R. Thelle, "A Barthian Thinker between Buddhism and Christianity," *Japanese Religions,* 8, no. 4 (October 1975), 54. The writer is indebted to Gerald Anderson for calling attention to this quotation.

70. Germany, *Protestant Theologies*, p. 112.

71. The "umbrella" metaphor is from Nels Ferré, *The Sun and the Umbrella* (New York: Harper, 1953). A visit of Dr. Ferré to Tokyo Union Seminary ca. 1962 was very stimulating for the TUTS faculty, including the present writer.

72. The section on Prof. Kazō Kitamori was based on an interview, Tokyo, March 2, 1973, and on many other occasions at TUTS. There has also been influence from works already mentioned by Germany and Kumazawa. Cf. Michalson, *Japanese Contributions*, chap. 3, "The Theology of the Pain of God," on Kitamori, and the English translation of Kazō (Kazoh) Kitamori, *Theology of the Pain of God* (Richmond, Va.: John Knox Press, 1965).

73. Germany, *Protestant Theologies*, chap. 2.

74. Yoshio Noro, "Transcendence and Immanence in Contemporary Theology," *NEAJT,* no. 3 (September 1969), pp. 54ff.

75. See Fritz Buri, "My Encounter with Buddhist Thought in Contemporary Japan," *NEAJT,* no. 3 (September 1969): 38ff.; "The Fate of the Concept of God in the Philosophy of Keiji Nishitani," *NEAJT,* no. 8 (March 1972): 49–56.

76. Interview with Prof. Jürgen Moltmann, Tokyo, March 1973: *JCAN,* March 16, 1973, p. 1.

77. Kumazawa, in Anderson, *Asian Voices*, p. 195.

78. Interview with Prof. Yoshio Noro, Tokyo, June 6, 1972.

79. Kumazawa, in Anderson, *Asian Voices*, p. 195.

80. Interview with Prof. Yoshinobu Kumazawa, Tokyo, April 6, 1972, and through the writer's attendance at the Kyōdan's Extraordinary General Assembly at the Yamate Church in Tokyo, Nov. 25–26, 1969.

81. Joseph L. Van Hecken, *The Catholic Church in Japan since 1859* (Tokyo: Enderle, 1963), pp. 161ff.

82. This section is based on an interview with Prof. Masao Matsumoto, Tokyo, Feb. 17, 1975.

83. Masao Matsumoto, *Shingaku to Tetsugaku no Jidai* [An Era of Theology and Philosophy] (Tokyo: Chūō Shuppansha, 1968), p. 3.

84. Tomonobu Yanagita, *Japan Christian Literature Review,* 2 vols. (Sendai: Seisho Tosho Kankōkai, 1958, 1960), pp. B51, B53.

85. Article on "Tsugio Tsutada," in "One Hundred Figures," p. 86.

86. Article on "Minoru Okada" in "One Hundred Figures," p. 69; Yanagita, *Japan Christian Literature*, p. C8.

87. Article on "Kōkichi Kurosaki," in "One Hundred Figures," p. 75.

88. Yanagita, *Japan Christian Literature*, pp. B11, D31, D32, D25.

89. Ibid., p. D25.

90. Interview with Dr. Yasuo Carl Furuya, Tokyo, July 13, 1972.

91. Interview with Fr. Peter Nemeshegyi, Tokyo, Sept. 2, 1974.

92. Interview with Prof. Yoshio Noro, Tokyo, Aug. 18, 1974.

10

Epilogue:
The View toward the Future

As this study draws to a close and we cast a glance toward the future, the writer is drawn into some reflections on the writing of this work, which has been a full decade in the making. When work on this study began, in the midst of the university crises that gripped Japan in the late 1960s and foreshadowed the end of the period of almost uninterrupted economic growth since 1952, the course the nation has taken in the past decade could not have been predicted. To be sure, Japanese society has surmounted the university struggles without too great difficulties, but as the continuing conflicts within many segments of Japanese society have indicated—and especially within the Kyōdan as the nation's largest Protestant church—the reappraisals and challenges that arose in the 1960s are still far from being completely resolved. The oil shock of 1973–74 has triggered economic dislocations that extend the need for reevaluation. If anything, the reappraisals became more significant in the late 1970s than they were in the late 1960s, for they no longer involve only a relatively small group of leftist students and intellectuals, but now include broad segments of the whole of Japanese society. The use of violence and struggle tactics are no longer condoned, but fundamental questions about social structures are being asked by more people than before. Although some observers of the Japanese scene might debate the precise dating of the turning points, few doubt that the nation has now entered into a prolonged period of challenge and reappraisal.

It is not without significance that the Christian churches have been wounded by the onset of this period of reappraisal more seriously than almost any other segment of Japanese society. For even though some schools and universities, labor unions, corporations, and opposition political parties were also initially torn by currents similar to those affecting the churches, these other groups have been able to pull themselves out of the doldrums, so

274

to speak, while there are those in the churches who still find any resolution of their problems a thing of the distant future.

This may be a good time, then, to reflect on the entire course that the Christian community in Japan has walked since 1945. The nine chapters have examined different aspects of the work of the Christian community in contemporary Japan, and it is natural that there should have been different points of departure for each of these topics. The time has come to examine some of the common themes underlying the entire study.

Some Common Themes in Japanese
Christianity's Contemporary History

Chapter 1 on the historical context set the basic framework for subsequent developments. It is significant that this framework was given almost entirely by external developments, and not by the internal dynamics of the Christian community itself. This is not unusual for churches anywhere, of course, especially for a minority religious group like the Christians in a large and dynamic culture like that of Japan. Furthermore, Japan's Christians have from the beginning found their energies directed primarily to reacting to external events in their society, and only occasionally and in limited ways being able to help shape the agenda for that society. Contemporary Japan has seen this pattern reiterated in new ways. The period 1945–52 found the Japanese nation as a whole and the Christian community in particular responding to the pressures of the Occupation. For some Christians this meant the restoration of patterns that had been interrupted by an imperialist-militarist interlude. For others it meant brand-new starts, both for individuals and for Christian groups as a whole.

It is striking that many of the leaders of the Japanese Christian community in the 1970s were converted to Christianity in the immediate postwar period, when they personally cast in their lot with a different group of people and a way of life that "seemed to have the future in their bones." The era 1952–68 was a time for the expansion or specialization or professionalization of some of the directions that had been established during the Occupation. The capital accumulated at the earlier period was here invested in a number of ways, figuratively speaking, and the buoyancy that an expanding economy provided made it possible for growth to take place for Christian projects that sustained their momentum, even though in modest ways. Churches managed to grow during most of this period in unpretentious fashion, while Christian schools and social work agencies experienced remarkable expansion, although often at the cost of crowding and somewhat more impersonal operations. It was only with the period of challenge and reappraisal from about 1968 that aspects of the entire postwar legacy of Japanese Christianity—and of society as a whole—were seriously opened to scrutiny. Even so, the scrutiny was apt to be one of economic feasibility rather than theological or spiritual strength, for the era of economic growth had accustomed people to measure things by economic yardsticks. When the fragile nature of the Japanese economy was exposed in numerous ways, Japanese Christians as well as many of their fellow citizens were no longer sure that they were measuring things properly. This has contributed to the sense of optimism mixed with malaise that characterizes the Japanese Christian community at the present time.

In chapter 2 the varying attitudes and roles of Japanese Christians in the political life of their country were examined, and it was shown how Christians tended to serve like gatekeepers on a slalom ski course, to mark the extremes both to the left and the right beyond which it was dangerous for Japan's fast-moving society to swerve. The issues of religious liberty and the significance of the new postwar constitution were at the head of the agenda, but Japan's Christians were also examining the dimensions of their nation's "welfare society," questioning the government's handling of national security arrangements with the United States, and seeking to establish new contacts with Japan's neighbors in Asia who watched the renewal of Japan's strength from the postwar ashes, phoenix-like, with a mixture of admiration and fear. Christian universities and churches were among the first to become embroiled in the conflicts of the late 1960s, and at the present writing, although most Christian organizations have emerged from such troubles, the Kyōdan is still deeply polarized by them. Japan's Christians have indeed been wounded in the political arena, and that makes them confront the future with sobering realism.

Christians and education were surveyed in chapter 3, where we noted the striking increases in the statistics of the Christian schools in the postwar period as they responded to an education boom of unprecedented proportions. The statistics may seem impressive, but case studies sometimes indicated that the expansion took place at a considerable cost. During the period of economic growth, it was possible to disguise many of the underlying problems by expanding facilities and taking in more students. But when the goals of education were questioned either by the conservatives' use of *The Image of the Ideal Person*, or by the radicals' struggle tactics, the Christian schools had little to offer different from that of their secular counterparts. In fact, because the Christian schools and universities had presumed to offer idealistic alternatives to the government or secular private universities, the Christian schools sometimes found themselves the primary targets of idealistically inclined leftist students and faculty. The agonizing episodes of campus struggles in 1968–70 brought few underlying changes to Japan's schools and universities, and because of the difficulties experienced by Christian and other private schools in balancing budgets and in dealing with campus disorders, the initiative in educational planning passed almost by default back to the government.

Christians in social work had a somewhat different record, as chapter 4 indicated. They were in the unique position in the postwar period of helping to establish guidelines for the nation's new social-welfare legislation, and also for helping to carry out these measures in fields where they had pioneering experience. Since the Christian social work leaders decided early in the postwar period that they would work in partnership with the government, they were more accustomed than their counterparts in the Christian schools to dealing with the government both with cooperation and with caution. Although they were increasingly hampered by the rising costs that were particularly hard on their operations, many Christians in social work have been able to continue in the pioneering and soul-searching tasks for which they have been justly renowned in the past.

In chapter 5 it was seen how Christian outreach programs took different forms in the postwar decades, whether in the Sinai-type of church extension which was a carryover from the prewar period, in Zion-type social action programs in response to what people held God had already done in the nation, or in Jubilee-type liberation efforts, which emphasized discontinuity rather than continuity with historical patterns. The perceptive novelist Shūsaku Endō compared Japan with a swamp that is able to swallow up forces for change. Contemporary Japan has seen continuing examples of the swamp's absorbing church-extension efforts and deflecting social action programs into other channels. It is too soon to take an accurate measure of either of the first two types of outreach, or of the Jubilee-type that operates in tensions with them.

The roles of foreign missionaries in contemporary Japan were examined in chapter 6. There was no single pattern by which foreign missionaries of different groups related to the Japanese Christian communities with which they worked, but Protestant, Catholic, and Orthodox groups gradually developed various working patterns to safeguard the selfhood of both the Japanese Christians and the foreign missionaries. That such arrangements could be worked out amicably for the most part, in the face of very real tensions that in other countries sometimes sent foreign missionaries packing, was evidence of the maturity of both legal and theological aspects of the "missionary riddle," which must be faced squarely if future relationships are to be as productive as those of recent decades.

Chapter 7 examined ecumenicity's unsteady course in the postwar decades, as the figure of *yajirobē* swung round and round on his pedestal in going through the familiar ecumenical motions, but making little discernible progress. To use Max Weber's categories, where ecumenism was promoted by charismatic leaders it seemed to get somewhere, but it fell flat whenever attempts were made to institutionalize the spirit. The example of the well-intentioned Christian Pavilion at Expo '70 was in many ways symptomatic of what could happen in this era of new possibilities, but also of what could go wrong.

Chapter 8 showed how biblical studies came out of the ivory tower of purely academic research to become the focus of controversy in both schools and churches. While many Japanese Christians, both laity and clergy, were surprised to find their sacred texts involved in such acrimonious controversy, this was the price of taking the Scriptures seriously in Japanese society. The outcome of the controversies—which is far from clear at the present writing—will doubtless be influenced by the serious attention that ordinary Christians give the Scriptures, as well as by the searching questions that scholars bring to their studies of them.

Theology in Japan, in chapter 9, is a sequel to the chapter on biblical studies, and ranges across the entire theological scholarship agenda. Here it was seen how Japanese theology was greatly influenced by foreign models in the immediate postwar period, when Japanese Protestants in their "Germanic captivity" looked to Barthianism and Catholics to Thomism to provide a normative systematic framework for their theological tasks. But the jarring conflicts engendered by the era of reappraisals after 1968 indicated that the time was over when one theological system could be considered the dominant and normative theological pattern for a Christian community in Japan. Instead, there was a growing recognition of theological pluralism, in which voices of all sorts would be carefully studied and heeded, but with the assumption that the whole truth lay beyond the grasp of any particular system.

Some Signs of Anguish

When we turn from our survey of the recent past to consider the future, this is done with considerable trepidation, for predictions are always suspect. Rather than attempt any such guesses, we shall begin by examining some signs of anguish about the future for the Christian community of Japan.

The first factor that strikes one is the growing domestic and international insecurity of the Japanese people, as the nation is plagued by a marked inflation that threatens to undo many of the social gains made by the nation during the period of rapid economic growth. To be sure, economic policies in Japan have resulted in lower rates of unemployment and seemingly less social dislocation than has been true in other countries. But inflation threatens to reintroduce some of the wide chasms between the rich and the poor that plagued prewar Japanese society. For better or for worse, the Christian churches of Japan have been predominantly middle-class enclaves, and the further enervation of the middle classes by rampant inflation would inevitably have adverse repercussions on the Christian community. Furthermore, the very fragility of the Japanese "economic miracle," which has been especially evident since the oil shock of 1973–74, has caused concern about the precarious nature of the freedoms enjoyed by the Japanese in the postwar decade.[1] If the economy should take a serious downswing in the days to come, would this mean a curtailment of the freedoms that postwar Japanese have tasted? In particular, would this lead to limitations on the religious liberty that has enabled the Japanese Christian communities in the nation to stand on their own feet for the first time?

A second and related source of concern is the continuation and gradual strengthening of the forces of militarism and reaction in Japanese society. Whether these forces are symbolized by the annual efforts in the Diet to nationalize Yasukuni Shrine, by the increasing role that the Self-Defense Forces play in national decision-making, or by the gradual encroachments on academic inquiry and human freedom in many related fields, some thoughtful Japanese Christians are frankly concerned about what seems to be an increasing slide of their nation toward authoritarianism. The patterns of the 1930s may not be repeated in carbon-copy fashion, but they might recur in new and unanticipated ways. While some Japanese and foreign observers point out the dangers of encroachments from the left, a more commonly heard view among Japanese Christians is that the growing strength of the Communists and other leftists of many different sorts would in any emergency situation be quickly neutralized by a revival of the right. The role of the emperor is seen as crucial in these developments, for even as the emperor was utilized to sanction the moves toward fascism in the 1930s, an analogous development could take place again sometime in the future. And while such events would not signal the disappearance of the Christian community in Japan, they could mean that Christians would again have to live under various forms of social repression, as was the case so often before 1945.

A third sign on the horizon, which brings no little cause for concern, is the growing ethnocentrism or "national selfishness," which thoughtful people have discerned in recent years. To be sure, one can discern elements of ethnocentrism in almost every nation. But Japanese Christians have noted indications of how the traditional appeal to their nation's uniqueness is often being twisted into a justification of the practice of riding roughshod over other nations, especially those neighboring countries in East Asia which are now beset with many problems. Even in the era of economic expansion, "Japan, Inc." was a catchword to symbolize a disposition for Japanese businessmen and government officials to look out after their own nation's interests first, and to have little concern for others. Also, Japanese Christians have agonized over the fact that their nation was able to prosper from both the Korean and the Indochina wars, benefiting from the catastrophes of their neighbors and neglecting the victims of these tragedies. If such a mood of national self-centeredness should continue unchallenged, it would serve to undo much of the idealism and hope engendered by Japan's postwar constitution, by which the nation pledged itself to domestic welfare and international peace. The fact that the postwar constitution has often been characterized by its critics as an American imposition on Japan, which should be revised or scrapped, serves for some Japanese Christians as a sign of how dangerous the mood of national self-centeredness has become.

When Japanese Christians try to list their problems, the tabulation can be almost endless, and such might be the case here as well. But the last source of anguish about the future that we shall mention is the mood of many of the Japanese churches themselves. Japanese Catholics have experienced a number of setbacks since Vatican Council II, which in the eyes of some Catholics have jeopardized the gains from that era of renewal. The decline in priestly vocations is only a symptom of a malaise of disrespect for authority that has infected the church in recent years. And for Japanese Protestants, the continuing divisions within the Kyōdan are a source of vexation for other Protestant groups, and for Catholics and Orthodox as well. It has been a full decade since the onset of the Kyōdan's divisions, and the end is nowhere in sight.[2] Conservative Protestant churches have registered some gains within this recent period, but they are not immune to similar difficulties in due course. In view of the rapid changes that have been taking place in Japanese society during this period, and that lie in the future, it is indeed a calamity that both Catholic and Protestant groups should be found so enervated at such a crucial time.

During the course of conducting interviews for this study, the writer very often encountered Japanese Christians' pessimism about the future, for some of the reasons just mentioned. But there is another and more positive side of the picture to which our attention must be turned as well.

Some Signs of Hope

Discerning the signs of hope, like enumerating the signs of anguish, must necessarily be a highly subjective matter. For this participant observer, however, the list must begin with reference to the great potential for the future of Christianity in Japan that lies with students. This may come as a surprise to those who have grown accustomed to seeing students as the posers of problems for which the answers may be both elusive or unclear. But for anyone such as this writer, who has had the privilege of working with Japanese students, the potential for great good is all the more clear. To be sure, the full potential of students is not being tapped by most of the institutional structures of the Japanese Christian community at present—the Christian schools and universities, the organized religious groups for students, the local churches' student study groups, the Christian-sponsored dormitories and student centers. But with some prayerful creativity, great things with students can happen, as has so often been the case in the past.

A second sign of hope lies with those involved in Urban Industrial Mission in Japan. The very commitment of these men and women has put them in touch with some of the most troublesome and nauseating aspects of postwar capitalism, as well as with the Marxist critics of many sorts who proclaim and promote capitalism's imminent demise. While they have paid close attention to the critiques of modern Japanese industrial society that Marxists and others have offered, many Christians involved in Urban Industrial Mission in Japan have never lost sight of the human dimensions of their situation and have maintained at great personal and professional cost the international contacts with Christians in other countries who are engaged in similar tasks. Surely something of the future lies with these people.

A third area in which Christians have made and will doubtless continue to make hopeful contributions is in the area of personal counseling. New Religions like Risshō Kōseikai seemed to have a head start with their *hōza* sessions for group counseling, based on traditional Japanese methods of problem-solving.[3] But Christian groups have demonstrated, for instance, through the Inochi no Denwa telephone counseling services and in counseling centers in many places, that they have some significant contemporary contributions to make in this field.

Lay movements are another source of hope, although their appearance in many Christian groups has often been stifled by continuing patterns of clerical dominations. It is remarkable that the Japanese Christian community, whether in its Catholic or Protestant form, has remained one of the most highly pastored and clergy-dominated groups in the world. Lay persons, both men and women, have had difficult times breaking out of the control of their pastors in order to carry out their unique ministries in society, but they have been able to do so in some encouraging instances, and many more will doubtless appear in the future.

Particular emphasis must be placed at this point on the Christian women of Japan, for even as they have been the bulwark of the Christian community in the past, they will continue to demonstrate rich resources for leadership, devotion, and courage in many areas. The women's organizations of the days to come will hardly be carbon copies of past women's groups, but will be able to show new ways for bringing their unique contributions to the problems of their own time.

Christian social work also holds out signs for hope, even though the social workers themselves realize the increasingly trying plight they are facing, with rising costs, problems of unionization, governmental regulations, and undermined morale. Perhaps these very crushing predicaments have enabled a remarkable group of Japanese Christian social workers to continue to make some of the pioneering contributions of which they are capable. This may be yet another example of how humans' extremity is God's opportunity.

Another hopeful area is in the work of Christian groups devoted to peace action and human rights. Our study has indicated how efforts for "peace" or "justice" have sometimes been derailed into various political or ideological sidetracks, and yet there have been Christians who have persisted in their convictions, despite the odds and adverse criticisms. That is not to say that every person who adds slogans about peace and justice to a banner is in reality promoting such goals. But the earnest efforts of those who are sincerely dedicated to such ends with Christian inspiration will not be without significance.

An eighth sign of hope lies with the work of Christian artists and writers. In a society that has always honored the artist even when ordinary people were bent on pursuing mammon and ugliness, the self-conscious groups of Christian painters, novelists, playwrights, dancers, poets, and essayists have found opportunities for expression and communication of the Christian gospel that go far beyond those open to clergy. We noted that although there were a number of writers influenced by Christianity in the Meiji era, most of them became disillusioned and gave up the faith. This has not been the case with the remarkable group of Japanese Christian artists since 1945, however, who have continued to express their faith in diverse—and controversial—ways. Surely here is a solid sign of hope.

Christian teachers hold out a firm ray of encouragement, even if the institutions where they work are sometimes in disarray. From the yōchien teachers who deeply care for their preschool youngsters, through the high school teachers who carry out their duties faithfully, to the university professors who maintain their commitments both to faith and to truth, the Christian community will doubtless continue to marshal one of its principal strengths. In the past the Christian schools have often been the fostering parents of the churches, and in the days ahead, the task may fall more directly on the committed teachers themselves, as they sow the seeds for the churches' modest but vital harvests.

A tenth source of hope lies with Japan's scholars in Bible and theology. While there has always been the temptation for scholars anywhere to keep their studies in an academic ivory tower, developments in Japan's postwar history have from time to time forced theological scholars and their research out into the world, with fearsome but also positive results. With the high respect that the Japanese have always shown for serious study, it is a sign of encouragement that the Christian community has produced such a brilliant group of scholars, who are in good positions to make their continuing contributions to the strengthening of tomorrow's Christian community in Japan.

Every list must come to an end, even though it can never claim to be exhaustive. For our eleventh and final source of hope, we look to the small but significant body of men and women who seek to deepen the spiritual life of Christians. Their efforts take many forms, covering the entire range of liturgies, sacraments, music, prayers, retreats, meditations, and the like. In the last analysis, the lives of individuals and of nations are moved decisively by such people, and the Japanese Christian community is fortunate to be blessed by numbers of them.

With such a list of signs of anguish and of hope, our view toward the future draws to a close. We bring to mind again the words of the psalmist (Ps. 113:3), which give the title to this book:

> From the rising of the sun to its setting
> the name of the Lord is to be praised!

The record of the Christian community in contemporary Japan shows that the Lord's name has been faithfully praised in the land of the rising sun, and we confidently trust that this will continue to be the case, until suns shall rise and set no more.

NOTES

1. See Frank Gibney, *Japan: The Fragile Superpower* (Tokyo: Tuttle, 1975). The fragility of Japan's situation was forcefully anticipated by Zbigniew Brzezinski's *The Fragile Blossom: Crisis and Change in Japan* (New York: Harper & Row, 1972). Brzezinski's book was largely a reply to Herman Kahn's euphoria in *The Emerging Japanese Superstate: Challenge and Response* (Englewood Cliffs, N.J.: Prentice-Hall, 1970).

2. See *JCQ* 45, no. 3 (Summer 1979), which has the theme "A Decade of Dispute in the United Church of Christ in Japan."

3. See Kenneth J. Dale, *Circle of Harmony: A Case Study in Popular Japanese Buddhism, with Implications for Christian Mission* (Tokyo: Seibunsha, 1975).

Bibliographical Notes:
On the History of Christianity
in Contemporary Japan

Several difficulties immediately confront anyone wanting to do detailed study of the history of Christianity in Japan since 1945. Initially one encounters all the problems that face the student of contemporary history in any land: the period is still too close to gain adequate perspectives for an analytical presentation, there are many records and reminiscences not yet available, and what is familiar and recent is seemingly not so interesting as what is remote or exotic. But there are particular problems that one encounters for the topic under consideration. Christianity in Japan since World War II seems to suffer by comparison with the heroic days of Catholic missions during the "Christian century" following the arrival of Saint Francis Xavier to Japan in 1549, or with the pioneering days of the Meiji era when Christians challenged their nation with projects and visions that caught the imagination of people then and now. A third disability that might be mentioned is that even though Japanese Christians—who are best qualified to tell the story—have written extensively about Christian faith and activity in almost every other era and every place under the sun, their accounts and interpretations of Christianity in their own land in modern times have been done almost as afterthoughts, when they have written them at all.

But when such problems have been fully recognized, the fact is that the study of Christianity in contemporary Japan is of more than ordinary interest. Indeed, one could maintain that the experiences of this era are in some sense a microcosm of those of Christianity around the world during these years. Rarely have so many diverse experiences and challenges been crowded into so short a time. And although the statistical record of Christianity's growth in Japan during this era is far from impressive—as those who measure "progress" in statistical terms have often pointed out—there is material here to stir the faith and reflection of Christians in any land.

General Surveys of Christianity in Contemporary Japan

We begin with general introductions to Christianity in Japan that have sections dealing with the period since 1945. We shall not attempt here to place such studies in the wider framework of Japanese national history during this time, or to refer to the many studies in Japanese sociology, economics, politics, law, and so forth that have appeared. But a careful student ought not to neglect such resources, which are amply catalogued elsewhere. In regard to the following church-history surveys, one notices that most of them deal primarily with earlier eras and that the events of 1945 are merely tacked on at the end, so to speak. It is understandable that they should be written in this way, but that should not make us overlook the fact that the earlier eras had terms of social reference quite different from those since 1945 and must therefore be read with certain correctives. (In the following listings, the practice of giving names differs from that of the book itself. Here the surnames of the writers, both Japanese and Westerners, are given first.)

Hiyane Antei, *Nihon Kirisutokyō Shi* [A History of Christianity in Japan], (Tokyo: Kyōbunkwan, 1949), is typical of the older approach to historical writing, with the listing of many names and dates but with little interpretive framework. Yanagita Tomonobu, *A Short History of Christianity in Japan* (Sendai: Seisho Tosho Kankōkai, 1957), has almost the opposite disability, in being overly dogmatic in its very conservative approach; yet it contains much valuable material. Katazokawa Chiyomatsu, *Nihon Purotesutanto Hyakunen no Ayumi* [The Course of Japanese Protestantism over One Hundred Years], (Tokyo: Nihon YMCA Dōmei, 1957), was one of the volumes prepared for the 100th anniversary of Protestant work in Japan, which most groups observed in 1959. Such volumes contain helpful insights, but often suffer from a "triumphalist" approach. Iglehart, Charles, *A Century of Protestant Christianity in Japan* (Tokyo: Tuttle, 1959), presents a still solid and comprehensive picture of Japanese Protestantism, although the lack of footnotes and bibliography makes it difficult in many cases to trace further the sources of his judgments. Kami Yoshiyasu, ed., *Purotesutanto Hyakunen Shi Kenkyū* [Studies of a Century of Protestant History], (Tokyo: Kyōdan Shuppanbu, 1961), is not a narrative history but a series of essays on a wide range of topics, written mainly from a Presbyterian–Reformed perspective. Van Hecken, Joseph L., *The Catholic Church in Japan since 1859* (Tokyo: Enderle, 1963), is valuable as a reference book for checking details about the Catholic dioceses of Japan and specific projects, but its arrangement and style make it a cumbersome book to read. Ishiwara Ken, *Nihon Kirisutokyō Shi Ron* [Essays on the History of Christianity in Japan], (Tokyo: Shinkyō Shuppansha, 1967), contains frank insights on many topics, by the outstanding church historian of Japan. Ebisawa Arimichi and Ōuchi Saburō, *Nihon Kirisutokyō Shi* [A History of Christianity in Japan], (Tokyo: Kyōdan Shuppanbu, 1970), contains a section on Catholicism by Ebisawa and one on Protestantism by Ōuchi, the latter dealing mostly with the United Church of Christ in Japan (or the Nihon Kirisuto Kyōdan, usually referred to simply as "the Kyōdan"). A short pamphlet, giving a brief introduction to present-day Christian groups in Japan, designed to be sold at the Christian Pavilion at Expo'70 in Osaka, is Spae, Joseph J., *Christians of Japan* (Tokyo: Oriens, 1970). Drummond, Richard H., *A History of Christianity in Japan* (Grand Rapids, Mich.: Eerdmans, 1971), is the best general survey of the entire field now available, and the first such survey one should read to gain an overall understanding of the topic. It makes use of materials no longer generally available. A more recent, briefer study is Dohi Akio, "Christianity in Japan," in Thomas, T. K., ed., *Christianity in Asia: North-East Asia* (Singapore: Christian Conference of Asia, 1979).

Histories of Particular Denominations in Japan

There are a number of denominational histories available. The Lutheran story is surveyed in Huddle, B. Paul, *History of the Lutheran Church in Japan* (New York: Board of Foreign Missions of the United Lutheran Church in America, 1958), while the Southern Baptists are covered in Garrott, W. Maxfield, *Japan Advances* (Nashville, Tenn.: Convention Press, 1958) and in the convention's own official seventy-year history, *Nihon Baputesuto Renmei Shi (1889—1959)* [A History of the Baptist Convention in Japan, 1889-1959], (Tokyo: Yorudan Sha, 1959). The Kyōdan's official history, written mostly by Yamaya Shōgo, is *Nihon Kirisuto Kyōdan Shi* [A History of the United Church of Christ in Japan], (Tokyo: Kyōdan Shuppanbu, 1967). Four recent studies of the development of Protestant churches are Katō Tsuneaki, *Fukuinshugi Kyōkai Keisei no Kadai* [The Task of Formation of the Evangelical Church] (Tokyo: Shinkyō Shuppansha, 1973); Amemiya Eiichi, *Nihon no Kokuhaku Kyōkai no Keisei* [The Formation of the Confessional Church in Japan] (Tokyo: Shinkyō Shuppansha, 1975); Dohi Akio, *Nihon Purotesutanto Kyōkai no Seiritsu to Tenkai* [The Organization and Development of the Protestant Church in Japan] (Tokyo: Nihon Kirisuto Kyōdan Shuppankyoku, 1975); and Furuya Yasuo, *Kirisutokyō no Gendaiteki Tenkai* [The Contemporary Development of Christianity] (Tokyo: Shinkyō Shuppansha, 1969). A very useful study of the early days of the Kyōdan is Carrick, Malcolm, "The Kyōdan and the IBC: A Study in Ecumenical Cooperation in Japan" (unpublished Th. M. thesis, San Francisco Theological Seminary, 1956). The Kyōdan has also published, in English, *Policy Statements and Statistics of the United Church of Christ in Japan* (Tokyo: United Church of Christ in Japan, 1968).

Among Catholic studies, one written just at the outset of the Occupation holds fascination for its view of that period: Taguchi, Paul Yoshigorō, *The Catholic Church in Japan* (Kyoto: Mainichi Shimbun, 1946). Another short general survey, with some descriptive sociological material, is Spae, Joseph

J., *Catholicism in Japan* (Tokyo: ISR Press, 1964). Personal reminiscences of a Japanese Catholic priest are contained in Shimura Tatsuya, *Kyōkai Hiwa* [The Hidden Story of the Church] (Tokyo: Chūō Shuppansha, 1971). A very readable study of the Southern Presbyterian work in Japan, set within the broader context of Japanese Christianity as a whole, is Cogswell, James A., *Until the Day Dawn* (Nashville, Tenn.: Board of World Missions, Presbyterian Church U.S., 1957). Non-Church Christianity is surveyed through the life of its founder in Jennings, Raymond P., *Jesus, Japan and Kanzō Uchimura* (Tokyo: Kyōbunkwan, 1958). The Nihon Seikōkai (the Anglican Church in Japan) has, as its centennial history, Miyakoda Tsunetarō, *Nihon Seikōkai Hyakunen Shi* [A History of a Century of the Anglican Church in Japan] (privately mimeographed, 1948).

Studies of Particular Periods and Problems

From a chronological standpoint, one might begin with Baker, Richard Terrill, *Darkness of the Sun* (Nashville, Tenn.: Abingdon, 1947), which gives a journalistic account of Christianity in Japan during the war years and immediately thereafter. The first postwar contacts of outsiders with Japanese Christians came from a deputation of four American church leaders, who told their story in *The Return to Japan,* Report of the Christian Deputation to Japan (New York: Friendship Press, 1946). The early Occupation days are well surveyed in a book that vividly presents the outlook of that period: Kerr, William, *Japan Begins Again* (New York: Friendship Press, 1949). A very thorough account of the religious policies of the Occupation, written by one who had a major hand in shaping them, is Woodard, William P., *The Allied Occupation of Japan 1945-1952 and Japanese Religions* (Leiden: E.J. Brill, 1972). Axling, William, *Japan at the Midcentury, Leaves from Life* (Tokyo: Protestant Publishing Company, 1955), contains the impressions of a leading Baptist missionary of the prewar and immediate postwar periods. The changing situation faced by the churches after the growth of Japan's postwar economy is the main theme of Germany, Charles, ed., *The Response of the Church in Changing Japan* (New York: Friendship Press, 1967).

There are many useful collections of essays dealing with the influence of Christianity on Japanese culture. Some are Sekine Bunnosuke, *Nihon Seishin Shi to Kirisutokyō* [The Spiritual History of Japan and Christianity] (Osaka: Sōbunsha, 1962); Corwin, Charles, *Biblical Encounter with Japanese Culture* (Tokyo: Christian Literature Crusade, 1967); Morino Zenemon et al., *Nihon no Kirisutokyō no Konnichiteki Jissen* [The Contemporary Practice of Christianity in Japan] (Tokyo: Nihon Kirisuto Kyōdan Shuppankyoku, 1972); and Reid, David, et al., *Kiku to Katana to Jūjika to* [Chrysanthemum, Sword, and Cross] (Tokyo: Nihon Kirisuto Kyōdan Shuppankyoku, 1976). Painful reflections on Japanese Christian attitudes toward war are contained in Morioka Iwao and Kasahara Yoshimitsu, *Kirisutokyō no Sensō Sekinin: Nihon no Senzen, Senchū, Sengō* [Christian Responsi-

288 BIBLIOGRAPHICAL NOTES

bility for War: Japan Before, During, and After World War II], (Tokyo: Kyōbunkwan, 1974). Critical essays on futurology as applied to the Christian community are in Shiozuki Kentarō, Shikama Yo, et al., *Mirai Shakai to Ningen* [Humans and Future Society] (Tokyo: Nihon Kirisuto Kyōdan Shuppanbu, 1975).

Collections of essays and materials about particular aspects of postwar Christianity in Japan have also been made. A book containing the tape-recorded discussions of a group of scholars reflecting on the postwar era, together with supplementary materials, is one volume in a series of discussions about Japanese Christian history: Kuyama, Yasushi, ed., *Gendai Nihon no Kirisutokyō* [Christianity in Contemporary Japan] (Tokyo: Sōbunsha, 1961). A later collection of essays on various topics related to Christianity is Miyakoda Tsunetarō, *Nihon Kirisutokyō Gōdōshikō* [Materials for a Study of Christianity in Japan] (Tokyo: Kyōbunkwan, 1967). Articles on various aspects of Japanese Christianity from the magazine *Japan Harvest* have been brought together in convenient form in Reynolds, Arthur, ed., *Japan in Review: Japan Harvest Anthology, 1955—1970,* vol. 1 (Tokyo: Japan Evangelical Missionary Association, 1970).

Church growth has been examined from various perspectives. A book in the series put out by Dr. Donald McGavran's Institute of Church Growth at Fuller Seminary, Pasadena, Calif., is Braun, Neil, *Laity Mobilized: Reflections on Church Growth in Japan and Other Lands* (Grand Rapids, Mich.: Eerdmans, 1971). While generally sound, some of Braun's materials, especially on the Spirit of Jesus Church, are to be read with the utmost skepticism. A more recent study is Yamamori Tetsunao, *Church Growth in Japan* (Pasadena: William Carey Library, 1974). The WCC's Commission on World Mission and Evangelism put out a series entitled "Churches in the Missionary Situation: Studies in Growth and Response," in which the book for Japan is Lee, Robert, *Stranger in the Land: A Study of the Church in Japan* (New York: Friendship Press, 1967). Another helpful survey is the Roman Catholic "Pro Mundi Vita" study: *Japan* (Study no. 34 in their series) (Brussels: Pro Mundi Vita, 1970). This pamphlet gives one of the most helpful and dependable surveys of the problems of church growth in Japan.

The entire field of Christianity and social problems has been examined in a number of books, of which we can give only a sampling. A survey of the field from a historical perspective from the Meiji era on is Sumiya Etsuji, ed., *Nihon ni Okeru Kirisutokyō to Shakai Mondai* [Christianity in Japan and Social Problems] (Kyoto: Misuzu Shōbō, 1963). One of the leading scholars in this field, whose books will probably be starting points for most future studies in their areas, is Sumiya Mikio, who has written *Nihon Shakai to Kirisutokyō* [Japanese Society and Christianity] (Tokyo: Tokyo Daigaku Shuppankai, 1954); *Kindai Nippon no Keisei to Kirisutokyō* [Christianity and the Formation of Modern Japan] (Tokyo: Shinkyō Shuppansha, 1950); *Gendai Nihon to Kirisutokyō* [Contemporary Japan and Christianity] (Tokyo: Shinkyō Shuppansha, 1962); *Nihon Shihonshugi to Kirisutokyō* [Christianity and Japanese Capitalism], (Tokyo: Tokyo Daigaku Shuppankai, 1962). A general introduction to Christian approaches to social issues is the very helpful book by Takenaka Masao, *Reconciliation and Renewal in Japan* (New York: Friendship Press, 1957, 1967 [2nd ed.]). And one should not overlook the article by Takenaka Masao, "Between the Old and New Worlds," and another by Chō, Kiyoko Takeda, "The Ideological Spectrum in Asia," in one of the preparatory volumes for the WCC Geneva Church and Society Conference, 1966, in de Vries, Egbert, ed., *Man in Community* (New York: Association Press, 1966). A historical approach to confessionalism and social issues is Hori Mitsuo, *Nihon no Kyōkai to Shinkō Kokuhaku* [The Japanese Churches and Confessions of Faith] (Tokyo: Shinkyō Shuppansha, 1970). A symposium on the Christian-Marxist dialogue in Japan is Nihon Kirisuto Kyōdan Senkyō Kenkyūjō [the Kyōdan's Research Institute on the Mission of the Church], *Deai: Nihon ni Okeru Kirisutokyō to Marukushugi* [Encounter: Christianity and Marxism in Japan] (Tokyo: Kyōdan Shuppankyoku, 1972).

Particular social problems in Japan are discussed within the framework of a Christian social ethics in Franklin, Sam H., *Christian Social Action* (Tokyo: Tokyo Union Theological Seminary, 1964; also in a Japanese edition). The "church-state conflict" in Japan, seen from a very conservative viewpoint, is Young, John M. L., *The Two Empires in Japan* (Tokyo: Bible Times Press, 1959). The Institute for the Study of Christianity and Culture at International Christian University has published collections of essays on social themes, a few of which deal with the contemporary period: Kokusai Kirisutokyō Daigaku Kirisutokyō to Bunka Kenkyūjō, *Kirisutokyō to Bunka* [Christianity and Culture] (Tokyo: ICU, 1966). And of considerable value for studies in this area in the Meiji era, but also with some materials on the postwar period, are the publications of the Study Committee of Christianity and Social Problems at Dōshisha University: *Kirisutokyō Shakai Mondai Kenkyū* [Studies of Christian Social Problems] (Kyoto: Dōshisha, published occasionally since 1959).

Christian education is a field deserving of its own separate bibliography. In passing, mention may be made of a reference book published by Kirisutokyō Hoiku Renmei [Christian Federation of Childhood Education], *Nihon Kirisutokyō Hoiku Hachijunen Shi* [A History of Eighty Years of Christian Childhood Education in Japan] (Tokyo: Kirisutokyō Hoiku Renmei, 1966). Two Christian schools of Methodist background, Aoyama Gakuin and Kwansei Gakuin, collaborated in publishing *Kirisutokyō Kyōiku no Risō to Genjitsu* [The Ideal and the Reality of Christian Education] (Tokyo: Sōbunsha, 1968). A history of student work in Japan, before the disruptions of 1968, is Nakabara Kenji, *Kirisutosha Gakusei Undō Shi* [A History of Christian Student Movements] (Tokyo: Nihon YMCA Dōmei Shuppanbu, 1962). A very interesting and readable survey of Roman Catholic catechetical materials, from Xavier's day to modern times, is Mueller, George A., *The Catechetical Problem in Japan (1549—1965)* (Tokyo: Oriens, 1967). Most Christian schools have at one time or another published anniversary histories, too numerous to mention here, which are sometimes of more than local interest.

There are a few studies of Christian work in rural areas, such as the pamphlet by Hitotsuyanagi, Merrell Voires, *The Evangelization of Rural Japan* (Omi-Hachiman: Omi Brotherhood, 1957); and Kroehler, Armin H., *The Renewal of the Church in Aizu* (privately printed, 1970).

Some personal accounts by missionaries are valuable: Maxey, Mark G., *Way Down Here* (Kagoshima: Kyūshū Christian Mission, 1972); and Neve, Lloyd R., *Japan: God's Door to the Far East* (Minneapolis: Augsburg, 1973).

Christianity and the Religions of Japan

The amount of material available on Japanese religions in general, and on Buddhism in particular, is truly astounding and should be consulted as background preparation for the study of Christianity in Japan. A general survey made for the Occupation authorities, now very much dated, is Bunce, William K., *Religions in Japan* (Tokyo: Tuttle, 1955). An older book brought up to date by a modern scholar is Anesaki Masaharu (revised by Kishimoto Hideo), *Religious Life of the Japanese People* (Tokyo: Society for Intercultural Relations, 1961). A recent reference work is Kasahara Kazuo, ed., *Nihon Shūkyōshi* [History of Japanese Religions], 2 vols. (Tokyo: Yamakawa, 1977). A Christian scholar's approach to the history of religion in Japan, done in the older style of historical writing, is Hiyane Antei, *Nippon Shūkyōshi* [History of Japanese Religions], (Tokyo: Kyōdan Shuppanbu, 1962). A readable account of "the Christian presence" in the midst of Japanese religion is Hammer, Raymond, *Japan's Religious Ferment* (London: SCM, 1961). A more lengthy historical survey is: Kitagawa, Joseph M., *Religion in Japanese History* (New York: Columbia University Press, 1966). A sociological approach to religion in modern times is Norbeck, Edward, *Religion and Society in Modern Japan: Continuity and Change* (Houston, Tex.: Tournaline Press, 1970). A recent survey, with helpful background essays on the major religious groups, is Hori Ichirō, et al., *Japanese Religion* (Tokyo: Kōdansha, 1972). The results of surveys of religious attitudes are reported in Basabe, Fernando M., *Religious Attitudes of Japanese Men* (Tokyo: Sophia-Tuttle, 1968); and *Japanese Youth Confronts Religion* (Tokyo: Sophia-Tuttle, 1968).

Special mention needs to be made of the writings of Joseph Spae, who has prepared over the years a number of articles in the *Japan Missionary Bulletin*, of which he was for many years the editor; these have been subsequently published in book form, all by the Oriens Institute for Religious Research, in Tokyo. They are *Christian Corridors to Japan* (1965); *Christianity Encounters Japan* (1968); *Japanese Religiosity* (1971); *Shinto Man* (1972); and *Buddhist-Christian Empathy* (1980). It is safe to predict that whatever work is done hereafter dealing with the relations between Christianity and the other religions of Japan will have to make use of these carefully written volumes by Spae.

Christian Theology in Japan

The field is so vast that it can be only briefly surveyed here, with emphasis on materials available in English. The only bibliography in English of Christian books in Japan, and that one badly out of date, is Yanagita Tomonobu, *Japan Christian Literature Review* (Sendai: Seisho Tosho Kankōkai, 1958, with *Supplement*, 1960). The Western world was introduced to some of the treasures of Japanese theology in the excellent study by Michalson, Carl, *Japanese Contributions to Christian Theology* (Philadelphia: Westminster Press, 1960). Later, a historical survey of the field appeared, which cannot be commended too highly: Germany, Charles, *Protestant Theologies in Modern Japan* (Tokyo: IISR Press, 1965). Of the many books mentioned in these two volumes, the only ones to appear thus far in English translation are Hatano Seiichi, *Time and Eternity* (Tokyo: Printing Bureau, National Government, 1963); and Kitamori Kazoh, *Theology of the Pain of God* (Richmond, Va.: John Knox Press, 1965). A general survey of Japanese theology, focusing mostly on the prewar writers, is Ishihara Ken, *Nihon no Shingaku* [Japanese Theology] (Tokyo: Kyōbunkwan, 1962). A more recent collection of essays is Satō Toshio, *Nihon no Kirisutokyō to Shingaku* [Japanese Christianity and Theology] (Tokyo: Kyōdan Shuppankyoku, 1968). Two important studies of preaching are Katō Tsuneaki, *Sekkyō* [Preaching] (Tokyo: Shinkyō Shuppansha, 1964); and, by the same author, *Nippon no Sekkyōja-tachi* [The Preachers of Japan] (Tokyo: Shinkyō Shuppansha, 1972). One should not overlook the theological themes that are dealt with in Piovesana, Gino K., *Recent Japanese Philosophical Thought, 1862—1962: A Survey* (Tokyo: Enderle, 1963). Excellent theological articles, as well as bibliographies of materials on Japanese theology, are to be found in Anderson, Gerald H., ed., *Asian Voices in Christian Theology* (Maryknoll: Orbis Books, 1976); and Elwood, Douglas J., ed., *What Asian Christians Are Thinking: A Theological Source Book* (Manila: New Day, 1976).

Biographies

There are only a few biographical works that deal with figures whose initial impact was made in the period since 1945. William Axling, an American Baptist missionary whose career spans the prewar and postwar eras, is the subject of Hine, Leland D., *Axling: A Christian Presence in Japan* (Valley Forge, Pa.: Judson Press, 1969). Ten figures from Japanese Christian history are dealt with in popular fashion in Prichard, Marianna, and Norman, *Ten against the Storm* (New York: Friendship Press, 1957). Miss Tomasine Allen, an American Baptist missionary, is commemorated in Hemphill, Elizabeth Anne, *A Treasure to Share* (Valley Forge, Pa.: Judson Press, 1964). The same author has also written about Paul Rusch, the founder of the Kiyosato Educational Experiment Project, in *The Road to KEEP* (Tokyo: Weatherhill, 1969). Hendricks, Kenneth C., *Shadow of His Hand: The Reiji Takahashi*

Story (St. Louis, Mo.: Bethany Press, 1971), tells of a pastor who worked with homeless refugees in postwar Japan and who subsequently founded a Christian social center.

By far the leading figure for biographical studies in this period is Kagawa Toyohiko. He has received uneven treatment in his biographies. Axling, William, *Kagawa* (New York: Harper, 1946) gives the impressions of one who worked close to Kagawa for many years. A hagiographical approach is taken in a book with a misleading subtitle: Simon, Charlie May, *A Seed Shall Serve: The Story of Toyohiko Kagawa, Spiritual Leader of Modern Japan* (London: Hodder & Stoughton, 1959). A somewhat more balanced approach is Davey, Cyril J., *Kagawa of Japan* (Nashville: Abingdon, 1960). Some lectures of Kagawa given during an American trip are featured in Bradshaw, Emerson O., *Unconquerable Kagawa* (St. Paul, Minn.: Macalester Park Pub. Co., 1952). Selections from Kagawa's writings are found in Trout, Jessie M., ed., *Kagawa, Japanese Prophet: His Witness in Life and Word* (World Christian Books no. 30) (London: Lutterworth, 1959). A biography in Japanese, written by a co-worker of many year's standing, is Yokoyama Shunichi, *Kagawa Toyohiko,* rev. ed. (Tokyo: Kirisuto Shimbunsha, 1960). Reminiscences about Kagawa's life and character are in Kuroda Shirō, *Ningen Kagawa Toyohiko* [The Man Toyohiko Kagawa], (Tokyo: Kirisuto Shimbun, 1970). An analysis of Kagawa's thought and activities is given in Sumiya Mikio, *Kagawa Toyohiko* (Tokyo: Kyōdan Shuppanbu, 1966). Kagawa's own writings in Japanese are in 24 volumes, under the editorship of Mutō Tomio, *Kagawa Toyohiko Zenshū* [The Complete Works of Toyohiko Kagawa] (Tokyo: Kirisuto Shimbunsha, 1962–64). Reminiscences of Kagawa's followers are to be found in *Kagawa Toyohiko to Sono Boranchia* [Toyohiko Kagawa and His Volunteers] (Kobe: Takeuchi, 1973). (The writer is indebted for information on Kagawa to Mr. Robert F. Hemphill, who is now working on a study of Kagawa in the postwar period.)

Collections of writings of other Christian theologians are also to be found, among which may be mentioned Watanabe Zenda, *Watanabe Zenda Zenshū* [Complete Works of Zenda Watanabe] (Tokyo: Kirisuto Shimbunsha, 1965–66); Suzuki Masahisa, *Suzuki Masahisa Sekkyōshu* [Collection of Sermons by Masahisa Suzuki], (Tokyo: Nihon Kirisuto Kyōdan Shuppankyoku, 1973); Kuwada Hidenobu, *Kuwada Hidenobu Zenshū* [Complete Works of Hidenobu Kuwada] (Tokyo: Kirisuto Shimbunsha, 1974–).

Periodicals

Before listing periodicals that are published in Japan, mention should be made of overseas periodicals that have carried articles on Japanese Christianity, such as *The International Review of Missions, The Ecumenical Review, Christianity Today, The Christian Century, Presbyterian Life* (later called *A.D.*), *Student World, Christianity and Crisis, Journal of Religion, Theology Today, New World Outlook,* etc.

We shall mention first some of the principal periodicals originating in Japan in the English language. *Breakthrough* (Kitakyūshū: mimeographed since 1967), a successor to the *Occupational Evangelism News Sheet*, deals with issues of urban industrial mission. *Contemporary Religions in Japan* (Tokyo: International Institute for the Study of Religions, since 1954) carries articles on Japanese religions. *Hayama Missionary Seminar Reports* (Tokyo: privately printed, since 1960) has papers presented at an annual missionary conference on subjects related to Christian mission. *Japan Christian Activity News* (Tokyo: National Christian Council of Japan, since 1952) is a biweekly and then monthly news sheet about Christian programs of all types. *Japan Christian Quarterly* (Tokyo: Kyōbunkwan, by that name since 1926), is the oldest journal in English in continuous circulation (except during the Pacific War), with articles on all phases of Japanese Christianity, published by the Fellowship of Christian Missionaries. *Japan Harvest* (Tokyo: Evangelical Missionary Association of Japan, since 1955), carries news and analysis of mission activities, generally from a conservative standpoint. *Japan Missions* (Tokyo: National Council of Nippon Seikōkai, 1952–71) reported on Anglican work in Japan. *Japan Missionary Bulletin* (Tokyo: Oriens Institute, since 1947) is a Roman Catholic missionary journal, with excellent articles in both English and Japanese, covering all phases of Christian work in Japan. *Japanese Religions* (Kyoto: NCC Center for the Study of Japanese Religions, since 1959) deals with the dialogue of Christianity and the religions of Japan. *Monumenta Nipponica* (Tokyo: Sophia University, since 1938) has articles on many aspects of Japanese society and culture, including religion. *The Northeast Asia Journal of Theology* (Tokyo: The North East Asia Association of Theological Schools, since 1968) covers developments in theology, seminaries, and church activities, in Korea, Taiwan, and Japan. *Tosei News* (Tokyo: Katorikku Shuppanbu, since 1948) is a news sheet about Roman Catholic activities in Japan.

As to Christian publications in Japanese, there is indeed an embarrassment of riches. It has been said about Christians in Japan that "where two or three are gathered together, there a publication results." The most widely circulated Christian newspaper is *Kirisuto Shimbun* [Christian Newspaper], (Tokyo: Kirisuto Shimbunsha, since 1946); it was founded by Kagawa Toyohiko to keep the entire Christian community in Japan informed of current developments in the churchs. *Kyōdan Shimpo* [in its English title, *Kyōdan Times*] (Tokyo: Kyōdan Shuppanbu, since 1944) is a house organ for the Kyōdan. *Katorikku Shimbun* [The Catholic Newspaper] (Tokyo: Chūō Shuppansha, since 1928) covers Roman Catholic activities. Other denominations have their own periodicals.

Among theological journals in Japanese, the most widely circulated is *Fukuin to Sekai* [Gospel and World], (Tokyo: Shinkyō Shuppansha, since 1956); it was a merger of its predecessors, *Kirisutokyō Bunka* [Christian Culture] and *Fukuin to Jidai* [Gospel and the Times], which both ran from 1946 to 1956. Several universities publish theological journals, among which may be mentioned *Kirisutokyō Kenkyū* [Studies in Christianity] (Kyoto: Doshisha, since 1923); *Kirisutokyō Ronshū* [Essays on Christianity] (Tokyo: Aoyama Gakuin Daigaku Kirisutokyō Gakkai, since 1953); *Seiki* [The Century] (Tokyo: Jōchi Daigaku, since 1949); and *Shingaku* [Theology] (Tokyo: Tokyo Shingaku Daigaku, since 1947).

The essays presented at the annual conference of the Japan Society of Christian Studies are published as *Nihon no Shingaku* [Japanese Theology] (Tokyo: Nihon Kirisutokyō Gakkai, 1945–62 in one volume, then annually from 1962).

Reference Works

There are yearbooks and directories published by Christian groups, and these sometimes have valuable general survey or historical articles. Roman Catholic listings of names and organizations are contained in the *Catholic Directory* (Tokyo: National Catholic Committee, published occasionally since 1953), and the *Catholic Year Book* (Tokyo: Katorikku Kyōku Renmei, since 1948), published in English and Japanese editions. *Kiristokyō Nenkan* [Christian Yearbook] (Tokyo: Kirisuto Shimbunsha, since 1914) has statistics of all Christian groups, and survey articles covering each year's events. In English, the *Japan Christian Yearbook* (Tokyo: National Christian Council of Japan, 1950–70, with predecessors going back to 1903) contains valuable reports on many different aspects of Christian work in Japan.

Two major Christian dictionaries are useful reference works: *Katorikku Daijiten* [Dictionary of Catholicism] (Tokyo: Jōchi Daigaku, 1954) covers Catholic subjects; *Kirisutokyō Daijiten* [Dictionary of Christianity] (Tokyo: Kyōbunkwan, 1963), compiled by Protestant writers.

(The writer is indebted to Robert M. Fukada and David L. Swain for calling his attention to publications not included in the original version of this article, published in the *Japan Christian Quarterly*.)

Index

(Titles have been used with some Japanese names, for more ready identification. Such titles have been omitted from most Western names.)